Philosophy and the Spontaneous Philosophy of the Scientists

&

Other Essays

◆

LOUIS ALTHUSSER

Edited with an Introduction by
Gregory Elliott

Translated by
Ben Brewster
James H. Kavanagh
Thomas E. Lewis
Grahame Lock
Warren Montag

VERSO
London · New York

Verso
UK: 6 Meard Street, London W1V 3HR
USA: 29 West 35th Street, New York, NY 10001-2291

Verso is the imprint of New Left Books

British Library Cataloguing in Publication Data

Althusser, Louis
    Philosophy and the spontaneous philosophy of scientists and other essays.
    1. Marxism. Theories of Althusser, Louis
    1. Title II. Elliot, Gregory, *1960–*
    335.4'092'4
ISBN 0-86091-244-2
ISBN 0-86091-956-0 (pbk.)

US Library of Congress Cataloging-in-Publication Data

Althusser, Louis.
    [Selections. English. 1990]
    Philosophy and the spontaneous philosophy of the scientists & other essays/Louis
    Althusser; edited and with an introduction by Gregory Elliott; translated by Ben
    Brewster . . . [et al.].
    p. cm.
ISBN 0-86091-244-2
ISBN 0-86091-956-0 (pbk.)
    1. Philosophy. 2. Philosophy, Marxian. I. Elliott, Gregory.
II. Title
B29.A48 1990
194—dc20

Typeset by Leaper & Gard Ltd, Bristol
Printed in Finland by Werner Söderström Oy

Contents

Introduction

I am only a philosopher ...

Louis Althusser, 'Machiavelli's Solitude'

It is an indication of the acuity of the current crisis of Marxism that it should be necessary to justify the publication of writings from the 1960s and 70s by a – perhaps the – major Marxist philosopher of the post-war period, Louis Althusser, whose work but lately enjoyed great prestige and resonance, not only in France but throughout Western Europe and beyond (especially in Latin America).

Althusser himself would not deny the existence of such a crisis (one that implicates his work). Indeed, he notoriously announced it, at a conference in Venice in November 1977 organized by the far-left Italian newspaper *Il Manifesto*.[1] Today, however, it is merely a subset of a general crisis of working-class politics, in its traditional forms (social-democracy, socialism, Communism), organizations (the Second and Third Internationals, trade-union movements), and ideologies. The twentieth anniversary of 1968, heralded at the time as a return of the revolutionary repressed to advanced capitalism, served only to under-score the extent to which the French May was 'less the portent of the future than the high point of an historical era of unfulfilled hopes'.[2] According to its author, Althusserian Marxism had aspired to 'help put some substance back into the revolutionary project here in the West'.[3] It is the less surprising that it should have receded from the horizon along with that project. If one secret of the Althusserian ascendancy lay in its

---

1. See 'The Crisis of Marxism', in *Il Manifesto, Power and Opposition in Post-Revolutionary Societies*, London 1979, pp. 225–37.
2. Martin Jay, *Marxism and Totality*, Oxford/Cambridge 1984, p. 359.
3. Quoted from *Le Nouvel Observateur* in *Radical Philosophy* 12, Winter 1975, p. 44.

combination of political radicalism and philosophical modernism, which
seemingly imparted an actuality to Marxist theory, a decade later, when
revolutionary expectations had been confounded at home and abroad,
he was triply vulnerable – as a Communist, a Marxist and a 'structural'
(i.e. Spinozist) Marxist – to prevalent Parisian suspicion of the intellectual pretensions (let alone political intentions) of historical materialism, culmination of modernity's *grande histoire* of human emancipation.
As that suspicion has been diffused, from the Latin Quarter to Rome
and Frankfurt, Madrid and London, so Althusserianism and Marxism
have been widely supplanted among progressive intellectuals by one or
another species of post-structuralist and 'post-modernist' thought.

In its anti-humanism and anti-evolutionism, Althusserianism had
itself represented a critique of Enlightenment Marxism. Yet as a
Marxism, however heretical, Althusser's system of thought would soon
come to 'appear very dated and, like the Beatles' music and Godard's
first films, inevitably evokes a recent but vanished past'.[4] Thus it proved
a transitional philosophical formation, the product of a specific
theoretical and political conjuncture whose mutation helps to explain its
fate. Echoing Althusser's reflections on Machiavelli's solitude,[5] it might
be said that this is the ultimate point in his own: the fact that he occupied a unique and precarious place in modern intellectual history
between a tradition of Marxism which he subjected to radical criticism
and sought to reconstruct, and a 'post-Marxism' which has temporarily
submerged its predecessor, and wherein the majority of the class of '68
has discovered its self-image.

'One is never obliged to publish old texts,' Althusser wrote in the fore-
word to a Hungarian collection of his work in 1968.[6] So why publish
these old texts twenty years later? Three reasons.

The first concerns Althusser's intellectual biography – an adequate
appreciation of his philosophical evolution (where he was coming from
and where he was going, to paraphrase his Hungarian preface). At
present this is impeded by several factors. Two volumes published by
New Left Books in the 1970s – *Lenin and Philosophy* (1971) and
Essays in Self-Criticism (1976) – have long been out of print, either in
Britain or the United States, and only a small proportion of their
contents feature in the Verso selection *Essays in Ideology* (1984). This

---

4. Luc Ferry and Alain Renaut, *La Penseé 68*, Paris 1985, p. 200.
5. See 'Machiavelli's Solitude', *Economy and Society*, vol. 17, no. 4, November
1988, pp. 468–79; and my own 'Althusser's Solitude', in ibid., pp. 480–98.
6. *Marx – az elmélet forradalma*, Budapest 1968, p. 11 (published in part in French
in Saül Karsz, *Théorie et politique: Louis Althusser*, Paris 1974, p. 316).

means that a considerable amount of valuable material is no longer readily available to English readers; from it, we have been able to reprint two texts, 'Lenin and Philosophy' (1968) and 'Is it Simple to be a Marxist in Philosophy?' (1975).[7] Next – and most important – Althusser's key transitional work after *Reading Capital, Philosophie et philosophie spontanée des savants (1967)* (belatedly released in 1974), was, for whatever reason, not published in English. As its best critic to date has argued, 'This gap in the corpus of Althusser translations means that the full novelty, subtlety and fragility of the new position [in and on philosophy – GE] has not been widely appreciated';[8] with this volume the gap is at last filled. Finally, numerous other items of interest in the Althusser canon, early and late, were never translated; a representative sample of the philosophical literature is offered here.[9] (It is hoped to publish some of the political writings, in the not too distant future, under the title *Positions and Interventions 1966–1978.*)

The rationale for the present collection, however, transcends 'Althusserological' considerations. For the writings that follow possess a wider historical significance; they too are 'inscribed ... in history'.[10] What Althusser said, here and elsewhere, helped several generations of students – among them Balibar and Establet, Lecourt and Macherey, Pêcheux and Rancière – 'to orientate themselves in thought'. Moreover, to borrow a distinction proposed in *For Marx* to encapsulate Marx's debt to Hegel, even where Althusser's teaching did not supply, or no longer offers, a *'theoretical formation'*, it performed the role of a *'formation for theory,* ... [an] education of the theoretical intelligence' for many prominent contemporary intellectuals, French and non-French.[11] In this sense (it is not the sole one), Althusser's influence has survived the recession of Althusserianism.

Althusser would not want his teaching to be divorced from the revolutionary cause it was intended to serve; and it would be wrong to

---

7. This leaves 'Cremonini, Painter of the Abstract' (1966), 'Philosophy as a Revolutionary Weapon' (1968), 'Preface to *Capital* Volume One' (1969), 'Lenin before Hegel' (1969) – all from *Lenin and Philosophy,* out of print in the UK; and *Elements of Self-Criticism* (1974) – from *Essays in Self-Criticism,* out of print in both the UK and USA.

8. Timothy O'Hagan, 'Althusser: How to be a Marxist in Philosophy', in G.H.R. Parkinson, ed., *Marx and Marxisms,* Cambridge 1982, p. 244 no.2 – an excellent short guide to Althusser's project in philosophy.

9. But only a sample; see the 'Bibliography of the Writings of Louis Althusser' in my *Althusser – The Detour of Theory,* London 1987, pp. 342–51. By contrast, virtually the totality of this material is in the process of being published in a six-volume *Schriften,* edited by Peter Schöttler and Frieder Otto Wolf, by Argument-Verlag of Hamburg.

10. Cf. Althusser's comments on the leading French Hegel scholar, Jean Hyppolite, in 'Marx's Relation to Hegel' (1968), *Montesquieu, Rousseau, Marx,* London 1982, p. 164.

11. See *For Marx,* London 1982, p. 85.

try to do so. Recollecting his days at the École Normale Supérieure from a Bolivian prison cell, Régis Debray was to recall the

> glorious chance that had brought us into contact with the philosophy teacher who guided our work and our reading. He tactfully gave us the chance of working with him, in such a way that we did not realize that it was he who actually did the work, that he was working for us. We knew he was a Communist, and under his influence, though without telling him, we became so too. But with him it was a wholehearted conviction, as could be seen not only from his written works, but from the affection and generosity with which he guided our steps in that direction. For what his students saw as his personal qualities were in fact those of every activist.[12]

Ten years later, in a less personal register, another French Marxist summed up Althusser's significance for herself and her peers thus:

> For a whole generation of 'young intellectuals' who had come to politics through the Algerian War ... Althusser represented a rupture and a historical opportunity ... a liberation which made it possible to think as a Marxist again. In a theoretical renewal of the first importance, his work ... buried the false French dilemma of the critical-engaged intellectual (of the non-Communist left) and the pedagogical intellectual, the ideologue purely and simply interiorizing the norms and theoretico-political ideology of the Party (Communist intellectuals during a phase of their history). . . . Because Marx's philosophy was 'still largely to be constituted', because it inaugurated a *labour* (theoretical practice) that was historically unfinished and theoretically novel, it was no longer enough to reproduce the political ideology of the Party in philosophical-practical ideology. In sum, no 'official philosophy' in the Party ...[13]

Althusser's writings, in other words, are the record of a certain history – that of the de-Stalinization of Marxist theory after the Twentieth Congress of the Soviet Communist Party (1956). Yet whilst that history was indeed shared with other Communist philosophers, these texts could not have been written by any one of them.[14] For not every such philosopher was Louis Althusser – and this for the reasons so well expressed by a non-Althusserian and non-Marxist philosopher,

---

12. Régis Debray, 'In Settlement of All Accounts' (1967), *Prison Writings*, London 1973, pp. 197–8.
13. Christine Buci-Glucksmann, 'Sur la critique de gauche du stalinisme', *Dialectiques* 15–16, 1976 (special issue on Althusser), p. 28.
14. Cf. Althusser's own statements in *Marx – az elmélet forradalma*, p. 12; Karsz, p. 316.

Alasdair MacIntyre. Reviewing an account of modern French philosophy in 1981, he entered the following reservation:

> What [it] does not sufficiently emphasise ... is the profound gratitude that we
> all owe to Althusser for having brought French Marxism back into dialogue
> with the rest of French philosophy.... So far as French philosophy was
> concerned, he de-Stalinized Marxism more thoroughly than any other Marxist
> did.[15]

We can go further. If, as Althusser suggested, 'Marx ... opened up to
scientific knowledge the continent of History',[16] then this partisan and
artisan of Marxism was among those who reopened it, following the
Stalinist closure and in the face of pronounced opposition from the
leadership of his Party.[17] The effect of what Fredric Jameson has called
'the Althusserian revolution'[18] was to stimulate a body of work, much of
it of lasting value, across a whole range of disciplines. No amount of
amnesia, no number of settlements of account can alter this fact;
wherever radical intellectuals are going today, this is where a significant
proportion of them came from.

Temporal succession is not invariably intellectual progression (the
Beatles' music may be superior to Duran Duran's, Godard's first films to
Jean-Claude Beineix's). At all events, neither the texts presented below,
nor Althusser's other writings, are of purely antiquarian interest. On the
contrary, notwithstanding their contemporary devaluation, they retain
theoretical significance today – the third motive for publishing a new
selection.

Althusser's achievement has been examined at length elsewhere.[19]
But to recapitulate briefly, it might be said that the enduring merits of
Althusserianism are essentially fivefold. First, its critique of the Hegelian
dialectic, and its Marxist avatars, as intrinsically teleological is correct,
and constitutes a point of no return. Secondly, its periodization of

---

15. Alasdair MacIntyre, review of Vincent Descombes, *Modern French Philosophy*
(Cambridge 1981), *London Review of Books*, 16 April – 6 May 1981, p. 16.
16. See 'Lenin and Philosophy', below, p. 180.
17. See, e.g., *Cahiers du Communisme* 5–6, 1966, 'Débats sur les problèmes idéolo-
giques et culturels', containing the interventions made at a PCF Central Committee meet-
ing at Argenteuil in March 1966. According to his successor as the Party's philosophical
authority, Lucien Sève, Roger Garaudy had vetoed publication of *Pour Marx* and *Lire le
Capital* by the PCF's imprint, Editions Sociales, in 1965 (whereupon Althusser turned to
the leftist publisher François Maspero); see *L'Humanité*, 24 April 1976, and *Le Monde*,
25–26 April 1976.
18. *The Political Unconscious*, London 1981, p. 37.
19. See Alex Callinicos, *Althusser's Marxism*, London 1976; Ted Benton, *The Rise
and Fall of Structural Marxism*, London 1984; and *Althusser – The Detour of Theory*.

Marx's *œuvre* rightly privileges *Capital* and foregrounds the emergence of a new theory of history, *c.* 1845–46, as the decisive development in his thought. Thirdly, its philosophy *for* science both registers the autonomy of the sciences and vindicates the possibility – and specificity – of science as the production of objective knowledge of the natural and social worlds alike. Fourthly, its systematic reconstruction of historical materialism, in addition to reclaiming it as a scientific research programme from Stalinist positivism and Western-Marxist anti-naturalism, respects the constitutive complexity of social formations, domesticating 'the concept of difference, of the irreducible heterogeneity of the material world . . . within Marxism'[20] – at a cost to historical messianism, but to the benefit of historical materialism. Fifthly, and finally, as intimated by MacIntyre, its recasting of Marxism reconnected it with non-Marxist currents of thought (e.g. psychoanalysis), facilitating a series of new departures (e.g. in the theory of ideology).

Althusser himself was acutely conscious of the problematic character of some of his alternatives to the actually existing Marxism he had subverted, in the process awakening many of its adherents from a dogmatic slumber (whether voluntary or enforced) and making reversion to pre-Althusserian forms of it, orthodox or heterodox, difficult. If he essayed the construction of a theoretical system in *For Marx* and *Reading Capital*, thereafter, as Pierre Macherey has remarked, he was preoccupied with 'deconstructing this system – not destroying it purely and simply, but trying to develop its internal contradictions, and to say some very different things'.[21] That auto-deconstruction is operative in the texts published below, which (to borrow O'Hagan's title) are variously concerned with the question of *how to be a Marxist in philosophy*, with the modalities of the Marxist practice of philosophy. Readers will come to their own conclusions about the value of this attempted rectification, and how it compares with Althusser's initial system. Taken as a whole, however, Althusser's *œuvre* may be said to constitute one of the most original and productive enterprises in the Marxist tradition – one ripe not only for revaluation, but also (and concurrently) further elaboration.

Whether this will transpire, whether posterity's judgement will be more clement than that of the present, are open questions; in a saying of

20. Alex Callinicos, *Marxism and Philosophy*, Oxford 1983, p. 95.

21. Interview with Étienne Balibar and Pierre Macherey, *Diacritics* 12, Spring 1982, p. 46. See also Étienne Balibar's remarkable article, 'Schweig weiter, Althusser!' in the special issue of *KultuR Revolution* (no. 20, December 1988, pp. 6–12) devoted to the philosopher on the occasion of his seventieth birthday.

de Gaulle's which Althusser was fond of quoting, 'the future lasts a long time'. Pending its verdict, we may be grateful to this mere philosopher.

A word on the contents of this volume, which are arranged in chronological order and printed without revision, except for the insertion of editorial footnotes offering some additional bibliographical guidance.

The first two items – 'Theory, Theoretical Practice and Theoretical Formation: Ideology and Ideological Struggle' (1965) and 'On Theoretical Work: Difficulties and Resources' (1967) – are contemporaneous with *For Marx* and *Reading Capital.* Louis Althusser has pointed out that they predate his criticism and revision of certain theses proposed in those works, and share what he has characterized as their 'theoreticist' tendency.[22] Their publication is justified even so, since they did didactically expound the positions to whose rectification the remainder of the collection is devoted. They serve as pedagogical introductions to high Althusserianism, and thus permit the reader to see where Althusser was coming from.

'Theory, Theoretical Practice and Theoretical Formation' was drafted one month after the Introduction to *For Marx*, in April 1965, and was an important text for Althusser's pro-Chinese students in the *Union des étudiants communistes*, engaged as they were in *la lutte interne* against the PCF's 'revisionism'. Never published in France, it was circulated within the Althusserian milieu and then translated – without its author's permission – by the Cuban *Casa de las Americas* in Havana in 1966. As soon as Althusser had completed *For Marx* and *Reading Capital,* he began to rewrite them in more accessible form, and it is likely that 'Theory ...' was intended to form part of a projected popular manual of Marxist theory designed to replace stereotyped Soviet and French versions.[23] In at least one respect – its discussion of ideology – it illuminates aspects of Althusser's previous work, elaborating on the controversial thesis of the permanence of ideology advanced in 'Marxism and Humanism'[24] and arguing the necessity of social science in consequence.

'On Theoretical Work', written in December 1966 and published in *La Pensée* the following April (but not included in any of Althusser's

---

22. Letter to the editor, 12 February 1987. Cf. *Elements of Self-Criticism*, in *Essays in Self-Criticism*, London 1976, pp. 101–50.

23. It overlaps with another pedagogical text, 'Matérialisme historique et matérialisme dialectique', *Cahiers marxistes-léninistes* (journal of the Cercle des étudiants communistes de l'École Normale Supérieure) 11 April 1966, pp. 90–122, composed of extracts from a longer work that was announced, yet did not appear.

24. See *For Marx*, pp. 231–6.

subsequent collections outside Hungary), provides an inventory of the 'difficulties and resources' bequeathed Marxist intellectuals by a century-old tradition and explored in detail in Althusser's earlier writings.[25] Once again, however, it contains some innovations – the differentiation between levels of theoretical abstraction and, in particular, between 'theoretical concepts' (bearing on 'abstract-formal objects' – e.g. the capitalist mode of production) and 'empirical concepts' (bearing on 'real-concrete objects' – e.g. capitalist France in 1966); and the fertile notion, developed subsequently, of the combination/articulation of different modes of production in particular historical social formations.

Seven months after the publication of 'On Theoretical Work', together with some of his students, Althusser convened the celebrated 'Philosophy Course for Scientists' at the École Normale Supérieure, which ran from November 1967 to May 1968. A second instalment of Alain Badiou's contribution, scheduled for 13 May 1968, was 'happily interrupted'[26] by non-theoretical events in Paris, and neither it nor the envisaged 'Provisional Conclusion' was ever delivered, for the Course did not resume after the Gaullist restoration of order. A sub-series entitled *Cours de philosophie pour scientifiques* was opened within Althusser's *Théorie* collection at Maspero, with the intention to publish the Course in its entirety. Of the six volumes initially planned, however, only three materialized.[27]

---

25. A complementary initiative, 'La Tâche historique de la philosophie marxiste' (April–May 1967), was written for *Voprossy Filosofi* on the fiftieth anniversary of the Russian Revolution and the centenary of the first volume of *Capital*. Declined by the Soviets, it never appeared in France but was published as 'A marxista filozófia történelmi feladata' in *Marx – az elmélet forradalma*, pp. 272–306.

26. Louis Althusser, 'Avertissement' to Alain Badiou, *Le Concept de modèle*, Paris 1969, p. 7.

27. In addition to Althusser's 'Introduction' (5 lectures), the *Cours* comprised: Pierre Macherey, 'The Empiricist Ideology of the "Object of Science"' (3); Étienne Balibar, 'From the "Experimental Method" to the Practice of Scientific Experimentation' (3); François Regnault, 'What is an "Epistemological Break"?' (1); Michel Pêcheux, 'Ideology and the History of the Sciences' (2); Michel Fichant, 'The Idea of a History of the Sciences' (2); Alain Badiou, 'The Concept of Model' (1).

The original publishing programme was as follows:

I.   *Introduction* (Althusser);
II. *Expérience et expérimentation* (Macherey, Balibar);
III. *La 'Coupure épistémologique'* (Regnault, Pêcheux);
IV. *Le Concept de modèle* (Badiou);
V.   *L'Idée d'une histoire des sciences* (Fichant);
VI. *Conclusion provisoire*.

Regnault's contribution having been withdrawn, the course by Pêcheux was amalgamated

Althusser's introduction, ninety or so single-spaced typed pages, circulated widely in mimeograph. A revised version was eventually published by Maspero in autumn 1974 as *Philosophie et philosophie spontanée des savants (1967)*. Apart from the consignment of the fourth lecture (devoted to biologist Jacques Monod's inaugural lecture at the Collège de France) to an Appendix, the major difference between the texts of 1974 and 1967 is the exclusion from the former of the fifth lecture (twenty-three pages, or a quarter of the total). This contained an anatomy of the determinate relationship between the sciences and philosophy (the correlation between scientific and philosophical revolutions, etc.) and of philosophy's inversion of it in the theory of knowledge (in its empiricist and formalist variants).[28] In so far as it displays certain continuities with positions recently retracted by Althusser, its inclusion in 1974 – the year in which *Eléments d'autocritique* appeared[29] – would doubtless have induced confusion. Nevertheless, it is a matter for regret that it has not been made public.

Philosophy and the Spontaneous Philosophy of the Scientists is the centrepiece of this volume. As Althusser notes in his Preface (p. 71), it represents a 'turning point in [his] research on philosophy in general and Marxist philosophy in particular'. Hitherto the latter had been defined as a scientific discipline, the 'Theory of theoretical practice'.[30] *Philosophy* introduces a new set of theses – that philosophy is not a science, that it has no object of its own, that it does not produce knowledge but states theses, that its relation to the sciences constitutes its 'specific determination', etc. – and propounds a new conception of 'the relations which philosophy *should* maintain with the sciences if it is to serve them rather than enslave them' (p. 73). Althusser retheorizes 'dialectical materialism', realigning it as a new practice within the 'necessary circle of philosophy' (pp. 101–2), which functions by practico-political intervention in the realm of theory to defend the sciences against their exploitation or deformation at the hands of ideology.

---

with Fichant's to form a new Vol. III, *Sur l'Histoire des sciences*, prefaced by a set of definitions by Pêcheux and Balibar resuming Regnault's exposition.

In the event, only the volumes by Badiou and Fichant/Pêcheux were published, as planned, in 1969. Extracts from the second were translated in *Theoretical Practice* 3/4 Autumn 1971, pp. 10–12, 38–67.

28. It concludes with a four-page appendix ('Sur Desanti et les pseudo "problèmes de troisième espèce"') responding to an article by the philosopher of mathematics (and former Communist) Jean-Toussaint Desanti. I am grateful to Timothy O'Hagan for kindly providing me with a copy of Althusser's Introduction.

29. See, e.g., *Elements of Self-Criticism*, p. 124, n.19, for Althusser's rejection of the project of epistemology; and pp. 148–50 for his retraction (in the case of Marx at least) of the notion that philosophy invariably arrives *post festum*.

30. See 'On the Materialist Dialectic' (1963), *For Marx*, pp. 161–218.

Althusser's *Cours* was a transitional moment not only in his own philosophical project but also in the intellectual development of a younger generation, poised to abandon the seminar room for the barricades. That is to say, it was a formative text of the pre-May period, whose critique of the 'interdisciplinary' approach as a substitute for scientificity in the human sciences, and identification of the majority of the latter as '*ideological techniques of social adaptation and readaptation*' (p. 98), were to be taken up in an influential pamphlet by the Nanterre radicals who founded the 22 March Movement.[31]

Post-May, by contrast, Althusser's persistent defence of the scientificity of the sciences (including Marxism) against ultra-leftist relativism was discordant with much radical French intellectual culture.[32] His new political definition of philosophy had already proved unwelcome to his academic colleagues just before the Events. On 24 February 1968, at the invitation of the Société française de Philosophie, Althusser delivered a lecture at the Sorbonne on 'Lénine et la philosophie'. Published in the October–December number of the Society's *Bulletin* together with the ensuing discussion,[33] it was issued as a short book by Maspero the following year, without the interventions by Jean Hyppolite, Paul Ricœur *et al.* and Althusser's responses to them. 'Lenin and Philosophy' is a rereading of Lenin's *Materialism and Empirio-criticism*, from which Althusser draws his new definition of philosophy: 'Philosophy represents politics in the domain of theory ... and, vice versa, philosophy represents scientificity in politics' (p. 199).[34] Its adumbration of a 'non-philosophical theory of philosophy' (p. 171) both retrospectively criticized the 'theory of theoretical practice', and sharply repudiated traditional conceptions of philosophy (Althusser's citation of Lenin's denunciation of philosophy professors as, in Dietzgen's words, '*graduated flunkeys*' (p. 173) aroused the irritation of a section of his

---

31. See Daniel Cohn-Bendit, Jean-Pierre Duteuil, Bertrand Gérard and Bernard Granautier, 'Why Sociologists?', in A. Cockburn and R. Blackburn, eds, *Student Power*, Harmondsworth 1969, p. 375. See also Gabriel and Daniel Cohn-Bendit, *Obsolete Communism – The Left-Wing Alternative*, Harmondsworth 1968, p. 38.

32. For Althusser's awareness of this, see the 'Avertissement' to Badiou, p. 8. In a substantial unpublished manuscript dating from 1969, *De la Superstructure (Droit–Etat–Idéologie)*, Althusser insists, *à contre-courant*, that 'there can exist a "knowledge" utterly different from authoritarian-repressive knowledge – ... scientific knowledge, which, since Marx and Lenin, has become an emancipatory scientific knowledge ...' (pp. 125–6).

33. *Bulletin de la Société française de Philosophie* 4, October–December 1968, pp. 125–81.

34. See also the contemporary interview, 'Philosophy as a Revolutionary Weapon', *Lenin and Philosophy and Other Essays*, London 1971, pp. 13–25. *De la Superstructure* represents part of an unfinished book devoted to the revolutionary character of Marxist philosophy, on which Althusser was working in the spring of 1969 and from which the ISAs essay was later extracted.

audience, obliging chairman Jean Wahl to intervene to placate them.[35] Marx was still credited with a dual theoretical revolution, scientific (historical materialism) and philosophical (dialectical materialism). The latter, however, was no longer conceived as the advent of a new philosophy as such, but rather as the inauguration of a new, materialist practice of philosophy, characterized by its 'partisanship' for scientificity.

After 1968, Althusser was to introduce a further modification into his definition of philosophy in a text published elsewhere, *Reply to John Lewis* (1972): '*philosophy is, in the last instance, class struggle in the field of theory.*'[36] The rationale for the adjustment was explained in *Elements of Self-Criticism* (written at the same time). Where the theory of theoretical practice had '*theoretically* overestimat[ed] philosophy [and] underestimated it *politically*', the conception of it *c.*1967–68 as 'politics in the realm of theory', representing the sciences and politics equally, had amounted to a 'semi-compromise' disadvantageous to the last instance: class struggle.[37] The next two items in the present collection – 'Is it Simple to be a Marxist in Philosophy?' (1975) and 'The Transformation of Philosophy' (1976) – bear the imprint of this change in emphasis.

'Is it Simple to be a Marxist in Philosophy?' was published in *La Pensée* in October 1975 and reprinted in the collection *Positions* the following year. It is a revised version of Althusser's *Soutenance* for the degree of *Doctorat d'État* at the University of Picardy in June 1975.[38] One of those present in the audience of five hundred at Amiens was *Le Monde*'s philosophy correspondent, who reported that

> Althusser turned in an astonishing performance: in an hour and a half he offered an account retracing his itinerary and synthesizing his thought, with such skill that it will henceforth be impossible to write anything worthwhile about him without reference to it.... For four hours the questions flowed ... for teachers and students alike, the University had come alive again.[39]

The least that can be said about Althusser's *Soutenance* is that it offers a fascinating retrospective on his recasting of Marxism. In it he explains that his philosophical interventions were 'the work of a member

---

35. See *Bulletin de la Société française de Philosophie* 4, p. 132.
36. *Essays on Ideology*, London 1984, p. 67 (note the riders attached on pp. 67–8 n.).
37. *Elements of Self-Criticism*, pp. 149–50.
38. Among the jurors was the distinguished Marxist historian Pierre Vilar. For the record, Althusser was awarded a *mention très honorable*.
39. *Le Monde*, 2 July 1975.

of the Communist Party, acting within ... the Labour Movement and for it'; that he had emulated Machiavelli, speaking in the name of a non-existent Prince so as to influence the existing Prince (the PCF); and that he had followed Lenin's example, 'bending the stick' in the direction of a theoreticism and theoretical anti-humanism *à l'outrance* in order to challenge prevalent constructions of Marxism. As to the objective of the 'class struggle in theory' Althusser professes himself to have practised, *Le Nouvel Observateur*'s account of Amiens quotes him as divulging:

> I would never have written anything were it not for the Twentieth Congress and Khrushchev's critique of Stalinism and the subsequent liberalization. But I would never have written these books if I had not seen this affair as a bungled de-Stalinization, a right-wing de-Stalinization which instead of analyses offered us only incantations; which instead of Marxist concepts had available only the poverty of bourgeois ideology. My target was therefore clear: these humanist ravings, these feeble dissertations on liberty, labour or alienation which were the effects of all this among French party intellectuals. And my aim was equally clear: to make a start on the first *left-wing* critique of Stalinism, a critique that would make it possible to reflect not only on Khrushchev and Stalin but also on Prague and Lin Piao; that would above all help put some substance back into the revolutionary project here in the West ... for me philosophy is something of a battlefield. It has its frontlines, its entrenched positions, its strongholds, its frontiers. I have made use of Hegel in order to launch an assault on the fortress of Descartes. I have turned the weapon of Spinoza against Hegel. I have always been rough in my use of references and quotations. But that was not the problem. The urgent thing was to 'think at the limit' and ... to bend the rod of theory in the other direction, to open the way, against the dominant ideas, for completely new political thought.[40]

The implied answer to the question posed in the title of Althusser's *Soutenance* is itself straightforward: no. The reasons are many and complex, among the most salient being the prior history of Marxist philosophy itself and, in particular, the version of it as Science of the sciences promulgated under Stalin.[41] Althusser's original philosophical project – to secure the cognitive autonomy of theory – had been inspired by the counter-example of its instrumentalization during the Zhdanov-ism and Lysenkoism of the Cold War in theory (with which Althusser's

---

40. Quoted in *Radical Philosophy* 12, Winter 1975, p. 44. See also Althusser's illuminating comments on 'theoretical rhetoric', and on his philosophical 'extremism', in a letter from 1974 recently published by Jean Guitton in *Lire*, 1987, pp. 86–7.

41. See especially J.V. Stalin, *Dialectical and Historical Materialism*, Moscow 1941 – a pamphlet extracted from chapter 4 of the notorious *History of the Communist Party of the Soviet Union (Bolsheviks) – Short Course* (Moscow 1939).

adherence to the PCF coincided). Yet as the passing reference to *Dialectical and Historical Materialism* in 'On Theoretical Work' (p. 53) attests Althusser was at first reluctant explicitly to reject the Stalinist theoretical legacy wholesale. The 1970s witnessed a change in this respect, as he came publicly to identify 'Diamat' – an ontology of matter, whose laws are stated by the dialectic and exemplified in (or applied by) the different sciences – as a prime obstacle to Marxist philosophy fulfilling its vocation as a 'revolutionary weapon'.[42]

Althusser's opposition to philosophy-as-ontology is expounded in the next piece in this collection, 'The Transformation of Philosophy' – the unedited transcript of a lecture on the paradoxes of Marxist philosophy delivered before a large audience at the University of Granada in March 1976, and published in Spain (but nowhere else) shortly afterwards. Althusser analyses the politics that constitute philosophy, conceiving it as the continuation of the class struggle at the level of theory in so far as the abstract discourse of philosophy indirectly contributes to the ideological hegemony of the dominant class. Contrary to traditional philosophical systems, and their re-edition in Marxism (especially in Soviet 'dialectical materialism', *ancilla rei publicae*), Marxist philosophy, it is argued, must be a 'non-philosophy', a new practice of philosophy which serves working-class struggle by challenging bourgeois ideological hegemony and promoting, rather than inhibiting, 'the liberation and free development of social practices' (p. 265).

The final text included here, 'Marxism Today', was commissioned by the Italian publisher Garzanti for the entry on Marxism in Volume VII of its *Enciclopedia Europea* (1978) and has not previously appeared outside Italy.[43] A companion piece to Althusser's contribution to the Venice conference mentioned above, it is marked by the conviction of a '*general crisis of Marxism* – political, ideological and theoretical' (p. 27), which nevertheless represents a historical opportunity for Marxism, in liaison with popular struggles, to settle accounts with its former philosophical conscience. The predominantly critical balance sheet of historical materialism drawn up by Althusser stands in arresting contrast to that supplied twelve years earlier in the first item in this collection, 'Theory, Theoretical Practice and Theoretical Formation' – a fact not unconnected with recent political developments in Europe and China (particularly the discrediting of the Cultural Revolution). Moreover, the optimism of its conclusion was shortly afterwards to be belied

---

42. See, for example, Althusser's Introduction (1976) to Dominique Lecourt, *Proletarian Science? The Case of Lysenko*, London 1977, pp. 7–16.

43. 'Il Marxismo oggi', reprinted in Louis Althusser, *Quel che deve cambiare nel partito communista*, Milan 1978, pp. 107–26.

by the defeat of the French Union of the Left in spring 1978, provoking trade-union leader Edmond Maire to remark that 'Henceforth it will be necessary to conjugate May '68 with March '78', and Marxist philosopher Louis Althusser to issue the summons of his party to rectitude[44] which proved to be his final – and in some respects his finest – word.

***

Preparation of this volume for publication has proved to be a collective effort. I am greatly indebted to Louis Althusser for his co-operation with the project; to Michael Sprinker for his support and encouragement; to Jim Kavanagh, Warren Montag and Thomas Lewis for undertaking the new translations; to Gillian Beaumont, Ruth Carim, Liz Heron, Lucy Morton and, above all, David Macey for sharing the editing; to Peter Osborne for sharing his enviable knowledge of German philosophical literature with me; to Étienne Balibar and Peter Schöttler for all their help over the last two-and-a-half years; and to the friends – Bill Massey and Frances Coady, in particular – who made completion possible amid one or two distractions.

Gregory Elliott
London, 31 January 1989

44. 'What Must Change in the Party', *New Left Review* 109, May/June 1978, pp. 19–45.

1

Theory, Theoretical Practice and Theoretical Formation: Ideology and Ideological Struggle*

*Théorie, pratique théorique et formation théorique. Idéologie et lutte idéologique, April 1965. Unpublished typescript. Translated by James H. Kavanagh.

These reflections are designed to present, in as clear and systematic a form as possible, the theoretical principles that found and guide the practice of Communists in the domain of theory and ideology.

1. Marxism is a Scientific Doctrine

A famous title of Engels's underscores the essential distinction between Marxism and previous socialist doctrines: before Marx, socialist doctrines were merely *utopian*; Marx's doctrine is *scientific*.[1] What is a *utopian* socialist doctrine? It is a doctrine which proposes *socialist* goals for human action, yet which is based on non-scientific principles, deriving from religious, moral or juridical, i.e. *ideological*, principles. The ideological nature of its theoretical foundation is decisive, because it affects how any socialist doctrine conceives of not only the *ends* of socialism, but also the *means* of action required to realize these ends. Thus, utopian socialist doctrine defines the *ends of socialism* – the socialist society of the future – by moral and juridical categories; it speaks of the reign of equality and the brotherhood of man; and it translates these moral and legal principles into utopian – that is, ideological, ideal and imaginary – economic principles as well: for example, the complete sharing-out of the products of labour among the workers, economic egalitarianism, the negation of all economic law, the immediate disappearance of the State, etc. In the same manner it defines utopian, ideological and imaginary *economic and political means* as the appropriate means to realize socialism: in the economic domain, the workers' co-operatives of Owen, the phalanstery of Fourier's disciples, Proudhon's people's bank; in the political domain, moral education and reform – if not the Head of State's conversion to socialism. In constructing an ideological representation of the *ends* as well as the *means* of socialism, utopian socialist doctrines are, as Marx clearly showed, prisoners of bourgeois and petty-bourgeois economic, juridical, moral and political principles. That is why they cannot really break with the

---

1. *Socialism: Utopian and Scientific*, in Karl Marx and Frederick Engels, *Selected Works*, vol. 3, Moscow 1970, pp. 95–151. [Ed.]

3

bourgeois system, they cannot be genuinely revolutionary. They remain *anarchist* or *reformist.* Content, in fact, to oppose the bourgeois politico-economic system with bourgeois (moral, juridical) principles, they are trapped – whether they like it or not – within the bourgeois system. They can never break out towards revolution.

Marxist doctrine, by contrast, is *scientific.* This means that it is not content to apply existing bourgeois moral and juridical principles (liberty, equality, fraternity, justice, etc.) to the existing bourgeois reality in order to criticize it, but that it criticizes these existing bourgeois moral and juridical principles, as well as the existing politico-economic system. Thus its general critique rests on other than existing ideological principles (religious, moral and juridical); it rests on the *scientific knowledge* of the totality of the existing bourgeois system, its politico-economic as well as its ideological systems. It rests on the knowledge of this ensemble, which constitutes an organic totality of which the economic, political, and ideological are organic 'levels' or 'instances', articulated with each other according to specific laws. It is this *knowledge* that allows us to define the *objectives* of socialism, and to conceive socialism as a new determinate mode of production which will succeed the capitalist mode of production, to conceptualize its specific determinations, the precise form of its relations of production, its political and ideological superstructure. It is this knowledge that permits us to define the appropriate *means of action* for 'making the revolution', means based upon the nature of historical necessity and historical development, on the determinant role of the economy in the last instance on this development, on the decisive role of class struggle in socioeconomic transformations, and on the role of consciousness and organization in political struggle. It is the application of these scientific principles that has led to the definition of the working class as the only radically revolutionary class, the definition of the forms of organization appropriate to the economic and political struggle (role of the unions; nature and role of the party comprised of the vanguard of the working class) – the definition, finally, of the forms of ideological struggle. It is the application of these scientific principles that has made possible the break not only with the *reformist objectives* of utopian socialist doctrines, but also with *their forms of organization and struggle.* It is the application of these scientific principles that has allowed the definition of a revolutionary tactics and strategy whose irreversible first results are henceforth inscribed in world history, and continue to change the world.

In 'Our Programme', Lenin writes:

We take our stand entirely on the Marxist theoretical position: Marxism was the first to transform socialism from a utopia into a science, to lay a firm foundation for this science, and to indicate the path that must be followed in further developing and elaborating it in all its parts. It disclosed the nature of modern capitalist economy by explaining how the hire of labour, the purchase of labour-power, conceals the enslavement of millions of propertyless people by a handful of capitalists, the owners of the land, factories, mines, and so forth. It showed that all modern capitalist development displays the tendency of large-scale production to eliminate petty production and creates conditions that make a socialist system of society possible and necessary. It taught us how to discern – beneath the pall of rooted customs, political intrigues, abstruse laws, and intricate doctrines – the *class struggle*, the struggle between the propertied classes in all their variety and the propertyless mass, the *proletariat*, which is at the head of all the propertyless. It made clear the real task of a revolutionary socialist party: not to draw up plans for refashioning society, not to preach to the capitalists and their hangers-on about improving the lot of the workers, not to hatch conspiracies, *but to organize the class struggle of the proletariat and to lead this struggle, the ultimate aim of which is the conquest of political power by the proletariat and the organization of a socialist society.*[2]

And, having condemned the Bernsteinian revisionists who 'have ... not ... advanced ... by a single step ... the science which Marx and Engels enjoined us to develop', Lenin adds:

There can be no strong socialist party without a revolutionary theory which unites all socialists, from which they draw all their convictions, and which they apply in their methods of struggle and means of action.[3]

From one end of Lenin's work to the other, the same theme is tire-lessly repeated: '*without revolutionary theory, no revolutionary practice*'.[4] And this revolutionary theory is exclusively defined as the scientific theory produced by Marx, to which he gave most profound form in his 'life's work' – the work without which, says Engels, *we would still 'be groping in the dark'*: *Capital*.[5]

2. Marx's Double Scientific Doctrine

Once we advance the principle that the revolutionary action of Communists is based on scientific Marxist theory, the following question must be addressed: *what is Marxist scientific doctrine?*

---

2. *Collected Works*, vol.4, Moscow 1960, pp. 210–11.
3. Ibid., p. 211.
4. See, for example, *What is to be Done?*, *Collected Works*, vol.5, Moscow 1961, p. 369. [Ed.]
5. 'Speech at the Graveside of Karl Marx', *Selected Works*, vol.3, p. 162.

Marxist scientific doctrine presents the specific peculiarity of being composed of *two scientific disciplines*, united for reasons of principle but actually distinct from one another because their objects are distinct: historical materialism and dialectical materialism.

Historical materialism is the science of history. We can define it more precisely as the *science of modes of production*, their specific structure, their constitution, their functioning, and the forms of transition whereby one mode of production passes into another. *Capital* represents the scientific theory of the *capitalist* mode of production. Marx did not provide a developed theory of other modes of production – that of primitive communities, the slave, 'Asiatic', 'Germanic', feudal, socialist, and Communist modes of production – but only some clues, some outlines of these modes of production. Nor did Marx furnish a theory of the forms of transition from one determinate mode of production to another, only some clues and outlines. The most developed of these outlines concerns the forms of transition from the feudal to the capitalist mode of production (the section of *Capital* devoted to primitive accumulation, and numerous other passages). We also possess some precious, if rare, indications concerning aspects of the forms of transition from the capitalist to the socialist mode of production (in particular, the 'Critique of the Gotha Programme', where Marx insists on the phase of the dictatorship of the proletariat). The first phase of these forms of transition is the object of numerous reflections by Lenin (*State and Revolution*, and all his texts of the revolutionary and post-revolutionary period). In fact, the scientific knowledge in these texts directly governs all economic, political and ideological action directed towards the 'construction of socialism'.

A further clarification is necessary concerning historical materialism. The theory of history – a theory of the different modes of production – is, by all rights, the science of the organic totality that every social formation arising from a determinate mode of production constitutes. Now, as Marx showed, every social totality comprises the articulated ensemble of the different levels of this totality: the economic infra-structure, the politico-juridical superstructure, and the ideological superstructure. The theory of history, or historical materialism, is the theory of the specific nature of this totality – of the set of its levels, and of the type of articulation and determination that unifies them and forms the basis both of their dependence *vis-à-vis* the economic level – '*determinant in the last instance*' – and their degree of '*relative autonomy*'. It is because each of these levels possesses this 'relative autonomy' that it can be objectively considered as a '*partial whole*', and become the object of a relatively independent scientific treatment. This is why, taking account of this 'relative autonomy', one can legitimately study the economic 'level', or the political 'level', or this or that ideological, philosophical, aesthetic or scientific formation of a given mode of production, separately. This specification is very important, because it is the basis of the possibility of a theory of the history (relatively autonomous, and of a degree of variable autonomy according to the case) of the levels or the respective realities – a theory of the history of politics, for example, or of philosophy, art, the sciences, etc.

This is also the basis of a relatively autonomous theory of the 'economic level' of a given mode of production. *Capital*, as it is offered to us in its incompleteness (Marx also wanted to analyse the law, the State, and the ideology of the capitalist mode of production therein), precisely represents the scientific analysis of the *'economic level' of the capitalist mode of production*; this is why *Capital* is generally and correctly considered as, above all, the theory of the *economic system* of the capitalist mode of production. But as this theory of the economic 'level' of the capitalist mode of production necessarily presupposes, if not a developed theory, at least some adequate theoretical elements for other 'levels' of the capitalist mode of production (the juridico-political and ideological levels), *Capital* is not limited to the 'economy' alone. It far exceeds the economy, in accordance with the Marxist conception of the reality of the economy, which can be understood in its concept, defined and analysed only as a level, a part, a partial whole organically inscribed in the totality of the mode of production under consideration. This is why one finds in *Capital* fundamental theoretical elements for the elaboration of a theory of the other levels (political, ideological) of the capitalist mode of production. These elements are certainly undeveloped, but adequate for guiding us in the theoretical study of the other levels. In the same way one finds in *Capital*, even as it proposes to analyse only 'the capitalist mode of production', theoretical elements concerning the knowledge of other modes of production, and of the forms of transition between different modes of production – elements that are certainly undeveloped, but adequate for guiding us in the theoretical study of these matters.

Such, very schematically presented, is the nature of the first of the two sciences founded by Marx: historical materialism.

In founding this science of history, at the same time Marx founded another scientific discipline: *dialectical materialism*, or *Marxist philosophy*. Yet here there appears a *de facto* difference. Whereas Marx was able to develop historical materialism very considerably, he was not able to do the same for *dialectical materialism*, or *Marxist philosophy*. He was able only to lay its foundations, either in rapid sketches (*Theses on Feuerbach*) or in polemical texts (*The German Ideology, The Poverty of Philosophy*), or again in a very dense methodological text (the unpublished Introduction to the *Contribution to the Critique of Political Economy*, 1857) and in some passages of *Capital* (particularly the Postface to the second German edition). It was the demands of the ideological struggle on the terrain of philosophy that led Engels (*Anti-Dühring, Ludwig Feuerbach and the End of Classical German Philosophy*) and Lenin *(Materialism and Empirio-criticism, Philosophical Notebooks*, the latter unpublished by Lenin) to develop at greater length the principles of dialectical materialism outlined by Marx. Yet none of these texts, not even those by Engels and Lenin – which are also, essentially, polemical or interpretative texts (Lenin's *Notebooks*) – displays a degree of elaboration and systematicity – and hence scientificity – in the least comparable to the degree of elaboration of historical materialism that we possess in *Capital*. As in the case of historical materialism, it is necessary carefully to distinguish between what has been given to us and what has not, so as to take stock of what remains to be done.

Dialectical materialism, or Marxist philosophy, is a scientific discipline distinct from historical materialism. The distinction between these two scientific disciplines rests on the distinction between their *objects*. The object of historical materialism is constituted by the modes of production, their constitution and their transformation. The object of dialectical materialism is constituted by what Engels calls '*the history of thought*', or what Lenin calls the history of the '*passage from ignorance to knowledge*', or what we can call the history of the production of knowledges – or yet again, the historical difference between ideology and science, or the specific difference of scientificity – all problems that broadly cover the domain called by classical philosophy the '*theory of knowledge*'. Of course, this theory can no longer be, as it was in classical philosophy, a theory of the formal, atemporal conditions of knowledge, a theory of the *cogito* (Descartes, Husserl), a theory of the a priori forms of the human mind (Kant), or a theory of absolute knowledge (Hegel). From the perspective of Marxist theory, it can only be a *theory of the history of knowledge* – that is, of the real conditions (material and social on the one hand, internal to scientific practice on the other) of the *process of production of knowledge*. The 'theory of knowledge', thus understood, constitutes the heart of Marxist philosophy. Studying the real conditions of the specific practice that produces knowledges, Marxist philosophical theory is necessarily led to define the nature of non-scientific or pre-scientific practices, the practices of ideological 'ignorance' (ideological practice), and all the real practices upon which scientific practice is founded and to which it is related – the practice of the transformation of social relations, or political practice; and the practice of the transformation of nature, or economic practice. This last practice puts man in relation to nature, which is the material condition of his biological and social existence.

Like any scientific discipline, Marxist philosophy presents itself in two forms: a *theory* which expresses the rational system of its theoretical concepts; and a *method* which expresses the relation the theory maintains with its object in its application to that object. Of course, theory and method are deeply united, constituting but two sides of the same reality: the scientific discipline in its very life. But it is important to distinguish them, in order to avoid either a dogmatic interpretation (pure theory) or a methodological interpretation (pure method) of dialectical materialism. In dialectical materialism, it can very schematically be said that it is *materialism* which represents the aspect of *theory*, and *dialectics* which represents the aspect of *method*. But each of these terms includes the other. *Materialism* expresses the effective conditions of the practice that produces knowledge – specifically: (1) the *distinction between the real and its knowledge* (distinction of reality), correlative of a correspondence (adequacy) between knowledge and its object (correspondence of knowledge); and (2) *the primacy of the real over its knowledge, or the primacy of being over thought.* None the less, these principles themselves are not 'eternal' principles, but the principles of the *historical nature of the process in which knowledge is produced.* That is why materialism is called *dialectical*: dialectics, which expresses the relation that theory maintains with its object, expresses this relation not as a relation of two simply distinct terms but as a relation within a process of transformation, thus of real production.

This is what is affirmed when it is said that dialectics is the law of transformation, the law of the development of real processes (natural and social processes, as well as the process of knowledge). It is in this sense that the Marxist dialectic can only be *materialist*, because it does not express the law of a pure imaginary or thought process but the law of real processes, which are certainly distinct and 'relatively autonomous' according to the level of reality considered, but which are all ultimately based on the processes of material nature. That Marxist materialism is necessarily dialectical is what distinguishes it from all previous *materialist* philosophies. That Marxist dialectics is necessarily materialist is what distinguishes the Marxist dialectic from all idealist dialects, particularly Hegelian dialectics. Whatever historical connections might be invoked between Marxist materialism and anterior 'metaphysical' or mechanical materialisms, on the one hand, and between Marxist and Hegelian dialectics, on the other, there exists a fundamental difference in kind between Marxist philosophy and all other philosophies. In founding dialectical materialism, Marx accomplished as revolutionary a work in philosophy as he effected in the domain of history by founding historical materialism.

3. Problems Posed by the Existence of these Two Disciplines

The existence of these two scientific disciplines – historical materialism and dialectical materialism – raises two questions: (1) Why did the foundation of historical materialism necessarily entail the foundation of dialectical materialism? (2) What is the proper function of dialectical materialism?

1. Very schematically, it can be said that the foundation of historical materialism, or the science of history, necessarily provoked the foundation of dialectical materialism for the following reason. We know that in the history of human thought, the foundation of an important new science has always more or less overturned and renewed existing philosophy. This applies to Greek mathematics, which to a great extent provoked the recasting that led to Platonic philosophy; to modern physics, which provoked the recastings that led first to the philosophy of Descartes (after Galileo), then of Kant (after Newton); and also to the invention of infinitesimal calculus, which to a great extent provoked Leibniz's philosophical recasting, and the mathematical logic that put Husserl on the road to his system of Transcendental Phenomenology. We can say that the same process occurred with Marx, and that the foundation of the science of history induced the foundation of a new philosophy.

We must go further, however, to show how Marxist philosophy occupies a privileged place in the history of philosophy, and how it has transformed philosophy from the condition of an *ideology* into a *scientific discipline*. In fact, Marx was in some sense *compelled*, by an implacable logic, to found a radically new philosophy, because he was the first to have thought scientifically the *reality of history*, which all other philosophies were incapable of doing. Thinking the reality of history scientifically, Marx was obliged, and able, to situate and treat philosophies – for the first time – as realities which, while aiming for 'truth', while speaking of the conditions of knowledge, belong none the less to history, not only because they are conditioned by it but also because they play a social role in it. Whether idealist or materialist, classical philosophies were incapable of thinking about their own history: either the simple fact that they appeared at a determinate moment in history; or, what is much more important, the fact that they have an entire history behind them and are produced in large part by this *past history, by the relation of properly philosophical history to the history of the sciences and the other social practices.*

Once a genuine knowledge of history had finally been produced, philosophy could no longer ignore, repress or sublimate its relation to history; it had to take account of, and think about, this relation. By means of a theoretical revolution it had to become a new philosophy, capable of thinking – in philosophy itself – its real relation to history, as well as its relation to the truth. The old philosophies of consciousness, of the transcendental subject – just like the dogmatic philosophies of absolute knowledge – were no longer possible philosophically. A new philosophy was necessary, one capable of thinking the *historical insertion* of philosophy in history, its real relation to scientific and social practices (political, economic, ideological), while taking account of the *knowledge-relation* it maintains with its object. It is this theoretical necessity that gave birth to dialectical materialism, the only philosophy that treats knowledge as the historical process of production of knowledges and that reflects its new object at once within materialism and within dialectics. Other transformations in philosophy were always based upon either the ideological negation of the reality of history, its sublimation in God (Plato, Descartes, Leibniz), or an *ideological* conception of history as the realization of philosophy itself (Kant, Hegel, Husserl): they were never able to attain the reality of history, which they always misunderstood or left aside. If the transformation imposed on philosophy by Marx is genuinely revolutionary from a philosophical point of view, this is because it took the reality of history seriously for the first time in history, and this simple difference comprehensively overturned the bases of existing philosophy.

2. As for the proper function of philosophy, and its absolute necessity for Marxism, this too is based on profound theoretical reasons. Lenin expounded them very clearly in *Materialism and Empiriocriticism*. He showed that philosophy always played a fundamental theoretical role in the constitution and development of knowledge, and that Marxist philosophy simply resumed this role on its own account, but with means that were, in principle, infinitely purer and more fertile. We know that knowledge – in its strong sense, scientific knowledge – is not born and does not develop in isolation, protected by who-knows-what miracle from the influences of the surrounding world. Among these are social and political influences which may intervene directly in the life of the sciences, and very seriously compromise the course of their development, if not their very existence. We are aware of numerous historical examples. But there are less visible influences that are just as pernicious, if not still more dangerous, because they generally pass unnoticed: these are *ideological* influences. It was in breaking with the existing ideologies of history – at the end of a very arduous critical labour – that Marx was able to found the theory of history; and we know, too – from Engels's struggle against Dühring and Lenin's against the disciples of Mach –

that, once founded by Marx, the theory of history did not escape the onslaught of ideologies, did not escape their influence and assaults.

In fact, every science – natural as well as social – is constantly submitted to the onslaught of existing ideologies, and particularly to that most disarming – because apparently non-ideological – ideology wherein the scientist 'spontaneously' reflects his/her own practice: 'empiricist' or 'positivist' ideology. As Engels once said, every scientist, whether he wants to or not, inevitably adopts a philosophy of science, and therefore cannot do without philosophy. The problem, then, is to know *which philosophy* he must have at his side: an ideology which deforms his scientific practice, or a scientific philosophy that accounts for it? An ideology that enthrals him to his errors and illusions, or, on the contrary, a philosophy that frees him from them and permits him really to master his own practice? The answer is not in doubt. This is what justifies the essential role of Marxist philosophy in regard to all knowledge: if based upon a false representation of the conditions of scientific practice, and of the relation of scientific practice to other practices, any science risks slowing its advance, if not getting caught in an impasse, or finally taking its own specific crises of development for crises of science as such – and thereby furnishing arguments for every conceivable kind of ideological and religious exploitation. (We have some recent examples with the 'crisis of modern physics' analysed by Lenin.[6]) Furthermore, when a science is in the process of being born, there is a risk that it will put the ideology in which it is steeped into the service of its bad habits. We have some striking examples with the so-called human sciences, which are all too often merely techniques, blocked in their development by the empiricist ideology that dominates them, prevents them from perceiving their real foundation, defining their object, or even finding their basic principles in existing disciplines which are rejected because of ideological prohibitions or prejudices (like historical materialism, which should serve as the foundation of most of the human sciences).

What goes for the sciences holds in the first place *for historical materialism itself, which is a science among others and holds no privilege of immunity in this matter.* It too is constantly threatened by the dominant ideology, and we know the result: the different forms of revisionism which – in principle, and whatever form they take (economic, political, social, theoretical) – are always related to deviations of a

---

6. In *Materialism and Empirio-criticism, Collected Works*, vol.14, Moscow 1962, chapter 5. [Ed.]

philosophical character: that is, to the direct or indirect influence of distorting philosophies, of ideological philosophies. In *Materialism and Empirio-criticism*, Lenin clearly demonstrated this, affirming that the *raison d'être* of dialectical materialism was precisely to furnish principles that enable us to distinguish ideology from science, thus to unearth the traps of ideology, in interpretations of historical materialism as well. In this way, he demonstrated that what he calls 'partisanship in philosophy' – that is, the refusal of all ideology, and the precise consciousness of the *theory of scientificity* – was an absolutely imperative requirement for the very existence and development not only of the natural sciences but of the social sciences, and above all of historical materialism. It has aptly been said that Marxism is a 'guide to action'.[7] It can act as this 'guide' because it is not a false but a *true* guide, because it is a science – and for this reason alone. Let us say, with all the precautions required by this comparison, that in many circumstances the sciences also require a 'guide', not a false but a *true* guide; and among them, historical materialism itself has a vital need for this 'guide'. This 'guide' is dialectical materialism. And since there is no other 'guide' over and above dialectical materialism, we can understand why Lenin attributed an absolutely decisive importance to the adoption of a scientific position on philosophy; we can understand why dialectical materialism demands the highest consciousness and the strictest scientific rigour, the most careful theoretical vigilance: because it is the last possible recourse in the theoretical domain – at least for men and women who, like us, are liberated from religious myths of divine omniscience, or their profane version: dogmatism.

4. Nature of a Science, Constitution of a Science, Development of a Science, Scientific Research

If, as we think, Marx's doctrine is a scientific doctrine, if all the goals and all the means of action of Communists are based on the application of the results of Marx's scientific theories, our first duty clearly concerns the *science* that furnishes us with the means to understand the reality of the historical world and to transform it.

We thus have a categorical duty to treat Marx's theory (in its two domains: historical materialism, dialectical materialism) as what it is – a true science. In other words, we must be fully aware of what is implied

---

7. A standard characterization of Marxism in the ranks of the Third International. [Ed.]

by the nature of a science, its constitution, its life, i.e. its development.

Today, this duty involves some specific demands. We are no longer in Marx's position, quite simply because we no longer have to do the prodigious work that he accomplished. Marxist theory exists for us first of all as a result, contained in a certain number of theoretical works and present in its political and social applications.

In an existing science, the theoretical work that produced it is no longer visible to the naked eye; it has completely passed into the science as constituted. There is a hidden danger here, because we may be tempted to treat constituted Marxist science as a *given* or as a set of finished truths – in short, to fashion an *empiricist* or *dogmatic* conception of science. We may consider it as an absolute, finished knowledge, which poses no problem of development or research; and then we shall be treating it in a *dogmatic* fashion. We may also – in so far as it gives us a knowledge of the real – believe that Marxist science *directly and naturally reflects the real,* that it sufficed for Marx to *see* clearly, to *read* clearly – in short, to *reflect* in his abstract theory the essence of things given in things – without taking into account the enormous work of theoretical production necessary to arrive at knowledge; and we shall then be treating it in an *empiricist* fashion. In the two interpretations – dogmatic and empiricist – we will have a false idea of science, because we will consider the knowledge of reality to be the knowledge of a pure given, whereas knowledge is, on the contrary, a *complex process of production of knowledges. The idea we have of science is decisive for Marxist science itself.* If we have a dogmatic conception we will do nothing to develop it, we will indefinitely repeat its results, and not only will the science not progress, it will wither. If we have an empiricist conception we risk being equally incapable of making the science progress, since we will be blind to the nature of the real process of the *production of knowledges,* and will remain in the wake of facts and events – in the wake, that is to say, lagging behind. If, on the contrary, we have a correct idea of science, of its nature, of the conditions of the production of knowledges, then we can develop it, give it the life that is its right, and in the absence of which it would no longer be a science but a dead, fixed dogma.

1. To know what a science is, is above all to know *how* it is constituted, how it is *produced:* by an immense, specific theoretical labour, by an irreplaceable, extremely long, arduous and difficult theoretical practice.

There is no royal road to science, and only those who do not dread the fatiguing climb of its steep paths have a chance of reaching its luminous summit.[8]

This practice presupposes a whole series of specific theoretical conditions, into whose details it is not possible to enter here. The important point is that a science, far from reflecting the immediate givens of everyday experience and practice, is constituted only on the condition of calling them into question, and breaking with them, to the extent that its results, once achieved, appear indeed as the *contrary* of the obvious facts of practical everyday experience, rather than as their reflection. 'Scientific truth,' Marx writes, 'is always paradoxical, if judged by everyday experience, which captures only the delusive appearance of things.'[9]

Engels says the same thing when he declares that the laws of capitalist production

prevail although those involved do not become aware of them, so that they can be abstracted from everyday practice only by tedious theoretical analysis ... [10]

This theoretical work is not an abstraction in the sense of empiricist ideology. To know is not to extract from the impurities and diversity of the real the pure essence contained in the real, as gold is extracted from the dross of sand and dirt in which it is contained. To know is to *produce* the adequate concept of the object by putting to work means of theoretical production (theory and method), applied to a given raw material. This *production* of knowledge in a given science is a *specific practice*, which should be called *theoretical practice – a specific practice, distinct, that is, from other existing practices* (economic, political, ideological practices) *and absolutely irreplaceable at its level and in its function.* Of course this theoretical practice is organically related to the other practices; it is based on, and articulated with, them; *but it is irreplaceable in its domain.* This means that *science develops by a specific practice – theoretical practice – which can on no account be replaced by other practices.* This point is important, because it is an empiricist and idealist error to say that *scientific* knowledges are the product of 'social practice

8. Letter to Maurice La Châtre, 18 March 1872, in Karl Marx and Frederick Engels, *Letters on 'Capital'*, London 1983, p. 172 (translation modified). [Ed.]

9. *Wages, Price and Profit*, in Karl Marx and Frederick Engels, *Selected Works*, vol.2, Moscow 1969, p. 54.

10. 'Supplement and Addendum to Volume 3 of *Capital*', in Karl Marx, *Capital*, volume 3, Harmondsworth 1981, p. 1037.

in general', or of political and economic practice. To speak only of practice in general, to speak solely of economic and political practice, without speaking of *theoretical practice as such*, is to foster the idea that non-scientific practices – *spontaneously, by themselves* – produce the equivalent of scientific practice, and to neglect the irreplaceable character and function of scientific practice.

Marx and Lenin put us on guard on this point, in showing us that the economic and political practice of the proletariat was, by itself, incapable of producing the *science* of society, and hence the science of the proletariat's own practice, but was capable only of producing utopian or reformist ideologies of society. Marxist–Leninist science, which serves the objective interests of the working class, could not be the spontaneous product of proletarian practice; it was produced by the theoretical practice of intellectuals possessing a very high degree of culture (Marx, Engels, Lenin) and 'introduced from without'[11] into proletarian practice, which it then modified and profoundly transformed. It is a leftist theoretical error to say that Marxism is a 'proletarian science', if by this one means that it was or is produced *spontaneously by the proletariat.* This error is possible only if one passes over in silence the existence and irreplaceable functions of *scientific practice*, as the practice productive of science. A fundamental condition of this scientific practice is that it works on the 'givens' of the experience of the economic and political practice *of the proletariat and other classes.* But this is only *one* of its conditions, for all *scientific work* consists precisely in producing, by starting from the experience and results of these concrete practices, *knowledge of them*, which is the result of another practice, an entire, specific theoretical labour. And we can get an idea of the immense importance and considerable difficulties of such work by reading *Capital,* knowing that Marx worked for thirty years to lay its foundations and develop its conceptual analyses.

It must be remembered, then, that *no science is possible without the existence of a specific practice, distinct from other practices: scientific or theoretical practice.* It must be remembered that this practice is irreplaceable, and that – like any practice – it possesses its own laws, and requires its own means and conditions of activity.

2. To know what a science is, is simultaneously to know that it can live only on condition that it *develops*. A science that repeats itself, without discovering anything new, is a dead science – no longer a science, but a fixed dogma. A science lives only in its development –

---

11. See Lenin, *What is to be Done?*, pp. 383–4. [Ed.]

that is, from its discoveries. This point is likewise very significant because we may be tempted to believe that we possess completed sciences in historical and dialectical materialism as they are given to us today, and to be suspicious on principle of any new discovery. Naturally, the working-class movement has cause to be on guard against revisionisms that are always decked out in the robes of 'novelty' and 'renovation', but this necessary defence has nothing to do with suspicion of the discoveries of a living science. Were we to fall into this error, it would govern our attitude towards the sciences in question, and we would save ourselves the bother of what we nevertheless *must* do: devote all our efforts to developing these sciences, forcing them to produce new knowledges, new discoveries.

Marx, Engels and Lenin expressed themselves on this issue without any ambiguity. When, in a celebrated outburst, Marx said he was '*not a Marxist*',[12] he meant that he considered what he had done as simply the commencement of science, and not as a completed knowledge – because a completed knowledge is a non-sense that sooner or later leads to a non-science. Engels said the same when he wrote, for example, in 1877:

> With these discoveries [by Marx] socialism became a science. The next thing was to work out all its details.[13]

> Political economy ... as the science of the conditions and forms under which the various human societies have produced and exchanged and on this basis have distributed their products – political economy in this wider sense has still to be brought into being. Such economic science as we possess up to the present is limited almost exclusively to the genesis and development of the capitalist mode of production ...[14]

Lenin states this even more forcefully, if possible, in 1899:

> There can be no strong socialist party without a revolutionary theory which unites all socialists, from which they draw all their convictions, and which they apply in their methods of struggle and means of action. To defend such a theory, which to the best of your knowledge you consider to be true, against unfounded attacks and attempts to corrupt it is not to imply that you are an enemy of *all* criticism. We do not regard Marx's theory as something completed and inviolable; on the contrary, we are convinced that it has only laid the foundation stone of the science which socialists *must* develop in all

---

12. See Engels's letter of 5 August 1890 to Conrad Schmidt, in Marx/Engels, *Selected Correspondence*, Moscow 1975, p. 393. [Ed.]
13. *Anti-Dühring*, Moscow 1947, p. 39.
14. Ibid., p. 185.

directions if they wish to keep pace with life. We think that an independent
elaboration of Marx's theory is especially essential for Russian socialists; for
this theory provides only general *guiding* principles, which, *in particular*, are
applied in England differently than in France, in France differently than in
Germany, and in Germany differently than in Russia.[15]

This text of Lenin's contains several major themes.

1. In the theoretical domain, Marx gave us the 'foundation stone'
    and 'guiding principles' – i.e. the basic theoretical principles of a
    theory – *which absolutely must be developed.*

2. This theoretical development is a *duty* of all socialists *vis-à-vis*
    their science, failing which they would be remiss in their obli-
    gation towards socialism itself.

3. It is necessary to develop not only theory in general but also
    particular applications, according to the specific nature of each
    concrete case.

4. This defence and development of Marxist science presupposes both
    the greatest firmness against all who want to lead us back to a theor-
    etical condition short of Marx's scientific principles, and a real *free-
    dom of criticism and scientific research* for those who want to go
    beyond, exercised on the basis of the theoretical principles of Marx
    – an indispensable freedom for the life of Marxist science, as for any
    science.

Our position must consist in drawing theoretical and practical
conclusions from these principles. In particular, if both historical and
dialectical materialism are scientific disciplines, we *must* of necessity
develop them, make them produce new knowledges – expect from them,
as from any living science, some *discoveries*. It is generally admitted that
it must be thus for historical materialism, but *it is not always clearly
enough stated in the case of dialectical materialism*, because we do not
have a precise idea of the character of a scientific discipline, because we
remain fixed on the (idealist) idea that philosophy is not really a
discipline of a scientific character. In fact, we would be hard pressed to
indicate the discoveries produced since Lenin in the domain of dialectical materialism, which has remained in practically the same state that
Lenin brought it to in *Materialism and Empirio-criticism*. If this is so, it

---

15. 'Our Programme', *Collected Works*, vol.4, pp. 211–12.

is a state of affairs which must be examined very seriously, and then rectified. At the same time, if historical materialism has accrued the great theoretical discoveries of Lenin (the theory of imperialism, of the Communist Party, the beginning of a theory of the specific nature of the first phase of the forms of transition from the capitalist to the socialist mode of production), it has not subsequently been the site of important *theoretical* developments, which are, however, indispensable for solving the problems we face today – to name but one, the problem of the forms of transition between the complex modes of production combined in the so-called 'underdeveloped' countries and the socialist mode of production. In the same way, the difficulty of acccounting *theoretically* for a historical fact as significant as the 'cult of personality' makes the insufficient development of the theory of the specific forms of transition between the capitalist and socialist modes of production, perfectly apparent.

3. If to develop Marxist science (in its two domains) is a *duty* for Communists, this duty must be considered in its concrete conditions. For a science to be able to develop, it is first of all necessary to have a correct idea of the nature of science and, in particular, of the means by which it develops, and therefore of all the real conditions of its development. It is necessary to assure these conditions and, in particular, to recognize – theoretically and practically – the irreplaceable role of *scientific practice* in the development of science. It is necessary, then, clearly to define our theory of science, to reject all dogmatic and empiricist interpretations, and to make a precise conception of science prevail intellectually and practically. It is also necessary *practically* to assure the conditions of scientific freedom required by theoretical research, to provide the material means of this freedom (organizations, theoretical reviews, etc.). Finally, the real conditions of scientific or theoretical research in the domain of Marxism itself must be created. It is to this concern that the creation of the Centre d'Études et de Recherches Marxistes and the Institut Maurice Thorez must respond in France. But it is also necessary for these different measures to be co-ordinated, considered as parts of a whole, and for a comprehensive politics – which can only be the act of the Party – to be conceived and applied in the matter of theory and theoretical research, in order to give historical and dialectical materialism the chance to develop, to live a real scientific life, and thereby to produce new knowledges. It must also be recognized that theoretical research cannot consist in simply repeating or commenting upon already acquired truths, and, *a fortiori*, that it has nothing to do with developing simple ideological themes or mere personal opinions. Theoretical research begins only in the zone that separates those know-

ledges already acquired and deeply assimilated from knowledges not yet acquired. To do scientific research this zone must have been reached and crossed. Accordingly, it is necessary to recognize that theoretical research demands a very strong theoretical formation simply to be possible, that it therefore supposes possession of a high degree not only of Marxist culture (which is absolutely indispensable) but also of scientific and philosophical culture in general. It is therefore necessary to encourage by all means this general education, at the same time as encouraging *Marxist theoretical formation*, the indispensable preliminary basis for all Marxist theoretical and scientific research.

4. We risk no error in proposing that the development of Marxist theory, in all its domains, is a primary, urgent necessity for our times, and an absolutely essential task for all Communists – and for two different kinds of reason.

The first kind of reason has to do with the very nature of the new tasks that 'life' – that is, history – imposes upon us. Since the 1917 Revolution and the era of Lenin, immense events have turned world history upside down. The growth of the Soviet Union, the victory against Nazism and Fascism, the great Chinese Revolution, the Cuban Revolution and Cuba's passage into the socialist camp, the liberation of the former colonies, the revolt of the Third World against imperialism, have overturned the balance of forces in the world. But at the same time these events pose a considerable number of new, sometimes unprecedented problems, for whose solution the development of Marxist theory – and especially the Marxist theory of the *forms of transition* from one mode of production to another – is indispensable.

This theory not only concerns the *economic* problems of transition (forms of planning, the adaptation of the forms of planning to different specific stages of the transition, according to the particular condition of the countries considered); it also concerns the *political* problems (forms of the State, forms of the political organization of the revolutionary party, the forms and nature of the revolutionary party's intervention in the different domains of political, economic and ideological activity) and the *ideological* problems of transition (politics in the religious, moral, juridical, aesthetic and philosophical, etc., domains). The theory to be developed not only concerns the problems posed by so-called 'underdeveloped' countries in their transition to socialism, it also concerns the problems of countries already engaged in the socialist mode of production (the USSR) or close to it (China) – all the problems of planning, the definition of new legal and political forms in close correspondence with new relations of production (pre-socialist, socialist, Communist) and, of course, all the problems posed by the existence of a socialist camp in which complex economic, political and ideological relations exist as a function of the *uneven* development of the different countries. Finally, the theory to be developed concerns the current nature of imperialism, the transformations of the capitalist mode of production in the new conjuncture, the development of the productive forces, the new forms of economic concentration and government of the monopolies, and all the strategic and tactical problems of Communists in the current phase of the class struggle. All these problems open onto the future of socialism, and must be posed and resolved as a function of our definition of socialism and its appropriate structures. With all these problems, we are on the very terrain knowledge of which Lenin enjoined Communists to produce for each country, by developing Marxist theory on the basis of the knowledges already produced, as marked out by the 'foundation stone' of Marx's discoveries.

But it is not only the new face of history and its problems which obliges us resolutely to develop Marxist theory. We are confronted with a *second kind of reason* that has to do with the theoretical time lag that built up during the period of the 'cult of personality'. Lenin's slogan 'to develop theory in order to keep pace with life' is especially cogent here. If we would be hard pressed to cite any discoveries of great calibre in many areas of Marxist theory since Lenin, this is due in large part to the conditions in which the international working-class movement was enmeshed by the politics of the 'cult', by its countless victims in the ranks of very valuable militants, intellectuals and scientists, by the ravages inflicted by dogmatism on the intellect. If the politics of the 'cult' did not compromise the development of the material bases of socialism, it did, for many years, literally sacrifice and block all development of Marxist–Leninist theory; it effectively ignored all the indispensable conditions for theoretical reflection and research and, with the suspicion it cast on any theoretical novelty, dealt a very serious blow in practice to the freedom of scientific research and to all discovery.

The effects of dogmatic politics as far as theory is concerned can still be felt today, not only in the residues of dogmatism but also, para-doxically, in the often anarchic and confused forms assumed by the attempts of numerous Marxist intellectuals to regain possession of the freedom of reflection and research of which they were deprived for so long. Today this phenomenon is relatively widespread, not only in Marxist circles but in the Marxist parties themselves, and even in the socialist countries. What is most painful – and directly expressed in these generous, if often ideologically confused, essays – is how the period of the 'cult', far from contributing to their formation, on the contrary, prevented the theoretical formation of an entire generation of Marxist researchers, whose work we cruelly miss today. Time is required – a great deal of it – to form real theoreticians, and all the time lost in forming them costs in terms of a dearth of works, a delay, a stagnation, if not a regression, in the production of science, of knowledge. This is all the more true, since the positions that Marxists did not know how to occupy in the domain of knowledge have not remained vacant: they are occupied – especially in the domain of the 'human sciences' – by bourgeois 'scientists' or 'theoreticians', under the direct domination of bourgeois ideology, with all the practical, political, and theoretical consequences whose disastrous effects can be observed – or rather, whose disastrous effects *are not always even suspected.* Not only, then, do we have to make good our own delay, but we have to reoccupy on our own behalf the areas that fall to us by right (to the extent that they depend on historical materialism and dialectical materialism) and we have to reoccupy them in difficult conditions, involving a clear-minded struggle against the prestige of the results apparently achieved by their actual occupants.

For these two kinds of reason – historical and theoretical – it is clear that the task of developing Marxist theory in all its domains is a political and theoretical task of the first order.

5. Ideology

To be able, as rigorously as possible, to draw out the *practical* conse-quences of what has just been said about Marxist scientific theory, it is now necessary to situate and define an important new term: *ideology.*

We have already seen that what distinguishes *Marxist* working-class organizations is the fact that they base their socialist objectives, their means of action and forms of organization, their revolutionary strategy and tactics, on the principles of a *scientific* theory – that of Marx – and not on this or that anarchist, utopian, reformist, or other ideological theory. Therewith, we have underscored *a crucial distinction and opposi-tion between science on the one hand, and ideology on the other.*

But we have also foregrounded an actual reality, as real for the break that Marx had to effect with ideological theories of history in order to found his scientific discoveries as for the struggle waged by any science against the ideology that assaults it: not only does ideology precede every science, but ideology survives after the constitution of science, and despite its existence.

Furthermore, we have had to remark that ideology manifests its exist-ence and its effects not only in the domain of its relations with science, but in an infinitely wider domain – that of society in its entirety. When we spoke of the 'ideology of the working class', to say that the *ideology* of the working class – which was 'spontaneously' anarchist and utopian at the outset, and then became generally reformist – was gradually transformed by the influence and action of Marxist theory into a *new ideology*; when we say that today the ideology of large sectors of the working class has become an ideology of a Marxist–Leninist character; when we say that we have to wage not only an economic struggle (through the unions) and a political struggle (through the Party) but an *ideological struggle* among the masses – when we say all this, it is clear that under the term *ideology* we are advancing a notion that involves *social realities*, which, while having something to do with a certain representation (and thus a certain 'knowledge') of the real, go far beyond the simple question of knowledge, to bring into play a properly *social* reality and function.

We are aware, then, in the practical use we make of this notion, that *ideology* implies a double relation: with knowledge on the one hand, and with society on the other. The nature of this double relation is not simple, and requires some effort to define. This effort of definition is indispensable if it is true, as we have seen, that it is of primary importance for Marxism to define itself unequivocally as a *science* – that is, as a reality distinct from *ideology* – and if it is true that the action of revolutionary organizations based upon the scientific theory of Marxism must develop in society, where at every moment and stage of their struggle, even in the consciousness of the working class, they confront the social existence of *ideology*.

In order to grasp this important but difficult problem, it is vital to step back a little and return to the principles of the Marxist theory of *ideology*, which form part of the Marxist theory of society.

Marx showed that every social formation constitutes an 'organic totality', comprised of three essential 'levels': the economy, politics, and *ideology* – or '*forms of social consciousness*'.[16] The ideological 'level', then, represents an objective reality, indispensable to the existence of a social formation – an objective reality: that is, a reality independent of the subjectivity of the individuals who are subject to it, even whilst it concerns these individuals themselves; this is why Marx used the expression 'forms of social consciousness'. How does the objective reality and social function of *ideology* present itself?

In a given society, people participate in *economic* production whose mechanisms and effects are determined by the *structure of the relations of production*; people participate in *political* activity whose mechanisms

---

16. See the Preface to *A Contribution to the Critique of Political Economy*, in Karl Marx, *Early Writings*, Harmondsworth 1975, pp. 425–6. [Ed.]

and effects are governed by the *structure of class relations* (the *class struggle*, law and the State). These same people participate in other activities – religious, moral, philosophical, etc. – either in an active manner, through conscious practice, or in a passive and mechanical manner, through reflexes, judgements, attitudes, etc. These last activities constitute *ideological activity*; they are sustained by voluntary or involuntary, conscious or unconscious, adherence to an ensemble of representations and beliefs – religious, moral, legal, political, aesthetic, philosophical, etc. – which constitute what is called the 'level' of *ideology*.

Ideological *representations* concern nature and society, the very world in which men live; they concern the life of men, their relations to nature, to society, to the social order, to other men and to their own activities, including economic and political practice. Yet these representations are not *true knowledges* of the world they represent. They may contain some *elements* of knowledge, but they are always integrated into, and subject to, a total *system* of such representations, a system that is, in principle, orientated and distorted, a system dominated by a *false conception* of the world or of the domain of objects under consideration. In fact, in their real practice, be it economic or political, people are effectively determined by *objective structures* (relations of production, political class relations); their practice convinces them of the *existence* of this reality, makes them perceive *certain objective effects* of the action of these structures, but conceals the essence of these structures from them. They cannot, through their mere practice, attain *true knowledge* of these structures, of either the economic or political reality in whose mechanism they nevertheless play a definite role. This knowledge of the *mechanism of economic and political structures* can derive only from *another practice*, distinct from immediate economic or political practice, *scientific practice* – in the same way that knowledge of the laws of nature cannot be the product of simple technical practice and perception, which provide only empirical observations and technical formulae, but is, on the contrary, the product of specific practices – *scientific practices* – distinct from immediate practices. None the less, men and women, who do not have knowledge of the political, economic and social realities in which they have to live, act and perform the tasks assigned them by the division of labour, cannot live without being guided by some *representation* of their world and their relations to this world.

In the first instance men and women find this representation ready-made at birth, existing in society itself, just as they find – pre-existing them – the relations of production and political relations in which they will have to live. Just as they are born 'economic animals' and 'political animals', it might be said that men and women are born 'ideological animals'. It is as if people, in order to exist as conscious, active social beings in the society that conditions all their existence, needed to possess a certain *representation* of their world, a representation which may remain largely unconscious or, on the contrary, be more or less conscious and thought out. Thus, ideology appears as a certain '*representation of the world*' which relates men and women to their conditions of existence, and to each other, in the division of their tasks and the equality or inequality of their lot. From primitive societies – where classes did not exist – onwards, the existence of this *bond* can be observed, and it is not by chance that the first form of this ideology, the reality of this bond, is to be found in *religion* ('bond' is one of the possible etymologies of the word *religion*). In a class society, ideology serves not only to help people live their own conditions of existence, to perform their assigned tasks, but also to 'bear' their condition – either the poverty of the exploitation of which they are the victims, or the exorbitant privilege of the power and wealth of which they are the beneficiaries.

The representations of ideology thus consciously or unconsciously accompany all the acts of individuals, all their activity, and all their relations – like so many landmarks and reference points, laden with prohibitions, permissions, obligations, submissions and hopes. If one represents society according to Marx's classic metaphor – as an edifice, a building, where a juridico-political *superstructure* rests upon the infrastructure of economic foundations – ideology must be accorded a very particular place. In order to understand its kind of effectivity, it must be situated in the *superstructure* and assigned a relative autonomy vis-à-vis law and the State; but at the same time, to understand its most general form of presence, ideology must be thought of as sliding into all the parts of the edifice, and considered as a distinctive kind of *cement* that assures the adjustment and cohesion of men in their roles, their functions and their social relations.

In fact, ideology permeates all man's activities, including his economic and political practice; it is present in attitudes towards work, towards the agents of production, towards the constraints of production, in the idea that the worker has of the mechanism of production; it is present in political judgements and attitudes – cynicism, clear conscience, resignation or revolt, etc.; it governs the conduct of individuals in families and their behaviour towards others, their attitude towards nature, their judgement on the 'meaning of life' in general, their different cults (God, the prince, the State, etc.). Ideology is so much present in all the acts and deeds of individuals that it is *indistinguishable from their 'lived experience'*, and every unmediated analysis of the 'lived' is profoundly marked by the themes of ideological obviousness. When he

thinks he is dealing with pure, naked perception of reality itself, or a
pure practice, the individual (and the empiricist philosopher) is, in truth,
dealing with an impure perception and practice, marked by the invisible
structures of ideology; since he does not *perceive* ideology, he takes his
perception of things and of the world as the perception of 'things themselves', without realizing that this perception is given him only in the veil
of unsuspected forms of ideology.

This is the first essential characteristic of ideology: like all social
realities, it is intelligible only through its *structure*. Ideology comprises
representations, images, signs, etc., but these elements considered in
isolation from each other, do not compose ideology. It is their
systematicity, their *mode of arrangement and combination*, that gives
them their meaning; it is their *structure* that determines their meaning
and function. The *structure* and mechanisms of ideology are no more
immediately *visible* to the people subjected to them than the *structure* of
the relations of production, and the mechanisms of economic life
produced by it, are visible to the agents of production. They do not
perceive the ideology of their representation of the world *as ideology*;
they do not *know* either its structure or its mechanisms. They *practise*
their ideology (as one says a believer practises his religion), they do not
know it. It is because it is determined by its *structure* that the reality of
ideology exceeds all the forms in which it is subjectively lived by this or
that individual; it is for this reason that it is irreducible to the individual
forms in which it is lived; it is for this reason that *it can be the object of
an objective study*. It is for this reason that we can speak of the nature
and function of ideology, and study it.

Now a study of ideology reveals some remarkable characteristics.

1. We notice, first of all, that the term *ideology* covers a reality which
– while diffused throughout the body of society – is divisible into distinct
areas, into *specific regions*, centred on several different themes. Thus, in
our societies, the domain of ideology in general can be divided into
relatively autonomous regions: religious ideology, moral ideology,
juridical ideology, political ideology, aesthetic ideology, philosophical
ideology. Historically, these regions have not always existed in these
distinct forms; they only appeared gradually. It is to be expected that
certain regions will disappear, or be combined with others, in the course
of the development of socialism and Communism, and that those which
remain will participate in the internal redivisions of the general domain
of ideology. It is also important to remark that, depending upon the
historical period (that is, the mode of production), and within identical
modes of production, according to the different social formations in
existence, and also, as we shall see, the different social classes, this or

that *region of ideology* dominates the others in the general domain of ideology. This explains, for example, the remarks of Marx and Engels on the dominant influence of religious ideology in all the movements of peasant revolt from the fourteenth to the eighteenth centuries, and even in certain early forms of the working-class movement; or, indeed, Marx's remark (which was not in jest) that the French have a head for politics, the English for economics, and the Germans for philosophy[17] – a significant remark for understanding certain problems specific to the working-class traditions in these different countries. The same kind of observations might be made regarding the importance of religion in certain liberation movements in former colonial countries, or in the resistance of Blacks to white racism in the United States. Knowledge of the different regions within ideology, knowledge of the *dominant ideological region* (whether religious, political, juridical, or moral), is of prime importance for the strategy and tactics of ideological struggle.

2. We note as well another essential characteristic of ideology. In each of these regions, ideology, which always has a determinate structure, can exist *in more or less diffuse or unthought forms, or, contrariwise, in more or less conscious, reflected, and explicitly systematized forms – theoretical forms.* We know that a religious ideology can exist with rules, rites, etc., but without a systematic theology; the advent of theology represents a degree of theoretical systematization of religious ideology. The same goes for moral, political, aesthetic ideology, etc.; they can exist in an untheorized, unsystematized form, as customs, trends, tastes, etc., or, on the contrary, in a systematized and reflected form: ideological moral theory, ideological political theory, etc. The highest form of the theorization of ideology is *philosophy*, which is very important, since it constitutes the laboratory of *theoretical abstraction*, born of ideology, but itself treated as theory. It is as a theoretical laboratory that philosophical ideology has played, and still plays, a very significant role in the birth of the sciences, and in their development. We have seen that Marx did not abolish philosophy; by a revolution in the domain of philosophy he transformed its nature, rid it of the ideological heritage hindering it and made of it a scientific discipline – thus giving it incomparable means with which to play its role as the theory of real scientific practice. At the same time, we must be aware that – with the

---

17. Althusser's gloss on Marx's discussion of the German status quo in 'A Contribution to the Critique of Hegel's Philosophy of Right. Introduction', *Early Writings*, pp. 243–57. [Ed.]

exception of philosophy *in the strict sense* – ideology, in each of its domains, is irreducible to its *theoretical* expression, which is generally accessible only to a small number of people; it exists in the masses in a theoretically unreflected form, which prevails over its theorized form.

3. Once we have situated ideology as a whole, once we have marked out its different regions, identified the region that dominates the others, and come to know the different forms (theorized and untheorized) in which it exists, a decisive step remains to be taken in order to understand the ultimate meaning of ideology: *the meaning of its social function.* This can be brought out only if we understand ideology, with Marx, as an element of the *superstructure* of society, and the essence of this element of the superstructure in its relation with the *structure of the whole* of society. Thus, it can be seen that the function of ideology in class societies is intelligible only on the basis of the existence of social classes. In a classless society, as in a class society, ideology has the function of assuring the *bond* among people in the totality of the forms of their existence, the *relation* of individuals to their tasks assigned by the social structure. In a class society, this function is *dominated* by the form taken by the division of labour in distributing people into *antagonistic classes*. It can then be seen that ideology is destined to assure the cohesion of the relations of men and women to each other, and of people to their tasks, in the general structure of class exploitation, which thus prevails over all other relations.

Ideology is thus destined, *above all,* to assure the domination of one class over others, and the economic exploitation that maintains its preeminence, by making the exploited accept their condition as based on the will of God, 'nature', moral 'duty', etc. But ideology is not only a 'beautiful lie' invented by the exploiters to dupe the exploited and keep them marginalized; it also helps *individuals of the dominant class* to recognize themselves as dominant class subjects, to accept the domination they exercise over the exploited as 'willed by God', as fixed by 'nature', or as assigned by a moral 'duty'. Thus, it likewise serves them as a bond of social cohesion which helps them *act as members of the same class,* the class of exploiters. The 'beautiful lie' of ideology thus has a double usage: it works on the consciousness of the exploited to make them accept their condition as 'natural'; it also works on the consciousness of members of the dominant class to allow them to exercise their exploitation and domination as 'natural'.

4. Here we touch on the decisive point which, in class societies, is at the origin of the *falsity* of ideological *representation.* In class societies, ideology is a representation of the real, but necessarily distorted,

because necessarily biased and tendentious – tendentious because its aim is not to provide men with *objective knowledge* of the social system in which they live but, on the contrary, to give them a mystified representation of this social system in order to keep them in their 'place' in the system of class exploitation. Of course, it would also be necessary to pose the problem of the function of ideology in a classless society – and it would be resolved by showing that the deformation of ideology is socially necessary as a function of the nature of the social whole itself, as a function (to be more precise) of *its determination by its structure*, which renders it – as a social whole – opaque to the individuals who occupy a place in society determined by this structure. The opacity of the social structure necessarily renders *mythic* that representation of the world which is indispensable for social cohesion. In class societies this first function of ideology remains, but is dominated by the new social function imposed by the *existence of class division*, which takes ideology far from the former function.

If we want to be exhaustive, if we want to take account of these two principles of necessary deformation, we must say that in a class society, ideology is necessarily deforming and mystifying, both because it is produced as deforming by the opacity of the determination of society by its structure and because it is produced as deforming by the existence of class division. It is necessary to come to this point to understand why ideology, as representation of the world and of society, is, by strict necessity, a *deforming and mystifying* representation of the reality in which men and women have to live, a representation destined to make men and women accept the place and role that the structure of this society imposes upon them, in their *immediate* consciousness and behaviour. We understand, by this, that ideological representation imparts a certain '*representation*' of reality, that it makes *allusion* to the real in a certain way, but that at the same time it bestows only an *illusion* on reality. We also understand that ideology gives men a certain 'knowledge' of their world, or rather allows them to 'recognize' themselves in their world, gives them a certain 'recognition'; but at the same time ideology only introduces them to its *misrecognition. Allusion-illusion* or *recognition-misrecognition* – such is ideology from the perspective of its relation to the real.

It will now be understood why every science, when it is born, has to break from the mystified-mystifying representation of ideology; and why ideology, in its *allusive-illusory* function, can survive science, since its object is not knowledge but a social and objective misrecognition of the real. It will also be understood that in its social function science cannot replace ideology, contrary to what the *philosophes* of the Enlightenment believed, seeing only illusion (or error) in ideology without seeing its *allusion* to the real, without seeing in it the social function of the initially disconcerting – but essential – couple: *illusion* and *allusion*, recognition and misrecognition.

5. An important remark concerning class societies must be added. If in its totality ideology expresses a representation of the real destined to sanction a regime of class exploitation and domination, it can also give rise, in certain circumstances, to the expression of the *protest of the exploited classes* against their own exploitation. This is why we must now specify that ideology is not only divided into regions, but also *divided into tendencies* within its own social existence. Marx showed that 'the ruling ideas of each age have ever been the ideas of its ruling class'.[18] This simple phrase puts us on the path to understanding that just as there are dominant and dominated classes in society, so too there are dominant and dominated ideologies. Within ideology in general, we thus observe the existence of *different ideological tendencies* that express the 'representations' of the different social classes. This is the sense in which we speak of bourgeois ideology, petty-bourgeois ideology, or proletarian ideology. But we should not lose sight of the fact that in the case of the capitalist mode of production these petty-bourgeois and proletarian ideologies remain *subordinate* ideologies, and that in them – even in the protests of the exploited – it is always the ideas of the dominant class (or bourgeois ideology) which get the upper hand. This scientific truth is of prime importance for understanding the history of the working-class movement and the practice of Communists. What do we mean when we say, with Marx, that bourgeois ideology dominates other ideologies, and in particular working-class ideology? We mean that working-class protest against exploitation expresses itself *within the very structure of the dominant bourgeois ideology*, within its *system*, and in large part with its representations and terms of reference. We mean, for example, that the ideology of working-class protest 'naturally' expresses itself in the form of bourgeois law and morality.

The whole history of utopian socialism and trade-union reformism attests to this. The pressure of bourgeois ideology is such, and bourgeois ideology is so exclusively the provider of raw ideological material (frames of thought, systems of reference), *that the working class cannot, by its own resources, radically liberate itself from bourgeois ideology*; at best, the working class can express its protest and its aspirations by using certain elements of bourgeois ideology, but it remains the prisoner of that ideology, held in its dominant structure. For 'spontaneous' working-

---

18. *Manifesto of the Communist Party*, in Karl Marx, *The Revolutions of 1848*, Harmondsworth 1973, p. 85. [Ed.]

class ideology to transform itself to the point of freeing itself from bourgeois ideology it must *receive, from without, the help of science*; it must transform itself under the influence of a new element, radically distinct from ideology: science. The fundamental Leninist thesis of the 'importation' of Marxist science into the working-class movement is thus not an arbitrary thesis or the description of an 'accident' of history; it is founded in necessity, in the nature of ideology itself, and in the absolute limits of the natural development of the 'spontaneous' ideology of the working class.

Very schematically summarized, these are the specific characteristics of ideology.

6. The Union of Marx's Scientific Theory and the Working-class Movement

What has just been said regarding, on the one hand, the scientific theory of Marx and, on the other, the nature of ideology, allows us to understand in exactly what terms to pose the problem of the historical emergence, and the existence and action, of Marxist–Leninist organizations.

1. *The first cardinal principle* was formulated by Marx, Engels, Kautsky and Lenin: the principle of the *importation* into the existing working-class movement of a scientific doctrine produced *outside the working class* by Karl Marx, an intellectual of bourgeois origin who rallied to the cause of the proletariat. The working-class movement of 1840s Europe was then subject to either proletarian (anarchist) or more or less petty-bourgeois and utopian (Fourier, Owen, Proudhon) *ideologies.* By itself, the working class could not break out of the circle of an *ideological* representation of its goals and means of action; and we know that by virtue of the relay of moralizing, utopian, and thus reformist petty-bourgeois ideology, this ideological representation was, and remained, subjugated by the dominant ideology – that of the bourgeoisie. Even today, social-democratic working-class organizations have remained in this reformist ideological tradition. To conceive the scientific doctrine of socialism, the resources of scientific and philosophical culture, as well as exceptional intellectual capacities, were required. An extraordinary sense of the need to break with ideological forms, to escape their grip, and to discover the terrain of scientific knowledge was necessary. This discovery, this foundation of a new science and philosophy, was the work of Marx's genius, but it was also an unrelenting work, in which – in the most abject poverty – he used all his energies and sacrificed everything to his enterprise. Engels carried on

his work, and Lenin developed it anew. This, then, is the scientific doctrine which, in the course of a long and patient struggle, was *imported from without* into a working-class movement still given over to ideology, and transformed that movement's theoretical foundations.

2. *The second cardinal principle* concerns the nature of the *historical union* sealed between Marx's scientific theory and the working-class movement. This historical union, whose effects dominate all of contemporary history, was by no means an accident, even a happy one. The working-class movement existed *before* Marx conceived his doctrine; its existence did not, therefore, depend on Marx. The working-class movement is an objective reality, produced by the very necessity of the resistance, the revolt, the economic and political struggle of the working-class – itself produced as an exploited class by the capitalist mode of production. Now, we notice an incontestable historical fact, which has not only survived the worst ordeals (the crushing of the Commune, imperialist wars, suppression of working-class organizations in Italy, Germany and Spain, etc.) but been prodigiously reinforced over the course of time: the most important part – by far – of the working-class movement *adopted Marx's scientific theory as its doctrine*, and successfully applied this theory in its strategy and tactics as well as in its means and forms of organization and struggle. This adoption was not painless. It took dozens and dozens of years, experiences, trials and struggles for this adoption to be sealed. And even today the struggle continues: the struggle between so-called 'spontaneous' ideological conceptions of the working class – anarchistic, Blanquist, voluntarist, and other ideologies – and the scientific doctrine of Marx and Lenin.

If, then, the working-class movement adopted Marx's scientific doctrine *against* its incessantly resurgent 'spontaneous' ideological tendencies, and if the working-class movement made this adoption *of its own accord*, without compulsion, this is because a profound necessity presided over this adoption – over the union of the working-class movement and the scientific doctrine of Marx. This necessity resides in the fact that Marx produced *objective knowledge* of capitalist society, that he understood and demonstrated the necessity of class struggle, the necessity and the revolutionary role of the working-class movement, and thus provided the working-class movement with the knowledge of the objective laws of its existence, of its goals, and its action. It is because the working-class movement *recognized* in Marxist doctrine the objective theory of its existence and its action; it is because the working-class movement recognized in Marxist theory the theory that enabled it to understand the reality of the capitalist mode of production and its own struggles; it is because the working-class movement recognized, by experience, that this doctrine was true, that it imparted to its struggle an objective foundation and genuinely revolutionary objective means – it is for these reasons that the working-class movement adopted Marxist theory. *It is because the working-class movement knew itself in Marxist theory that it recognized itself in it.* It is the scientific truth of Marxist theory that has sealed its union with the working-class movement and made this union definitive. There is nothing fortuitous in this historical fact; everything here is a matter of *necessity, and of its comprehension.*

3. *The third cardinal principle* concerns the process by which this union was finally produced and by which it must unceasingly be maintained, reinforced, and extended. If the 'importation' of Marxist theory required a long haul and a great effort, this is precisely because it was effected through a protracted labour of *education and formation in Marxist theory* and, at the same time, a long *ideological struggle.* Marx and Engels had patiently to convince the best – the most dedicated and the most conscious – working-class militants to abandon existing ideological foundations and adopt the scientific foundations of socialism. This protracted work of education took many forms: direct political action by Marx and Engels, theoretical formation of militants in the course of the struggle itself (during the revolutionary period 1848–49), scientific publications, conferences, propaganda, etc.; and naturally, very quickly – once the conditions existed – *organizational measures,* on the national and then the international plane. In these terms, we can see the history of the First International as the history of the long struggle waged by Marx, Engels and their partisans to make the fundamental principles of Marxist theory prevail in the working-class movement. But at the same time as they were performing this work of education and formation in scientific theory, Marx, Engels and their partisans were constrained to wage a long, patient but harsh struggle *against the ideologies* that then dominated the working-class movement and its organizations, and against the religious, political and moral ideology of the bourgeoisie. *Theoretical formation* on the one hand, *ideological struggle* on the other – these are the two absolutely essential forms, two absolutely essential conditions, which governed the profound transformation of the spontaneous ideology of the working-class movement. These are two tasks which have never ceased, and will never cease, to impose themselves as vital tasks, indispensable to the existence and development of the revolutionary movement in the world – tasks which today condition the passage to socialism, the construction of socialism, and will later condition the transition to Communism.

Theoretical formation, ideological struggle – two notions which must now be examined in more detail.

7. Theoretical Formation and Ideological Struggle

The problem we now examine is distinct from the problem of the nature of Marxist science, distinct from the conditions of the exercise and development of its theoretical practice. We are now presupposing that Marxist science exists as a true living science, which continues to grow and to enrich itself with new discoveries, vis-à-vis the questions that the working-class movement and the development of the sciences pose to it. We are considering Marxist science as existing, as possessing at a given moment of its development a definite body of theoretical principles, analyses, scientific demonstrations, and conclusions – that is, know-ledges. And we are asking ourselves the following question: *by what means* can and must one make this science pass into the working-class movement? *By what means* can this scientific doctrine be made to pass into the consciousness and the practice of working-class organizations?

To answer this question it is necessary to step back again, this time to examine what the *practice* of the working-class movement in general consists of, independently of the scientific character of the principles brought to it by Marx.

As soon as the working-class movement gained a certain strength, and endowed itself with a minimum of organization, its *practice* was subject to objective laws, founded on the class relations of capitalist society as well as the total overall structure of society. The practice of the working-class movement, even in its utopian and reformist organiz-ational forms, unfolds in three planes, corresponding to the three 'levels' constitutive of society: the *economic*, the *political*, and the *ideological*. Nor is this law specific to the working-class movement; it applies to any political movement, whatever its social nature and objectives. Of course, the class nature of different political movements or parties causes the forms of existence of this general law to vary considerably, but this law, with its variations, imposes itself on all political movements. The action of the working-class movement thus necessarily takes the form of a triple struggle: *economic* struggle, *political* struggle, *ideological* struggle.

We know that the *economic struggle* developed first, in sporadic fashion initially, then in more and more organized forms. In *Capital*, Marx shows us that the first phases of the proletariat's economic struggle unfolded around several themes, the most important of which were the struggles for the reduction of the working day, to defend and raise wages, etc. Other themes have intervened in the subsequent history of the working-class movement: the struggle for job security, for social benefits (social security), for paid holidays, etc. In all these cases, we are dealing with a struggle waged on the terrain of *economic exploitation*, and thus at the level of the *relations of production* themselves. This struggle corresponds to the immediate practice of the workers, to the sufferings imposed on them as victims of economic exploitation, to their direct experience of this exploitation, and to their direct understanding – in this experience – of the economic *fact* of exploitation. In large-scale modern industry, wage workers, concentrated by the technical forms of production, directly perceive the class relation of economic exploitation, and they see in the capitalist boss the person who exploits them and benefits from their exploitation. Direct experience of wage labour and economic exploitation cannot furnish *knowledge of the mechanisms* of the economy of the capitalist mode of production, but is sufficient to make the workers aware of their exploitation and organize and engage in their economic struggle. This struggle is developed in *trade unions*, created by the workers themselves, without the intervention of Marxist science; these unions can survive and fight without recourse to Marxist science, and that is why trade-union action constitutes the chosen ground for economic *reformism* – a conception that anticipates the revolutionary transformation of society *from economic struggle alone*. It is this 'trade-unionist', apolitical-syndicalist conception that feeds the *anarcho-syndicalist* tradition, with its suspicion of politics, in the working-class movement. This is why Marx could say that trade unionism – that is, the organization of economic struggle on reformist premises, and the reduction of the struggle of the working-class movement to economic struggle – constitutes the furthest extent, the limit-point of the evolution of the working-class movement 'left to its own devices'.

Whether it wants to or not, however, economic struggle always runs up against *political realities* that intervene directly and violently in the course of the economic struggle – if only in the form of the *repression* of protests, strikes and revolts during the workers' economic struggle by the forces of the bourgeois State and law: the police, the army, the courts, etc. From this experience, produced by the economic struggle itself, derives the necessity for a *political struggle*, distinct from the economic struggle. Here things become more complicated, for workers cannot have an *experience* of *political reality* comparable to their everyday experience of the reality of economic exploitation, because the forms of intervention of class political power are often – with the exception of intermittent displays of overt violence – concealed under cover of the 'law', and juridical, moral, or religious justifications of the existence of the State. This is why the political struggle of the working class is much more difficult to *conceive* and to *organize* than its economic struggle. To lead and organize this struggle on its real terrain, it is necessary to have recognized – at least partially – the nature and role of the State in the class struggle, the relation between political domination and its juridical cover on the one hand, and economic exploitation on the other. For this, something more than intermittent, blind experience of certain effects of the existence of the class State is required: a *knowledge* of the mechanism of bourgeois society. In this domain, the 'spontaneous' conceptions of the proletariat, which govern their political actions, are significantly influenced by bourgeois conceptions, by the juridical, political and moral categories of the bourgeoisie. Whence the utopianism, anarchism and political reformism which can be observed not only at the outset of the political struggle of the working-class movement, but throughout its history. This anarchism and political reformism are incessantly perpetuated and renewed in the working class under the influence of the institutions and ideology of the bourgeoisie.

In the early stages of its political struggle, and in the very limits of that struggle, the working-class movement thus confronts *ideological realities*, dominated by the ideology of the bourgeois class. This accounts for the third aspect of the struggle of the working-class movement: *ideological struggle*. In social conflicts the working-class movement, like all other political movements, experiences this fact: every struggle implies the intervention of people's 'consciousness'; every struggle involves a conflict between *convictions, beliefs,* and *representations of the world*. Economic struggle and political struggle also imply these ideological conflicts. Ideological struggle is not limited, then, to a particular domain. By means of the representation people have of their world, their place, their role, their condition and their future, ideological struggle embraces the totality of human activities, all the domains of their struggle. Ideological struggle is ubiquitous, because it is indissociable from the conception that people have of their condition in all the forms of their struggle; it is indissociable from the ideas in which people live their relation to society and to its conflicts. There can be no economic or political struggle unless people commit their ideas to it as well as their strength.

Nevertheless, ideological struggle can and must also be considered as a struggle in a *specific domain: the domain of ideology*, the domain of religious, moral, juridical, political, aesthetic and philosophical ideas. In this regard, ideological struggle is distinct from other forms of struggle: its object is the terrain of the objective reality of *ideology*, and its goal is, as far as possible, to free this domain from the domination of bourgeois ideology and transform it, in order to make it serve the interests of the working-class movement. Considered thus, ideological struggle is also a specific struggle which unfolds in the domain of ideology and must take account of the nature of this terrain, of the nature and laws of ideology. Without *knowledge* of the nature, laws and specific mechanisms of ideology; without knowledge of the distinctions within ideology, of the dominance of one region over others, of the different degrees (theorized, untheorized) of the existence of ideology; without knowledge of the class nature of ideology; without knowledge of the law of the domination of ideology by the ideology of the dominant class – without all this, ideological struggle is waged blindly. It can obtain some partial results, but never profound and definitive results. It is here that the limits of the natural, 'spontaneous' potential of the working-class movement are most strikingly revealed because, lacking scientific knowledge of the nature and social function of ideology, the 'spontaneous' ideological struggle of the working class is conducted on the basis of an ideology subjected to the insurmountable influence of the ideology of the bourgeois class. It is in the domain of ideological struggle that the necessity of an external intervention – *that of science* – is felt above all. This intervention is revealed to be even more important given that, as we have just seen, ideological struggle accompanies all other forms of struggle, and inasmuch as it is thus absolutely *decisive* for all forms of working-class struggle, since the *inadequacy of the ideological conceptions* of the working class left to itself produces anarchist, anarcho-syndicalist and reformist conceptions of its economic and political struggle.

We can sum up this analysis as follows. Independent of any influence by Marx's scientific theory, the very nature of the working-class movement commits it to a triple struggle: economic struggle, political struggle, ideological struggle. In the unity of these three distinct struggles, the general orientation of the struggle is fixed by the working class's representation of the nature of society and its evolution, the nature of the goals to be attained, and the means to be employed to wage the struggle successfully. The general orientation depends, then, on the *ideology* of the working-class movement. It is *this ideology* that directly governs the conception the working class has of its ideological struggle, and thus the manner in which it conducts the struggle to transform existing ideology; it is the ideology of the working class that directly governs its conception of its economic and political struggles, of their relations, and thus of the manner in which it conducts these struggles. At this level, everything depends on the *content of the ideology* of the working-class movement. Now, we know that this ideology remains a prisoner of the fundamental categories (religious, juridical, moral, political) of the dominant bourgeois class, *even in the way the 'spontaneous' ideology of the working class expresses its opposition to the dominant bourgeois ideology.*

Accordingly, everything depends on the *transformation* of the ideology of the working class, on the transformation which can extricate working-class ideology from the influence of bourgeois ideology and submit it to a new influence – that of the *Marxist science of society*. It is precisely upon this point that the intervention of Marxist science in the working-class movement, and the union of Marxist science and the working-class movement, are founded and justified. And it is the very nature of ideology and its laws that determines the appropriate means to assure the transformation of the 'spontaneous' reformist ideology of the working-class movement into a new ideology, of a scientific and revolutionary character.

The necessity of this *transformation* of existing ideology, first of all in the working class itself, and then in the social strata that are its natural allies, allows us to comprehend the nature of the *means* of this transformation – *ideological struggle* and *theoretical formation*. These means constitute *two decisive links* in the union of Marxist theory and the working-class movement, and thus in the practice of the Marxist working-class movement.

Ideological struggle can be defined as struggle waged *in the objective domain of ideology, against* the domination of bourgeois ideology, *for* the transformation of existing ideology (the ideology of the working class, the ideology of the classes which may become its allies), in a way that serves the objective interests of the working-class movement in its struggle for revolution, and then in its struggle for the construction of socialism. Ideological struggle is a struggle *in* ideology; to be conducted on a correct theoretical basis, it presupposes knowledge of Marx's scientific theory as its absolute condition – it presupposes, then, *theoretical formation*. These two links – ideological struggle and theoretical formation – while both decisive, are thus not on the same plane; they imply a relation of domination and dependence. It is *theoretical formation* that governs ideological struggle, that is the theoretical and practical foundation of ideological struggle. In everyday practice, theoretical formation and ideological struggle constantly and necessarily intertwine. One may therefore be tempted to confuse them and misjudge their difference in principle, as well as their hierarchy. This is why it is necessary, from the theoretical perspective, to insist at once on the *distinction in principle* between *theoretical formation* and *ideological struggle*, and on the *priority in principle of theoretical formation* over ideological struggle.

It is through theoretical formation that Marx's scientific doctrine has been able to penetrate the working-class movement; it is by permanent theoretical education that it continues to penetrate, and to reinforce itself in, the working-class movement. Theoretical formation is an essential task of Communist organizations, a permanent task, which must be pursued without respite and must be incessantly updated, taking account of the development and enrichment of Marxist scientific theory.

It is easy to understand how absolutely indispensable this theoretical formation was in the past in winning the working-class movement to the scientific theory of Marx. Its importance is perhaps less clear *today*, when Marxist theory directly inspires the most important working-class organizations and the entire life of socialist countries. Nevertheless, despite these spectacular historical results, our theoretical task is not finished, and never can be. When we say that the ideology of the working class has been transformed by Marxist theory, this cannot mean that the working class, which was otherwise 'spontaneously' reformist, has become definitively Marxist today. Only the vanguard of the working class, its most conscious part, possesses a Marxist ideology. The great mass of the working class is still in part subject to an ideology of a reformist character. And among the vanguard of the working class itself, which forms the Communist Party, there exists great unevenness in the degree of theoretical consciousness. Among the vanguard of the working class only the best militants have a genuine theoretical formation – in the area of historical materialism at least – and it is among them that theoreticians and researchers capable of advancing Marxist scientific theory can be recruited. This constant unevenness in the degree of theoretical consciousness underlies the demand for a continually renewed and updated effort of theoretical formation in today's Marxist organizations. This reality also dictates an exact conception of theoretical formation, defined as rigorously as possible.

By *theoretical formation*, we understand the process of education, study and work by which a militant is put in possession – *not only of the conclusions* of the two sciences of Marxist theory (historical materialism and dialectical materialism), *not only of their theoretical principles*, not only of some detailed analyses and demonstrations – but of *the totality* of the theory, of all its content, all its analyses and demonstrations, all its principles and all its conclusions, in their indissoluble scientific bond. We literally understand, then, a *thorough study and assimilation* of all the scientific works of primary importance on which the knowledge of Marxist theory rests. We might use a striking formula of Spinoza's to represent this objective: Spinoza said that a science solely of conclusions is not a science, that a true science is a science of premises (principles) and conclusions in the integral movement of the demonstration of their necessity. Far from being an initiation to simple conclusions, or to principles on the one hand and conclusions on the other, theoretical formation is the thorough assimilation of the demonstration of conclusions on the basis of principles, the assimilation of the profound life of science in its spirit, in its very methods; it is a formation that endows those who receive and acquire it with the very scientific spirit that constitutes science, without which science would not be born, and would be unable to develop. Theoretical formation is thus something entirely different from simple economic, political or ideological formation. These must be preliminary stages of theoretical formation; they must be clarified by theoretical formation and founded upon it, but cannot be confused with it, because they are only *partial* stages of it. Practically speaking, there is no real theoretical formation without the study of Marxist science (theory of history, Marxist philosophy) in its purest existence – *not only in the texts of Lenin, but also in the work on which all Lenin's texts were based, and to which they constantly refer: Capital.* There is no real theoretical formation without an attentive, reflective and thorough study of the most important text of Marxist theory that we possess, a text which is far from having yielded to us all its riches.

Doubtless, theoretical formation thus defined may be considered an ideal – not accessible to everyone, given the great theoretical difficulties of reading and studying *Capital,* the degree of intellectual formation of militants, and the limited time we have to dedicate ourselves to this work. We can, and absolutely must, concretely envisage the successive and progressive degrees of theoretical formation, and strike a balance between them, according to people and circumstances. But arranging and realizing this balance itself presupposes the effective recognition of theoretical formation, its nature and its necessity; *it presupposes an absolutely clear knowledge of the ultimate objective of theoretical formation*: to form militants capable of one day becoming men and women of science. To attain this goal one cannot aim too high, and by aiming well and truly it will be possible to define precisely the degrees and appropriate means of progression conducive to this objective.

Why attach such importance to theoretical formation? Because it represents the *decisive intermediary link* by which it is possible both to develop Marxist theory itself, and to develop the influence of Marxist theory on the entire practice of the Communist Party and thus on the profound transformation of the ideology of the working class. It is this double reason that justifies the exceptional importance which Communist Parties have attributed in their past history, and must attribute in their present and future history, to theoretical formation. It is, in fact, by means of well-conceived theoretical formation that Communist militants – whatever their social origin – can become intellectuals in the strong sense of the term – that is, men and women of science, capable one day of advancing Marxist theoretical research. It is also the precise knowledge of Marxist science which *theoretical* formation represents that makes it possible to define and implement, on the basis of Marxist–Leninist science, the Party's economic and political activity and its ideological struggle (its objectives and its means).

The Party is not content to *proclaim* its loyalty to the principles of Marxist–Leninist science. What radically distinguishes the Party from other working-class organizations is not this simple proclamation; it is the concrete, practical *application* of Marxist scientific theory – in the Party's forms of organization, in its means of action, in its scientific analyses of concrete situations. Not content with proclaiming principles, but applying them in action – this is what distinguishes the Party from other workers' organizations. What finally distinguishes the Party is that – even while recognizing the specificity and necessity of theory, of theoretical practice and theoretical research, and the proper conditions of their existence and exercise – the Party refuses to reserve the knowledge of theory as a monopoly for some specialists, leaders and intellectuals, thereby relegating its practical *application* to other militants. On the contrary, consistent with Marxist theory itself, the Party wants to unite theory with its practical application as widely as possible, for the good of theory and practice alike.

That is why it must want to extend the broadest possible *theoretical formation* to the greatest possible number of militants; it must want to educate them constantly in theory, to make them militants in the full sense of the term – capable of analysing and understanding the situation in which they have to act, and thus of helping the Party to define its politics; and also capable, in their own practice, of making new observations and new experiences that will serve as already elaborated raw material on which other, more theoretically formed militants and the best Marxist theoreticians and researchers will work. To say that the entire orientation, and all the principles of action, of the Party rest on Marxist–Leninist theory; to say that practical experience of the political action of the masses and of the Party is indispensable to the development of theory – this is to affirm a fundamental truth which makes sense only if it takes a *concrete form*, if *a real and fruitful bond* is created in both directions – through necessary organizational measures – between theory and its development on the one hand, and the economic, political and ideological practice of the Party on the other. Creation of this bond is the Party's task. And the first, absolutely decisive, link of this bond is constituted by the most thorough *theoretical formation* of the greatest possible number of militants.

In all these matters, it is as imperative to conceive the *overall unity* of the organic process that relates scientific theory and revolutionary practice in both directions as it is to conceive the specific *distinction* of the different moments, and the articulation of this unity. Such a double conception is indispensable, as we have just seen, for *positive* reasons that are at once theoretical and practical. It is equally imperative to be on guard against *negative* confusions both in the domain of theory and in that of practice. We will fall into *idealism* pure and simple if theory is severed from practice, if theory is not given a practical existence – not only in its application, but also in the forms of organization and education that assure the passage of theory into practice and its realization in practice. We will fall into the same idealism if theory is not permitted, in its specific existence, to nourish itself from all the experiences, from all the results and real discoveries, of practice. But we will fall into another, equally grave form of idealism – *pragmatism* – if we do not recognize the irreplaceable specificity of *theoretical practice*, if we confuse theory with its application, if – not in words, but in *deeds* – we treat theory, theoretical research and theoretical formation as purely and simply auxiliary to practice, as 'servants of politics', if we construe theory as pure and simple commentary on immediate political practice. In these two forms of idealism, it can clearly be seen that disastrous practical consequences correspond to the errors of conception, consequences that can – as the history of the working-class movement has shown and still shows – gravely distort not only the working class's own practice, which may succumb to sectarianism or opportunism, but also theory itself, which may be doomed to the stagnation and regression of dogmatic or pragmatic idealism.

The correct distinction between theoretical formation and ideological struggle is thus essential in order to avoid falling into confusions which *all ultimately come down to taking ideology for science, and thus reducing science to ideology.*

At the end of our analysis, then, we rejoin the cardinal principle with which we began: *the distinction between science and ideology.* Without this distinction it is impossible to understand the specificity of Marxism as a science, the nature of the union of Marxism and the working-class movement, and all the theoretical and practical consequences that flow therefrom.

It would be as well to remember that this analysis cannot pretend to be exhaustive; that it had to proceed by simplification and schematization; that it leaves a number of important problems unresolved. We hope that it may nevertheless furnish a correct idea of the decisive importance of the distinction between science and ideology, and of the light that this distinction sheds on a whole series of theoretical and practical problems which working-class and popular Marxist organizations have to confront and resolve in their struggle for the revolution, and for the transition to socialism.

Paris, 20 April 1965

2

On Theoretical Work: Difficulties and Resources*

*Sur le travail théorique. Difficultés et ressources, La Pensée 132, April 1967. Translated by James H. Kavanagh.

I would like to expound, in some rapid pages, some of the difficulties encountered by any work of theoretical exposition of Marxist principles, before proceeding to an inventory of the resources – some well known, others sometimes misunderstood – at our disposal.

1. Difficulties

Whatever the simplicity of its language and the clarity of its exposition, any Marxist theoretical treatise presents some specific and inevitable difficulties: inevitable because they pertain to the specific nature of theory or, more precisely, *theoretical discourse.*

A. *Difficulty of the Terminology of Theoretical Discourse*

Marxism is at once a science (historical materialism) and a philosophy (dialectical materialism). Scientific discourse and philosophical discourse have their own requirements: they use the words of everyday language, or composite expressions constructed with the words of everyday language, but these words always function *otherwise* than they do in everyday language. In theoretical language, words and expressions function as *theoretical concepts.* To be precise, this implies that the meaning of words in such a language is not fixed by their ordinary usage but by the relations between theoretical concepts within a conceptual system. It is these relations that assign to words, designating concepts, their *theoretical meaning.* The peculiar difficulty of theoretical terminology pertains, then, to the fact that its *conceptual* meaning must always be discerned behind the usual meaning of the word, and is always different from the latter. Now this difficulty is concealed for the unaware reader when the theoretical term purely and simply *reproduces* an ordinary term. For example, everyone thinks they immediately know what Marx means when he uses so ordinary a word as 'labour'. Yet it requires a great effort to discern, behind the common (ideological) obviousness of this word, the Marxist *concept* of labour – or better still, to see that the word 'labour' can designate *several* distinct concepts – the concepts of the labour process, labour power, concrete labour, abstract labour, etc.

45

When it is clear – that is, when it is firmly fixed and well marked off – a theoretical terminology assumes the precise function of preventing confusion between the normal meaning of words and the theoretical (conceptual) meaning of the same words. It performs this role above all by forging *composite expressions* that prevent the ideological confusion: thus labour process, abstract labour, mode of production, relations of production, etc.; in each of these expressions one finds only ordinary words (labour, concrete, abstract, mode, production, relations, etc.). It is their specific *conjunction* that produces a new, precise meaning, which is the theoretical concept. Something can be obtained from a theoretical discourse only on condition that it produces these specific expressions, which designate theoretical concepts. This is why, on our own account, we have had to propose some new expressions, as and when necessary, to designate concepts indispensable to the definition of our object (e.g. knowledge-effect, mode of theoretical production, etc.). We have done this with the greatest care, but we had to do it.

B. *Difficulty of Theoretical Discourse*

The terminological difficulty is itself only the index of another, more profound difficulty, which has to do with the *theoretical* nature of our discourse.

What is a theoretical discourse? In the most general sense, it is a discourse that results in the *knowledge* of an object.

At this point, in order to make what follows intelligible, we must offer a few clarifications, anticipating theoretical developments that will be published later.

We shall say that, in the strong sense of the term, only particular real and concrete objects exist. At the same time, we shall say that the ultimate purpose of any theoretical discourse is 'concrete' knowledge (Marx) of these particular real and concrete objects. This is the sense in which abstract history or history in general does not exist (in the strong sense of the term) but only the real, concrete history of those concrete objects that are the particular concrete social formations we can observe in the accumulated experience of humanity. It is in this sense that production in general, abstract production, does not exist (Marx),[1] but only this or that concrete–real conjunction-combination of hierarchically structured modes of production in this or that determinate social formation: the France of 1848 (Marx, *The Eighteenth Brumaire, Class*

---

1. See the 1857 Introduction, in Karl Marx, *Grundrisse*, Harmondsworth 1973, pp. 84 ff. [Ed.]

Struggles in France); the Russia of 1905 or 1917 (Lenin); etc. All knowledge, and hence any theoretical discourse, has as its ultimate goal the knowledge of these particular concrete real objects: either their individuality (the structure of a social formation) or the modes of this individuality (the successive conjunctures in which this social formation *exists*).

However – and this is the decisive point – we know that knowledge of these particular, concrete, real objects is not an immediate given, nor a simple abstraction, nor the *application* of general concepts to specific data. These are the positions of empiricism and idealism. Knowledge of particular, concrete, real objects is the result of an entire *process* of production of knowledge, whose outcome is what Marx calls 'the synthesis of many determinations' – this synthesis being the 'concrete knowledge' of a concrete object (1857 *Introduction*).[2] What does this 'synthesis', as Marx calls it, consist in? And what are these 'determinations'?

This synthesis consists in the correct combination-conjunction of *two types* of elements (or determinations) of knowledges, which, for the sake of clarity, we will for the moment call *theoretical* elements (in the strong sense) and *empirical* elements – or, in other terms, *theoretical* concepts (in the strong sense) and *empirical* concepts.[3]

Theoretical concepts (in the strong sense) bear on abstract-formal determinations or objects. Empirical concepts concern the determinations of the singularity of concrete objects. Thus, we will say that the concept of *mode of production* is a theoretical concept which concerns the mode of production in general – an object which does not *exist* in the strong sense but is indispensable to the knowledge of any social formation, since every social formation is structured by the combination of several modes of production. In the same way, we will say that the concept of the *capitalist* mode of production is a theoretical concept, that it concerns the capitalist mode of production in general – an object that has no existence in the strong sense (in the strong sense, the capitalist mode of production does not exist, but only social formations dominated by the capitalist mode of production) but is none the less indispensable for the knowledge of any social formation characterized by the domination of what we call the capitalist mode of production, etc. The same goes for all Marx's theoretical concepts: mode of production, productive forces (or technical relations of production), social relations

---

2. Ibid., p. 101. [Ed.]
3. I am using the expression 'empirical concept' *provisionally*. We shall need to replace it with a different, more adequate term at a later date.

of production, the political instance, the ideological instance, the concept of determination in the last instance by the economy, the concept of the articulation of instances, the concept of social formation, the concept of conjuncture, the concept of practice, of theory, etc. These concepts do not give us concrete knowledge of concrete objects, but knowledge of the *abstract-formal* determinations or elements (we will say objects) that are indispensable to the production of concrete knowledge of concrete objects. In saying that these are *abstract-formal* objects, we are only noting the terminology used by Marx himself, who, in *Capital*, engaged in 'abstraction' and produced knowledge of 'forms' and 'developed forms'.[4]

Empirical concepts bear on the determinations of the singularity of concrete objects – that is, on the *fact* that such a social formation presents such and such a configuration, traits, particular arrangements, which characterize it as *existing*. Empirical concepts thus add something essential to concepts that are theoretical in the strong sense: precisely the determinations of the existence (in the strong sense) of concrete objects. It might be thought that with this distinction we have reintroduced, under the guise of theoretical concepts, something resembling empiricism – namely, *empirical* concepts. This term (which will be modified in subsequent works to avoid any ambiguity) must not lead us into error. Empirical concepts are not pure *givens*, not the pure and simple tracing, not the pure and simple immediate reading, of reality. They are themselves the result of a whole process of knowledge, containing several levels or degrees of elaboration. Of course, these empirical concepts express the absolute requirement that no concrete knowledge can do without observation, experiment, and the data they provide (this corresponds to the gigantic empirical research, bearing on 'the facts', of Marx, Engels and Lenin, and to the concrete *investigations* and *inquiries* that sustained every 'concrete analysis of a concrete situation' for all the great leaders of the working-class movement. But at the same time they are irreducible to the pure data of an immediate empirical investigation. An investigation or an observation is in fact never passive: it is possible only under the direction and control of theoretical concepts directly or indirectly active in it – in its rules of observation, selection, classification, in the *technical* setting that constitutes the field of observation or experiment. Thus, an investigation or an observation, even an experiment, first of all only furnishes the *materials* which are then worked up into the *raw material* of a subsequent labour

---

4. See Preface to the First Edition of *Capital*, vol.1, Harmondsworth 1976, pp. 89–90. [Ed.]

of transformation that is finally going to produce *empirical* concepts. By 'empirical concepts', then, we do not mean the initial *material* but the result of successive elaborations; we mean the result of a process of knowledge, itself complex, wherein the initial material, and then the raw material obtained, are transformed into empirical concepts by the effect of the intervention of *theoretical concepts* – present either explicitly, or at work within this transformative process in the form of experimental settings, rules of method, of criticism and interpretation, etc.[5]

In no case is the relation of theoretical concepts to empirical concepts a relation of exteriority (theoretical concepts are not 'reduced' to empirical data), or a relation of deduction (empirical concepts are not deduced from theoretical concepts), or a relation of subsumption (empirical concepts are not the complementary *particularity* – the specific cases – of the *generality* of theoretical concepts). Rather, it should be said (in a sense close to Marx's expression when talking about the 'realization of surplus-value') that empirical concepts 'realize' theoretical concepts in the concrete knowledge of concrete objects. The dialectic of this 'realization' – which has nothing to do with the Hegelian concept of the speculative 'realization' of the Idea in the concrete – will obviously demand sustained clarification, which can be produced only on the basis of a theory of the practice of the sciences, and of their history. Be that as it may, we can say that the concrete knowledge of a concrete object indeed appears to us as the 'synthesis' of which Marx spoke: a synthesis of the requisite theoretical concepts (in the strong sense) combined with elaborated empirical concepts. There is no concrete knowledge of a concrete object without the necessary recourse to the knowledge of those specific objects that correspond to the abstract-formal concepts of theory in the strong sense.

For the moment, these specific points suffice for introducing an important distinction between the possible objects of a theoretical discourse. If we retain the distinction just advanced between abstract-formal objects and concrete-real objects, we may say that a theoretical discourse can, according to its *level*, bear either on abstract and formal objects, or on concrete and real objects.

For example, the *scientific* analysis of a concrete historical reality – the French social formation in 1966 – will indeed constitute a theoretical discourse in the general sense, since it provides us with a knowledge. But in that case, it will be said that the discourse concerns a *real-concrete*

_____

5. The concrete or empirical history, empirical sociology, and 'concrete analyses of concrete situations' carried out by Communist Parties offer an example of this work of elaboration.

object. On the other hand, Marx's *Capital* does not analyse a social formation (a real concrete society), but *the capitalist mode of production*; it will be said that it concerns a *formal* or *abstract* object. We can conceive of a large number of theoretical discourses bearing on formal or abstract objects: on the concept of mode of production, for example; or on the instances that constitute a mode of production (economic, political, ideological); or on the forms of transition from one mode of production to another; etc. A discourse on the general principles of Marxist theory also bears on a formal or abstract object: it does not treat some concrete object (this social formation, that conjuncture of the class struggle) but the principles – i.e. the theoretical concepts – of Marxism, *formal-abstract* objects.

If all discourses that produce knowledge of an object can be called, in general, *theoretical*, we must accordingly make a very important distinction between discourses concerning real-concrete objects, on the one hand, and discourses concerning formal-abstract objects, on the other. It will be helpful to designate as theoretical discourse, or *theory in the strong sense*, discourses bearing on formal-abstract objects. This distinction is necessary: on the one hand, the first kind of discourse (concrete) presupposes the existence of the second (abstract); on the other, the *scope* of the second kind of discourse (abstract) infinitely exceeds the object of the first kind. This is quite clear in the case of Marx's theoretical discourse in *Capital*. The *theory* of the capitalist mode of production (a formal-abstract object) – theory in the strong sense – in fact permits knowledge of a great number of real-concrete objects, in this case knowledge of all social formations, all real societies, structured by the capitalist mode of production. On the other hand, the (concrete) knowledge of a real object (e.g. France in 1966) does not *ipso facto* allow knowledge of another real object (England in 1966) unless one makes recourse to the *theory* (in the strong sense) of the capitalist mode of production – that is, unless one extracts from the first concrete knowledge the abstract knowledge at work therein.

From these remarks – difficult, to be sure, but clear, I hope – we can draw two conclusions.

First, that a discourse on the general principles of Marxism is, in its very limits, a *theoretical* discourse *in the strong sense*, since it does not address some real-concrete object (e.g. the class struggle in France, or the history of the 'cult of personality', etc.), but a formal-abstract object: the fundamental principles of Marxism, considered independently of any real-concrete object.

Second, that the specificity of *theory in the strong sense* is precisely to be concerned with a formal-*abstract* object or objects – that is, not to produce 'concrete' knowledge of real-concrete objects, but knowledge of formal-abstract or theoretical objects (in the strong sense), of concepts of theoretical relations and conceptual systems, which then can and must intervene, at a second stage, to work towards the knowledge of real-concrete objects. To say that a theoretical knowledge, or theory in the strong sense, concerns formal-abstract objects, concepts and theoretical conceptual systems means that it possesses the specific capacity to provide the theoretical instruments indispensable to the concrete knowledge of a whole series of *possible* real-concrete objects. In having formal-abstract objects for its object, theory in the strong sense thus bears on *possible* real objects: both on some current, present social formation or 'concrete situation' (Lenin) here and now, but *also* on some other past or future social formation or concrete situation, in some other place – as long as those real objects do indeed come under the abstract concepts of the theory in question.

Such is the difficulty of *theory*. We must never lose sight of the fact that, understood in the strong sense, theory is never reducible to the real examples invoked to *illustrate* it, since it goes beyond any given real object, since it concerns all *possible* real objects within the province of its concepts. The difficulty of theory in the strong sense derives, then, from the abstract and formal character not just of its concepts, but of its *objects*. To do Marxist theory in the strong sense, to define the fundamental theoretical principles of Marxism, is to work on abstract objects, to define abstract objects – for example, the following abstract objects: materialism, historical materialism, dialectical materialism, science, philosophy, dialectic, mode of production, relations of production, labour process, abstract labour, concrete labour, surplus-value, the structure of the economic, the political, the ideological and theoretical mode of production, theoretical practice, theoretical formation, union of theory and practice, etc., etc.

Naturally, the knowledge of formal-abstract objects has nothing to do with a speculative and contemplative knowledge concerning 'pure' ideas. On the contrary, it is solely concerned with *real* objects; it is meaningful *solely* because it allows the forging of theoretical instruments, formal and abstract theoretical concepts, which permit production of the knowledge of real-concrete objects. Of course, this knowledge of formal-abstract objects does not fall from the sky or from the 'human spirit'; it is the product of a *process of theoretical labour,* it is subject to a material history, and includes among its determinant conditions and elements non-theoretical practices (economic, political and ideological) and their results. But, once produced and constituted, the formal-theoretical objects can and must serve as the object of a theoretical labour in the strong sense, must be analysed, thought in their necessity, their internal relations, and developed in order to draw from them all the consequences – that is, all their wealth.

Marx provided us with an example of such work in *Capital*: there, an analysis of a formal-abstract object (the capitalist mode of production) is used to develop all its '*forms*', and to draw out all its consequences. It is because Marx accomplished this theoretical work, in the strong sense – i.e., produced knowledge of the formal-abstract object that is the capitalist mode of production, of all its '*forms*' and consequences – that we can *know* what happens in *real* objects – social formations which fall under the capitalist mode of production. We must go still further. In working on the theoretical object *capitalist mode of production*, Marx also and at the same time worked on a more general theoretical object: the concept of *mode of production*. This permits us, in turn, to work on this object, then on other objects, knowledge of which the concept makes possible – modes of production other than the capitalist mode of production, the feudal mode of production, the socialist mode of production, etc. – and even on an object required by Marx's thought, although he never arrived at it: the concept of *theoretical mode of production* and subsidiary concepts. This, on the condition that we know that in working on these other concepts of modes of production, we are *still* working on formal-abstract objects.

Such is the fundamental difficulty of *theory*, of any theoretical discourse, in the strong sense. Naturally, this difficulty offends common sense, because it introduces a paradoxical innovation: the idea that one can attain the knowledge of real-concrete objects only on the condition of working also and at the same time on formal-abstract objects. Therewith, this difficulty introduces the idea of a very specific form of existence: that of formal-abstract objects, distinct from the form of existence of real-concrete objects. It is not *easy* to grasp this idea, which is the very idea of theory in the strong sense. Above all, it is not *easy* to take this idea into account, practically and constantly, when reading a theoretical text. It requires a real effort to resist the temptations of empiricism (for which only real-concrete objects exist), to adopt the critique of its ideological 'facts', genuinely to criticize them, and to situate oneself at the level of *theory* – i.e. of its formal-abstract objects.

C. *Difficulty of Theoretical Method*

Another difficulty specific to theory pertains not to its object but to *the way* in which it treats its object – that is, to its *method*. It is not enough, in fact, that a discourse treats a theoretical (formal-abstract) object for it to be called theoretical in the strong sense. A theoretical object can, for example, just as well be treated by an ideological or pedagogical discourse. What distinguishes these discourses is their *mode* of treating their theoretical object, their *method.* For example, a discourse like Stalin's little treatise (on dialectical and historical materialism),[6] which played a big role, since it taught Marxism to millions of militants over dozens of years, treats its object by a pedagogical method. It expounds the fundamental principles of Marxism, and in a generally correct manner. It offers the essential definitions, and above all makes the essential distinctions. It has the merit of being clear and simple, and thus accessible to the broad masses. But it exhibits the great defect of *enumerating* the principles of Marxism, without demonstrating the necessity of the 'order of exposition' (Marx) – that is, without demonstrating the internal necessity that links these principles, these concepts. Now the order (of exposition), which connects these concepts to each other, pertains to their necessary relations, these relations to their very properties: this order constitutes their *system,* which gives its real meaning to each of the concepts. For example, if the *distinction* between Marxist science (historical materialism) and Marxist philosophy (dialectical materialism) is clearly marked in Stalin's text, their internal relation and the specific necessity of their relation are not really thought through and demonstrated. For example, if the principles of materialism and of the dialectic are indeed affirmed, their internal, necessary relation is neither expounded nor demonstrated in its specific content.

For practical, *de facto* reasons a pedagogical method of exposition can assuredly leave certain of these relations – if not the necessary system that links the concepts and gives them their sense – in the shade. For *de jure* reasons, a theoretical method of exposition cannot do this. It must rigorously expound the necessity of these relations; that is its purpose. Marx was perfectly conscious of this in *Capital,* when he said that the '*method of exposition*', as distinct from the method of investigation (or method of research and discovery) was an integral part of all scientific (we can add: and philosophical) discourse – that is, of all theoretical discourse.[7]

The difficulty of a theoretical discourse in the strong sense derives, on the one hand, from the formal-abstract nature of its object, and on the other, from the rigour of its 'order' – that is, its method of exposition. What was said of the object must equally be said of the method: like the object, it is necessarily formal-abstract.

Of course, this does not mean that a theoretical discourse must constantly remain at the level of theoretical abstraction alone. It can be illustrated by a great many possible 'concrete' examples. Here again,

6. *Dialectical and Historical Materialism,* Moscow 1941. [Ed.]
7. See Postface to the Second German Edition of *Capital,* vol.1, p. 102. [Ed.]

Marx showed us the way in *Capital*: he continually *illustrates* his analysis of the capitalist mode of production with examples drawn from a real-concrete object, the nineteenth-century British social formation. We have a perfect right to resort to this method of illustration, which is pedagogically sound and may play an important role in certain conditions. But we may do this only on the condition that we carefully distinguish the theoretical analysis of our theoretical (abstract) object from all its concrete 'illustrations', that we know that the object of theory in the strong sense cannot be reduced to, or *confused with*, the real objects used to illustrate it.

If care is not taken to treat illustrations for what they are – illustrations only, and not concrete knowledges in the sense we have defined along with Marx – one risks falling into misunderstandings, like the celebrated misunderstanding to which many historians who read *Capital* fall victim. A historian looks for the concrete knowledge of a concrete object: some social formation in some conjuncture or in the dialectic of conjunctures that cover an entire period. Now *Capital apparently* contains some chapters of concrete history: on labour in England and the history of manufacture and industry; on primitive accumulation, etc. One may be tempted to see in this the Marxist theory of history at work in empirical concepts produced and displayed before our very eyes. Now if these chapters have so fascinated historians, it is precisely because they are *not* chapters of concrete Marxist history in the proper sense; it is because they bear a fraternal resemblance to the empirical chronological descriptions in which ordinary ideological history abounds. Marx does not in fact present them to us as chapters of a Marxist history, but as simple *illustrations* of *theoretical* concepts: the concepts of absolute and relative surplus-value, and of the non-capitalist origin of capitalism. In these pseudo-chapters of concrete history, he confined himself to giving us what he had to: facts designed to illustrate – that is, to repeat in empirical reality – a concept (labour in England) or partial genealogies (the transition from primitive accumulation to large-scale industry). As has been powerfully demonstrated,[8] these are elements for a concrete history – either materials or raw material for a Marxist history – but not chapters of Marxist history. If we want examples of concrete Marxist history, we must look for them where they are to be found: in Marx's historical works (*The Eighteenth Brumaire*, etc.), or in Lenin's historical analyses (*The Development of Capitalism in Russia*, etc.) and the great political analyses from 1917 to 1922. On this condition, we will avoid

---

8. See Étienne Balibar, 'The Basic Concepts of Historical Materialism', *Reading Capital*, London 1979, chapter 4.

the confusions between a concrete illustration of a theoretical concept and Marxist history.

D. *Final Difficulty: the Revolutionary Novelty of the Theory*

To conclude this section on difficulties, we must offer yet another reason – the most important – for the difficulty of Marxist theoretical work.

A theoretical text on Marx contains another difficulty besides that which pertains to the theoretical nature of its object or its method. This further difficulty is the revolutionary novelty of *Marxist* theory.

We have seen what threatens the *words* used by a theoretical discourse: a rapid reading may construe them as having the same meaning they would possess in everyday life, when they actually have an entirely different meaning – that of *theoretical concepts*. We have seen what threatens the object of a theoretical discourse in the strong sense: a rapid reading can take this object as a real-concrete object, when it actually possesses an entirely different nature – that of a formal-abstract object. In these two cases, the specificity of theoretical language (terminology) and of the theoretical object is reduced and destroyed by the intervention of familiar 'obvious facts': those of 'everyday' ideology – i.e., of empiricist ideology.

We cannot have any illusions about this: it cannot be otherwise for Marxist theory. It is not only Marxist theory's sworn adversaries who loudly proclaim that it has *contributed nothing new*; it is also Marxism's partisans, when they read Marx's texts and 'interpret' Marxist theory through the established 'self-evident truths', those of the reigning ideological theories. To take only two examples, Marxists who *spontaneously* – without difficulties, scruples, or hesitation – read and interpret Marxist theory within the schemes of *evolutionism* or *humanism in fact* declare that Marx contributed nothing new – at least in philosophy and, by implication, in science – regarding the method of conceiving theoretical objects, and hence their structure. These Marxists reduce the prodigious philosophical novelty of Marx's thought to existing, ordinary, 'obvious' forms of thought – that is, to forms of the dominant theoretical ideology. In order clearly to perceive and grasp the revolutionary novelty of Marxist philosophy and its scientific consequences, it is necessary lucidly to resist this ideological reduction, to combat the ideology that supports it, and to state what distinguishes the specificity of Marx's thought, what makes it a revolutionary thought, not only in politics, but also in theory.

This is where the last difficulty resides. For it is not easy to break with the 'self-evident truths' of theoretical ideologies like evolutionism or 'humanism', which have dominated all of Western thought for two hundred years. It is not easy to say that Marx was not Hegelian

(Hegelianism is the 'rich man's' evolutionism), that Marx was not evolutionist, that Marx was not theoretically 'humanist'; it is not easy to show *positively how* Marx, because he is neither Hegelian nor 'humanist', is something else entirely, something which must then be *defined*. And when one tries to show this, it is not easy to make it understood and have it acknowledged.

Any theoretical text, however limited, that treats Marxist principles *inevitably* contains this fundamental difficulty. Unless we are going to cede to the false 'self-evidence' of the dominant theoretical ideologies (whether evolutionism, humanism, or other forms of idealism) and thus betray the most precious aspect of Marx's thought – what makes it *theoretically* revolutionary – we must confront this difficulty, and struggle against the ideologies that continually threaten to suffocate, reduce and destroy Marxist thought. This is not an imaginary difficulty; it is an objective historical difficulty, as real in its way as the difficulties of revolutionary practice. The world does not undergo 'fundamental' change *easily*[9] – neither the social world, nor the world of thought.

We know that a revolution is first of all required for the social world to 'change fundamentally'. But after the revolution, it is further necessary to undertake an extremely long, arduous struggle, in politics and ideology, to establish and consolidate the new society, and make it prevail. The same goes for the world of thought. Following a theoretical revolution, another extremely long and arduous struggle is required, in theory and ideology, to establish the new thought, have it recognized and make it prevail, especially if a form of thought that founds a new ideology and a new political practice is involved. Prior to the success of this struggle, the revolution in society, like the revolution in thought, runs a very great risk: of being smothered by the old world and, directly or indirectly, falling back under its sway.

It will be understood why, again today, it would require a real effort to represent accurately the theoretical revolution accomplished by Marx in philosophy and in science, against the old ideologies that tend constantly to submit this revolution to their own law – that is, to smother and destroy it.

This is why, although one certainly wants to take account of the bad reasons (errors, omissions, awkwardness and limits), any theoretical work will also have good reasons, inevitable and necessary reasons, for sometimes being *difficult* – reasons that pertain on the one hand to the theoretical nature of its object and its method, and on the other to the revolutionary novelty of Marx's thought.

---

9. Althusser is alluding to the following line of the *Internationale: 'le monde va changer de base'*. [Ed.]

2. Resources

But another question arises here. When we propose to attempt to define and expound the principles of Marxism, we do not claim to invent them but to resume them, to analyse and develop them. In order to be available for definition and exposition, these principles must already exist and be at our disposal, in some way or another.

This condition seems obvious. We are reflecting on what Marx gave us. In order to speak of the principles of Marxist theory and practice, it seems sufficient, then, to obtain these principles *from where they are to be found*: in Marxist theory and Marxist practice.

Yet this response, in its simplicity, poses a certain number of important problems, which touch on the very nature of the principles of Marxism.

1. We will first of all obtain Marxist principles where they are produced and set forth: in the theoretical works of Marx and his important disciples.

Yet we need only know a little about these works to see that reading them immediately raises a certain number of difficulties.

The first of these difficulties concerns the works of Marx himself. In fact, there are some very tangible theoretical differences between Marx's first works (the so-called 'philosophical' or 'Early' works) and the later works, such as the *Manifesto*, the *Poverty of Philosophy*, the *Contribution to the Critique of Political Economy, Capital,* etc. Similarly, there are tangible differences in *object* between these two groups of works. For example, Marx talks directly and at length about philosophy and ideology in the works of his youth and in *The German Ideology*, but talks of these very little, if at all, in *Capital.* If we want to obtain some Marxist principles concerning philosophy or ideology, to which texts do we refer? To the texts that speak of these directly and explicitly, whatever their date, or to other, subsequent texts that have the great inconvenience of speaking very little, or not at all, about such concerns?

To obtain the principles of Marxism from Marx, then, we must have posed and resolved this preliminary problem: which of Marx's texts can be taken as Marxist? In other words, we must have asked Marx himself a simple and perfectly natural question: from what moment, from which work, did Marx – who, like any bourgeois intellectual of the 1840s necessarily thought in the dominant (idealist) ideology – break with that ideology, at what moment did he lay the foundations of his revolutionary theory? It is evident that if we take the content and the letter of the texts prior to this rupture and this revolution as Marxist – for example, the idealist and humanist texts of his youth – we remain fascinated by the fetishism of the *signature*, and regress to a pre-Marxist position; it is not Marx's signature but Marx's 'thought', in the strong sense, which authenticates a text as Marxist.

To identify the pre-Marxist and the Marxist texts, clearly to distinguish these two series of texts – this is a project that presupposes an entire labour of critique on Marx's work itself. This indispensable critical work has been commenced.[10] It must be understood that any discourse on Marxist theory *presupposes* this preliminary work of critique.

If we take this preliminary work seriously, this implies that we are then able to answer a second question: can we derive certain Marxist principles from the Marxist works of Marx (e.g. *Capital*), even if these works do not directly or explicitly treat or state these principles? By what right, and via what procedures, may we do this? Let us consider, for example, the Marxist conception of *philosophy*: the question of philosophy abounds in the Early Works, and in *The German Ideology*, but little, if anything, is said about it in *Capital*. If we know that the works of Marx's youth are not 'Marxist', we will not take their formulations on philosophy as Marxist; we will not be able to retain them. We will turn to *Capital* in search of what defines Marxist philosophy. Now, *Capital* does not give us the principles of Marxist philosophy in person, since it does not treat philosophy; the capitalist mode of production, not philosophy, is its object.

Nevertheless, Marxist philosophy is very much present in *Capital*, which is a '*realization*' of it. We will say, then, that Marxist philosophy can be found there, because it is *at work* there. We will say that Marxist philosophy exists in *Capital* '*in the practical state*', that it is present in the theoretical practice of *Capital* – to be precise, in the *way* the object of *Capital* is conceived, in the *way* its problems are posed, in the *way* they are treated and resolved. The expression '*in the practical state*' should not mislead us. In this case, the expression designates a mode of existence of philosophy in a *scientific* work, in a theoretical practice, thus a *theoretical* mode of existence, and not (something we shall encounter shortly) a mode of existence in a *political* and historical work, hence 'practical' in the usual sense of the term. The existence of Marxist philosophy '*in the practical state*' in *Capital* designates the particular modality of the existence of the object, the problems, the scientific and thus theoretical method, of *Capital*. To say that Marxist philosophy is found in a practical state in *Capital* signifies, then, that the content of Marxist philosophy is indeed present in *Capital*, but that it lacks its

---

10. Cf. *For Marx* and *Reading Capital*, where distinctions inherited from the Marxist tradition are resumed and developed.

theoretical *form*. Dialectical materialism (Marxist philosophy) is not dealt with there in its own right, as a distinct entity independent of historical materialism (science of history), but in, by, and through this chapter of historical materialism, which analyses the essence of the capitalist mode of production.

It is the existence of Marxist philosophy 'in the practical state' in *Capital* that authorizes us to 'derive' the Marxist conception of philosophy from *Capital*. If Marxist philosophy were not present in *Capital*, we could not derive it therefrom. If it were present there, not only in its content but also in its form, spelled out explicitly, we would not need to 'derive' it. Since it is present therein in the 'practical state' (content), but not in the theoretical state (form), we must endow its content with its proper form. To do that we must identify its content, and give it its corresponding form.

This work is a real theoretical work: not merely a work of simple *extraction, abstraction* in the empiricist sense, but a work of elaboration, transformation and production, which requires considerable effort. At least we can carry out this work, once we know that Marxist philosophy can really exist, in actuality, *in the practical state*, independently of its form and thus of its *theoretical* formulation. And when we affirm this possibility, we should know that we are affirming not only a fact ('it is thus') but a fundamental principle of Marxism itself, a principle that ultimately concerns the relation between a philosophy and a science, the relation between theory and practice: the principle which holds that philosophy exists first of all in the *practice* of the sciences, before existing for itself.

Everyone will understand that what has just been said regarding the principles of Marxist philosophy applies to a great many other principles of Marxism: we often find ourselves obliged to 'derive' them, by a protracted labour of theoretical elaboration, transformation and production, from the 'practical state' in which they are given to us in the texts of Marx and his successors. What applies to certain essential principles (e.g. philosophy, the union of theory and practice, etc.) obviously applies, *a fortiori*, to their consequences. Marx did not 'say everything', not only because he did not have the time, but because to 'say everything' makes no sense for a scientist: only a religion can pretend to 'say everything'. On the contrary, a scientific theory, by definition, always has *something else* to say, since it exists only in order to discover, in the very solution of problems, as many, if not more, problems than it resolves. Thus, in order to define certain Marxist concepts and their consequences, we will often have to 'derive' them from the works of Marx and his successors, and to extend their effects by a complex labour of theoretical elaboration and production.

This indispensable and difficult work has been begun elsewhere, in a rudimentary and imperfect form.[11] But we must understand that any discourse on Marxist theory presupposes this work, without which we would go no further than resetting and rededicating the 'foundation stone' (Lenin)[12] laid by Marx.

Of course – and this is an absolutely determinant remark – we are not alone before Marx's works, and before *Capital.* The work of elaboration to which I have just alluded has been under way for a long time, and its results are to be found in the theoretical works of Marx's main disciples. For example, we find something in Engels and Lenin that explicitly and directly takes up certain of the principles which are found only in the 'practical state' in *Capital. Anti-Dühring, The Dialectics of Nature*, and *Materialism and Empirio-criticism* allow us to pose in much more explicit terms the problem of the nature of Marxist philosophy, of the relation between theory and practice, etc., that remained implicit in *Capital.* The same applies to other principles pertaining to historical materialism – for example the concept of *social formation*, the concept of the *combination of several modes of production in every social formation*: Lenin formulated these, 'deriving' them from Marx through a rigorous theoretical examination, etc.

Any work on Marxist theory must commence by carefully identifying and recording the results we owe to Marx and to his successors, and furthering this effort within the objective and subjective limits of possibility. Of course, we must apply the same method of theoretical 'extraction-elaboration' to the works of Marx's successors. We will thus come to 'derive' such-and-such theoretical elements present in the 'practical state' in these works, in order to impart an adequate theoretical form to their theoretical content.

It will be understood that this work – if it is not a simple 'extraction', but a genuine elaboration – is rarely limited to the production of a made-to-order *form*, just the right match for a ready-and-waiting *content*. To believe that it is simply a matter of *identifying* an already adequate *content*, in order then to provide it with the appropriate form, as one chooses a suit according to the size of a customer, is insufficient. There is no pure content. Any content is always already given in a certain form. To give an adequate form to a theoretical content existing 'in a practical state' almost always presupposes, then, two conjoint operations: the critical rectification of the old form and the production of the new, in one and the same process. This means that the production

---

11. Cf. *For Marx* and *Reading Capital.*
12. See Lenin, 'Our Programme', *Collected Works*, vol.4, Moscow 1960, p. 211. [Ed.]

of the new, *more* adequate, theoretical form presupposes the critique of the old – the perception of its inadequacy and of the reasons for that inadequacy. This means that a work of theoretical elaboration – even one bearing on theoretical contents existing in a theoretical discourse in the 'practical state' – presupposes a critical rectification of what is given in the practical state. There is nothing surprising about this: this is how any theoretical discipline proceeds in its development. A science or philosophy that is new, even revolutionary, always begins somewhere – in a certain universe of extant, and thus historically and theoretically determined, concepts and words; it is by means of the available concepts and terms that any new, even revolutionary, theory must find what it requires in order to think and express its radical novelty. Even in order to think *against* the content of the old universe of thought, any new theory is condemned to think its new content in *certain* of the forms of the existing theoretical universe which it is going to overturn. Neither Marx nor his successors escaped this condition, which governs the dialectic of all theoretical production. This is why we have not only to remove the pre-Marxist content of the thought of the young Marx, but also to criticize, in the name of the logic and coherence of the system of Marxist principles, certain of the *forms* in which the new content is presented. Evidently, this rule also applies to certain *forms* of existence of Marxist theoretical principles 'in the practical state' in the mature works of Marx and his successors. This is why any production of an adequate form for a theoretical content 'in the practical state' is in fact, at the same time, a critical *rectification* of the old form, wherein this content existed 'in the practical state'.

The important thing to grasp here is that this operation of critical rectification is not imposed *from without* on the works of Marx and his successors, but results from the *application* of these works *to themselves*; very specifically, it results from the *application* of their more elaborated forms to their less elaborated forms – or, if one prefers, of their more elaborated concepts to their less elaborated concepts, or again, of their theoretical system to certain terms of their discourse, etc. This operation reveals some 'blanks', 'plays on words', lacunae, inadequacies, which rectification can then reduce. All this work proceeds concurrently: it is by bringing to light the most elaborated forms and concepts, the theoretical system, etc., that rectification can be carried out, and it is rectification that foregrounds forms, concepts and systems which determine its objects. Is it necessary to give some examples? It is the *application* of the conceptual system of *Capital* to the conceptual system of the young Marx's *Economic and Philosophical Manuscripts* that makes visible the theoretical break between the two texts; it is in this way, to be quite precise, by the application of the concept of 'wage labour' (which figures in *Capital*) to the concept of 'alienated labour' (which figures in the Paris *Manuscripts*), that the ideological, non-scientific character of the concept of 'alienated labour' – and thus of the concept of 'alienation' that supports it – becomes visible. In the same way, within *Capital* itself, it is by the *application* of the well-defined concepts of labour process, labour-power, concrete labour, abstract labour, wage labour, etc., to the concept of '*labour*' (also found in *Capital*), that one discovers this concept of 'labour' (by itself) to be, *in Capital*, only a word, one of the old *forms* belonging to the conceptual system of classical political economy and Hegelian philosophy. Marx made use of it, but to lead to some new concepts which, in *Capital* itself, render this form superfluous and constitute its critique. It is extremely important to know this in order to avoid taking this word (labour) for a Marxist concept; otherwise, as many current examples attest, one may be tempted to erect upon it all the idealist and spiritualistic interpretations of Marxism as philosophy of labour, of the 'creation of man by man', of humanism, etc.

Such, then, is the *first response* that can be given to the question: where are we to obtain the principles of Marxism? – *from the theoretical works of Marx and his successors.* On condition, first of all, of having accurately identified those works of Marx that are Marxist. On condition, next, of knowing that Marxist principles can be given to us in those works either in person, in an adequate theoretical form, or in another form, in the practical state. On condition, finally, of knowing that to 'derive' certain of the principles of Marxism from the works of Marx and his successors, especially when those principles are there in a practical state, presupposes an elaboration that must sometimes take the form of a work of critical *rectification*.

2. All this, however, concerns only the *theoretical* works among the classics of Marxism. We must now speak of something else: the *practical* works of Marxism – that is, the political practice of the organizations of class struggle born of the union of Marxist theory and the workers' movement, and its results.

We have shown that Marxist principles can exist 'in the practical state' in the *theoretical* works of Marxism. Now it must be shown that they can also exist 'in the practical state' in the *practical* works of Marxism.

The political practice of Communist Parties can in fact contain, in the practical state, certain Marxist principles, or certain of their theoretical consequences, which are not to be found in existing theoretical analyses. From the viewpoint of the *theoretical content* itself, the political practice of organizations of class struggle can thus find itself – in certain cases and on certain points, and sometimes very considerably – *in advance* of existing theory. One can then 'derive', from the political practice that contains them, theoretical elements in advance of the state of existing theory.

Of course, it is not a matter of just any 'spontaneous' practice, but of the practice of revolutionary parties that base their organization and their action on Marxist theory. Of course, it is not a matter of just any of these practices 'based' on Marxist theory, but of a practice whose relation to Marxist theory is correct.[13] With this dual qualification in mind, the political practice of a revolutionary party, the structure of its organization, its objectives, the forms of its action, its leadership of the class struggle, its historical achievements, etc., constitute the *realization* of Marxist theory in determinate real-concrete conditions. As these principles are theoretical, if this realization is *correct*, it inevitably produces results of *theoretical* value. Among these results, some simply represent the application of theoretical principles already known and stated by theory; others, by contrast, can represent theoretical elements – some new theoretical effects or even principles – that do not figure in the actual state of theory. Under the conditions just mentioned, it is in this way that the political practice of revolutionary Marxist parties can contain, *in the practical state*, theoretical elements, effects, or principles *in advance* of existing theory.

This is why, to the question: where do we find the principles of Marxism?, we can answer: *at once* in the *theoretical* works or the classics of Marxism, and in the *practical* works of the Communist Parties.

Let us clarify what is meant by the 'practical works' or political practice of Communist Parties.

These can be *political* analyses of the concrete situation, *resolutions* fixing the party line, political discourses defining it and commenting on it, *programmatic slogans* recording political decisions or drawing out their conclusions. These can be *actions* undertaken, the *way* they are conducted as well as the results obtained. These can be *forms of organization* of the class struggle, the distinction between its different levels and between the corresponding different organizations. These can be *methods of leadership* of the class struggle and of the union with the masses, the *way* problems of the union of theory and practice in the

---

13. Take, for example, the political practice of the parties of the Second International at the beginning of the twentieth century: its mechanistic, economistic and evolutionist relationship to Marxist theory was essentially *false*. Hence one will not find in it positive *theoretical effects* in the 'practical state' but negative, regressive effects whose theoretical examination would be valuable, as long as it is conceived as the examination of a form of historical *pathology*.

Party, between the leadership and the base, between the Party and the masses, etc., are resolved.

These are so many *forms* of the political practice of the Communist Parties. It is these forms that may contain, in the practical state, new theoretical elements or effects, which can 'realize' and thus produce *principles* as yet absent from theory itself. These new theoretical elements must be sought not only in analyses, decisions, political discourses or actions undertaken, but also in the forms of organization, and in the methods of leadership of the class struggle.

Let us take an example.

It is normal to look for the development of the theoretical principles of Marxism in the *theoretical* works of Lenin. Everyone knows what Lenin contributed to the working-class movement with his theory of imperialism. Yet he contributed still more. And if we wish to identify the most important *theoretical* events produced since Marx and Engels, we must look not so much in Lenin's *theoretical* texts as in his *political* texts. Lenin's deepest and most fertile theoretical discoveries are contained, above all, in his *political* texts, in what constitutes, then, the 'résumé' of his *political practice*. To take only *one* example, Lenin's political texts (analyses of the situation and its variations, decisions taken and analyses of their effects, etc.) give us, with dazzling insistence, *in the practical state*, a *theoretical* concept of capital importance: the concept of the 'present moment' or 'conjuncture'. This concept (or principle), produced by Lenin in the activity of a Marxist party, in order to lead its struggle, is an absolutely fundamental Marxist principle, not only for historical materialism but also – as will be shown below – for dialectical materialism; yet it did not explicitly figure in existing Marxist theory.

Only a little attention is needed to grasp the decisive import of this new theoretical concept. Not only does it retrospectively cast light on the distinctiveness of the Marxist theory of history, on the forms of *variation in dominance* within the social structure on the basis of deter-mination in the last instance by the economic, and thus on historical periodization (that 'cross' of the historians); not only does it for the first time permit the enunciation of a theory – that is, a genuine conceptualiz-ation – of the possibility of political action, detached at last from the false antinomies of 'freedom' and 'necessity' (the 'play' of the variations in dominance in the conjuncture), and of the real conditions of political practice, in designating its object (the balance of class forces engaged in the struggle of the 'present moment'); not only does it allow us to think the articulation of the different instances whose combination of over-determined effects can be *read* in the conjuncture – but it also allows us to pose, in a concrete manner, the problem of the union of theory and practice – that is, one of the most profound questions of dialectical materialism, not only in the domain of political practice but also in the domain of theoretical practice (for, in its relation with the non-theoretical, and especially the political, conjuncture, the theoretical conjuncture defines the link that allows us to think, in the necessity of its 'play', the nature of theoretical practice).

That a principle of such theoretical fecundity and importance was contained in the practical state in Lenin's political analyses and interventions from 1917 to 1923 is an incontestable fact. That this principle remained in a practical state, no one being sufficiently advised to 'derive' it from Lenin's political works, is, unfortunately, also a fact. A theoretical treasure was there, within reach, in Lenin's political works; no one 'discovered' it, and it remained sterile. Even the officially proclaimed primacy of practice, and of political practice, did not inspire systematic research on Lenin's political works. There have certainly been important lessons drawn from them in the practice of the Communist Parties. But, leaving aside Stalin's *Questions of Leninism*, no systematic theoretical work was derived, bearing on Lenin's political principles. Moreover, there has been no systematic theoretical work drawn from Lenin's political practice, bearing on the theoretical concepts of historical materialism and dialectical materialism and thus on the important theoretical, even philosophical, discoveries produced by Lenin's *political practice*. In the same way, a number of theoretical concepts remained in the 'practical state' in the works of Marx himself. To what do we owe this regrettable situation, whose effects can be painfully felt today? Without a doubt, to the urgency of the political tasks of the working-class movement, which was not allowed the leisure of calm study by its class enemy. But also to the conception of Marxism constructed by 'intellectuals of the working class', cut off as they were either from its real practice or from the practice that produced its theory, and thus subject, despite their political loyalty, to bourgeois ideologies – empiricism, evolutionism, humanism, pragmatism – which they projected on to the great classical texts, as they did on to the great deeds of the working-class movement. Be that as it may, this situation lays a precise task before us: to draw from Marx, from Lenin, and from the great Communist leaders, not only what they said in their theoretical works, but also whatever these works contain in the practical state, as well as whatever their political works contain by way of theoretical discoveries. An urgent task.

Thus, important theoretical events do not always or exclusively occur in theory: it happens that they also occur in *politics*, and that as a result, in certain of its sectors, political practice finds itself in advance of theory. It happens that theory does not take notice of these theoretical events, which occur outside its official, recognized field, even though they are decisive, in many respects, for its own development.[14]

If, to reprise an excellent formula (applied to Galileo by Georges Canguilhem), we declare that the peculiarity of theory is to '*speak the truth*' [*dire le vrai*], in the strong sense of the word – to isolate, define, state and demonstrate it with theoretical arguments; thus in a *discourse* subject, as Marx wished, to a rigorous 'order of exposition' – we must note, at the same time, that one can '*be in the truth*' [*être dans le vrai*], without therewith being able to 'speak the truth'.[15] This distinction may be understood in a very broad sense: one 'is in the truth' not only when one 'tells' it but also when one produces a theoretical content 'in the practical state', without at the same time producing its theoretical form, the form of its 'telling', or of its theoretical discourse. We have seen that one can thus be in the truth *in theory* itself, without in the same breath being able to *speak* the truth therein. It is thus that Marxist philosophy is found in the practical state in *Capital*: *Capital* is indeed in Marxist philosophy, without also being able to 'speak' it, without producing its rigorous discourse. We have just seen that one could thus 'be in the truth' in political practice, without being able to 'speak' this truth there, in the strong sense of theoretical discourse.

This possibility of being in the truth without saying the truth, the distinction between a theoretical content in the practical state and a theoretical content in the theoretical state – all these propositions are not conveniences or devices of an expository *rhetoric*; they are propositions that directly concern Marxism itself, because they involve the relation of theory and practice, they affirm the 'primacy of practice' – in theory as well as in practice – and, most crucially, they also show us the variations of this relation, which can oscillate between the extremes of a false relation and a correct relation.

Just because a new theoretical content can exist in the practical state in Marxist theory or in the practice of Communist Parties, it does not follow that everything existing there in a 'practical state' has a theoretical value. It is not true that one is in the truth solely by virtue of the fact that one is in 'practice', just as it is not true that one is in the truth solely by virtue of the fact that one decides to 'speak' it – that is, solely by virtue of the fact that one has a discourse with a 'theoretical' appearance, or

---

14. To take another example, it is clear that Marxist theory has still not drawn all that it should from the theory-practice and leadership-masses dialectic contained in Lenin's decision to adopt the slogan of 'Soviets', or his analysis of the transition phases of the revolutionary period.

15. See Georges Canguilhem, 'Galilée: la signification de l'œuvre et la leçon de l'homme', *Études d'histoire et de philosophie des sciences*, Paris 1968, p. 46. [Ed.]

that one 'does' theory. If this were true, all chatterboxes would be scientists, as Feuerbach said. One can 'do' bad practice, just as one can 'do' bad theory. In the practical as in the theoretical order, we have a renowned example, to which Lenin drew our attention: the theoretical and political revisionism of the Second International.

But this example leaves us with a final theoretical problem: in the theoretical practice of Marxism, as in its political practice, what conditions must be observed to assure a *correct union* of theory and practice – that is, to assure this union against the deviations to which it is exposed? The answer to this question depends on a *general* theory of the union of theory and practice, both in the field of theoretical practice and in the field of political practice, and on a theory of the *articulation* of these two fields; this theory can be *general* only on condition that it includes the theory of the extreme limits of the variability of this union (false union, correct union). We are no longer bereft of the means with which to pose and resolve this difficult and urgent problem: we have at our disposal the entire experience of the ideological struggle (Engels's and Lenin's struggle against theoretical dogmatism and revisionism) and of the political struggle (against political dogmatism and revisionism) of the Communist Parties. There, again, we have at our disposal an experience that undoubtedly contains, in the practical state, historical protocols of the greatest theoretical import. We need only go to work.

In this work, the resources far outweigh the difficulties.

Philosophy and the Spontaneous Philosophy of the Scientists (1967)*

*_Philosophie et philosophie spontanée des savants (1967)_, François Maspero, Paris 1974. Translated by Warren Montag.

PREFACE

This introduction to the 'Philosophy Course for Scientists' was delivered in October–November 1967 at the École Normale Supérieure.

At that time I and a group of friends concerned with problems in the history of the sciences, and with the philosophical conflicts to which it gives rise, intrigued by ideological struggle and the forms it can take among the intellectuals of scientific practice, decided to address our colleagues in a series of public lectures.

This experiment, inaugurated by the present exposition and continued by the interventions of Pierre Macherey, Étienne Balibar, François Regnault, Michel Pêcheux, Michel Fichant and Alain Badiou, was to last up to the eve of the great events of 1968.

The texts of the lectures were immediately mimeographed and soon began to circulate. Later, on the initiative of students, certain of them were even reproduced in the provinces (Nice, Nantes).

From the beginning we had planned, perhaps precipitately, to publish the lectures. To this end, a 'series' was created in the *Théorie* collection, and in 1969 the lectures by M. Pêcheux and M. Fichant (*Sur l'Histoire des sciences*) and by A. Badiou (*Le Concept de modèle*) appeared. For various reasons the other lectures, although announced, could not be published.

It is in response to numerous requests that I have today, after a long delay, published my 1967 Introduction to *Philosophy and the Spontaneous Philosophy of the Scientists.*

With the exception of part of the first lecture and the critique of Jacques Monod, which I have reproduced unchanged, I have revised the remainder of the text to make more readable what was nothing more than a hasty improvisation and also to develop certain formulae that had not been worked out and were often enigmatic.

But I have, on the whole, been careful to respect the theoretical *limitations* of this essay, which should be read as a *dated* work.

I am also publishing it as a retrospective testimony. In it may be found the initial formulations that 'inaugurated' a turning point in our research on philosophy in general and Marxist philosophy in particular. Previously (in *For Marx* and *Reading Capital*), I had defined philosophy as 'the theory of theoretical practice'. But in this course new formulae

71

appear: philosophy, which has no *object* (in the sense that a science has an object), has *stakes*; philosophy does not produce knowledges but states *Theses*, etc. Its *Theses* open the way to a *correct* position on the problems of scientific and political practice, etc.

These formulae remain schematic and much work will be necessary to complete them and render them more precise. But at least they indicate an order of research the trace of which may be found in subsequent works.

Louis Althusser
14 May 1974

Lecture I

Our poster announced an introductory course on philosophy for scientists.

I see among you mathematicians, physicists, chemists, biologists, etc., but also specialists in the 'human sciences' and, if they will forgive me, in what are, by convention, known simply as 'the arts'. Little matter: it is either a real experience of a scientific practice or the hope of giving your discipline the form of a 'science' that brings you together, as well as, naturally, the question: what is to be expected of philosophy?

You see before you a philosopher: philosophers took the initiative of organizing this course, having judged it possible, opportune, and useful.

Why? Because, being familiar with works on the history of philosophy and of the sciences and having friends who are scientists, we have arrived at a certain idea of the relations that philosophy necessarily maintains with the sciences. Better still: a certain idea of the relations that philosophy *should* maintain with the sciences if it is to serve them rather than enslave them. Better still: because, as a result of an experience external to philosophy and to the sciences but indispensable to an understanding of their relationship, we have arrived at a certain idea of *which* philosophy can serve the sciences.

And since it is we philosophers who have taken this initiative, it is fitting that we take the first step: by first speaking of our own discipline, philosophy. I will therefore attempt, using terms that are as clear and simple as possible, to give you an initial idea of philosophy. I do not propose to present to you a theory of philosophy but, far more modestly, a description of its manner of being and of its manner of acting: let us say of *its practice*.

Hence the plan of this first lecture. It will consist of two parts:

1. A 'putting into place' of basic notions, culminating in the statement of twenty-one philosophical Theses.

2. The summary examination of a concrete example in which we will be able to see the majority of these Theses exercise their proper philosophical 'function'.

I BASIC NOTIONS

This lecture will begin with the statement of a certain number of didactic and dogmatic propositions. These adjectives, I am quite aware, do not have good reputations, but that does not matter: we must not give in to either the fetishism or the counter-fetishism of words.

Didactic propositions: for no lecture escapes the circle of pedagogical exposition. To give an idea of a question, it is necessary to begin and hence first to give apparently arbitrary definitions which will only subsequently be justified or demonstrated.

Dogmatic propositions: this adjective pertains to the very nature of philosophy. Definition: I call dogmatic any proposition that assumes the form of a *Thesis*. I will add: 'Philosophical propositions are Theses' and therefore dogmatic propositions.

This proposition is itself a philosophical Thesis.

Hence *Thesis 1*. Philosophical propositions are Theses.

This Thesis is stated in a didactic form: it will be explained and justified later, as we go along. But at the same time I specify that it is a Thesis, that is, a dogmatic proposition. I therefore insist: a philosophical proposition is a dogmatic proposition and not simply a didactic proposition. The didactic form is destined to disappear into the exposition, but the dogmatic character persists.

We have straight away touched a sensitive point. What does 'dogmatic' really mean, not in general but in our definition? To give a first elementary idea, I will say this: philosophical Theses can be considered dogmatic propositions *negatively*, in so far as they are not susceptible to demonstration in the *strictly* scientific sense (in the sense that we speak of demonstration in mathematics or in logic), nor to proof in the *strictly* scientific sense (in the sense that we speak of proof in the experimental sciences).

I then derive from *Thesis 1* a *Thesis 2* that explains it. Not being the object of scientific demonstration or proof, philosophical Theses cannot be said to be 'true' (demonstrated or proved as in mathematics or in physics). They can only be said to be 'correct' [*justes*].

Thesis 2. Every philosophical Thesis may be said to be correct or not.

What might 'correct' signify?

To give an initial idea: the attribute 'true' implies, above all, a relationship to theory; the attribute 'correct' above all a relationship to practice. (Thus: a correct decision, a just [*juste*] war, a correct line.)

Let us stop a moment.

I am simply trying to give you some idea of the *form* of our lecture. Being a lecture, it states didactic propositions (which are justified later). But being a lecture on philosophy, it didactically states propositions that are necessarily dogmatic propositions: Theses. It will be noted that in so far as they are Theses, philosophical propositions are *theoretical* propositions, but in so far as they are 'correct' propositions, these theoretical propositions are haunted by *practice*. Let me add a paradoxical remark. An entire philosophical tradition since Kant has contrasted 'dogmatism' with 'criticism'. Philosophical propositions have always had the effect of producing 'critical' distinctions: that is, of 'sorting out' or separating ideas from each other, and even of forging the *appropriate* ideas for making their *separation* and its necessity visible. Theoretically, this effect might be expressed by saying that philosophy 'divides' (Plato), 'traces lines of demarcation' (Lenin) and produces (in the sense of making manifest or visible) distinctions and differences. The entire history of philosophy demonstrates that philosophers spend their time *distinguishing* between truth and error, between science and opinion, between the sensible and the intelligible, between reason and the understanding, between spirit and matter, etc. They always *do* it, but they do not say (or only rarely) that the practice of philosophy consists in this demarcation, in this distinction, in this drawing of a line. *We say it* (and we will say many other things). By recognizing this, by saying it and thinking it, we separate ourselves from them. Even as we take note of the practice of philosophy, we exercise it, but *we do so in order* to transform it.

Therefore philosophy states Theses – propositions that give rise neither to *scientific* demonstration nor to proof in the strict sense, but to *rational justifications* of a particular, distinct type.

This Thesis has two important and immediate implications:

1. Philosophy is a discipline different from the sciences (as the 'nature' of its propositions will suffice here to indicate).

2. It will be necessary to explain and justify this difference, and in particular to think the proper, specific *modality* of philosophical propositions: what distinguishes a Thesis from a scientific proposition?

From the outset, we can see that we have touched on an important primary problem: what is philosophy? What distinguishes it from the sciences? And what makes it distinct from them?

I will leave these questions to one side. I simply wanted in two Theses to give you an initial idea: what might these philosophers who are speaking to you be thinking of? A few preliminary words were necessary. But if we were now to get acquainted?

You scientists did not come here to hear what I said a moment ago. You did not really know what to expect. You came for different reasons: let us say out of friendship, interest, curiosity.

Let us leave aside friendship and all that might pertain to the comforts of this place: the École Normale. You came out of curiosity and interest. Difficult feelings to define.

I do not believe I am wrong, however, in saying that your interest and your curiosity centre around two poles: one negative, the other positive. And that whilst the negative is well defined, the positive is rather vague. Let us see.

1. The Negative Pole

Let us be good sports. Philosophers at work! It is well worth going out of your way to have a close look at such a spectacle! What spectacle? Why, comedy. Bergson (*Le Rire*)[1] has explained and Chaplin has shown that, ultimately, comedy is always a matter of a man missing a step or falling into a hole. With philosophers you know what to expect: at some point they will fall flat on their faces. Behind this mischievous or malevolent hope there is a genuine reality: ever since the time of Thales and Plato, philosophy and philosophers have been 'falling into wells'. Slapstick. But that is not all! For ever since Plato philosophy has been falling within its own realm. A second-degree fall: into a philosophical theory of 'falling'. Let me spell it out: the philosopher attempts *in* his philosophy to descend from the heavenly realm of ideas and get back to material reality, to 'descend' from theory and get back to practice. A 'controlled' fall, but a fall nevertheless. Realizing that he is falling, he attempts to 'catch' his balance in a theory of falling (a descending dialectic, etc.) and falls just the same! He falls twice. Twice as funny.

Let us be good sports. Philosophers make a lot of fuss about nothing. They are intellectuals without a practice. Far removed from everything.

---

1. Paris 1920; translated as *Laughter. An Essay on the Meaning of the Comic*, London 1921. [Ed.]

Their discourse is nothing but a commentary on, and a disavowal of, this distance. They try, at a remove, to grasp the real in their words, to insert it in systems. Words succeed words, systems succeed systems, while the world continues its course as before. Philosophy? The discourse of theoretical impotence on the real work of others (scientific, artistic, political, etc., practice). Philosophy: what it lacks in titles it makes up for in pretension. This pretension produces beautiful discourses. So: philosophy as pretension will figure among the fine arts. An art. We are back to the spectacle. This time it is dance: dancing so as not to fall.

Yes, we are going to fall flat on our faces. Note that scientists (like all men engaged in a real practice) can also fall flat on their faces. But they do so in a particular way: when they fall, they calmly register the fact, ask themselves why, rectify their errors and get on with their work. But when a philosopher falls flat on his face, things are different: for he falls flat on his face within the very theory which he is setting forth in order to demonstrate that he is not falling flat on his face! He picks himself up *in advance*! How many philosophers do you know who admit to *having been mistaken*? A philosopher is never mistaken!

In short, your air of amused curiosity masks a certain comic and derisive idea of philosophy – the conviction that philosophy has no practice, no object, that its domain is but words and ideas: a system that might be brilliant, but which exists in a void.

You have to admit that even if, out of politeness, you refrain from saying so, you do derive a certain pleasure from entertaining such ideas, or at least analogous ones.

Well, I will say right away that for my part I endorse *all these ideas*: for they are neither gratuitous nor arbitrary. But I will, naturally, take them up, in the form of *Theses*, for in their way they are philosophical and contribute to the definition of philosophy.

Thesis 3. Philosophy does not have as its object real objects or a real object in the sense that a science has a real object.

Thesis 4. Philosophy does not have an object in the sense that a science has an object.

Thesis 5. Although philosophy has no object (as stated in Thesis 4), there exist 'philosophical objects': 'objects' internal to philosophy.

Thesis 6. Philosophy consists of words organized into dogmatic propositions called Theses.

Thesis 7. Theses are linked to each other in the form of a *system*.

Thesis 8. Philosophy 'falls flat on its face' in a particular, different, way: for others. In its own view, philosophy is not mistaken. There is no philosophical error.

Here again I am proceeding didactically and dogmatically. The explanations will come later. But you suspect that, when I grant all your points, I am holding something back. You naturally suspect that in advancing Theses on philosophy *in general*, and in stating them as *Theses*, I am saying what is, but at the same time keeping my distance: I am already adopting a philosophical position with regard to philosophy in general. What position? That too will become clear later.

2. The Positive Pole

In truth, you have not come here solely for the pleasure of seeing us perform our comically clumsy acrobatics. For my own part, I agree with you that we have come to 'fall flat on our faces', but in an unexpected manner that distinguishes us from the majority of philosophers and knowing it perfectly well: *so as to disappear into our intervention*. You see that we are already beginning to distance ourselves from Thesis 8.

And what about you? What attracts you and keeps you here? I would say: a sort of expectation, questions that have not been formulated and to which you have no answers, some well founded, others perhaps false. But each one expecting or demanding an answer: either a positive answer or an answer that exposes the pointlessness of the question.

In a very general sense, this expectation (coming as much from scientists as from specialists in the arts) can be stated in the following form. Leaving details to one side (we will come back to them), all these unanswered questions give rise to the following question: *is there not, after all, in spite of everything, something to be hoped for from philosophy?* When all is said and done, might there not be in philosophy something of relevance to our concerns? To the problems of our scientific or literary practice?

This kind of question is undoubtedly 'in the air', because you are here. Not simply out of curiosity but because it might be in your interests to be here.

With your permission, we are going to proceed in order: going from the most superficial to the most profound – and to this end, to distinguish three levels in the reasons for this interest.

A. *First Level*

First of all, there is what can only be called the fashion for interdisciplinarity. These days, an encounter between representatives of different disciplines is supposed to hold all the promise of a miracle cure. Scientists are already holding such meetings, and the CNRS[2] itself

---

2. Centre National de la Recherche Scientifique. [Ed.]

recommends them. It is virtually the main slogan of modern times. Cities have already been built, conceived for the sole purpose of housing large communities of scientists (Princeton, Atomgorod). Interdisciplinarity is also very much the 'done thing' at all possible levels in the human sciences. So why not here? Why not an encounter between philosophers, scientists and literary specialists? Let us go further: would not the presence of philosophers give meaning to this interdisciplinary encounter? Given that he is eccentric to all scientific disciplines, might not the philosopher, by his very *nature*, be the artisan of interdisciplinarity because he is, whether he likes it or not, a 'specialist' in interdisciplinarity?

Behind the term interdisciplinarity, there may certainly be undeniably definite and important objective achievements. We will speak of them. But behind the generality of the slogan of interdisciplinarity, there is also an *ideological* myth.

For the sake of clarity, I will take note of this by stating three Thesis:

Thesis 9. An ideological proposition is a proposition that, while it is the symptom of a reality other than that of which it speaks, is a false proposition to the extent that it concerns the object of which it speaks.

Thesis 10. In the majority of cases, the slogan of interdisciplinarity is a slogan that today expresses an *ideological* proposition.

Thesis 11. Philosophy is neither an interdisciplinary discipline nor the theory of interdisciplinarity.

I will indicate in passing: it is clear that with these Theses we are moving ever further from the domain of a definition of philosophy in general. We are taking part in debates internal to philosophy concerning a *stake* [*enjeu*] (interdisciplinarity) in order to mark our own philosophical *position*. Is it possible to define philosophy without adopting a position within philosophy? Remember this simple question.

B. *Second Level*

Here we encounter the problems posed by the massive development of the sciences and technologies, and this is a much more serious matter. Problems internal to each science, and problems posed by the relations between different sciences (relations of the application of one science to another). Problems posed by the birth of new sciences in zones that might retrospectively be said to be border zones (e.g. chemistry, physics, biochemistry, etc.).

There have always been problems internal to scientific practice. What is new is that today they seem to be posed in *global* terms: recasting earlier sciences, redrawing former borderlines. They are also posed in global terms from the social point of view: the theoretical problems of

strategy and tactics in research; the problems of the material and
financial conditions and implications of this strategy and tactics.

And so one wonders: can there be strategy and tactics in research?
Can there be a direction of research? Can research be directed, or must
it be free? In accordance with what ought it to be directed? Purely scientific objectives? Or *social* (that is, *political*) objectives (the prioritization
of sectors), with all the financial, social and administrative consequences
that implies: not only funding but also relations with industry, with
politics, etc.?

And if these questions are successively resolved on a general level,
what will their possible and necessary effects be at the level of research
itself? It is possible to think a strategy and tactics internal to each research
programme? Are there methods, methods of scientific discovery, that
permit research to be 'guided'?

These are all problems before which scientists are hesitant or divided.
One has only, for example, to read the official and technocratic
discourses from the *Colloque de Caen* and the criticisms voiced by the
young scientists of *Porisme*. Two extreme positions: absolute freedom
on the one hand, planned research on the other. Between the two, the
technocratic solution of Caen, inspired by American and Soviet
'models'. On the horizon, the Chinese solution.

When faced with the complexity and difficulty of these massive
problems, where it is no longer simply a question of immediate scientific
practice (the researcher in his laboratory) but of the social process of the
production of knowledges, of its organization and its politics (the
question of who will govern it), one wonders: might not the philosopher
by chance have something to say; a semblance of an answer to these
questions? Something to say, for example, on the important theoretical
and political alternative of freedom or planning in research? On the
social and political conditions and goals of the organization of research?
Or even on the method of scientific discovery?

Why not? Because such an expectation responds precisely to something that pertains to the pretension of philosophy. Those who laugh-
ingly say that philosophers 'dabble' in everything may find that the joke
is on them. To put it in more elevated terms, these dabblers in everything may have certain ideas about *the Whole*, about the way things are
linked to each other, about the 'totality'. This is an old tradition that
goes back to Plato, for whom the philosopher is the man who *sees* the
connection and articulation of the Whole. The philosopher's object is
the Whole (Kant, Hegel ...), he is the specialist of the 'totality'.

Similar expectations are found amongst literary specialists who are
trying to give birth to sciences. Might not the philosopher have some
idea about the way the sciences, the arts, literature, economics and

politics are related to each other, interconnected and articulated into a Whole?

There is a certain truth behind this expectation and in this tradition. The philosopher is certainly concerned with *questions* that are not unrelated to the *problems* of scientific practice, to the problems of the process of the production of knowledges, to political and ideological problems, to the problem of relations between all these problems. Whether he has the *right* to be so concerned is another question: he *is*.

But philosophical *questions* are not scientific *problems.* Traditional philosophy can provide answers to its own *questions*, it does not provide answers to scientific, or other, *problems* – in the sense in which scientists solve their problems. Which means: philosophy does not resolve scientific problems in the place of science; philosophical questions are not scientific problems. Here again, we are adopting a position within philosophy: philosophy is not a science, nor *a fortiori* Science; it is neither the science of the crises of science, nor the science of the Whole. Philosophical questions are not *ipso facto* scientific problems.

I will immediately record this position in the form of Theses.

Thesis 12. Philosophy states Theses that effectively concern most of the sensitive points regarding the problems of 'the totality'. But because philosophy is neither a science nor the science of the Whole, it does not provide the solution to these problems. It intervenes in another way: by stating Theses that contribute to *opening the way* to a *correct* position with regard to these problems.

Thesis 13. Philosophy states Theses that assemble and produce, not scientific concepts, but philosophical categories.

Thesis 14. The set of Theses and philosophical categories that they produce can be grouped under, and function as, a *philosophical method.*

Thesis 15. In its modality and its functioning, philosophical method is different to a scientific method.

C. *Third Level*

Here, finally, are the last reasons for your interest in philosophy.

Behind purely scientific problems we have all felt the presence of historical events of immense import. Official vocabulary sanctions this fact: 'mutations' in the sciences, 'moving into the space age', 'the revolution in civilization' (from Teilhard de Chardin to Fourastié). All the political problems that are known to be more or less linked to these questions, the backdrop, the USA, the USSR, China. Real political and social revolutions. The feeling that we have reached a 'turning point' in the history of humanity gives renewed force to the old question: where do we come from? Where are we? And behind those questions, the question of questions: *where are we going?*

A question to be understood in every sense of the term, and in all its aspects. It interrogates not only the world and science – where is history going? Where is science going (exploitation, well-being, nuclear war)? – but also each one of us: what is our place in the world? What place can we occupy in the world today, given its uncertain future? What attitude should we adopt with regard to our work, to the general ideas that guide or hinder our research and may guide our political action?

Behind the question: where are we going?, there is an urgent, crucial practical question: how do we *orientate* ourselves? Which direction should we follow? What is to be done?

For intellectuals, scientists or literary specialists, the question takes a precise form: what place does our activity occupy in the world, what role does it play? What are we as intellectuals in this world? For what is an intellectual if not the product of a history and a society in which the division of labour imposes upon us this role and its blinkers? Have not the revolutions that we have known or seen announced the birth of a *different* type of intellectual? If so, what is our role in this transformation?

The meaning of history, our place in the world, the legitimacy of our profession: so many questions which, whenever the world shatters old certitudes, touch upon and always end up reviving the old religious question of *destiny*. Where are we going? And that soon becomes a different question. It becomes: what is man's destiny? Or: what are the ultimate ends of history?

We are then close to saying: philosophy must have something of an answer in mind. From the Whole to the Destiny, origins and ultimate ends, the way is short. The philosophy that claimed to be able to conceive of the Whole also claimed to be able to pronounce upon man's destiny and the Ends of history. What should we do? What may we hope for? To these moral and religious questions traditional philosophy has responded in one form or another by a theory of 'ultimate ends' which mirrors a theory of the radical 'origin' of things.

We will not play on this expectation. Once again I will respond with Theses, by taking sides, as always, in philosophy. Everyone will understand that the philosophy in question in these Theses is not philosophy in general nor *a fortiori* the philosophy of 'ultimate ends'.

Thesis 16. Philosophy does not answer questions about 'origins' and 'ultimate ends', for philosophy is neither a religion nor a moral doctrine.

Thesis 17. The question of 'origins' and of 'ultimate ends' is an *ideological* proposition (cf. Thesis 9).

Thesis 18. Questions of 'origins' and 'ultimate ends' are ideological propositions drawn from religious and moral ideologies, which are *practical ideologies.*

Thesis 19. Practical ideologies are complex formations which shape notions–representations–images into behaviour–conduct–attitude– gestures. The ensemble functions as practical norms that govern the attitude and the concrete positions men adopt towards the real objects and real problems of their social and individual existence, and towards their history.

Thesis 20. The primary function of philosophy is to draw a line of demarcation between the ideological of the ideologies on the one hand, and the scientific of the sciences on the other.

See what has happened. The question of the meaning of history, of the destiny of man, has projected a new character to the front of the stage: the *ideological.* Not in the form that we have already encountered in Thesis 9 (an ideological proposition is ...) – which was purely formal – but in another form: that which relates an ideological proposition to its 'birth place': *practical* ideology, thus to a *social* reality foreign and external to scientific practice.

And see what happens. With ideology (as related to practical ideologies), a third character enters the stage. Up to now we have had two of them: philosophy and science, and our central question was: what distinguishes philosophy from the sciences? What gives philosophy its own nature, distinct from the nature of the sciences? Now a new question arises: what distinguishes the scientific from the ideological? A question that must be either confronted or replaced by another but which, from the outset, has its effects upon philosophy. For the philos- ophy within which we have taken a position is truly haunted by practical ideologies! – since it reflects them in its theory of 'ultimate ends', be they religious or moral.

Let us simply note this point: from now on, philosophy is defined by a double relation – to the sciences and to practical ideologies.

This is not speculation. If we hope to receive anything from philos- ophy, we must know what it can impart, and in order to know that, we must know how it is done, upon what it depends and how it functions. We advance, step by step: we discover what philosophy is *by practising it.* There is no other way. And our position is coherent: we have said that philosophy is above all *practical.*

You see the result. Simply taking seriously and examining not only, shall we say, the negative, or in any case mischievous, reasons, but also the positive reasons, however imprecise, that you might have had to come and hear a philosopher in the discharge of his public duties, has provoked this result: an avalanche of Theses! Do not be frightened: we will enter into the details.

II AN EXAMPLE

The best way to avoid the aridity of Theses is, of course, to show how
they function with an example. This is not an illustration: philosophy
cannot be illustrated or applied. It is *exercised*. It can be learned only by
being practised, for it exists only in its practice. This point could be
stated in the form of a Thesis, but I leave that to you. It will be a good
'practical' exercise.

In order to show how philosophy functions, how it traces critical lines
of demarcation in order to clear a correct way, we will therefore take an
example: that of an *ideological* proposition, that of the slogan of *interdisciplinarity*.

You will see that it is not by chance that the example we have chosen
is that of an *ideological* proposition.

I remind you: interdisciplinarity is today a widely diffused slogan
which is expected to provide the solution to all sorts of difficult
problems in the exact sciences (mathematics and the natural sciences),
the human sciences, and other practices.

I remind you: an ideological proposition is a proposition which, whilst
it is the symptom of a reality other than that of which it speaks, is a false
proposition to the extent that it concerns the object of which it speaks
(Thesis 9).

What will the work of philosophy on this ideological proposition
consist in? Drawing a line of demarcation between the ideological
pretensions of interdisciplinarity and the realities of which it is the
symptom. When we have surveyed these realities, then we will see what
remains of these ideological pretensions.

It is clear that something like interdisciplinarity corresponds to an
objective and well-founded necessity when there exists a 'command' that
requires the co-ordinated co-operation of specialists from several
branches of the division of labour.

When the decision is taken to build a housing estate somewhere or
other, a whole series of specialists is gathered together according to the
precise needs that dictate their intervention: economists, sociologists,
geologists, geographers, architects and various kinds of engineers.
Whatever the results (sometimes such schemes come to nothing), in
theory no one contests the need to go through that process. The interdisciplinarity defined by the technical requirements of a *command* thus
appears to be the obverse of the division of labour – that is, its
recomposition in a collective undertaking.

May not the same be said of intellectual interdisciplinarity in the
sciences when the 'commands' are justified? Formally, yes. Thus,
physicists appeal to mathematicians, or biologists call upon the services

of mathematicians and chemists: but they always do so to resolve *specific problems* whose solution requires the intervention of specialists from other disciplines.

If what I say is correct (at least as a first approximation, for these are simple notations), I am in the process of making a 'distinction', therefore of 'drawing a line of demarcation' between a justified recourse to technical and scientific co-operation (which may be defined by the precise demands addressed to specialists from other disciplines for the solution of problems that have emerged in a given discipline) and a different, unwarranted use of the slogan of interdisciplinarity.

However, if the generalized, undefined slogan of interdisciplinarity expresses a proposition of an ideological nature (Thesis 9), we must consider it as such: false in what it claims to designate, but at the same time a symptom of a reality other than that which it explicitly designates. What, then, is this other reality? Let us see. It is the reality of the effective relations that have either existed for a long time between certain disciplines, whether scientific or literary, or which are in the process of being constituted between older and newer disciplines (e.g. between mathematics, etc., and the human sciences).

Let us examine the case a little more closely. We will differentiate between these cases:

1. relations between disciplines belonging to the exact sciences;

2. relations between the exact sciences and the human sciences;

3. relations between literary disciplines.

1. Relations between the Exact Sciences

Very schematically, and bearing in mind possible objections, I propose to say that there exist two fundamental types of relations: relations of *application* and relations of *constitution*.

A. *Relations of Application*

I will distinguish between two such relations: the application of mathematics to the exact sciences and the application of one science to another. As you can see, I am making a *distinction*. I am drawing a line of demarcation between these two types of application. This distinction is made by philosophy.

Relations between mathematics and the natural sciences: let us immediately note the double aspect of this relation. On the one hand, all the natural sciences are mathematicized: they cannot do without mathematics. This relation of mathematics to the natural sciences might at first sight be considered a relation of application. But a philosophical question immediately arises: how is this application to be conceived?

We all have in our heads the common and convenient notion (in reality, an ideological notion) of application as the effect of an impression: one 'applies' a signature under a text, a design on fabric, a stamp on an envelope. An appliqué is a thing that can be posed *on* or *against* something else. The original image of this notion is that of super-imposition–impression. It implies the duality of objects: what is applied is different from that to which it is applied; and the *exteriority*, the *instrumentality* of the first is relative to the second. The common notion of application thus takes us back to the world of *technology*.

Thus, I draw a line of demarcation. It is clear that mathematics is not applied to mathematical physics, nor to experimental physics, nor to chemistry, biology, etc., according to the mode of exteriority and instrumentality: according to the mode of *technology*. Mathematics is not, for physics, a simple 'tool' to be used when necessary, or even an 'instrument' (at least given the usual sense of the word: for example, when one speaks of a 'scientific instrument' – and even that remains to be seen). For mathematics is the very existence of theoretical physics, and it is infinitely more than a mere instrument in experimental physics. You can see the practical *point* of drawing this line of demarcation: in the space that it opens up it makes visible something that *could not be seen*. What? *Questions*: what are we to understand by the category of the *application* of mathematics to the natural sciences? First question. We will attempt to discuss it, if only to see what philosophy has been able to perceive and what it has missed (and why. Why has it necessarily missed something?). But this first question implies another, its counterpart, since by drawing a line we see that 'application' conceals 'technology': what is technology? What is its field of validity? For this word obviously covers several realities: no doubt there are also differences between the technology of the blacksmith, that of the engineer, and the technical problems that currently dominate a whole series of branches of natural science (physics, chemistry, biology), and therefore lines of demarcation to be drawn. We shall try.

But the relationship between mathematics and the natural sciences works both ways. The natural sciences pose problems for mathematics: they have always done so. The application of mathematics to the sciences therefore conceals another, inverse, relation: that by which mathematics is obliged, in order to meet the demands of the sciences, to formulate problems that may be either those of 'applied' mathematics or those of pure mathematics. It is as though mathematics gave back, in a more elaborated form, to the sciences what it received from them. Can we still speak of 'application' in this organic exchange? Should we not rather speak another language, and say that there exists between mathematics and the natural sciences another relation, a relation of *constitution* – mathematics being neither a tool nor an instrument, nor a method, nor a language at the service of the sciences, but an *active participant* in the existence of the sciences, in their constitution?

One word in place of another: *constitution* in place of *application*: it does not seem like much. Yet this is how philosophy proceeds. One word is enough to open up the space for a question, for a question that has not been posed. The new word throws the old words into disorder and creates a space for the new question. The new question calls into question the old answers, and the old questions lurking behind them. A new view of things is thus attained. It may be the same with the word 'constitution', if it is 'correct'.

B. *Relations of Constitution*

Let us take the case in all its generality: the intervention of one science, or a part of a science, in the practice of another science.

These relations are typical of contemporary scientific phenomena. Increasingly, so-called 'neighbouring' disciplines are brought into play in 'zones' which were once considered to be definitive 'frontiers'. From these new relations new disciplines are born: physical chemistry, biophysics, biochemistry, etc. These new disciplines are often the indirect result of the development of new branches within the classical disciplines: thus atomic physics had its effects on chemistry and biology; in conjunction with the progress of organic chemistry, it contributed to the birth of biochemistry.

These exchanges are organic relations constituted between the different scientific disciplines without external philosophical intervention. They obey purely scientific necessities, purely internal to the sciences under consideration.

One thing is sure: *these relations do not constitute what contemporary ideology calls interdisciplinary exchanges*. The new disciplines (physical chemistry, biochemistry) were not the product of interdisciplinary 'round tables'. Nor are they 'interdisciplinary sciences'. They are either new branches of classical sciences or new sciences.

We are therefore obliged to draw a *line of demarcation* between interdisciplinary ideology and the effective reality of the process of the mutual application and constitution of sciences. The act of drawing such a line of demarcation has both theoretical and practical implications. *Theoretically*, this line of demarcation clearly reveals *philosophical questions*: what is the application of mathematics to the sciences? What is technology? What is the application of one science to another? Why is it necessary (at first) to speak of constitution rather than of application? What concrete dialectic is at work in these complex relations? These philosophical questions can open the way to *scientific problems* (of the history of the sciences, or rather the conditions of the processes of constitution of the sciences). *Practically*, this line of demarcation can have *real effects*: avoiding conceptions, tendencies or temptations which might lead to unthinking 'interdisciplinary' collaboration, and encouraging every productive practice.

I will draw one final conclusion. There are false ideas about science, not simply in the heads of philosophers but in the heads of scientists themselves: false 'obviousnesses' that, far from being means of making progress, are in reality 'epistemological obstacles' (Bachelard).[3] They must be criticized and dispelled by showing that the imaginary solutions they offer in fact conceal real problems (Thesis 9). But it is necessary to go still further: to recognize that it is not by chance that these false ideas reign in certain regions within the domain of scientific activity. They are non-scientific, ideological ideas and representations. They form what we will provisionally call scientific ideology, or the ideology of scientists. A philosophy *capable* of discerning and criticizing them can have the effect of drawing the attention of scientists to the existence and efficacy of the epistemological obstacle that this spontaneous scientific ideology represents: the representation that scientists have of their own practice, and of their relationship to their own practice. Here again philosophy does not substitute itself for science: it intervenes, in order to clear a path, to open the space in which a correct line may then be drawn.

From this I draw *Thesis 21*. Scientific ideology (or the ideology of scientists) is inseparable from scientific practice: it is the 'spontaneous' ideology of scientific practice.

Here again I anticipate. I will explain. I have only one more word to say about this 'spontaneous' ideology: we will see that it is 'spontaneous' *because it is not.* One of philosophy's little surprises.

2. Relations between Scientific and Literary Disciplines

These relations are proliferating in a spectacular manner. To make them visible we will again 'bring into play' the difference between our two categories: application and constitution.

For example: formally, one might compare the public relationship

---

3. See especially Gaston Bachelard, *La Formation de l'esprit scientifique* (1938), Paris 1980. [Ed.]

between mathematics and the human sciences to the relationship just discussed between mathematics and the natural sciences. But there is a great difference: in the case of the human sciences the relationship with mathematics is manifestly, in whole or in part, an external, non-organic relationship; in short, a *technical* relation of application. In the natural sciences, the question of the *conditions* of application of mathematics and hence of the legitimacy of this application, and of its technical forms, is not a problematic question; philosophy can pose questions, but it does not create problems for scientific practice. In contrast, in the human sciences this question is most often *problematic*. Some (spiritualist) philosophers contest the very possibility of a mathematicization of the human sciences; others contest the technical forms of this application.

It is this problematic character, this hesitation, that is expressed in the *wish* for interdisciplinarity and in the expression 'interdisciplinary exchange'. The notion of interdisciplinarity indicates not a solution but a *contradiction*: the fact of the relative exteriority of the disciplines placed in relation. This exteriority (mathematics as a tool, a 'tool' that is to a greater or lesser extent adaptable) expresses the problematic character of these relations or of their technical forms (*what* use is being made of mathematics in 'psychology', in political economy, in sociology, in history . . .? What complicities are in fact being established behind the prestige of the use of mathematics?). As we go on asking questions, we finally arrive at the conclusion that this exteriority expresses and betrays the *uncertainty* which the majority of the human sciences feel concerning their theoretical status. This *generalized impatience* to embrace mathematics is a symptom: they have not attained theoretical maturity. Is this simply an 'infantile disorder', to be explained by the relative youth of the human sciences? Or is it more serious: is it an indication that the human sciences, for the most part, 'miss' their object, that they are not based on their true distinctive foundation, that there is a sort of misrecognition between the human sciences and their pretensions, that they miss the object that they claim to grasp because, paradoxically, this object (or at least the *object* they take as their *own*) *does not exist*? All these questions are supported by the real experiences from which Kant, in another time, had drawn the lesson (for theology, but also for rational psychology and rational cosmology): *there may exist sciences whose objects do not exist, there may exist sciences without an object* (in the strict sense).[4]

_____

4. See Immanual Kant, *Critique of Pure Reason* (1781, 1787), London 1929, The Transcendental Doctrine of Method, chapter 3, 'The Architectonic of Pure Reason', pp. 662–3. [Ed.]

New distinctions should be made here, but, as always, I must anticipate. I will therefore take the risk of pronouncing upon the phenomenon as a whole, and take a position. I say: in *the majority* of the human sciences mathematizing inflation is not a childhood illness but a desperate attempt to fill a fundamental gap: *with some distinct exceptions* the human sciences are sciences without an object (in the strict sense). They have a false or equivocal theoretical base, they produce long discourses and numerous 'findings', but because they are too confident that they know *of what* they are the sciences, in fact they do not 'know' *what* they are the sciences *of*: a misunderstanding.

But let us leave relations of application, and move on to relations of constitution. These may be seen today in a discipline traditionally considered a branch of philosophy: logic. Today logic has become mathematical logic, making it, in fact, independent of philosophy. It has a status of its own. In a certain sense it might be compared to the new borderline disciplines that are to be seen in the natural sciences, such as physical chemistry or biophysics. Mathematical logic is a branch of mathematics, but as a scientific discipline it functions above all in the human sciences. It is, or can be, the object of applications in a whole series of literary disciplines (linguistics, semiology, psychoanalysis, literary history). Here too there is a whole series of questions.

From these summary and general remarks, some conclusions may be drawn. It may be said:

– That between the human sciences and the natural sciences, and above all between the human sciences and mathematics, on the one hand, and mathematical logic, on the other, there exist relations *formally* similar to the relations that exist between the exact sciences, with the double phenomena that we have observed: application and constitution;

– But that this relation is far more external, and therefore technical (non-organic), than the relations that exist between the exact sciences themselves. That this exteriority seems to authorize an expression such as the notion of 'interdisciplinary' exchanges and therefore the notion of interdisciplinarity, but that this notion is in all probability an illusory name for a problem entirely different to the problem it designates;

– That, at the same time, the use of *certain philosophies* by the human sciences seems necessary to the establishment of this relation. Here again we see a new and important index. Whereas in the exact sciences everything proceeds without any *visible* intervention on the part of philosophy and its apparatus, in the human sciences the structure of relations between the sciences and the human sciences seems to require, for ill-explained and therefore confused reasons, the intrusive intervention of this third character that is philosophy: in person.

Let us note an important point here. (1) The human sciences use philosophical categories and subordinate them to their objectives. They get through a lot of philosophy, but the initiative *seems* not to come from philosophy. *Appearances* suggest that this is not a matter of a critical intervention on the part of philosophy in the ideological problems of the human sciences, but, on the contrary, an *exploitation* by the human sciences of certain philosophical categories or philosophies. (2) It is not a question of 'philosophy' in general, but of very determinate categories or philosophies, idealist (positivist, neo-positivist, structuralist, formalist, phenomenological, etc.) or spiritualist. (3) The philosophies or philosophical categories thus 'exploited' by the human sciences are used practically by them as an *ideological substitute* for the theoretical base they lack. (4) But then the following question may be posed: is not the philosophical practice *borrowed* by the human sciences at the same time an appearance? Should we not reverse the order of things? And in the necessary complicity between the human sciences and these idealist philosophies, *are not the philosophies in command*? Are not the human sciences sciences without an object because they do no more than 'realize' in their 'object' determinate idealist philosophical tendencies rooted in the 'practical ideologies' of our time, that is, of our society? Are sciences without objects simply philosophies disguised as sciences? After all, that would seem to be a fairly convincing argument since, as we know, philosophy has no object.

In any event, the Thesis that philosophies serve as an ideological substitute for the theoretical foundations that the human sciences lack holds for the majority of the human sciences: not for all, for there are exceptions (e.g. psychoanalysis and, to a certain extent, linguistics, etc.). I remind you also that this thesis does not imply that certain aspects, procedures and even certain findings of the human sciences cannot possess a positive value. Each case has to be examined in detail: but that is no more than an internal and minor aspect of an *overall* investigation.

It follows from this that the proportion of 'dubious' ideas increases as we move from relations between the exact sciences to relations between the exact sciences and the human sciences. We dealt earlier with localized and localizable false ideas. Now we have no real grounds for speaking of false ideas, but we can speak of generalized suspect ideas. The exploitation of certain philosophies is in direct proportion to the suspect character of these ideas. What we might call scientific ideologies and philosophical ideologies assume an extreme importance in the domain of the human sciences. Not only do these ideologies exist and have great importance in our world, but they directly govern the scientific practices of the human sciences. They take the place of theory in the human sciences.

Hence the importance of a philosophy capable of drawing a line of demarcation which will traverse the domain of the majority of human sciences: to help distinguish 'true' sciences from would-be sciences and to distinguish their *de facto* ideological foundations from the *de jure* theoretical foundations (provisionally defined in negative terms) which might make them something other than sciences without an object. Hence the importance of our position, which now becomes clear: this task cannot be undertaken and successfully completed in the name of the philosophies that the human sciences think they are exploiting, whereas they are in fact their garrulous slaves. It can be undertaken only in the name of another, completely *different*, philosophy. *The line of demarcation thus runs through philosophy itself.*

3. Relations between Literary Disciplines

These relations have always been numerous and close. They are apparently in the midst of fundamental change. If this is true, it is because the disciplines of the human sciences are in the midst of fundamental change: at least, that is what they claim.

Let us take a closer look.

Traditionally, literary disciplines have rested on a very particular relation to their object: a practical relation of utilization, appreciation, of taste, or, if you prefer, consumption. *Belles lettres*, the humanities and the teaching practices and research that have been attached to them for centuries, make them a school of 'culture'. This means two things.

1. The relation between literary disciplines and their object (literature properly speaking, the fine arts, history, logic, philosophy, ethics, religion) has as its *dominant* function not so much the knowledge of this object but rather the definition and inculcation of rules, norms and practices designed to establish 'cultural' relations between the 'literate' and these objects. Above all: to know how to handle these objects in order to consume them 'properly'. To know how to 'read' – that is, 'taste', 'appreciate' – a classical text, to know how 'to apply the lessons' of history, to know how to apply the right method to think 'well' (logic), to know how to look to correct ideas (philosophy) in order to know where we stand in relation to the great questions of human existence, science, ethics, religion, etc. Through their particular relations, the arts or

humanities thus impart a certain *knowledge* [*savoir*]: not a scientific knowledge of their object, and not a scientific knowledge of the mechanism of their object, but – in addition to the particular erudition needed for familiarity – a *savoir-faire* or, to be more accurate, a *know-how-to-do* to appreciate–judge, and enjoy–consume–utilize this object which is properly 'culture': a knowledge invested in a knowing how to do in order to ... For in this couple, what is secondary (and, although not negligible, superficial, formal) is *knowledge*; what matters is the *knowing how to do in order to* ... Basically, the arts were therefore the pedagogical site *par excellence*, or, in other words, a site for cultural training: learning to think properly, to judge properly, to enjoy properly, and to behave properly towards all the cultural objects involved in human existence. Their goal? The well-bred gentleman, the man of culture.

2. The practical relation of consumption that exists between literary disciplines and their object cannot be considered a relation of scientific knowledge [*connaissance*]. The 'culture' provided by the humanities in their different forms (literature, logic, history, ethics, philosophy, etc.) was never any more than the commentary made on certain consecrated objects by the culture that exists in society itself. To understand the meaning of the 'culture' provided by the humanities, it is necessary to question not the humanities themselves, or not only the humanities, but the 'culture' which exists in the society that 'cultivates' these arts, the class functions of that culture, and therefore the class divisions of that society. The 'culture' taught in the schools is in fact never anything more than a *second-degree culture*, a culture that 'cultivates', for the benefit of a greater or lesser number of individuals in this society, and with reference to certain privileged objects (*belles lettres*, the arts, logic, philosophy, etc.), *the art of relating to those objects* as a practical means of inculcating in those individuals defined norms of practical behaviour with respect to the institutions and 'values' of that society and to the events that occur within it. Culture is the elite and/or mass ideology of a given society. Not the *real ideology of the masses* (for, as a result of class oppositions, there are several tendencies within culture) but the ideology that the ruling class seeks to inculcate, directly or indirectly, through education or other means, and on a discriminatory basis (one culture for the elite, one for the popular masses), into the masses they dominate. We are speaking here of an enterprise of *hegemonic* character (Gramsci): obtaining the *consent* of the masses through the diffusion of ideology (through the presentation and inculcation of culture). The dominant ideology is always imposed on the masses against certain tendencies in their own culture which are neither recognized nor sanctioned, but do resist.

This idea of the arts is not in accordance with the received idea. We should not be content to take the arts at their word and accept the definition they give of themselves. Behind the literary disciplines there is a long heritage: that of the humanities. To understand the humanities, we must seek out the meaning of the 'culture' they dispense *in the norms* of the *forms of behaviour* that are *dominant* in the society under consideration: religious, moral, juridical, political, etc., ideology – in short, in *practical ideologies*. With this implication: the literary culture dispensed by the teaching that goes on in schools *is not a purely academic phenomenon*; it is one moment in the ideological 'education' of the popular masses. Through its means and effects, it intersects with other ideologies mobilized at the same time: religious, juridical, moral, political, etc. The many ideological means by which the ruling class achieves hegemony and thus holds power are all grouped around the State over which the ruling class holds power. This *connection* – one might say this *synchronization* – between literary culture (which is the object-objective of the classical humanities) and the mass ideological action exercised by the Church, the State, law, and by the forms of the political regime, etc., are, of course, usually *masked*. But it comes to light during great political and ideological crises in which, for example, educational reforms are openly recognized as revolutions in the methods of ideological action deployed against the masses. At such times, it can be clearly seen that education is directly related to the dominant ideology and it is apparent that its conception, its orientation and control are an important stake in the class struggle. Some examples: the Convention's educational reform, Jules Ferry's educational reforms, the educational reforms that so preoccupied Lenin and Krupskaya, the educational reforms of the Cultural Revolution, etc.

But the sciences too are a teaching object. The arts – by which I mean the humanities, as defined by their long history – are therefore not the only 'subject matter' of 'cultural' – that is, ideological – training. The teaching of the sciences is also the site of a similar 'cultural' training, although it takes more subtle, infinitely less visible form. But *the way* the exact sciences themselves are taught implies a certain ideological relation to their existence and their content. There is no teaching of pure knowledge [*savoir*] that is not at the same time a *savoir-faire* – that is, the definition of a know-how-to-act-in-relation-to-this-knowledge, and to its *theoretical and social function*. This know-how ... implies a political attitude towards the object of knowledge, towards knowledge as object, and towards its place in society. All science teaching, whether it wants to or not, conveys an ideology of science and of its findings – that is, a certain knowing-how-to-act-in-relation-to-science and its findings, based on a certain idea of the place of science in society, and on a certain idea of the role of intellectuals who specialize in scientific knowledge and therefore of the division between manual and intellectual labour.

For intellectuals, nothing could be more difficult than perceiving the ideology conveyed by education, and by its curriculum, its forms and its practices. This applies to the sciences as well as the arts. Intellectuals live in culture, just as fish live in water; but fish cannot see the water in which they swim. Everything about them militates against their having any accurate perception of the social position of the culture in which they are steeped, of the teaching which dispenses it, or of the disciplines they practise – to say nothing of the positions they occupy in this society as intellectuals, academics or research workers. Everything militates against it: the effects of the division of labour (primarily the division between manual and intellectual labour, but also divisions within intellectual labour; divisions between intellectual specialisms), the impressive immediacy of the object of their activity, which absorbs all their attention, and the character of their practice, which is at once extremely concrete and extremely abstract, etc. Their practice, which they carry out in a framework defined by laws that they do not control, thus spontaneously produces an ideology which they live without having any reason to break out of it. But matters do not end there. Their own ideology, the spontaneous ideology of their practice (their ideology of science or the arts) does not depend solely on their own practice: it depends mainly and in the last instance on the dominant ideological system of the society in which they live. Ultimately, it is this ideological system especially that governs the very forms of their ideology of science and of the arts. What seems to happen before their eyes happens, in reality, *behind their backs.*

But let us return to the arts. For some time – since the eighteenth century, but in an infinitely more rapid and accelerated fashion in the last few years – relations between literary disciplines have apparently undergone a fundamental change. It is a primarily *practical,* that is, ideological and political relation. From all sides the literary disciplines proclaim that this relationship has changed. It would seem to have become *scientific.* Even if it is highly inconsistent, this phenomenon is visible in the majority of the disciplines known as the human sciences. We are not speaking of logic: logic has been displaced and is now a part of mathematics. But linguistics, at least in some of its 'regions', seems to have become a science. Even the credentials of psychoanalysis, for a long time condemned and banished, have begun to be recognized. Other disciplines also claim to have attained the level of scientificity: political economy, sociology, psychology, history.... Literary history itself has been given a new lease of life, and has put the tradition of the humanities behind it.

It is on the basis of this contradictory situation that we can begin to understand the relations which are currently being tentatively established between the different literary disciplines. They lay claim to the name of 'human sciences', marking with the word *sciences* their claims to having broken off their old relationship with their object. Instead of a cultural – that is, ideological – relation, they want to install a new relation: scientific. On the whole, they think they have succeeded in this conversion and proclaim it in the name they give themselves, by baptizing themselves 'human sciences'. But a proclamation may be no more than a proclamation, an intention, or a programme. It may also be in part a myth designed to sustain an illusion, or a 'wish-fulfilment'.

It is not certain that the human sciences have really changed their 'nature' by changing their name and their methods. The relations that are currently being established between the literary disciplines are proof of that: the systematic mathematicization of a number of disciplines (economics, sociology, psychology); and the 'application' of disciplines manifestly more advanced in scientificity to others (the pioneering role of mathematical logic and especially linguistics, the equally intrusive role of psycho-analysis, etc.). Contrary to what has occurred in the natural sciences, in which relations are generally organic, this kind of 'application' remains external, instrumental, technical and therefore suspect. The most aberrant contemporary example of the external application of a 'method' (which in its 'universality' is following fashion) to any object whatsoever is 'structuralism'. When disciplines are in search of a universal 'method', we may wager that they are a little too anxious to demonstrate their scientific credentials really to have earned them. True sciences never need to let the world know that they have found the key to becoming sciences.

Another sensitive point in this equivocal process appears in the relation that exists between this relation (between disciplines) and philosophy. The human sciences that are being constituted openly *exploit* certain philosophies. They seek in these philosophies (for example in phenomenology, whose influence is on the wane; in structuralism; not to mention in Hegelianism and even Nietzscheanism) a base of support and a way of orientating themselves. That is what they are looking for in philosophy, even when they aggressively reject all philosophy; though, given their current state, theirs is a *philosophical* rejection of philosophy (a variety of positivism). As we have seen, this relation may be reversed: it is only because they themselves realize the dominant ideology that the human sciences can exploit philosophy or the other disciplines that stand in for philosophy (thus linguistics and psychoanalysis function increasingly as 'philosophies' for literary history, 'semiology', etc.). In all this to-ing and fro-ing something appears, if we are willing to see it, as an absence, a lack – the very thing which the sciences need if they are to deserve the name of science: a recognition of their theoretical base.

These relationships, whether direct or indirect, bring us back to our term and our question: *interdisciplinarity*. This myth enjoys a wide currency in the human sciences and in general. Sociology, economics, psychology, linguistics and literary history constantly borrow notions, methods and procedures from existing disciplines, whether literary or scientific. We are speaking of the eclectic practice of holding inter-disciplinary 'round tables'. All the neighbours are invited, no one is forgotten – one never knows. Inviting everyone so as to leave no one out means that we do not know precisely who to invite, *where* we are or *where* we are going. The practice of 'round tables' is necessarily accompanied by an ideology of the virtues of interdisciplinarity, of which it is the counterpoint and the mass. This ideology is contained in a formula: when one does not know what the world does not know, it suffices to assemble all the ignorant: science will emerge from an assembly of the ignorant.

Am I joking? This practice is in flagrant contradiction with what we know of the process of constitution of real sciences, including new sciences. They are never born out of specialists' 'round tables'. In fact, this practice and its ideology are in accordance with what we know of the *processes of domination of ideologies*. When everyone is invited, it is not the hoped-for new science that is being invited (for it is never the result of a gathering of specialists who are ignorant of it), but a character no one has invited – and whom it is not necessary to invite, since it invites itself! – the *common theoretical ideology* that silently inhabits the 'consciousness' of all these specialists: when they gather together, it speaks out loud – through their voice.

Apart from certain specific cases, most often technical, where this practice has its place (when a discipline makes a justified request of another on the basis of real organic links between disciplines), inter-disciplinarity therefore remains a magical practice, in the service of an ideology, in which scientists (or would-be scientists) formulate an imaginary idea of the division of scientific labour, of the relations between sciences and the conditions of 'discovery', to give the impression of grasping an object that escapes them. Very concretely, inter-disciplinarity is usually the slogan and the practice of the spontaneous ideology of specialists: oscillating between a vague spiritualism and technocratic positivism.

Concerning all this, there are false ideas to be avoided in order to open the way to the correct ideas.

Once again, it is necessary to ask what the application of one science to another, of determinate methods to a new object in the literary disciplines, might consist of. Once again, it is even more necessary to examine the nature of the pre-existing ideology and to penetrate its current disguises. Finally, it is necessary to pose the question of questions: are the human sciences, with certain limited exceptions, what they think they are – that is, sciences? Or are they in their majority something else, namely *ideological techniques of social adaptation and readaptation*? If this is in fact what they are, they have not, as they claim, broken with their former ideological and political 'cultural' function: they act through other, more 'sophisticated', perfected techniques, but still in the service of the same cause. It will suffice to note the direct relation they maintain with a whole series of other techniques, such as *human relations* and modern forms of mass media, to be convinced that this hypothesis is not an imaginary one.

But then, it is not simply the status of the human sciences that is in question but the status of the theoretical basis that they claim to have provided for themselves. Question: what makes up the *apparatus* that permits disciplines to function as ideological techniques? This is the question that philosophy poses.

Let us summarize the lessons that can be drawn from this simple example: *interdisciplinarity*. What in fact does the slogan of interdisciplinarity mask?

1. Certain real practices, perfectly founded and legitimate: practices that remain to be defined, in cases that remain to be defined. To define them is to distinguish them from others. The first line of demarcation.

2. In the interior of these practices and these real problems, there are new distinctions to be made (application, constitution) and therefore new lines of demarcation to be drawn.

3. Outside these real practices, we encounter the pretensions of certain disciplines that declare themselves to be sciences (human sciences). What are we to make of their pretensions? By means of a new line of demarcation we distinguish between the real function of most of the human sciences and the ideological character of their pretensions.

4. If we go back to the slogan of interdisciplinarity, we are now in a position to state (on the basis of certain resistant symptoms) that it is massively *ideological* in character.

The 'lesson' to be drawn from this brief summary? We have made our definition of philosophy 'function': philosophy states Theses which draw lines of demarcation. We have been able to show that this practice, however 'wild' [*sauvage*] (as in this lecture), produces results.

Everyone can agree on one thing: we have not once, for a single moment, given in to the temptation of most philosophies and philosophers. We have not *exploited* the findings or difficulties of the sciences for the greater glory of *a* Truth or *the* Truth. In this way we have demarcated ourselves from the dominant philosophical currents and we have marked out our own position.

If we have respected the sciences and their findings, and if philosophy is an intervention, *where* have we intervened?

Note well: each time we have intervened, it has been to draw a line of demarcation. Further, each time we have drawn a line of demarcation, it has been to *make something appear* that was not visible before our intervention. What? The existence, reality, consistency and function of what we have called theoretical or scientific *ideology* – or, better still, the spontaneous *ideology* of the practice of scientists or supposed scientists. And behind these forms of ideology, other forms – practical ideologies and the dominant ideology.

But just as it makes the ideological appear, the line of demarcation makes it possible to recognize, on the other side of the divide, the *scientific* that is obscured by the ideological: by *extricating* it.

The ideological is something that relates to practice and to society. The scientific is something that relates to knowledge [*connaissance*] and to the sciences.

So, where have we intervened? Very precisely, in the 'space' where the ideological and the scientific merge but where they can and must be separated, to recognize each in its functioning and to free scientific practice from the ideological domination that blocks it.

Provisionally, we can say that the essential function of the philosophy practised on these positions is to draw lines of demarcation, all of which seem capable of introducing, in the last instance, a line of demarcation between *the scientific and the ideological.* From this follows

Thesis 22. All the lines of demarcation traced by philosophy are ultimately modalities of a fundamental line: the line between the scientific and the ideological.

We have thus shown that the result of these philosophical interventions is the production of new *philosophical questions*: what is the application of one science to another? The constitution of one science by another? Technology? Ideology? The relation between the ideological and the philosophical? Etc. *These philosophical questions are not scientific problems.* Philosophy does not encroach upon the domain of the sciences. But *these philosophical questions can help to pose scientific problems*, in the space that they open.

Such is the 'game' of philosophy, as we practise it – drawing lines of demarcation that produce new philosophical questions without end. Philosophy does not respond like a science to the questions it produces, with demonstrated solutions or proven findings (in the scientific sense of these words): it responds by stating Theses which are correct, not arbitrary, and which in turn draw new lines of demarcation, giving rise to new philosophical questions, *ad infinitum.*

This much is *obvious,* but behind the obvious something else happens. This operation – drawing lines of demarcation to produce philosophical questions; provoking new Theses, etc. – is not a speculative game. It is an operation that has *practical* effects. What are they? Let us summarize them in one word: the *line* (that takes the form of justified Theses, which in turn give rise to an intelligible discourse) that divides the scientific from the ideological has as its practical effect the 'opening of a way', therefore the removal of obstacles, opening a space for a 'correct line' *for the practices* that are at stake in philosophical Theses.

But I think this is enough for the first lecture.

Lecture II

I PHILOSOPHY AND CORRECTNESS

In this second lecture we will again take up our central question: what is philosophy? And this question will take us on a long journey.

But it will be objected: haven't I already answered this question? Yes and no.

Yes: I have put forward Theses on philosophy and I have even shown how philosophy 'functions' with a precise example: the slogan of inter-disciplinarity.

No: for it is not enough to put forward Theses on philosophy and to show how it 'functions' to settle the question. Things are not so simple.

For example, to begin at the end ('functioning'), and assuming that this kind of comparison is not too odious, it might be objected: it is not enough to *see* a machine 'function' – a combustion engine, for example – to understand its mechanism and, *a fortiori*, the physical and chemical laws that regulate the functioning of this mechanism.

For example, to go back to the beginning (Theses on philosophy): when I laid my cards on the table, you had the definite feeling that I was making a strange finesse. When, with my first words, I said: 'Philo-sophical propositions are *Theses*', and quickly added: '*This* proposition is itself a philosophical Thesis' by which I put Thesis 1 into play, you obviously noticed that my argument was circular: because I declared that the proposition by which I defined philosophical propositions as *Theses* was itself a *philosophical* Thesis.

This might have been an unperceived contradiction, a careless error or an evasion. However, I entered the necessary circle deliberately. Why? To show even crudely that whilst it is indispensable to leave philosophy in order to understand it, we must guard against the illusion of being able to provide a definition – that is, a knowledge – of philosophy that would be able *radically* to escape from philosophy: there is no possibility of achieving a science of philosophy or a 'meta-philosophy'; one cannot radically escape the *circle* of philosophy. All *objective* knowledge of philosophy is in effect at the same time a *position within* philosophy, and therefore a Thesis in and on philosophy; that is why you felt, on the contrary, that *I could speak of philosophy in general only from a certain position in philosophy*: demarcating myself, by distancing myself from *other* existing positions. There is no objective discourse about philosophy that is not itself philosophical, and therefore a discourse based upon certain positions *within* philosophy.

It is to mark this inescapable condition that I have inscribed it in the *circle* of a *Thesis that defines philosophical positions as Theses.* Accordingly, this circle is not inconsistent but entirely consistent: *I said what I was doing.* It is obviously impossible to explain in a few words the sense in which this circle is necessary and productive, not at all sterile like logical 'circles' – to explain, in other words, the sense in which it is not a circle at all. But this question holds some surprises.

To go back to my first Theses. I pronounced a certain little word which, as I know from the questions I was asked, held your attention and proved intriguing, if not worrisome. In effect, I said that philosophical propositions, unlike scientific propositions that are said to be true because they are proven or demonstrated, are declared *correct* (or incorrect). And I added that the 'true' relates to knowledge, while the 'correct' relates to practice. In passing, two words: common but singular.

They are even more singular in that philosophy has, throughout its history, always spoken of Truth and error, of the True and the false, and in that philosophers always begin with a 'Search for the Truth' and always wage their struggle in the name of the Truth: in that *philosophical propositions have never been qualified as correct.* And here I am claiming that they are *said* to be correct or not, but *by whom* are they said to be thus? – since no one in the whole of philosophy has used this adjective. The first 'finesse': they are not *said* to be correct but they certainly relate to this adjective: *correct.* If we wish to understand what happens in philosophy, we must consider that its propositions, regardless of their *declared* devotion to the presence and adequation of the Truth, are bound up with the world in which they intervene by a very different relation: that of *correctness.* They are not said to be *correct,* but we will say that they are correct, in part to understand why they are *said* by philosophers to be 'true'. *Correct* is the password that will permit us to enter into philosophy.

It is understood that *correct* [*juste*] is not the adjectival form of *justice* [*justice*]. When St Thomas Aquinas distinguished between just and unjust wars, he spoke in the name of *justice.* But when Lenin distinguished between correct and incorrect wars [*les guerres justes et les guerres injustes*], he spoke in the name of correctness [*justesse*]: of a correct line, of a correct assessment of the character of wars in the light of their class meaning. Of course, a politically correct war is waged by combatants who have a passion for justice in their hearts: but it is not only justice (an idealized notion under and in which men 'live' their relations to their conditions of existence and to their struggles) that made a war 'correct' for Lenin. A war is correct when it conforms to a correct position and line in the conjuncture of a given balance of forces: as a practical intervention in line with the class struggle, correct because it has been *aligned* with the meaning of the class struggle.

But even when we have left behind philosophical Truth and avoided the pitfalls of Justice, there still remains this little word: *correct* [*juste*] and its cognate: *correctness* [*justesse*]. And this question: what distinguishes the 'correct' from the 'true?'

And that question immediately provokes fear: is there not, in the philosophy that I have presented, a higher Authority which will decide what is *correct*? And is not the philosophy of which we speak the Judge or Last Judgement that renders unto Caesar that which is Caesar's *by dividing*? And in the name of what is it going to divide? But let us take care not to fall into the abyss of metaphor: for 'Judge' pertains to 'Justice', an institution of the State that pronounces and applies a pre-existing *Law*. In the codes of its Law, the Justice of the State inscribes, in the form of a pre-established order, the rules of the established Order, the rules of its reproduction. The correctness [*justesse*] of which we speak is not pre-established: it does not pre-exist the *adjustment*, it is its result.

Adjustment: that, for the moment, is the essential word. When philosophy in its practice 'draws a line of demarcation' to delineate practically, and state theoretically, a position that is a Thesis (Thesis = Position), philosophy may well appear to be appealing to pre-established Truths or Rules, to the Judgement to which it submits and conforms: even when it does this (and God knows it has done it often enough in its history: indeed, that's all it has ever done), in reality it *adjusts* its Thesis by taking account of all the elements that make up the existing political, ideological and theoretical conjuncture, by taking account of what it calls the 'Whole'.

But see how things are. This conjuncture is political, ideological and theoretical. We know that, and we can show that it is so: every great philosophy (Plato, Descartes, Kant, Hegel, etc.) has always taken into account the political conjuncture (the great events of the class struggle), the ideological conjuncture (the great conflicts between and within practical ideologies), *and* the theoretical conjuncture. But what does *theoretical* mean?

To limit ourselves to the essential, the domain of theory embraces the whole of science and the whole of philosophy. Philosophy itself is therefore part of the conjuncture in which it intervenes: it exists within this conjuncture, it exists within the 'Whole'. It follows that philosophy cannot entertain an external, purely speculative relation, a relation of pure knowledge to the conjuncture, because it *takes part in this ensemble.* That suggests that a *Thesis* does not have an 'object' but a *stake,* that the relationship between a Thesis and what is at stake in it cannot be simply a relation of 'Truth' (= a relation between a knowledge and its object) and therefore of pure knowledge, but that it must be a *practical* relation, a practical relation of *adjustment.* How should these terms be understood? (1) *Practical* relation does not mean only that this relation gives rise to practical effects (although it does). *Practical* relation signifies something else: the balance of power internal to a field dominated by contradiction and conflicts. (2) That gives the process of *adjustment* its very particular meaning: an adjustment *in struggle,* let us say, between the existing ideas – some dominant, others dominated. (3) It is at this point that *practical results* intervene: the new position delineated and established by the Thesis (Thesis = Position) modifies other positions and affects the realities that are the stake of the entire process of adjustment in struggle which results in the establishment of 'correct' (or incorrect) Theses.

If this is clear, it may be seen that we have escaped the worst pitfall of all. That pitfall pertains to the inevitable misunderstanding that arises as soon as the word 'practice' is pronounced. The misunderstanding results from a *pragmatist* conception of practice. For I know what is in store for us here. It will be said that the mechanic too adjusts a 'part' so that the motor will run! That the surgeon too must 'cut correctly' if he is to save the patient! And that Lenin too had to take into account all the elements of a conjuncture before fixing the correct line of political action. Now, there is something behind all these objections: a pragmatist represen-tation of action, according to which all these 'adjusters' adjust their part, their political line, their intervention to obtain a result, attain an end that governs their action from the exterior. According to this representation, action is the action of a *subject* who 'adjusts' or 'tinkers with' [*bricole*] his intervention with an *end* in view – that is, for the achievement of an *aim* that 'exists in his head' to be realized in the external world. If we accept that argument, we deserve to be called pragmatists, subjectivists, voluntarists, etc.

It is here that we must be careful with images. Of course the 'correct-ness' that results from an 'adjustment' is not unrelated to the practices invoked above, but that is primarily because this affinity of terms fore-grounds the relation between 'correctness' and practice – in its difference with another relation: between 'Truth' and theory. As for the rest, we will not allow ourselves to be trapped by these images. The mechanic who 'adjusts' his part knows very well that the motor pre-exists him and waits for his work to be completed to begin to run the engine again: it is completely external to him. So with the surgeon: it is certainly more complicated, but he is not part of the patient. In contrast, the political leader Lenin interests us for different reasons, and it is not by chance that we have borrowed his terms: 'drawing a line of demarcation', 'Thesis' (think of the 'April Theses') and 'correct'. These are *political* terms. But they suit our purposes, and it certainly suits our purposes that the practice which helps us to think the proper practice of philosophy as adequately as possible should be *political.* For in contrast to the mechanic and the surgeon, who are subjects who act on the basis of an 'idea in their mind' – (1) because they are *subjects* and (2) because this idea simply reflects the fact that the engine to be repaired or the patient to be operated on are *external,* 'existing outside their minds' – Lenin, the politician, the working-class leader, is well and truly *internal* to the conjuncture *in* which he must act if he is to be able to act *on* it. This is why Lenin's practice is not pragmatist (and hence subjectivist–voluntarist). He is not a 'subject' who has 'in mind' an 'idea that he will carry out' and wants to realize externally: he is the leader of a class struggle organization, the vanguard of the popular masses, and in so far as he defines a 'correct line' 'one step ahead of the masses and one step only', he is simply reflecting in order to inflect *a balance of forces in which he participates and takes sides.* Formally speaking, the philosophical practice that we have attempted to think under the Leninist terms 'drawing a line of demarcation', 'Theses', 'correct', etc., is thus on the same side as Lenin's practice: practical, but not pragmatist.

The fact remains, however, that philosophy is not simply politics.

If, at least on the basis of the positions that we are defending, philosophical practice 'functions' in many respects *like* Lenin's political practice, we must support ourselves on this 'like' to see over the wall: to see beyond how philosophy 'functions' in its own domain; to see how it functions *philosophically.* We must proceed further in the determination of the specificity of philosophy.

To do so, we must return to two of our Theses.

1. It is necessary to take seriously the fact that philosophy states *theoretical* propositions (philosophy is 'part' of 'theory') and that it intervenes in 'theory' – that is, in the sciences, in philosophy and in theoretical ideologies: it is this which distinguishes it from all other practices, including political practice.

2. We must restate Thesis 22: all the lines of demarcation traced by philosophy are ultimately modalities of a fundamental line: the line between the scientific and the ideological.

Remember my example of interdisciplinarity. It showed us how philosophy 'functions': by tracing lines of demarcation, making distinctions to clear the correct way, provoking new questions, and therefore new lines *ad infinitum*.
Our analysis of this example has brought out three points:

1. Philosophy functions by intervening not in matter (the mechanic), or on a living body (the surgeon), or in the class struggle (the politician), but *in theory*: not with tools or a scalpel or through the organization and leadership of the masses, but simply by stating *theoretical* propositions (Theses), rationally adjusted and justified. This intervention in theory provokes *theoretical* effects: the positions of new philosophical interventions, etc., and *practical* effects on the balance of power between the 'ideas' in question.

2. Philosophy intervenes in a certain reality: 'theory'. This notion perhaps remains a little vague, but we know what interests us in it. Philosophy intervenes in the indistinct reality in which the sciences, theoretical ideologies and philosophy itself figure. What are theoretical ideologies? Let us advance a provisional definition: they are, in the last instance, and even when they are unrecognizable as such, forms of practical ideologies, transformed within theory.

3. The result of philosophical intervention, such as we have conceived it, is to draw, in this indistinct reality, a line of demarcation that separates, in each case, the scientific from the ideological. This line of demarcation may be completely covered over, denied or effaced in most philosophies: it is essential to their existence, despite the denegation. Its denegation is simply the common form of its existence.

This analysis therefore brings out three essential terms:

1. the intervention of philosophy;
2. the reality in which this intervention takes place;
3. the result of this intervention.

I will go right to the heart of things by saying that the enigma of philosophy is contained in the difference between the reality in which it intervenes (the domain of the *sciences* + theoretical *ideologies* + philosophy) and the result that its intervention produces (the distinction between the *scientific* and the *ideological*).

This difference appears in the form of a difference between *words*. But (note the paradox!) the words that we employ to designate the 'reality' in which . . ., and the words we use to designate the 'result' of the line we have drawn, are *virtually the same*: on the one hand, the sciences and theoretical ideologies; on the other, the scientific and the ideological. On the one hand, nouns; on the other, their adjectival forms. Is this not the same thing? Are we not repeating in the result what we already have in the reality? It would seem that the same characters are in opposition: sometimes in the form of nouns, sometimes in the form of adjectives. Is this not simply a nominal distinction, a terminological difference and therefore merely apparent? Is the result produced by the philosophical intervention really distinguished from the reality in which it intervenes, if it is already inscribed in that reality? In other words, does not the whole of philosophy consist simply in repeating, in the same words, what is already inscribed in reality? Hence in modifying words without producing anything new?

Yes, philosophy does act by modifying words and their order. But they are theoretical words, and it is this difference between words that allows something *new* in reality, something that was hidden and covered over, to appear and *be seen*. The expression *the scientific* is not identical to the expression *the sciences*; the expression *the ideological* is not identical to the expression *theoretical ideologies*. The new expressions do not reproduce the older ones: they bring to light a contradictory couple, a *philosophical* couple. The sciences are sciences: they are not philosophy. Theoretical ideologies are theoretical ideologies: they are not reducible to philosophy. But 'the scientific' and 'the ideological' are *philosophical* categories and the contradictory couple they form is brought to light by philosophy: it is philosophical.

A strange conclusion, but we have to cling to it. We said: philosophy intervenes *in* this indistinct *reality*: the sciences + theoretical ideologies. And we discover that the *result* of the philosophical intervention, the line that reveals the scientific and the ideological by separating them, *is entirely philosophical*. A contradiction? No. For philosophy intervenes in reality only by producing results *within itself*. It acts *outside of itself* through the result that it produces *within itself*. It will be necessary to attempt to think through this necessary paradox one day.

Let us be content to record it with a new Thesis.

Thesis 23. The distinction between the scientific and the ideological is internal to philosophy. It is the result of a philosophical intervention. Philosophy is inseparable from its result, which constitutes the *philosophy-effect*. The philosophy-effect is different from the knowledge-effect (produced by the sciences).

But at the same time let us keep in mind that this internal result (the philosophy-effect) is inseparable from the intervention of philosophy in reality = the sciences + theoretical ideologies.

The first element in this reality is familiar to us: the sciences. They have a recognized historical existence and scientists are witnesses not only to their existence but to their practices, problems and their findings as well. The second element is not so familiar to us: *theoretical ideologies*. We will provisionally leave this element on one side. Because it would take a long analysis to attain knowledge of it: we would have to sketch out a theory of ideologies culminating in a distinction between practical ideologies (religious, moral, juridical, political, aesthetic, etc.), and theoretical ideologies, and in a theory of the relations between these two. But also because we will begin to get an initial idea of the theoretical ideologies as we go along. And finally because it is *indispensable* to dwell for some time on the philosophical question of the existence of the sciences and of scientific practice, before we can approach the problem of ideology.

This last reason is neither one of convenience nor simply of method. It not only concerns the theoretical ideologies, it is primarily concerned with philosophy itself. For we can advance only on one condition: that we enlighten philosophy as to its own nature.

I will therefore advance at this point a central Thesis that is going to command the remainder of this course.

Thesis 24. The relation between philosophy and the sciences constitutes the *specific* determination of philosophy.

I do not say: determination in the last instance, or primary determination, etc. Philosophy has other determinations that play a fundamental role in its existence, its functioning and its forms (for example, its relation with the world-views through practical or theoretical ideologies). I say *specific*, for it is proper to philosophy and pertains to it *alone.*

We must be quite clear as to what is meant by the relation of philosophy to the sciences. It does not mean that *only* philosophy *speaks* of the sciences. Science figures in other discourses: for example, religion, ethics and politics all speak of science. But they do not speak of it as does philosophy, because their relation to the sciences does not constitute the specific determination of religion, ethics, politics, literature. It is not their relation to the sciences that constitutes them as religion, ethics, etc. Similarly, that does not mean that philosophy speaks *only* of the sciences! It speaks, as everyone knows, of everything and of nothing (of nothingness), of religion, ethics, politics, literature, etc. The relation of philosophy to the sciences is not that of a discourse to its 'specific' themes, or even to its 'object' (since philosophy has no object). This relation is *constitutive* of the specificity of philosophy. *Outside of its relationship to the sciences, philosophy would not exist.*

In what remains of this lecture, I will restrict myself to commenting on Thesis 24.

I am going to adopt the only method possible in an introduction: proceeding by *empirical* analyses with the sole purpose *of showing*, making perceptible by *facts*, this specific relation and its importance.

I insist on this precise point: *empirical* analyses. Naturally, there is no such thing as a *pure* empirical analysis. Every analysis, even an empirical analysis, presupposes a minimum of theoretical references without which it would be impossible to present what are called facts: otherwise, we would not know why we accept and recognize them as *facts*. But to analyse the 'functioning' of philosophy in its relation to the sciences empirically is insufficient to furnish a *theory* of philosophy: that is merely a preliminary to such a theory. In a theory of philosophy, other realities (for example, practical ideologies) and other relations (relations of production) must also be taken into account. And it is above all necessary to 're-examine' the findings of empirical analyses from the viewpoint of the *overall* function (or functions) of philosophy in the history of social formations, which does not contradict empirical findings but rather *transforms* their meaning.

In this inquiry into the relation of philosophy to the sciences, we shall now explore the scientific side of things.

II ON THE SIDE OF THE SCIENCES: SCIENTIFIC PRACTICE

How does the relation of philosophy to the sciences appear on the side of the sciences or, more precisely, on the side of scientific practice?

Thesis 25. In their scientific practice, specialists from different disciplines 'spontaneously' recognize the existence of philosophy and the privileged relation of philosophy to the sciences. This recognition is generally unconscious: it can, in certain circumstances, become partially conscious. But it remains enveloped in the *forms* proper to unconscious recognition: these forms constitute the 'spontaneous philosophies of scientists' or '*savants*' (SPS).

To clarify this Thesis I will begin with a case in which this recognition is (partially) conscious.

The most famous and striking example of this recognition is furnished by the particular situations called 'crises'. At a certain moment in its development, a science confronts scientific problems which cannot be

resolved by the existing theoretical means or (and) that call into question the coherence of the earlier theory. As a first approximation, we
might speak either of a contradiction between a new problem and the
existing theoretical means, or (and) of a disturbance of the entire theoretical edifice. These contradictions can be lived as 'critical' or even
dramatic moments by scientists [*savants*] (cf. the correspondence of
Borel, Le Besgue, Hadamard).

Everyone knows famous examples of scientific 'crises': the crisis of
irrational numbers in Greek mathematics, the crisis of modern physics at
the end of the nineteenth century, the crisis triggered in modern
mathematics and mathematical logic by early set theory (between
Cantorian theory and that of Zermelo, 1900–08).

How do *savants* 'live' these crises? What are their reactions? How are
they expressed consciously, by what words, what discourse? How did
they act when faced with these 'crises that shake science'?

Three kinds of reaction may be noted.

First reaction. This is the reaction of scientists [*savants*] who keep a
cool head and confront the problems of science without abandoning the
realm of science. They struggle as best they can with their scientific difficulties and attempt to resolve them. If need be they accept their inability
to see clearly and advance into the darkness. They do not lose confidence. For them the 'crisis' is not a 'crisis of Science' that calls science
itself into question; it is rather a temporary episode, a test. Because in
general they have no sense of history, they do not say that every
scientific crisis is a 'growth crisis', but in practical terms they act as
though it were. In the great 'crisis' of physics in the nineteenth century
and the beginning of the twentieth, we see certain *savants* of this type
resisting the general contagion and refusing to accept the latest word:
'matter has disappeared'. But they were swimming against the tide, and
were not always very happy about arguing the case.

Second reaction. At the other extreme may be seen another kind of
scientists [*savants*] who do lose their heads. The 'crisis' catches them by
surprise, unprepared or, without even knowing it, so prejudiced that
their convictions are badly shaken; everything collapses around them
and, in their panic, they call into question not simply a given scientific
concept or theory so as to rectify or reformulate it, but the validity of
their practice itself: the 'value of science'. Instead of remaining deter-
minedly in the field of science to confront its unforeseen, surprising and
even disconcerting problems, they go over to 'the other side', leaving the
scientific domain to consider it *from the outside*: it is thus *from the
outside* that they render the judgement of 'crisis' and the word they
pronounce takes on a different meaning. Previously, 'crisis' meant in

practice: growing pains, or signs, perhaps critical, that a science was about to be recast. Now 'crisis' means the shattering of *scientific principles*, the fragility of the discipline – or, better still, the radical precariousness of any possible scientific knowledge because it is a human enterprise and, like human beings, limited, finite and prone to error.

And so these *savants* begin to do philosophy. It may not be very lofty, but it is philosophy. Their way of 'living' the crisis is to become 'philosophers' *in order to exploit it*. For they do not do just any philosophy. Especially when they think they have invented something new, they are simply picking up, as best they can, snatches and the refrains of the old *spiritualist* philosophical song, which is always lying in wait for the difficulties of 'science', so as to exploit its reversals, to lead it back to and confine it within its 'limits' as proof of human vanity, and which, from the depths of its nothingness, pays tribute to Spirit by admitting its defeats. It is scientists that we have to thank, for example, for the announcement of the latest news about the 'crisis' in modern physics: 'matter has disappeared!', 'the atom is free!' But religious spiritualism does not always speak so clearly in proclaiming the defeat of 'matter' and of 'necessity'. It also uses other discourses which confine science within its 'limits' to curb and control its pretensions. Restrictions on the 'rights' of science: to ensure that it remains within *its* borders (it is taken for granted that *someone* has established them from the outside, in advance and for ever, and by 'right'). Here again, the *savants* who adopt this discourse on the 'crisis' fall back upon an old agnostic–spiritualist tradition: but we have known since Pascal and Kant that behind the borders assigned science by philosophy there lurks religion.

These reactions offer us an unanticipated spectacle. In our naivety we thought it was philosophers who produced philosophy. But in a 'crisis' situation we discover that *savants* themselves can begin to 'manufacture' philosophy. *Inside every savant, their sleeps a philosopher*, who will awaken at the first opportunity. And perhaps in a pure religious delirium. Like Teilhard de Chardin, palaeontologist and priest, authentic scientist [*savant*] and authentic clergyman, exploiting science for the profit of his faith: directly.

But whilst these scientists [*savants*] who awaken as philosophers may prove that a philosopher sleeps in every scientist, they also demonstrate that the philosophy which speaks through them is, give or take a few individual variations, never anything more than a repetition of an unbroken spiritualist tradition in the history of philosophy which, as it does with all forms of human misery, throws itself upon the 'crisis' of sciences in order to exploit them to apologetic, ultimately religious, ends (Bergson, Brunschvicg, etc.). We must be aware that our history is profoundly marked, and remains so today, by a whole philosophical tradition that lies in wait for the difficulties, contradictions and crises internal to the sciences, because there are so many weaknesses that it can use (that is, exploit) – *ad majorem Dei gloriam* – just like Pascal who was, however, an authentic scientist, but used his science to justify his philosophy; and just like those members of the clergy who await the approach of death to throw themselves at the dying unbeliever and inflict on him, in his agony, the last rites (for his salvation, obviously, but also for the salvation of religion). It is necessary to know that there is within philosophy a whole tradition that survives only by the ideological exploitation of human suffering – of the sick or the dying, of cataclysms and wars – that hurries towards every crisis, including the crises that strike the sciences. It is difficult not to relate this *ideological* exploitation to another form of exploitation which has, since Marx, been known as the exploitation of man by man.

In the 'crisis' of a science, certain *savants* whose convictions have been shaken can thus be seen joining the ranks of those philosophers who want to 'save' science in their own way: by 'forgiving' it 'for it knows not what it does' – that is, by condemning it to its nothingness or to its limits, upon which may be built the kingdom of God or of the Spirit and its freedom.

The philosophy that we propose does not seek the 'salvation' of science. It invites scientists to distrust any philosophy that seeks the 'salvation' of science. It professes, on the contrary, that the question of 'salvation' is religious and has nothing to do with science and its practice; that the 'health' of science is the business of science itself; it has confidence in scientists to solve their own problems, no matter how 'critical'. Scientists should above all count on their own forces: but *their* forces are not a matter for them alone; a good proportion of these forces exists *elsewhere* – in the world of men, in their labour, their struggles and their ideas. I will add: philosophy – not just any philosophy, not that which exploits the sciences, but that which serves them – plays, or can play, a role here.

Third reaction. Leave on one side the two extremes: scientists who continue their work and those who believe the 'divine surprise'[1] that 'matter has disappeared'. There remains a third type of scientist.

They too set out to do philosophy. They too 'live' the 'crisis', not as

---

1. An allusion to the comments on the French defeat of 1940 by Charles Maurras, leader of *Action Française* – a royalist, anti-Semitic and ultranationalist political movement which attacked the Third Republic for 'decadence' and supported the Vichy government during the War. [Ed.]

the contradiction of a process of the recasting and growth of scientific practice and theory, but as a *philosophical* question. They too leave the field of science and, from the outside, ask science philosophical 'questions' about the conditions of the validity of its practice and its findings; about its *foundations* and *qualifications*. But they are not simply content, like the others, to place the homage of their defeats on the steps of the Temple. They are critical not so much of science and its practices as of the naive philosophical ideas in which they *discover* that they had hitherto lived. They recognize that the 'crisis' has awakened them from their 'dogmatism': or better, they *recognize, after the event*, once they are awakened to philosophy, that *because they are scientists, a philosopher has always slept within them*. But they have turned against the philosophy of that philosopher, condemning it as 'dogmatic', 'mechanistic', 'naive' and, in a word, as 'materialist'. In short, they condemn it as a bad philosophy of science and consequently attempt to give science the philosophy it lacks: *the good philosophy of science*. For them, the crisis is the *effect*, within science, of the *bad philosophy of scientists which, until then, reigned over science*. All they have to do now is to start working.

I said: these scientists too leave the realm of science. For us, this is true. But for them, no. As far as they are concerned, they remain *in* science and do not repudiate it. Indeed, they invoke their experience of their scientific practice, their experience of their scientific 'experience'. They invoke their scientific knowledge and it is *from within science* that they claim to speak of science, that they set out to manufacture, *with scientific arguments* borrowed from the sciences – physics, psychophysiology, biology – the good philosophy of science that science is claimed to need. And who is better placed than a scientist to speak of science and its practice? *A scientific philosophy of science* made *by scientists*. What more could anyone reasonably ask for?

Such is the spectacle furnished by the 'crisis' in modern physics at the end of the nineteenth century and the beginning of the twentieth: the appearance of the great *savants* Ostwald and Mach who, together with many scientists, attempted to provide *science* with the good scientific philosophy it needed to be able to 'criticize', 'overcome' and 'abolish' the cause of its crisis – the bad philosophy that scientists had in their heads and which 'caused science so much trouble' – in a word, *materialism*. Along with a number of other systems, Ostwald's energeticism and Mach's empirio-criticism are testimony to this prodigious adventure.

It is at this point that the situation is reversed, and becomes clear.

For note well this little fact: these *savants* who fashion a *savant*'s philosophy for science are not the only people to enter the lists! They

find an entire battalion of *philosophers* – and some major ones at that –
at their side, playing the chorus, repeating their 'scientific' arguments,
and lending them a hand in their search for the philosopher's stone. Thus
Avenarius, Bogdanov and a score of others. Why? It is simple. This
philosophy of scientists, scientific and critical, possessed all that was
necessary to seduce philosophers, for it was *critical.* In one sense,
because it *criticized* the illusions of the bad, 'dogmatist' and 'materialist'
philosophy of previous scientists. But also in another sense: because it
proposed, in sum, to elucidate, under phenomena, the conditions of
possibility which guarantee that scientific knowledge is truly the knowledge of the object of *its* 'experience', and which therefore found a
critical Theory of Knowledge. Something to gratify philosophers who,
since Kant, have had a weakness for 'criticism', and 'do' it in every
possible variant of the critical theory of knowledge. Is it surprising that
they supported Mach? They simply recognized themselves as *philosophers* in his *scientist*'s philosophy.

But if they recognize themselves in his philosophy, it is because they
are *at home* there. And because *savant*-philosophers who believe they
can extract their philosophy *purely* from their experience as scientists,
and *purely* from their scientific knowledges, are simply *endorsing* a
variation on the classical themes of the dominant philosophy, the
'philosophy of philosophers', in a language and with examples that
appear to be new. These philosophers may believe they are doing
revolutionary work, but even a little knowledge of the history of philosophy is enough to set the record straight. For these philosophies of
scientists are, *at bottom*, not new at all but in line with a long tradition,
and they give it both a new form and a new lease of life. The
philosophies of science of Mach and Ostwald, for example, are merely
new presentations of old and well-known philosophical tendencies: they
are variants, admixtures, combinations – sometimes extremely ingenious
– of empiricism, nominalism, pragmatism, criticism, etc., and, therefore,
of *idealism.* Their endeavours are underwritten by the entire constel-
lation of the themes of British *empiricism* of the eighteenth century,
which was dominated by Kantian criticism, combined with the 'scientific
findings' of the physics of sensation of the nineteenth century. For it so
happens that when late-nineteenth-century bourgeois ideology, for
reasons which surpass a simple 'crisis' of physics because they are fundamentally *political*, staged the great 'return to Kant' that took it beyond
Hegel and positivism, the *savant*-philosophers who thought they were
swimming against the current were, without realizing it, being carried
along and carried away by the current. It is hardly surprising that some
philosophers followed their example, for they had all been swept away
by the same current: that of the dominant philosophy in its 'return to Kant'.

The philosophies of scientists provoked by the 'crisis' in '*Science*' belong by rights to the history of *philosophy* which, without their knowing it, sustains them: they do not derive from a theory of the history of the sciences but from a theory of the history of philosophy, its tendencies, its currents and its conflicts.

Scientists in the grip of the 'crisis' means, more prosaically, scientists in the grip of philosophy. Let us say: when there arise scientific difficulties, internal to science and provoked by its contradictory growth, some scientists suddenly *discover* that they had always had a philosophy within them, and criticize it *only* to replace it with another – to them better – philosophy. We may translate: whereas others hasten to exploit the recasting of a science for religious ends, they declare science to be 'in crisis' and, having pronounced the verdict of 'crisis', fall headlong into what must be called a philosophical 'crisis' of their own. All this creates quite a row and since, in the world of the dominant ideology, it is the chanting in unison that makes something true, it is not surprising that it took someone as straightforward and cool-headed as Lenin, who had been formed in the class struggle, brutally to break the 'spell' of these complicities and to condemn the imposture.[2]

One last word: what about those scientists who continue working through the night of their ordeal and who, without exploiting the 'crisis' in science, either keep quiet or defend themselves with whatever words they possess, but remain determined to resolve their problems and contradictions? Are they philosophers too? And what kind? We shall see.

We may now return to our analysis. What have we done? We have grasped the *empirical* opportunity provided by an event observable in certain circumstances in the history of the sciences: that which is declared the 'crisis' of a science.

For in an experience like a 'crisis', something that is ordinarily concealed in shadow or written in small letters appears in the broad light of day or, as Plato said, written in capital letters. The 'crisis' acts as a 'developer' and shows clearly something that remains hidden, unrecognized or disavowed in the course of the everyday life of the sciences. Namely the fact that in every scientist there sleeps a philosopher or, to put it another way, that every scientist is affected by an ideology or a scientific philosophy which we propose to call by the conventional name: *the spontaneous philosophy of the scientists* (abbreviated as SPS).

---

2. See *Materialism and Empirio-criticism, Collected Works*, vol.14, Moscow 1962 – analysed by Althusser in 'Lenin and Philosophy' below, pp. 167–202. [Ed.]

We say that all scientists are, unbeknownst to them, permanently affected by it, even when there is no 'crisis' to make manifest revelations. '*No crisis*': to put it simply, this SPS functions silently and can take forms other than the spectacular forms typical of crises. '*Unbeknownst to them*': this must be said even of the spectacular philosophical forms of crises, for the scientists who suddenly set out to manufacture a philosophy of science, to construct 'the philosophy of science' needed to bring science out of its 'crisis', *no more believe in the existence of an SPS than the others*: they think they are simply denouncing a materialist philosophical *intrusion* into the sciences and giving science the philosophy it needs, by reacting to an *accident* that happened outside science, for they see science in its normal state as a pure science, free from any SPS.

We say that this SPS takes silent and invisible forms in the 'normal' course of scientific practice and spectacular forms in the case of a 'crisis' – which leads us to question the very meaning of the term 'scientific *crisis*'. Are there really 'scientific crises' that are not simply, as Lenin argued, 'growth crises', crises which, far from being *critical*, are on the contrary productive? And if there is such a 'crisis', is it not necessary to return the term against its authors – that is, against those who, one fine day, announce to the world that 'modern physics' or 'set theory' is 'in crisis'? After all, it is *they* who pronounce the judgement of 'crisis'! And it must be asked if all this takes place inside their heads – that is, in the ideologico-philosophical reaction they experience (jubilation or fear) before the emergence of a certain number of unforeseen or disconcerting *scientific* problems. Crisis for crisis: it must be asked if the crisis – not the productive crisis, but the *critical* crisis – far from being a crisis in science, is not rather a crisis of their own making and, in so far as they live the crisis in philosophy, *simply their philosophical crisis and nothing more.*

If this is so, then our hypothesis is reinforced: all scientific practice is inseparable from a 'spontaneous philosophy' which may, depending upon which philosophy is involved, be a materialist aid or an idealist obstacle; that this spontaneous philosophy alludes, 'in the last instance', to the secular struggle that unfolds on the battlefield (*Kampfplatz*, Kant[3]) of the history of philosophy between idealist tendencies and materialist tendencies; and that the forms of this struggle are themselves governed by other more distant forms, those of the ideological struggle

---

3. *Critique of Pure Reason*, Preface to the first edition, p. 7. Kant provides a small-scale map of the battlefield in the final section of the *Critique*, The Transcendental Doctrine of Method, chapter 4, 'The History of Pure Reason', pp. 666–9. [Ed.]

(between or within practical ideologies) and those of the class struggle.

It is to the forms of the class struggle that we must turn if we are really to understand what happens in the 'critique' of modern physics and the 'spontaneous philosophy of scientists' that reflects it. For why, in the last resort, have the scientific events of the development of modern physics taken the form of a 'crisis' and given rise to the exemplary discourses of *neo-Kantian* philosophy? It is because 'Kant is in the air', because the conjuncture has imposed a 'return to Kant'. The conjuncture ... after the great fear and the massacres of the Commune, bourgeois philosophers and ideologues and later, surrendering to the contagion, the ideologues of the labour movement itself, began to celebrate the 'return to Kant' so as to *struggle against 'materialism'*: the materialism of scientific practice and that of the proletarian class struggle. When modern physics becomes conscious of unforeseen and contradictory problems, it is merely taking its place in a pre-existing current that 'tails the movement'; while the scientists who have constructed neo-Kantian philosophy believe themselves to be the vanguard of history.

To denounce this mystification we need nothing less than Lenin (*Materialism and Empirio-criticism*). I have on several occasions cited Lenin in connection with philosophy. We know that this political leader (who described himself as an amateur in philosophy)[4] had a fairly good idea of what it is to struggle and of what relation links the political to the philosophical struggle, since he knew how to intervene (and who else did it? No one!) in this difficult matter, and to trace the appropriate lines of demarcation to open the way to a correct position of the problems of the 'crisis'. And at the same time, by way of example, he gave us the means to understand the *practice* of philosophy.

In other words, without Lenin and all that we owe him, this philosophy course for scientists could never have taken place.

---

4. See Lenin's letter to Gorky of 7 February 1908, in *Collected Works*, vol. 34, p. 381. [Ed.]

Lecture III

Now we are heading out to sea. Not only did we embark suddenly, without warning. We have already come a long way, or so it would seem, and we are already in uncharted waters. It is time to take our bearings in order better to know where we have come from and where we are going. But first, we must work out how far we have come.

We are still steering towards the question: *what about philosophy*? (I say *what about*?, instead of *what is*?, to satisfy certain philosophers who are irritated beyond measure by the question *what is*? But these are intra-philosophical matters, and I will not bore you with the details.)

We have been hugging the shores of the history of the sciences as closely as possible.

Why this cruise along the 'scientific shores'? Because we thought we could advance the Thesis that the relationship with the sciences consti- tutes what is *specific* to philosophy (remember: its specific determinant, not its determinant in the last instance). It is this Thesis that we are attempting to justify.

It was to this end that we took a look at what occurs in what seemed to us a privileged, because revealing, experience (or even experiment?) of what is known as a 'crisis in the sciences'. And from this we drew a certain number of conclusions that are undoubtedly difficult for our scientific friends to accept: we hit them with the 'revelation' that they have always been affected by a 'spontaneous philosophy of scientists', even when they were not wearing the historical hat of the Great Scientist Philosophers who, believing themselves 'assigned' to a historical Mission unprecedented in the history of philosophy, are simply chewing over, like hard-working but ingenious subordinates, the leftovers of an old philosophical meal which the ideological contradictions of the epoch made dominant and obligatory. By inflicting this 'revelation' on them we

119

have undoubtedly fallen foul of their convictions, their honesty – even if it is cloaked in a certain naivety (after all, to replace one cartoon image with another, whilst we recognized that philosophers are ridiculous characters who 'fall into wells' and drew conclusions from this, scientists are well aware that even if they do not fall in their disciplines as philosophers do in theirs, they do not always have their feet 'on the ground', but rather a certain naivety in their heads).

It is time to step back from this experience. If they examine these conclusions from a safe distance, our scientific friends will find that things fall into place, and that we will render them the justice they may fear we are denying them.

From this distance, what are we to retain of our analysis of the phenomena that the 'crises' of the 'sciences' 'reveal'? Two discoveries, two themes of the utmost importance:

1. There is such a thing as the *exploitation* of the sciences by philosophy.

2. There is within the 'consciousness' or the 'unconscious' of scientists such a thing as a *spontaneous philosophy of scientists* (SPS).

I will now take up these two points.

I THE EXPLOITATION OF THE SCIENCES BY PHILOSOPHY

More precisely: the vast majority of philosophies have always exploited the sciences for apologetic ends, ends extrinsic to the interests of scientific practice.

Note well: I am saying nothing new. I am merely taking up a theme that was evoked in relation to the 'crisis' of the sciences, specifically, when I spoke of the reaction of the *second* type of scientist (the spiritualists who turn the failure of science *ad majorem Dei gloriam*, as they do all human misery and suffering). But in taking up this theme, I will *generalize* it.

And to give it its *general* meaning, I am obliged to say: the vast *majority* of known philosophies have, throughout the history of philosophy, always *exploited* the sciences (and not simply their failures) to the profit of the 'values' (a provisional term) of *practical ideologies*: religious, moral, juridical, aesthetic, political, etc. This is one of the *essential* characteristics of idealism.

If this proposition is true, it must be capable of being concretely illustrated, and this is the case.

I believe there is no need to dwell at length on the example of *reli-gious* philosophies (dominated by religious ideology). All the scientific genius of Pascal did not prevent him from deriving beautifully eloquent flourishes of rhetoric, dedicated to the (slightly heretical) Christianity he professed, from the contradictions of the mathematical infinite itself, and from the religious 'terror' inspired in him by the new (Galilean) 'infinite spaces' of a world of which man was no longer the centre and from which God was 'absent' – which made it necessary, in order to save the very idea of God, to say that He was in essence a '*hidden* God' (because He was no longer anywhere to be found – neither in the world, nor in its order, nor its morality: one can only wait to be touched by His unpredictable and impenetrable grace). I say: all the genius of Pascal, for he was a very great scientist and, what is extremely rare (a paradox that must be pondered), an astonishing, almost materialist, philosopher of scientific practice. But he was too alone in his time, and like everyone else was subject to such contradictions, such stakes and such a balance of power (think of the violence of his struggle against the Jesuits) that he could not avoid the obligatory 'solution', which was also no doubt a consolation to him, of resolving *in religion* (his own) the most general and conflict-ridden contradictions of a science in which he laboured as a genuine materialist practitioner. And so, together with some admirable texts (on mathematics, on scientific experimentation), Pascal left us the corpus of a *religious philosophy* of which it must be said that its inspir-ation is the exploitation of the great theoretical contradictions of the sciences of his time to apologetic ends external to the sciences.

Next to a giant like Pascal, what is to be said in our time of a Teil-hard? The same thing, but without being able to find anything in his work to counterbalance the vacuous and deluded enterprise of a palae-ontologist dressed in a cassock who prides himself on being a priest as he draws risky conclusions from his science: open exploitation 'for the sake of heaven above'.

The case of *spiritualist* philosophies is a little more complex. They do not have the disconcerting, even moving, simplicity of certain religious philosophies. They are more cunning, for they do not pursue their ends directly but make a detour through the *philosophical categories* elabo-rated in the history of philosophy: Spirit, Soul, Freedom, the Good, the Beautiful, Values, etc.

And because at this point I bring the history of philosophy to bear, note well that all the philosophies of which we are speaking are still *con-temporary*: we still have among us 'representatives' of religious philos-ophy, spiritualist philosophy, idealist-critical philosophy, neo-positivism, materialism, etc. But these philosophies do not share the same 'date of birth' and most have not *always* existed. New philosophies have appeared *in opposition* to the older ones: they have prevailed over them in historical struggle. But the characteristic feature of this singular 'history' of philosophy is that the new philosophy that 'prevails over' an older one, which it comes to dominate after a long and difficult struggle, *does not destroy the older one*, which lives on beneath this domination and thus survives indefinitely, most often in a subordinate role, but sometimes recalled by the conjuncture to the front of the stage. If this is the case, it is because the 'history' of philosophy 'proceeds' very differently from the history of the sciences. In the history of the sciences a double process is constantly in play: the process of *the pure and simple elimination of errors* (which disappear totally) and the process of the *reinscription* of earlier theoretical elements and knowledges in the context of *newly* acquired knowledges and newly constructed theories. In sum, a double 'dialectic': the total elimination of 'errors' and the integration of earlier findings, still valid but transformed, into the theoretical system of the new insights.

The history of philosophy 'proceeds' very differently: via a *struggle for domination* by the new philosophical forms against those that were once dominant. The history of philosophy is a struggle between tendencies realized in philosophical formations, and it is always a struggle for domination. But the paradox is that this struggle results only in the replacement of one domination by another, and not in the pure and simple elimination of a past formation (as '*error*': for there is no error in philosophy, in the sense that there is in the sciences) – that is, of the adversary. The adversary is never totally defeated and *therefore never totally suppressed,* totally *erased from historical existence.* It is only *dominated* and it lives on under the domination of the new philosophical formation that has overcome it after a very protracted battle: it lives on as a *dominated* philosophical formation, and is naturally ready to re-emerge whenever the conjuncture gives the signal and furnishes the occasion.

These remarks were of course necessary to give the real meaning of our analysis of the different philosophical formations that we are examining. It is not a question of simply *enumerating* philosophies, asking why they exist or subsist alongside one another, but rather of examining the philosophical formations which, old as they may be, still exist today in subordinate but still living forms, *dominated* by other formations which have conquered in struggle, or are in the process of conquering, something that must be called 'power'.

I will now return to spiritualist philosophies. Not to give their 'date of birth', but to show that they were *dominant* throughout the entire period that preceded the establishment of bourgeois relations (to say nothing of their 'roots' in Antiquity): under feudalism, in the Middle Ages, only to be dominated subsequently by bourgeois idealist philosophy, from which they did not fail to take some of their own arguments, divorced from their classical idealist meanings (there is thus, as we shall see, a 'spiritualist interpretation' of Descartes, Kant, Husserl, etc.).

What distinguishes spiritualist philosophies from overtly religious philosophies is that they do not *directly* exploit the sciences (to speak only of what concerns us now) to the profit of overtly religious themes: *ad majorem Dei gloriam.* (They too may well pronounce the name of God, but it is the 'God of the philosophers' – a philosophical category.) They exploit the sciences for the profit of the Human Spirit, of Human Freedom, of Human Moral Values, etc. – or, bringing all these themes together, to the profit of the *Freedom* of the Human Spirit which, as everyone knows, is manifested in 'creation', be it scientific, moral, social, aesthetic or even religious. All philosophers know this.

But not only philosophers: for these philosophical themes, which famous academics have enshrined in 'immortal' works (and as nothing ever completely dies in philosophy, they do stand a chance of becoming immortal!), have passed into the 'vulgar' language of political speeches, sermons, magazine articles – in short, have ended up where all philosophy normally ends: in everyday life, to furnish arguments to justify the *practical* stands taken by these gentlemen.

Have we not heard enough about the '*supplément d'âme*' (Bergson), which our 'mechanical civilization' (see Duhamel[1]), and now our 'consumer society', seems to 'need'? From the '*supplément d'âme*' to the 'quality of life', the way is short and direct. Surely we heard enough about the '*Freedom*' of the Spirit, of culture, of the creative power of the human mind, of the Great (moral!) Values that justify the existence and the defence of our 'civilization' which is, apparently, not simply an organization of production (industrial societies!) but 'a soul' which, of course, struggles as best it can against the intrusions of matter, yet remains what it always has been: *a soul* which, naturally enough, must be saved and defended (against whom? Against an intrusive materialism? Which one? The materialism that speaks of mechanized matter? That poses no real threat: if we use 'the standard of living' and 'participation' to improve the 'quality of life', we will get by; but the *other* materialism of political materialists united in struggle poses a very different kind of threat).

If we leave these 'lower' regions to ascend to the heights of our spiritualist philosophers, we will easily begin to see how their thought is constructed. Bergson's whole career as a spiritualist was based upon the

---

1. See Georges Duhamel, *Civilisation*, Paris 1918. [Ed.]

exploitation of the 'difficulties' or, in the sense that we have discussed it, of the 'crisis' in the theory of cerebral localizations (*Matter and Memory*[2]), as well as modern physics (relativity) and Durkheimian sociology (*The Two Sources of Morality and Religion*[3]). Pretexts for developing, in a multitude of forms and in a vocabulary renovated to the profit of Spirit, the antagonism between (material) space and (spiritual) duration. A singular destiny: at the very moment of the 'return to Kant' that gave birth to the different forms of neo-criticism, Bergson chose another way. He knew almost nothing about Kant, and if he did read Kant, he understood him badly because he did not want to understand him. Bergson 'works' the old spiritualist vein and exploits the sciences in a spiritualist mode, supplemented with new arguments and new categories (intuition, *le mouvant*, spiritual energy, etc.). The mode is different, the result the same.

Brunschvicg (who, like Bergson, but at a higher level, wielded real autocratic ideological power in the university) is *apparently* something else. A 'great mind' (at least as far as the history of modern French philosophy is concerned), who spoke incessantly of Spirit.[4] The fact that he came to a miserable end in an occupied France whose government hunted down the Jews changes nothing of his official past. This man, who read Plato, Aristotle, Descartes, Spinoza, Kant, Fichte, and Hegel, possessed an 'impressive' culture, historical (unlike Bergson) and scientific (albeit only second-hand). And this man seemed to belong to the great critical idealist tradition since, in his eyes, everything was contained in Kant and Fichte, so much so that he thought Aristotle and Hegel retarded ('the mental age of a twelve-year-old'). Brunschvicg, Kantian and critical thinker? That would be going too far. It is true that when he read Descartes, he never stopped relating him to Kant. But he read Kant through Spinoza, a strange Spinoza who would turn in his grave if he knew he was being read as a spiritualist! The truth is that all these references are false, because they are deceptive. Brunschvicg may well have constantly invoked Kant, but he was not a *critical* philosopher. One has only to look at the astonishing *mélange* he made of Plato, Descartes, Spinoza and Kant to see the direction in which he *tended*. Brunschvicg was a spiritualist who (like many of his peers) knew how to make use of the prestige of certain arguments taken from the most disparate philosophers, and how to distort them for his own purposes. In the battle that is philosophy all the techniques of war, including

---

2. Originally published in Paris, 1896; translated London, 1911. [Ed.]
3. Originally published Paris, 1932; translated London, 1935. [Ed.]
4. See especially *Le Progrès de la conscience dans la philosophie occidentale*, Paris 1927. [Ed.]

looting and camouflage, are permissible. And when it was necessary no longer simply to 'comment' on an author but to express an opinion about the facts of the history of the sciences (mathematics, causality in physics), Brunschvicg revealed his true colours. He too exploited the sciences to compose hymns to the Human Spirit, to the Freedom of the Spirit, to moral and aesthetic Creation. The fact that he did not believe in a *personal* God (the spiritualist existentialist-Christian Gabriel Marcel reproached him for this at a famous congress on philosophy in Paris in 1937) changes nothing: this was a minor conflict between a religious philosopher and a spiritualist philosopher.

Are other names necessary? When Paul Ricœur writes a large book on psychoanalysis (*Freud and Philosophy*[5]), a scientific discipline yet again pays the price of a 'demonstration' of Freedom borrowed, this time, not from Descartes or Kant, but from Husserl. When someone like Garaudy, who had his moment of power, claims to find in Marx's scientific work a notion of 'freedom' (Marxism is a theory of 'historical initiative', a formula borrowed from Fichte), however Marxist and materialist he declares himself to be, he remains no less a spiritualist.[6] Others who abuse Marx to present his theory as 'humanist', however Marxist and materialist they declare themselves, are no less spiritualist. Lenin would have called them 'shamefaced' spiritualists, as this kind of spiritualism is hard to swallow and therefore hard to admit to. In every case, sciences (whether of nature, the unconscious, or history) are *exploited* by spiritualist philosophies for apologetic ends: to justify their 'objectives', no doubt because these 'objectives' are so lacking in guarantees that they must fraudulently obtain one from the prestige of the sciences.

As I said a moment ago: in the case of overtly *religious* philosophies it is the practical ideology of *religion* that, thanks to the good offices of these philosophies, exploits the sciences, their difficulties, problems, concepts or their existence, to its own ends. But in the case of *spiritualist* philosophies? I advance the following thesis: it is *moral* practical ideology. And this is verifiable in that all spiritualist philosophies culminate in a commentary on the Good, in a Morality, a Wisdom that is nothing more than an exaltation of human Freedom, whether contemplative or practical (practice = morality); in the exaltation of a creative Freedom at once moral and aesthetic. At this highest level, the Beautiful of aesthetic creation and the Good of moral creation (or even

---

5. Paris 1965; translated New Haven, 1970. [Ed.]
6. See, for example, Roger Garaudy, *Karl Marx – The Evolution of his Thought*, London 1967. [Ed.]

religious creation, in the sense that religion is the highest form of morality) exchange their weapons and their charms with the blessing of human Freedom and within its element.

I am well aware that *moral* practical ideology poses a problem, for it is most often 'floating' or 'drifting'. Either it is a by-product of social, economic, or political relations (for the Greek philosophers morality is a by-product of political ideology, and is political); or it is the by-product of religious ideology (as in the Middle Ages); or it is a by-product of juridical ideology (in the bourgeois period). In each of these cases, morality is an *ideological complement* or supplement that depends upon another ideology. Let us not forget, as we have seen in some of our authors, that morality may also be linked to an aesthetic ideology. But this practical ideology is in itself, in certain periods and conjunctures, endowed with a kind of privilege that permits it, through its *subordinate* form (which is nevertheless regarded as *autonomous* and *dominant*), to express 'values' that are difficult to defend, or at least difficult to defend in the name of an openly avowed practical ideology. To spell it out: when religion fails, it may be an advantage to be able to fall back upon morality: it makes no difference that the morality in question is bound up both with a declining religious ideology *and* with ascendant juridical ideology. To spell it out: when juridical ideology is too overt, and when espousing it might damage the cause you wish to defend, it may be an advantage to be able to fall back upon morality, its by-product, and to treat it as if it had more to do with religion than with juridical ideology, or, if not religion, then the Human Spirit and its freedom. Brunschvicg is typical of this latter case: he speaks of Freedom, but this is not the freedom of juridical ideology; it is another Freedom: the Freedom of the Human Spirit, which he slips in under the juridical by speaking simply of morality.

But we have not yet finished. For, in addition to religious philosophies and spiritualist philosophies, there remain the classical idealist philosophies from Descartes to Kant and Husserl: from *rationalist* idealism to *critical* idealism. As a first approximation, these philosophies may claim a very different 'relation' to the sciences from the religious and spiritualist philosophies. In fact, from Descartes to Husserl by way of Kant, this idealism can claim a real knowledge of scientific problems and a position with regard to the sciences that seems to demarcate it from other philosophies. Descartes himself was a mathematician; he gave his name to certain discoveries and wrote on 'method'. Kant denounced the imposture of 'sciences without an object', such as rational theology, rational psychology and rational cosmology; he took a close interest in problems of cosmology and of physics; in his *Metaphysical Foundations of Natural Science* he even inaugurated what would later be called epistemology. As for Husserl, we know that he was steeped in mathematics and mathematical logic.

However, although in a different, infinitely less crude form this rationalist and critical idealism claims to recognize the rights of science, it none the less exploits the sciences. In all its variants, philosophy appears to be the discipline that *establishes the rights* of the sciences, for it *poses the question of rights* and answers it by defining *legal rights* to scientific knowledge. This philosophy appears in every case as the juridical guarantee of both the *rights* and *limits* of science.

It is not by chance that the 'question of knowledge', and the corresponding 'theory of knowledge', have come (this has in no way always been the case) to occupy the central place in philosophy. *Who will guarantee me* that the (scientific) truth I possess is beyond doubt, that I am not being 'deceived' by a God who, like an 'evil demon', deceives me with the very obviousness of the presence of the true (Descartes)?[7] *Who will guarantee me* that the 'conditions of experience' give me the truth of experience itself? What then are the *limits* of any possible experience (Kant)?[8] What must be the 'modality' of consciousness *in order for* the object that is given to it to be 'present in person', and what is this 'consciousness' that is both 'my' 'concrete' consciousness and the consciousness of scientific ideality (Husserl)?[9] Although these questions seem *preliminary*, concerning only questions of 'right', allowing the sciences their autonomy, they involve philosophy in a 'theory of knowledge' that unfailingly leads to a philosophy of *Science* in which philosophy 'states the truth' about science, the 'truth' of science in a theory that relates science a human activity like any other, to the system of human activities in which, purely by coincidence, Freedom is realized in Morality, Art, Religion, and politics.

It is necessary to unmask the subtle deceptions of this rationalist– critical idealist procedure, which does not invoke the rights of science but asks science a *question of right* external to science in order to *furnish* its rightful qualifications: always from the outside.

What is this 'exterior'? Once again, a practical ideology. This time, *juridical* ideology. It might be said that the whole of bourgeois philosophy (or its great dominant representatives, for the subordinate tendencies that formulate religious or spiritualist philosophies behind the scenes must be given their due) is nothing more than a recapitulation of,

---

7. René Descartes, *Meditations on the First Philosophy* (1641), *Discourse on Method/Meditations*, Harmondsworth 1960, First Meditation, p. 100. [Ed.]

8. Introduction to *Critique of Pure Reason*, pp. 41–62. [Ed.]

9. Edmund Husserl, *Ideas* (1913), New York 1941. [Ed.]

and a philosophical commentary on, bourgeois juridical ideology. No one can contest the fact that the 'question of right', which opens up the royal road to the classical theory of knowledge, is relatively foreign to ancient philosophy (Plato, Aristotle, the Stoics and the core of scholasticism). If there is an element of a 'theory of knowledge' in these philosophies, it plays a subordinate and very different role to the role played by the 'theory of knowledge' of classical bourgeois philosophy. It is hardly open to argument that this 'question of right' at the heart of bourgeois philosophy itself is bound up with the domination of juridical ideology, although it is an unrecognized 'truth' – unrecognized for good reasons! But that the 'theory of knowledge' is entirely enclosed in the *presupposition* of this preliminary question, that the developments and therefore the results of this 'theory of knowledge' are at bottom governed and contaminated by this presupposition of external origin – this is more difficult to concede.

This, however, is something to reflect upon. It is not by chance that in response to the 'question of right', the classical theory of knowledge puts into play a category like that of the 'subject' (from the Cartesian *ego cogito* to the Kantian transcendental Subject to the 'concrete', transcendental subjects of Husserl). This category is simply a reproduction within the field of philosophy of the ideological notion of 'subject', itself taken from the juridical category of the 'legal subject'. And the 'subject–object' couple, the 'subject' and 'its' object, is merely a reflection within the philosophical field, and within a properly philosophical mode, of the juridical categories of the 'legal subject', 'owner' *of itself and* of its goods (things). So with consciousness: it is owner of itself (*self*-consciousness) and of its goods (consciousness *of its* object, of *its* objects). Critical idealist philosophy resolves this duality of right in a philosophical theory of *constitutive* (of itself and of its object) consciousness. Husserl explains this theory of constitutive consciousness as 'intentional' consciousness. Intentionality is the theory of the '*of*' (consciousness *of* self = consciousness *of* its object). Only one 'of': just like that, consciousness is *sure* of grasping itself when it grasps *its* object, and vice versa. Always the same need for a *guarantee*! I have given only a simple indication here, but it could easily be shown, by developing its logic, and by supporting it with all the connecting elements, that the demonstration is possible.

If this is the case, we can understand why critical–rationalist idealist philosophy subjects the sciences and scientific practice to a preliminary question that already contains the answer which it innocently claims to be seeking in the sciences. And because this answer, inscribed in the question of right, appears in law only because it appears elsewhere at the same time: in the entire structure of emerging bourgeois society and therefore in its ideology, in the practico-aesthetico-religious 'values' of this ideology, we can understand that what is being played out, in an apparently exclusive manner, in the little 'theatre' of the Theory of knowledge, and of the epistemology of rationalist and critical philosophies, concerns very different debates: for Kant, the destiny of law, morality, religion and politics in the epoch of the French Revolution; for Husserl, 'the crisis of the European Sciences' [*sic!*][10] under imperialism. Of course, the sciences exploited by idealism once again bore the cost of the operation.

The following points therefore emerge from this analysis: the vast majority of philosophies, be they religious, spiritualist or idealist, maintain a relation of *exploitation* with the sciences. Which means: the sciences are never seen for what they really are; their existence, their limits, their growing pains (baptized 'crises') or their mechanisms, as interpreted by the idealist categories of the most well-informed philosophies, are *used* from outside; they may be used crudely or subtly, but they are used to furnish arguments or guarantees for extra-scientific values that the philosophies in question objectively serve through their own practice, their 'questions' and their 'theories'. These 'values' pertain to *practical ideologies*, which play their own role in the social cohesion and social conflicts of class societies.

Obviously, I am aware of the objection that cannot fail to come to mind, for scientists will readily agree with my remarks. What scientist has not felt the very particular impression created by philosophy in its relation to the sciences, even when it declares its sincerity and honesty: the impression of blackmail and exploitation? Philosophers obviously do not have this impression: exploiters in general, and not simply in philosophy, never have the impression of being exploiters. And that does not make for easy relations between philosophers and scientists. But – and here is the objection – if every philosophy is, as has been shown, subordinate to certain values pertaining to practical ideologies, and if there is an almost organic link between philosophies and practical ideologies, *in the name of what philosophy do we denounce this exploitation*? Is the philosophy to which we adhere by chance an exception? Is it exempt from this link? Is it exempt from this dependency, and the shortcomings it implies, and is it therefore, and a priori, immune to the possibility that it might exploit the sciences?

In all honesty, my answer must be that we cannot offer you an absolute *guarantee*. And I will add: if we were to offer you such a guarantee (after what has been said concerning the abusive, harmful and

---

10. Cf. Edmund Husserl, *The Crisis of the European Sciences and Transcendental Phenomenology* (1936; 1954), Evanston 1970. [Ed.]

illusory function of the search for a philosophical 'guarantee'), it would be, in our eyes at least, suspect. Instead, we will offer you two means of control.

First, we offer the *practice* of our philosophy. The same scientists who are capable of 'feeling' from experience whether or not a given philosophy is treating the sciences in cavalier fashion, or abusing or exploiting the sciences, will be able to tell if we are *exploiting* the sciences or if, on the contrary, we *are serving* them in our philosophical practice. This is a *de facto* argument.

And here is a *de jure* argument. It is true that all the great philosophical currents we have briefly analysed are subordinated to the 'values' of the practical ideologies which exist in a conjuncture: to the values, let us say, of the dominant ideology (and, beneath it, the dominated ideologies). Let us go even further: it is highly probable that *every* philosophy, even if it is not religious, spiritualist or idealist, maintains an organic relation with the 'values' of some practical ideology, with the values in question in the ideological struggle (which takes place against the backdrop of the class struggle). Which implies that *materialist* philosophies, of which we have not spoken, obey the same law themselves. Even if they do not exploit the sciences to prove the existence of God or to shore up great moral and aesthetic values, even if they are devoted, as they most certainly are, to a materialist *defence* of the sciences, they are not without a relation to a *practical* ideology, usually *political* ideology even if, as in the Enlightenment of the eighteenth century, it is highly contaminated with juridico-moral ideology.

We must go that far. But it is necessary to go a lot further. For if this dependence of philosophy on practical ideologies and their conflicts is recognized, why should philosophy *passively* submit to dependence on these realities (practical ideologies) without being able to produce a knowledge both of the nature and of the mechanism of these realities? Now it so happens that the principles of this knowledge were furnished by Marx in historical materialism, and that this knowledge transformed the old materialism into a new materialism: dialectical materialism.[11] It has been seen that the philosophy to which we adhere – or, more exactly, the position we occupy in philosophy – is not unrelated to politics, to a certain politics, to Lenin's politics, so much so that Lenin's political formulae were of use to us in stating our theses on philosophy. There is no contradiction here: this politics is the politics of the workers'

---

11. This knowledge did not, as is all too often said, transform philosophy into a *science*: the new philosophy is still *philosophy*, but *scientific* knowledge of its relations with practical ideologies makes it a 'correct' philosophy.

movement and its theory comes from Marx, *just as the knowledge of practical ideologies that finally permits philosophy to control and criticize its organic link with practical ideology, and therefore to rectify the effects of this link by taking a 'correct' line, comes from Marx.* In the absence of an absolute guarantee (something that does not exist except in idealist philosophy, and we know what to think of that), here are the arguments that we can present. They are both practical (they can be judged by comparing the services which we can render the sciences) and theoretical (the critical check on the inevitable effects of ideology on philosophy through a knowledge of the mechanisms of ideology and ideological struggle: in particular, by a knowledge of their action on philosophy).

II THE SPONTANEOUS PHILOSOPHY OF SCIENTISTS (SPS)

We may now take up this second point.

The meaning of the manufacture of 'new' or 'true' philosophies of science' by scientists in the grip of a scientific 'crisis' will now perhaps be more readily understood. In so far as they simply adopt spiritualist or idealist themes that have been 'worked upon' for centuries in the history of philosophy, they too take their place, *even though they are scientists*, in the long tradition of those who exploit the sciences for apologetic ends, and naturally without the counterweight of materialism and without the critical checks that can be ensured, within materialism, by knowledge of the mechanism of ideology and the class conflicts within it.

But at the same time we can also understand something else: what we have described as the reaction of those stubborn and silent hard-working scientists who, even in the midst of the pseudo-crisis, obstinately pursue their work and defend it with arguments, always the same arguments, that the great philosophers of the 'crisis' call naive and materialist. We have spoken very little of this type of scientist (the first reaction). However, Lenin, who violently attacked other scientists, defended them by evoking their 'materialist instinct'. These scientists never proclaimed that 'matter' had disappeared: they thought that it continued to exist and that physical science does indeed produce a knowledge of the 'laws of matter'. These scientists have no need of a neo-critical philosophy to revitalize their idea of science and of the 'conditions of possibility' of scientific knowledge; they have no need of a philosophy to *guarantee* that their knowledges are truly knowledges – that is, *objective* (in a double sense: knowledge of its object and knowledge valid outside of any subjectivity). They defend themselves as best they can. Their arguments may seem 'simple' or even 'crude' to their adversaries; they may even be mistaken in their idea as to how to resolve the contradictions of modern physics: but who is *guaranteed* not to err? They represent a very different position to that of their peers, who are in the 'grip' of the philosophy they profess.

Their existence is important for us. For if we want to speak of the spontaneous philosophy of scientists in all its breadth and its contradiction, we must take into account both extremes: not only the scientists who construct a philosophy that exploits the difficulties of science, but also those scientists who obstinately fight, at considerable personal risk, on the basis of very different positions.

I will cut short these indispensable analyses in order to justify the details of the exposition and get down to basics.

1. By looking at the elements furnished by the experience of a 'crisis' in a science, we have come to the conclusion that there exists a relation between philosophy and the sciences, and that this first relation may be revealed in the work of scientists themselves in so far as they are bearers of what I have termed a spontaneous philosophy of scientists (SPS).

2. We understand this term (SPS) in a very strict and limited sense. By SPS we understand not the set of ideas that scientists have about the world (i.e., their 'world-view') but only the ideas that they have (consciously or unconsciously) concerning their scientific practice and science.

3. We therefore rigorously distinguish between (1) the spontaneous philosophy of scientists and (2) scientists' world-views. These two realities are united by profound ties, but they can and must be distinguished. Later, we will examine the notion of world-view. The SPS bears only on the ideas (conscious or unconscious) that scientists have of the scientific practice of the sciences and of 'Science'.

4. If the content of the SPS is analysed, the following fact may be registered (we are still at the level of empirical analysis): the content of the SPS is *contradictory*. The contradiction exists between two *elements* that may be distinguished and identified in the following manner:

A. An element of internal, 'intra-scientific' origin which we shall call ELEMENT 1. In its most 'diffuse' form, this element represents 'convictions' or 'beliefs' stemming from the experience of scientific practice itself in its everyday immediacy: it is 'spontaneous'. If it is elaborated philosophically, this element can naturally take the form of Theses. These convictions-Theses are of a materialist and objectivist character. They can be broken down as follows: (1) belief in the real, external and material existence of the *object* of the scientific knowledge; (2) belief in the existence and objectivity of the *scientific knowledges* that permit knowledge of this object; (3) belief in the correctness and efficacy of the procedures of scientific experimentation, or *scientific method*, capable of producing scientific knowledge. What characterizes the corpus of these convictions-Theses is that they allow no room for the philosophical 'doubt' that calls into question the validity of scientific practice; that they avoid what we have called the 'question of right', the question of the right to existence of the object of knowledge, of knowledge of that object, and of scientific method.

B. An element of external, 'extra-scientific' origin which we shall call ELEMENT 2. In its most diffuse form, this element too represents a certain number of 'convictions' or 'beliefs' that can be elaborated in philosophical Theses. It is, of course, *related* to scientific practice itself, but does not originate in it. On the contrary, it is a reflection *on* scientific practice by means of philosophical Theses elaborated *outside* this practice by the religious, spiritualist or idealist-critical 'philosophies of science' manufactured by philosophers or scientists. It is characteristic of the 'convictions-Theses' of Element 2 that they should subordinate the experience of scientific practice to Theses, and therefore to 'values' or 'instances', that are external to it and which, by exploiting the sciences, uncritically serve a certain number of objectives pertaining to practical ideologies. In appearance, they are as 'spontaneous' as the first set: in fact, they are highly elaborated and can be considered 'spontaneous' only because their dominance makes them immediately 'obvious'. To speak only of this case, in the nuance of their formulation they bear the trace of the 'question of right', which can take many forms: a calling into question of the external material existence of the *object* (replaced by *experience* or *experiment*); a calling into question of the objectivity of scientific knowledges and of theory (replaced by '*models*'); a calling into question of scientific method (replaced by 'techniques of validation'); or an emphasis on the 'value of science', the 'scientific spirit', its exemplary 'critical virtue', etc.

Having identified what is at stake in the conflict between scientists caught up in a pseudo-crisis of science (and it is manifestly *materialism*), we can reasonably call Element 1 the *materialist* element and Element 2 the *idealist* element (in the generic sense of the three philosophies – religious, spiritualist and critical – that we have rapidly examined).

5. In the spontaneous philosophy of scientists (SPS) the (materialist) Element 1 is, in the vast majority of cases, dominated by Element 2 (and the exceptions are therefore all the more noteworthy). This situation reproduces in the heart of the SPS the philosophical balance of power that exists between materialism and idealism in the world in which scientists known to us live, and the domination of idealism over materialism.[12]

Nothing is less 'obvious' than this last fact. And even if scientists are fairly knowledgeable about the nature of philosophy, about the internal conflicts played out within it, and the way in which they are related to the great political and ideological struggles of this world, were they to recognize that in social, political, ideological, moral, etc. terms, materialism is in fact massively dominated by idealism (which reproduces on the theoretical plane the domination of the exploited classes by the exploiting classes), they would be reluctant to admit that the same balance of power exists *within* their own SPS. And so we must try to demonstrate it to them.

It would take an extended theoretical and historical analysis to do so properly. Here again, however, given the lack of time, we must restrict ourselves to the production of simple *empirical* facts to make this decisive reality 'visible'. But even assuming that we can make it visible, I should not conceal the difficulty of the task: it is difficult because we must 'work' here in the element of 'spontaneity' – that is, in the forms of 'representation' that are given in an immediate obviousness which it will be necessary to break through or get around. And nothing is more difficult to break through or get around than the obvious.

Consider, for example, what happens between you, who are scientists, and me, a philosopher. When a philosopher speaks, as I am doing, of Element 1 of the SPS by calling it 'intra-scientific', he will easily be understood, for the majority of scientists do not *doubt* the existence of their object, the objectivity of their findings (knowledges), or the efficacy of their method. But if he calls Element 1 *materialist*, he will not be understood by *all* scientists. Some will understand: modern specialists in the earth sciences, naturalists, zoologists, biologists, physiologists, etc. For all these scientists, the words 'matter', 'materialism', and the adjective 'materialist' express something essential about their convictions as to their scientific practice: for them these words are 'correct'. But if we turn to other disciplines, things change considerably.

Leaving aside mathematicians (certain of whom even wonder

---

12. On all these questions, see the analysis of Monod in the Appendix.

whether their 'object' 'exists') and, with some exceptions, specialists in the human sciences (the majority of whom would not admit to being materialists), let us consider two sciences that do in fact deal with *matter*: physics and chemistry.

When it comes to talking about themselves, physicists and chemists are very modest and reserved. I will therefore attempt to speak on their behalf: and they will tell me later whether I was correct or not. And if we were now to tell physicists and chemists that they have a spontaneous philosophy of scientists, which is contradictory and contains both an 'intra-scientific' element and an 'extra-scientific' element – the one originating in their practice, the other imported from the outside – they would not deny it. They would not find that improbable. But when they are told that Element 1 (intra-scientific) is of a *materialist* character, and especially when it is explained that this element has as its kernel the unity of three terms – an external object with a material existence/ objective scientific knowledges or theories/scientific method, or, more schematically, object/theory/method – they have the impression of hearing not a scandalous language but a language that sounds foreign to them, that has nothing to do with the content of their own 'experience'. This means that, to them, things are *spontaneously* presented in other terms. And if they were asked to speak for themselves, the odds are that they would replace the little group *object/theory/method* with another, much more 'modern' little group, in which it would be a question of 'experimental data', of 'models', and of 'techniques of validation' – or, more schematically, *experiment/models/techniques.*

This does not seem like much: after all, words are just words. If we wish to change them, we have only to establish the right convention. But unfortunately, we are not free to establish our own conventions in these matters, nor are words substituted for one another without a reason. To take only one little word, perfectly innocent in appearance: *experience* (or '*experiential* data'). It has to be made known that this word has *expelled* another word from the place which it occupies in the second group: *a materially existing external object.* It is for this purpose that Kant put it in power against materialism and that it was returned to power by the empirio-critical philosophy of which we have spoken. When *experience* (which is, note well, something very different from experimentation) is promoted to the highest position, and when one speaks of *models* instead of *theory*, we are not simply changing two words: a slippage of meaning is provoked, or better, one meaning is *obscured* by another, and the first, materialist, meaning disappears under the second, idealist, meaning. It is in this equivocation, impercept- ible to most physicists and chemists, that the domination of Element 2 over Element 1 is achieved in their SPS – which proves that it is not

enough for a science to work with 'matter' for its practitioners to
recognize themselves as materialists. Which also proves, in fact, that a
strange dialectic is in play between the two elements of the SPS: since one
of these elements can obscure the other to the extent of making it
disappear entirely, whilst claiming that it is merely 'giving an account' of
the *same practice*.

However that may be, and to restrict discussion to the domination
provoked by this slippage of meaning: it has not always existed in the
history of physics and chemistry or any of the 'experimental' sciences
that think their practice in terms of 'experiment/model/technique'. A
hundred years ago, physicists and chemists employed a very different
language to speak of their practice, a language close to that used today
by earth scientists and life scientists. If our scientific friends took the
time to study the history of their discipline and of their own predecessors' representation of it, they would find interesting documents proving
how, and under what influences, this slippage in the terminology of their
SPS occurred, resulting in the domination of the extra-scientific Element
2 over the intra-scientific Element 1. It may be concluded from this that
to understand the content of an SPS, it is indispensable to return to the
history of the sciences and to the history of the spontaneous philosophies, which simultaneously depend upon the history of the sciences and
on the history of philosophy.

But let us attempt once again to make 'palpable' the fact of this
domination by means of another, 'inverse' example.

If we recognize the existence of these two contradictory elements in
the SPS and the dominance of Element 2 over Element 1, and if we
know that Element 2 is organically linked to the philosophies which
exploit the sciences to apologetic ends, for the benefit of the 'values' of
practical ideologies that are neither known nor criticized, it is clear that
it is in the interests of scientists to transform their SPS in a critical manner,
to dispel the illusions contained in Element 2, and to change the existing
balance of power so as to place the 'intra-scientific' and materialist
Element 1 in a position of dominance.

But if it is obviously in their interests to do so, it is also obvious from
experience that it is *practically impossible* (except perhaps in borderline
cases, which would have to be studied separately) for the internal play of
the SPS alone to bring about a shift in the balance of power within that
SPS or a critical transformation of that SPS. To put it another way: in
the (most general) situation in which Element 2 dominates Element 1, it
is impossible to reverse the balance of power *without external support*.
The domination of Element 1 by Element 2 cannot be overturned simply
through an internal *critical* confrontation. As a general rule, the SPS is
incapable of criticizing itself through the play of its internal content alone.

What might this external support be? This external force capable of changing the balance of power within the SPS? First, it can only be a force of the same nature as the forces that are in contention: a *philosophical* force. But not just any philosophical force: a force capable of criticizing and dispelling the idealist illusions of Element 2 by basing itself on Element 1; therefore a philosophical force related to the philosophical force of Element 1 – that is, a *materialist* philosophical force which, instead of exploiting, respects and serves scientific practice.

Scientists are perfectly well aware that this is a matter of philosophy, of the philosophical balance of power, and therefore, in the last instance, of philosophical struggle. If they know something of their past, they know perfectly well, for example, that the experimental sciences of the eighteenth century received considerable help from materialist philosophers. And under the umbrella of the Great and Glorious History of the Enlightenment they know the stakes of the struggle *in* the representations which the men of this time (priests and their intellectuals on one side, the materialist Encyclopaedists on the other) formed of the sciences and of scientific practice: it was a matter of freeing 'minds' from a false representation of science and knowledge, and of bringing about the triumph over it of a 'correct' or more 'correct' representation. It was a matter of struggling to transform the existing SPS: and in this struggle to change the balance of power, *the scientists needed philosophers* and relied upon them.

Of course things do not always happen in broad daylight. But just as our 'crisis in science' revealed to us the philosopher dormant in every scientist, so the open alliance of the scientists and *philosophes* of the Enlightenment, under the slogan of 'materialism', shows us *the condition* without which the balance of power between Element 2 and Element 1 within the SPS cannot be shifted. This condition is *the alliance of scientists with materialist philosophy*, which brings to scientists the extra forces needed so to reinforce the materialist element as to dispel the religious–idealist illusions that dominated their SPS. The circumstances were no doubt 'exceptional', but there again they have the advantage of showing us in 'bold print' what, in the 'normal' course of things, is 'writ small' in tiny or illegible letters. And since we are speaking of this Grand Alliance between materialist philosophy and the scientists of the eighteenth century, why not recall that slogan under which this alliance was sealed – *materialism* – was brought to the scientists by philosophers who wanted to serve them and who on the whole, despite the shortcomings of this materialism (mechanism, etc.), served them well?

But at the same time – to dwell on this example for a moment – it is also necessary to take stock of the objective limits of this alliance. For the 'materialism' that thus came to the aid of the sciences and scientists protected them, above all, from *religious* power and imposture. The 'historical line of demarcation' of this time was a line between a 'religious knowledge' that was no more than dogma and 'obscurantism', and sought to govern all the world's knowledge, and a scientific knowledge that was open and 'free' in the face of the infinite which it discovered in the mechanism of things. But this materialism was itself subject to the domination of another idealism because of its own representation of the 'Truth': a juridical, moral and political idealism. It is not by chance that the materialism of the eighteenth century was also the materialism of the 'Century of the *Enlightenment*'. In the great symbol of Enlightenment, which the German language renders more explicitly as *Aufklärung,* enlightenment, *illumination* (very different from the mysticism of 'illuminism'), the scientists and philosophers of this time themselves were also living a Great Illusion: that of the historical omnipotence of knowledge. An old tradition, stretching back centuries and linked no doubt to the power attributed, in the division of labour, to those who possessed 'knowledge' (but there is no 'power of knowledge' that is not bound up with 'power' proper): exalting the omnipotence of Knowledge over Ignorance. Truth has only to appear for all shadows, errors and prejudices to vanish, just as the break of day drives away the shades of night. This 'thought' has never ceased to haunt even modern scientists. In some corner of their mind they are certain that because they possess science and the experience of its practice, they possess exceptional truths: quite apart from the Truth, which they do not doubt will one day be recognized and transform the world, they possess the 'virtues' of its acquisition – honesty, rigour, purity and disinterestedness, which they are quite ready to fashion into an Ethics. And they think that all this derives from their practice itself! And why should they not think so, given that in their practice they are honest and rigorous and pure and disinterested? These 'obviousnesses' are the most difficult to overcome. For, to return to our detour through the eighteenth century, we may see 'as clearly as day', so to speak, that the conviction that scientific truth is omnipotent is closely bound up with something other than the sciences themselves: with the juridical, moral and political 'consciousness' of the *intellectuals* of a rising class which is confident that it can take power thanks to the obviousness of Truth and Reason, and which has already put Truth in power. In their Enlightenment philosophy, the scientists and *philosophes* of the eighteenth century, however materialist they may have been in their struggle against religion, were no less *idealist* in their conception of history. And their idealist conception of the omnipotence of scientific truth derives, in the last instance, from their historical (juridical, moral, political) idealism. Those (such as Monod) who even today take up in other forms the same exemplary themes and are, as their predecessors once were, convinced that they are speaking *solely* of their own experience as scientists, are in fact speaking of something very different: of what is now, for understandable reasons, a bitter and disillusioned philosophy of history. They simply reflect it in connection with their scientific experience, and it is reflected *in* their experience.

Why all these details? To come to the following conclusion: in the contradictory history of the materialism of the Enlightenment, we may see the *conditions* of a shift in the balance of power between Element 1 and Element 2 and the *limits* of that shift. The *conditions*: the materialism of the *philosophes* incontestably served the scientific practice of the times, by reinforcing Element 1 against the religious impostures of Element 2 that then dominated Element 1. The scientists' Alliance with materialism served the sciences. The *limits*: but at the same time, whilst it did modify the prior balance of power, the contradiction of the Enlightenment philosophers' materialism (they were idealists in history) in fact restored the former balance of power: by subordinating Element 1, the materialist element, to *a new Element 2*, to an idealist element. Yes, to a new Element 2 which, thanks to the illusion of the omnipotence of Truth, and therefore of scientific knowledge, could incorporate all the themes of the ruling empiricism of the day.

If this analysis, which is barely an analysis at all, has any indicative value, it is that it verifies, this time in an inverted and (which is even more interesting) a contradictory way, our Thesis on the domination of Element 2 over Element 1 and on the inability of an SPS to modify its internal balance of power, to criticize itself. For it goes without saying that the illusions of the *philosophes* and scientists of the Enlightenment have taken a beating from history. It was not their ideas that changed the world by 'reforming the understanding', by bringing 'Reason' to light, by bringing Truth to power; it was the 'unenlightened' popular peasant and plebeian masses when they rose up in rags during the Revolution. Just as it is not their 'enlightened' representations of scientific practice that has always allowed the sciences to advance, but rather the thankless labour of certain practitioners who do make progress – sometimes because of these ideas, but often in spite of them: because of *other* ideas. The ruse of 'Reason'.

If you are willing to bear with me, we will draw some conclusions from this episode.

I hope, first of all, to have made it clear that the balance of power within an SPS cannot be changed through an immanent critique: there must be a counterforce, and that counterforce can only be philosophical and materialist.

Further, I hope to have made it clear that neither the contradictory relation between the elements of the SPS, nor the materialist philosophy that may intervene in their conflict, is given from all eternity, and that they belong to a definite historical conjuncture. Coming into play are not only the state of the sciences, the scientific division of labour, relations between different sciences, and possibly the domination of one science over the others, imposing its own practice as the norm of scientific practice, etc., but also the state of the dominant SPS and the state of the existing philosophies, practical ideologies and class conflicts. If this *historical* reality, and its necessarily contradictory forms, are neglected, it is impossible to understand anything at all about the SPS and the conditions of its transformation.

Finally, I hope to have shown that the materialist philosophy which can so strengthen the forces of Element 1 as to transform in a critical manner the forces of Element 2 must be *other* than the materialist philosophy that allied itself with the scientists of the eighteenth century against the Church and religious philosophy and ideology. For this latter philosophy, materialist in one sense, was idealist in another, and the services it rendered the sciences on the one hand were paid for on the other by a restoration, *in a new form*, of the prior domination of idealism (Element 1) over materialism (Element 2).

If this is so, we may perhaps be able to define the *conditions* for a new Alliance between scientists and a materialist philosophy that respects and serves scientific practice.

1. They cannot be *general* conditions (edifying statements such as: scientists need philosophy), but must be *specific* conditions which above all take into account the *historical* balance of power.

It is not enough to recognize the existence within the SPS of two elements, and the contradiction between them; nor even to identify one as materialist and the other as idealist; nor, finally, to establish that as a general rule the second dominates the first. In every case we have to know the *actual historical form* of these two elements and their contradiction. For it is an observable fact that the form of the representation of scientific practice, the form of its contradiction, *varies* in history with the history of the sciences and the history of philosophy and, behind these two 'histories', with the history of political and ideological struggles that are ultimately reflected in these two elements. We therefore have to identify the actual historical form of the antagonism in the *dominant* SPS.

I say dominant, for it is also a fact of experience (we encountered it when examining the position of scientists belonging to different branches of scientific knowledge) that there is no such thing as a single, unique form of the SPS in a determinate epoch; there are *several*, one of which is in a dominant position, while the others, which have enjoyed their moment of power, must submit, although continuing to exist in a subordinate position. Thus, the mechanistic rationalism dominant in the seventeenth century, the empiricist rationalism dominant in the eighteenth century, and then the positivism dominant in the nineteenth century (if I may be forgiven these very schematic indications), although dominated today by the logical, neo-positivist SPS, subsist and survive even in our conjuncture – and one 'opportunity' is enough for them to return, in certain disciplines, to centre-stage (thus, Cartesian mechanistic rationalism serves the SPS well in Chomsky's linguistics or in avant-garde biology).

It will be understood that this enumeration does not in the least indicate a linear sequence. On the contrary, it is the trace of a *conflict-ridden* history in which different forms of the SPS clashed in protracted and harsh struggles: let us say, 'ways of thinking' scientific practice, 'manners of posing scientific problems' ('problematics'), and finally 'modes of resolving' the theoretical contradictions of the history of the sciences. It is because this history is *conflict-ridden* that it is necessarily resolved by *putting into power* a new 'form of thought' or a new SPS which, at a certain moment, begins to supplant those that preceded it.

But if we must speak of a conflict-ridden history of the SPS, then *every* conjuncture (including our own) must be considered conflict-ridden. And because in philosophy a conflict is never definitively or absolutely settled, in order to see this conflict clearly it is not only necessary to recognize the forces present: it is also necessary to identify the *tendential* resolution of this conflict, to know where it has come from in order to know where it is going, to which 'taking of power' it will lead. We must therefore take into consideration all the 'stratified' forms of the SPS which subsist and intervene, directly or indirectly, in the conflict and the forms that occupy centre-stage, and we must discern which is really the ascendant force and through what contradictory process it 'clears a path' to achieve domination. We shall see later what today's ascendant SPS is: logical neo-positivism.

2. The conditions of an Alliance between scientists and a new materialist philosophy must be particularly clear. I repeat that we are talking about an Alliance through which materialist philosophy brings its support to Element 1 of the SPS to help it struggle against Element 2 of the SPS: to alter the balance of power, currently dominated by the idealism of Element 2, in favour of Element 1.

Through this Alliance, materialist philosophy is authorized to intervene in the SPS and *only in the SPS*. Which means that philosophy intervenes *only* in philosophy. It refrains from making any intervention in science proper, in its problems, in its practice. This does not imply that there is a radical separation between science, on the one hand, and philosophy, on the other; or that science is a domain reserved for science alone. Rather, it means that the role of philosophical categories and even philosophical conceptions in science, a role of which we have not hitherto spoken,[13] is exercised, among other forms, through the intermediary of the SPS, and that the philosophical intervention of which we speak here is an intervention by philosophy in philosophy. Again, it is a question of shifting the balance of power within the SPS, in such a way that scientific practice is no longer *exploited* by philosophy, but *served* by it.

Now you will understand why we insist on the *novel* character of the materialist philosophy from which scientific practice may expect this service. For if it is to be able to serve scientific practice, this materialist philosophy must be prepared to combat all the forms of the idealist exploitation of the sciences; and if it is to be able to wage this combat *en connaissance de cause*, this philosophy must be capable of *mastering through knowledge and criticism* the organic link that binds it to the practical ideologies on which it, like any other philosophy, depends. We have seen under what conditions this critical control is possible: *only* in the case of a materialist philosophy connected to the discoveries through which Marx opened up the way to knowledge of the mechanisms of 'ideological social relations' (Lenin), and therefore a knowledge of the function of practical ideologies and their class antagonisms.

But if this is the case, it will also be understood *that it is not a question of simply 'applicating' a ready-made philosophy to a determinate SPS.* For even supposing that we are applying a ready-made philosophy, a philosophy that has been perfectly elaborated and has mastered all its categories, we ought not to expect a miracle. A balance of power is not reversed in an instant, and idealist illusions are not simply swept away. If we believed that, we would simply be reproducing, within a formally materialist philosophy, the essentials of the idealist conception of the Enlightenment: the omnipotence of the Truth dissipating the shadows of error. We might well have a materialist philosophy; but this would not be a *materialist practice* of that materialist philosophy. It would mean forgetting that this affair is a matter of *struggle.* The Alliance we propose cannot be reduced to a protocol agreement. Of course we should sign it and proclaim it. But thereafter everything remains to be

---

13. One may legitimately defend the idea that, when they are 'correct', philosophical categories function as *relations of production* and *reproduction* of scientific knowledge.

done: the protracted and arduous labour, amounting to a battle, to win terrain from the enemy, to foil his tricks and foresee his counterattacks, the long and arduous struggle to confront the unforeseeable forms that emerge from the development of scientific practice itself, and of which the enemy will always know how to take advantage. When allies agree to unite their forces, they must realize that they are engaged in a common struggle which is at the same time an interminable struggle. And the struggle is all the more difficult in that we still live in a situation in which idealism is dominant within the consciousness of intellectuals and will be so for a long time to come, even after the Revolution.

Throughout our argument we have assumed that materialist philosophy is complete, and armed with well-prepared arguments. But *this is not the case*. The scientists to whom we have proposed this Alliance must know the nature of the materialist philosophy with which they are allying themselves. If philosophy is a struggle, and if, in this struggle, it is idealist philosophy that is dominant, this inevitably means that *dialectical materialist philosophy must itself be constituted in the struggle*, and that in the course of this struggle it must gradually win its own positions against the enemy simply in order to exist, to acquire the existence of a historical force. Just as materialist philosophy does not possess the 'truth' about the sciences, so it does not claim to present itself as a completed truth. Of course, we are able to state a certain number of basic Theses that begin to constitute a corpus of categories; and these Theses are tested in the struggle against idealist Theses. But they do not constitute a 'system' as in the idealist philosophies: the system of a total and closed Truth. If dialectical materialist philosophy is genuinely a weapon in theory it must, on the basis of a minimum number of firm principles that assure its position, be mobile enough to take itself where battle calls and to be formed – that is, constituted – in the battle itself.

Have scientists ever been offered such an Alliance? It is truly unique: because it respects the sciences in their domain; because it calls on philosophy's help only to intervene in the philosophy that exploits the sciences; because, instead of promising a miracle, it calls for a struggle conducted *en connaissance de cause*, and a struggle without end; because, rather than speaking of the intervention of a completed, finished philosophy, it warns that philosophy is constituted in its intervention. Have you ever heard of a philosophy so modest in the way it offers its services?

And so we call upon you to join this Alliance. We do not expect miracles from it, and we are not promising you the earth, for we know the world we live in, a world where all the important things, even those which concern the spontaneous philosophy of scientists, are not decided in the minds of intellectuals but in the class struggle and its effects.

However, we may expect results from this Alliance: both for the scientists that you are and for the philosophers we are. By inviting you to draw a 'line of demarcation' in your SPS between Element 1 and Element 2, we are not acting as spectators or judges giving advice. By inviting you to form an Alliance with dialectical materialist philosophy, we are not acting like 'elders' who have the strength you need. For *we apply the same rule to ourselves that we recommend to you.* How? By 'drawing' our own 'line of demarcation' *in philosophy*; by occupying, within philosophy, positions that enable us to combat idealism.

If you have followed us this far, it seems likely that you have been convinced that such is indeed our practice. From the very beginning we have been able to speak of philosophy only by occupying a definite position in philosophy. For in philosophy we cannot, like Rousseau's Noble Savage in the *Discours sur l'origine et les fondements de l'inégalité parmi les hommes,* occupy an *empty* corner of the forest. In philosophy every space is always already occupied. Within it, we can only hold a position against the adversary who already holds that position. This is not an easy task. It is a matter of 'words'; we know that. And nothing could be more natural than hearing words. But these words are not arbitrary and, above all, they must 'hold together'; otherwise, they will flee in every direction and have no position or space of their own to hold. And that is what has happened here among us. At times you perhaps had the impression that we were delivering a speech prepared in advance. Pedagogically (didactically), perhaps: but philosophically, no. In truth, what we have succeeded in saying to you was won through a protracted, sustained effort: a work of reflection that was at the same time a struggle. And if we have set you an example, so be it: it is your turn now.

APPENDIX
On Jacques Monod

This Appendix is devoted to an analysis of excerpts from Monod's inaugural lecture at the Collège de France, published by Le Monde *on 30 November 1967.[1]*

This critique was initially the object of the fourth lecture. I reproduce it as delivered, without any alteration.

Monod's text is an exceptional document, of an unparalleled scientific quality and intellectual honesty. I speak of it with the greatest respect, and I hope to give proof of that throughout my analysis. It will be seen that I do not accord myself any right to intervene in its strictly scientific content, which I accept unreservedly as an absolute reference for any philosophical reflection. At the same time, it will be seen that I not only accord myself the right, but also the duty, even *vis-à-vis* Monod, to make a clear distinction between its strictly scientific content and the philosophical use of which it is the object – not on the part of philosophers external to Monod but on the part of Monod himself, in Element 2 of his SPS, in his philosophy and his world-view (WV).

I will discuss Monod's SPS, his philosophy and his WV in the most *objective manner* possible. In speaking of Monod and citing his declarations, I am not attacking Monod himself but the '*realities*' which appear in his own 'consciousness' as so many realities which appear in the 'consciousness' of all scientists, and therefore as so many objective realities independent of the subjective personality of the scientists.

---

1. The themes of Jacques Monod's lecture were subsequently developed in a book of the same title; see *Chance and Necessity – An Essay on the Natural Philosophy of Modern Biology* (1970), London 1972. [Ed.]

Through the analysis of Monod's text, I want to bring out objective *'general realities'*, the form of which varies according to the individuals, their disciplines, and the historical moment of their science, which dominate and govern the 'consciousness' of all scientists, usually without their knowing it. I speak of scientists in the strict sense; however, you will already have realized that what I say about them is infinitely more true of specialists in the human sciences and also, although with specific differences, of mere philosophers.

One last word concerning the particular form which those general elements take in Monod. As we shall see, they culminate in an idealist world-view that I do not share. But Monod's world-view represents an idealistic tendency whose *form* is quite particular: in terms of its *scientific content*, it may be considered *the richest form of idealism* to be found in this idealist tendency. I also see – another very important sign – an indication of this in the fact that the morality which dominates Monod's world-view is what he calls an ethics of knowledge – that is, an ethics closely linked to *scientific practice*.

Because of its scientific richness, its honesty and its nobility, Monod's text is in our opinion an exceptional text, to which I would like to pay public homage. This is only a philosopher's homage. I would be happy if it were taken for what it is – the homage of a philosopher, but a homage nevertheless.

For the clarity of the exposition, I will distinguish four elements in Monod's lecture:

1. modern biological science;

2. the spontaneous philosophy of the scientist (SPS);

3. philosophy;

4. world-view (WV).

1. Modern Biological Science

It is present in the explanation Monod gives of his most recent findings and fundamental principles (beginning of paragraph 2, paragraphs 4, 5, 6).

This exposition may be articulated in three 'moments', as follows:

(a) The statement of the content of the *'discovery'* which has transformed modern biology: deoxyribonucleic acid (DNA), 'the constituent of chromosomes, the guardian of heredity, and the source of evolution, the philosopher's stone of biology'.

(b) The reflection of this revolutionary scientific discovery in *the concepts of biological theory*: the concepts of *emergence* and of *teleonomy*. New key concepts of modern biological theory.

(c) Retrospectively: these new concepts show that the old concepts of classical theory (evolution, finality) have been preserved but transcended in a new form. In a parallel way, the old philosophical theories linked to biological concepts (vitalism, mechanism) and the philosophies exploiting the results or the difficulties of biology (religious philosophy, metaphysics) appear to have been transcended but rejected (paragraphs 2 and 3): transcended but not preserved: rejected without appeal.

2. The Spontaneous Philosophy of the Scientist (Biologist) (SPS)

It is present throughout the exposition of the findings of modern biology, of its reflection in biological theory, and of its retrospective effects. We may distinguish the presence of two elements: *Element 1*, intra-scientific, materialist; *Element 2*, extra-scientific, idealist.

Element 1 (of the SPS)

Basically *materialist,* basically *dialectical.* As a general rule, Element 1 is almost always, if not invariably, 'intricated' in the exposition of scientific findings and therefore mixed in the scientific material itself: it is not isolated, and the scientist does not make it the object of his thought. It is up to us to '*disintricate*' it, thus to make it appear in its distinction by drawing a philosophical line of demarcation. Element 1 appears, then, on the occasion of the exposition, and of the reasons adduced for it, as a *tendency* confronted by, and opposed to, other tendencies.

This fact is very striking in Monod's text, which is exemplary in this respect. Monod does not *declare* himself to be a materialist or a dialectical thinker. These words do not appear in his text. But everything he says about modern biology displays a profound materialist and dialectical tendency, visible in positive assertions coupled with determinate philosophical condemnations.

(a) MATERIALISM

Sensitive points:

— Definition of the *material reality* of the object of biology via a critique of the notion (scientifically outmoded and 'functioning' only in certain philosophies) of 'living matter'. This one-word denunciation is a denunciation of philosophical exploitation, and therefore of an anti-scientific tendency: very precisely, it is the denunciation of the *vitalist philosophy* which is implied in the notion of 'living matter'. The expression 'living matter' is meaningless. '*There are living systems. There is no living matter.*' It is a denunciation of the use of the ambiguous notion of 'living matter' by certain physicists themselves, and of the exploitation of this notion by metaphysics and religious philosophy (an attack on Teilhard).

— The rejection of the notion of 'living matter' does not in any sense take Monod back to spiritualism or idealism: *he remains a materialist.* Living systems have 'emerged' in the material world ('local emergence of complex structures' endowed with specific qualities). This emergence is thought in terms of an openly materialist tendency: this emergence possesses a '*physical* support', DNA.

It will be noted that Monod's materialist theses are presented in a manner which is both positive and polemical: he rejects the philosophical elements (exploitative) to 'clear the way' for the exposition of scientific findings. This operation is, in itself and because of its results, of a *materialist* tendency.

(b) DIALECTICS

Sensitive points:

— The critique of the ideological relation (philosophical exploitation) previously prevailing between emergence and 'teleonomy' (formerly known as teleology, finalism). Monod rejects all theories that subordinate emergence (the sudden appearance of life) to teleonomy. Thus he rejects in the clearest manner the spiritual–religious tendency which takes the view that if life appeared in the material world, it did so '*in order to*' realize a providential or natural end, to produce '*Spirit*'. Here again he is attacking Teilhard and all religious–spiritualist–idealist exploitation of biology.

— As before, this critique 'opens the way' to positive categories: especially to the category of *emergence*. *In fact*, the category of emergence functions in Monod not only as a purely scientific category but also as a category representing a possible theory of a *dialectic* which is at work in nature itself. A very important category: in effect Monod proposes in the concept of emergence a 'rational kernel'[2] of a purely *intra-scientific* origin, which is, because of its theoretical potential and the tendency of this potential, full of dialectical resonance. In practical terms, and provided that we take it seriously, it allows us to think through what a certain philosophical tendency is looking for in connection with what has been called the 'laws of the dialectic', and even the dialectics of nature. Traditionally, one speaks of the 'qualitative leap', of 'the dialectical transition from quantity to quality', etc. In the notion of emergence Monod offers something that allows us, to a partial extent, to restate this question with intra-scientific elements.

I recapitulate: materialism, dialectics. Such are the components of *Element 1* in Monod. In the case of the modern biologist that Monod is, Element 1 is in direct resonance with a definite philosophical tendency: dialectical materialism.

Element 2 (of the SPS)

I said that this element is extra-scientific and idealist. Here again, Monod is exemplary. Because *Element 2* appears in his work, almost in a pure state (this is not always the case with scientists), as a reprise of *Element 1 itself* under a modality and a tendency *completely opposed* to the modality and the tendency wherein we were able to locate *Element 1*. And in *Element 2* we are dealing with practically the same content as in *Element 1*, but there has been an inversion of meaning, an inversion of tendency. Let us take up the two components of *Element 1* – materialism and dialectics – to see what becomes of them in *Element 2*.

(a) MATERIALISM

In *Element 1*, Monod defined the materialist content of his tendency by eliminating mechanism and vitalism, by saying that there is no 'living matter' but only 'living systems', and by designating DNA the 'physical support' of those living systems.

But when Monod leaves the domain of biology – which he calls, using an already suspicious term, the 'biosphere' (a Teilhardian term) – to speak of what – using an even more suspicious term – he calls the 'noosphere' (a Teilhardian term), he no longer respects the rules which govern the materialist content of *Element 1*. At this point, we see that as

---

2. An ironic allusion to Marx's discussion of his relation to the Hegelian dialectic; see *Capital*, vol.I, Harmondsworth 1976, pp. 102–03 and cf. Althusser's critique in 'Contradiction and Overdetermination', *For Marx*, London 1979, especially pp. 89–94. [Ed.]

the concepts of *Element 1* are put to use, the *materialist* tendency that
ruled Element 1 is inverted and becomes an *idealist* and even spiritualist
tendency. The most striking symptom of this inversion is the inversion of
Monod's attitude to Teilhard: in Element 1, Monod is 100 per cent
against Teilhard. In Element 2, Monod resorts to two of Teilhard's
concepts: the '*noosphere*' and the 'biosphere'. As we shall see, the result
is that the dialectic component expressed by the concept of emergence
becomes idealist itself and lapses back into the very thing Monod
avoided in Element 1: namely, the spiritualism–mechanism couple.

To be precise, Monod proposes a theory of the birth of humanity:

> *only the latest of these accidents could lead to the emergence in the heart of*
> *the biosphere of a new realm, the noosphere, the realm of ideas and*
> *knowledge, which was born on the day when the new associations, the creative*
> *combinations in an individual could be transmitted to others, rather than dying*
> *with him.*

This thesis is then further specified: *language created man.* The realm of
man is the noosphere. The noosphere is '*the kingdom of ideas and*
knowledge'.

In making this extrapolation, Monod believes himself a materialist
because for him language is not a spiritual origin, but simply an
accidental emergence which has the informational resources of the
human central nervous system as its biophysiological support.

Yet in his theory of the noosphere Monod is *in fact* (though not
according to his stated convictions) idealist – to be precise, mechanistic-
spiritualistic. Mechanistic because he believes he can give an account of
the existence and content of the 'noosphere' in terms of the effects
triggered by the emergence of the biophysiological support of language
(the human central nervous system). In simple terms: he thinks he can
account for the content of the social existence of men, including the
history of their ideas, as a mere effect of the play of neurobiological
mechanisms. To extend, without any scientific justification, biological
laws to the social existence of mankind is mechanism. Monod insists on
the legitimacy of this arbitrary extension: '*Although it is immaterial, and*
populated only by abstract structures, the noosphere presents close
analogies to the biosphere from which it emerged.' And he does not beat
about the bush: he calls for the coming of the great mind 'who will be
able to write *a sequel to the work of Darwin: a natural history of the*
selection of ideas'. Monod does not even wait for this great mind to be
born; without even charging him for it, he gives him a basis for the work
to come: an astounding biologistic theory of ideas as endowed with the
specific qualities of living species, dedicated to the same function and

exposed to the same laws. There are ideas that possess an invasive power, others that are doomed to die out because they are parasitic species, still others ineluctably condemned to death by their rigidity.

We fall back with this great avant-garde biologist upon banalities which have existed for more than a century and which Malthus and Social Darwinism charged with ideological energy throughout the nineteenth century.

Theoretically speaking, Monod's *mechanism* resides in the following tendency: the mechanical application of the concepts and the laws of what he calls the biosphere to what he calls the 'noosphere', the application of the content of a materialism appropriate to the biological species to another real object: human societies. This is an idealist use of the materialist content of a determinate science (here, modern biology) in its extension to the object of another science. This idealist use of the materialist content of a determinate science consists of arbitrarily *imposing* upon another science – which possesses a real object, different from that of the first – the materialist content of the first science. Monod declares that the physical support of the biosphere is DNA. In the present state of biological science, this materialist thesis is unassailable. But when he believes himself to be materialist, by giving as the biophysiological basis of what he calls the 'noosphere' – that is to say, the social and historical existence of the human species – the emergence of the *neurobiological support of language*, he is not a materialist but, as we have already said, a 'mechanistic materialist' and in terms of a theory of human history, that now means that he is an *idealist*. For the mechanistic materialism that was materialism's historical representative in the eighteenth century is today no more than one of the representatives of the *idealist* tendency in history.

In so far as Monod is a *mechanist*, he is necessarily also a *spiritualist*. His theory that language created mankind might find a sympathetic audience among certain philosophers of anthropology, of literature and, indeed, of psychoanalysis. But we should be suspicious of sympathetic audiences: it is in their interest deliberately to misunderstand what is *said* to them in order to hear what they want to hear. They may be correct in what they want to hear, but they are wrong in hearing it in what is said to them. The theory that language created humanity is, *in Monod's lecture*, a spiritualist theory which ignores the specificity of the materiality of the object in question. To say that language created man is to say that it is not *the materiality of social conditions of existence*, but what Monod himself calls 'the *immateriality*' of the noosphere, 'this realm of ideas and knowledge', which constitutes the real base, and thus the principle, of the scientific intelligibility of human history. No essential difference separates these theses, which Monod believes to be scientific but which are in reality merely ideological, from the most classical theses of conventional spiritualism. Indeed, when one has given as the sole material base of the noosphere the biophysiological support of the central nervous system, one has to fill the void of the 'noosphere' with the help of the Spirit, because there is no other recourse – and certainly no scientific recourse.

It is in this manner that the *materialism* of *Element 1* is inverted into idealism in *Element 2* of Monod's SPS. The inversion of the tendency affects the same content (the same concepts): in Monod the idealistic tendency is constituted as an effect of the mechanism–spiritualism couple. The logical genealogy of this inversion can be retraced: materialism at the start, then mechanism–spiritualism, and finally idealism. In Monod's case, *mechanism* is the precise point of sensibility, the point where the inversion takes place. *A mechanistic use of biological materialism outside biology, in history, has the effect of inverting the materialist tendency into an idealist tendency.*

(b) DIALECTICS

The same inversion.

In *Element 1*, the dialectic is materialist; it is present in the concept of emergence. This concept of *emergence* functions adequately from the scientific point of view in the domain of biological science. It functions in a materialist way.

But when we leave the sphere of biology for the noosphere, the concept of emergence loses its original scientific content and is contaminated by the manner in which Monod thinks the nature of his new object: history. In history, the dialectic functions in an astonishing fashion.

First, emergence proliferates: a true *deus ex machina*. Each time something new happens – a new idea, a new event – Monod utters the magic word 'emergence'. As a general rule, it might be said that when a concept is used to think everything, it is in danger of not thinking anything at all. This is the failing Hegel once denounced in Schelling, who applied his theory of poles everywhere: *formalism*.[3]

Then, emergence functions in history not in the form appropriate to history but in the form proper to biology: witness the theory of the natural selection of ideas – an old imposture which Monod believes to be new.

Finally, whether we like it or not, and despite what Monod has said

---

3. See G.W.F. Hegel, *Phenomenology of Spirit*, Oxford 1977, Preface, pp. 8–9; *Lectures on the History of Philosophy*, vol.III, London 1955, pp. 512–45. [Ed.]

about the primacy of emergence over teleonomy, and despite the excellence of his criticisms of Teilhard and the finalists, *it is the emergence of the noosphere – in other words, the emergence of the Spirit – that forms the basis of history for Monod*; because the noosphere is, scientifically speaking, an empty concept; because emergence and the noosphere are constantly associated, in a repeated manner, there results an objective philosophical effect in the mind – not, presumably, in Monod's mind but in that of his listeners and readers. This empty repetition in fact produces the effect of an inversion of sense and tendency: *whether we like it or not, it is as though the noosphere were the most complex, finest and most extraordinary of the whole sequence of emergences*; thus it is a valorized product, if not *de jure* (Monod does not *say* so), then *de facto*. The sudden and miraculous multiplication of emergences in the noosphere is only a kind of empirical manifestation of this *de facto* privilege, which is a privilege none the less; the noosphere is the privileged sphere of the functioning of emergence. Thus the relationship is upset and it appears as if the sequence of emergences had, as its hidden end and teleonomy, the emergence of the noosphere. Monod might contest this interpretation. However, because he does not control the notions he manipulates in the domain of history, because he believes them to be scientific, whereas they are merely ideological, it is not surprising that he perceives only the *intention* of his discourse and not its *objective* effect. The dialectic, which is materialist in *Element 1*, has become idealist in *Element 2*: an inversion of tendency. I openly acknowledge that what I have just said has not really been proven, since I speak only of an 'effect' of listening or reading, which in itself is imperceptible outside a *convergence* of diverse effects: I will analyse *two more of these effects* to reinforce what has been said.

1. Monod provides a definition of emergence which in fact contains two very different definitions. His lecture opens with this definition. I quote: 'Emergence is the property of reproducing and multiplying highly complex ordered structures and of permitting the evolutionary creation of structures of increasing complexity.'

It would be fascinating to analyse closely this very thoughtful but lame formula because it contains two different definitions, two different characteristics, though in one and the same concept. Emergence is a double property: reproduction *and* creation. Everything is in the 'and'. For the property of reproduction is one thing, the property of creation another. It is clear that the latter has scientific meaning in biology only on the basis of the former: if living forms did not have the property of reproduction and multiplication, nothing new could appear among them, and be both alive and more complex. Thus there is a link between reproduction and creation. But there is also a difference or a break: the unexpected appearance of the new, more complex than what preceded it. The small word 'and' linking reproduction and creation in Monod may lead to two realities being confused; at any rate, it *juxtaposes* them.

Now, a juxtaposition might be insufficient from a scientific point of view. Thus Monod does not adequately think through, beginning with the definition which is manifestly intended to designate one of the essential components of *Element 1* of the SPS, what he has *said*. Monod does not really *distinguish* the two properties in his definition. And yet, in the domain of the biological sciences, his scientific practice makes a perfectly clear distinction between properties which his definition simply juxtaposes: there are reproduction–multiplication phenomena *and* the phenomenon of sudden appearances. When Monod causes the term emergence to intervene in his scientific exposé, it is practically always to designate the sudden appearance of new forms: reproduction always remains in the shadows. Indeed, it does not play any scientific role in thinking the sudden appearance of new forms: it only shows that we are dealing with life, with forms which reproduce and multiply. This question is resolved by DNA. Thus, in his practice Monod very clearly makes a *distinction* which he does not think in his definition, unless one considers that he thinks it under the form of the conjunction '*and*', which is insufficient. Hegel wrote many interesting things on the usage scientists make in their language and practice of that little word '*and*'. Scientists should read these pages, which directly concern them (*The Phenomenology of Mind*). As we proceed with this analysis, I hope that this definition of emergence will produce in its central silence (the word '*and*') an effect similar to that of the 'creation' (an unfortunate word) of new forms of 'increasing' complexity, that it will allow the notion of emergence to cease being something that remains unthought and functions as an unthought finality, and therefore to change tendency: from materialism to idealism.

2. Analogous considerations might be developed in relation to the concept of *chance* in Monod. In fact, the concept of emergence is clearly bound up with the concept of chance. In biology chance is in a sense a precise index of the conditions of possibility of emergence. So be it. Since Epicurus it has played a positive materialist role in combating finalist exploitations of biology. But we then find that Monod retains the concept of *chance* when he moves from biology to history, to the noosphere. Practically, then, the emergence/chance couple permits Monod to think as emergences based on *chance* phenomena that are perfectly explicable on the basis of a science of history, whose existence he neither mentions nor even suspects. In most of Monod's historical

examples (Shakespeare, Communism, Stalin, etc.), *chance* functions in a sense that is the *opposite* of the way it functions in biology: not as an index of the conditions of the existence of emergence, but as *a biologistic theory of history itself.*

A striking symptom of this inversion is provided by Monod's historical Darwinism. While he does not cause the theory of natural selection to intervene in biology, he resorts to it suddenly and on a grand scale in history, speaking of the great mind who will write a history of 'the selection of ideas'. It is unusual to see a notion like natural selection, a notion which biology has strictly delimited or even profoundly transformed, suddenly being put to full use in history. It is clear that for Monod the underdevelopment of history justifies an uncontrolled and excessive use of the concept, in a way which has nothing in common with the use biology itself makes of it. In any event, the result that interests us is this: through its uncontrolled use, chance changes its meaning and tendency. It has passed from a materialist to an idealist functioning. And as chance is bound up with emergence, emergence too is transformed.

I will therefore summarize in a word – or in little more than a word – what we have said in the course of analysing the content of *Elements 1* and *2* of Monod's SPS.

Monod's SPS is *a borderline SPS,* and it is exemplary in its simplicity and clarity. It is remarkable in that it reveals that the distinction introduced in our previous lectures between Element 1 and Element 2 affects not only the *conceptual content* of the two elements, but also *the different tendencies with which a single content may be invested.* The content of the two elements of Monod's SPS is essentially the same. It is constituted by a certain number of key concepts: in Monod's case, the concepts of matter, physical support, living system, chance, and emergence. These are the concepts common to the two elements. The concept of the *noosphere* is then added to *Element 2,* but because the concept of *biosphere* figures in *Element 1,* it might be thought that we are dealing with the complement that the concept of biosphere carries within it. The content of Elements 1 and 2 is therefore essentially the *same content.*

However, there is, as we have said, a *contradiction* between the two elements: *Element 1* is materialist and *Element 2* is idealist. This contradiction cannot affect the content of the two elements because the content is common to them: it therefore affects their *meaning,* the significance of the use made of them – that is, the *tendency* with which explicit or implicit use invests them.

From this we may conclude that the contradiction between Element 1 and Element 2 of Monod's SPS is *a contradiction between the materialist and idealist tendencies* in relation to his representation of the content of his scientific knowledges (the current state of biology), of the validity of the use and extension of his key concepts, and of the nature of scientific knowledge in general.

We may also note that the materialist tendency (*Element 1*) can be positively asserted *only* in the struggle against idealist, spiritualist and religious philosophical exploitations of the problems of biology (the struggle against Teilhard), and therefore that *Element 1* is not a pure statement of the reality of scientific practice, but a result that must be won in a polemical struggle. But we may note at the same time that the idealist tendency which, in the form of its representatives (Teilhard), was expelled from *Element 1*, in fact reappears in the idealist *Element 2*. The proof: we find that in *Element 2* one of Teilhard's key concepts has re-entered through the window: the concept of the *noosphere*. The idealist tendency against which Monod struggles, with all his strength, in order to make the materialist tendency in *Element 1* triumph, secretly re-enters through the window to triumph in *Element 2*. What is tragic is that it is Monod himself who opens the window. And because we cannot theoretically compare a scientist to a man who willingly opens a window to let the wind of idealism rush in, we say that it is the wind of idealism itself that opens the window. It has all the power necessary. All that may be said of Monod is that he does not *prevent the window from being opened.* He does not resist the idealist tendency; indeed, he gives in to it, thinking that he resists it. Which proves that *Element 2* is always stronger than *Element 1*. Which proves that the SPS cannot with its forces alone prevent the window from being opened. And which proves that the SPS needs the support of an external force, allied with *Element 1*, if it is to triumph over *Element 2*, the support of an external tendency that reinforces the materialist tendency of *Element 1* to reverse the meaning of the idealist tendency of *Element 2*.

We may finally take note of something important that recapitulates what I have said concerning the differential receptivity of scientists to certain terms, such as materialism, according to their discipline. In Monod's case – modern biology – the notions of *materialism* and of the *dialectic* not only pose no problems (at least in the branch in which Monod works) but they 'work' quite well with the content of Element 1. In the case of modern biology, or at least the branch to which Monod has devoted his work, the expression *dialectical materialism* may be admissible, at least provisionally and 'pending further information'.

But as I am speaking not only to an audience of biologists, but also to many other scientists and literary specialists, I can imagine what they are thinking. To address only those who are really and truly in a different world from Monod, I can guess what the mathematicians are thinking. What I have just said of a biologist may perhaps apply to biology. But mathematics? You know the famous passage from Sartre's *Words*, in which he explains that he has no 'superego'.[4] The superego, when it exists, is that of others. The SPS, when it exists, is that of others. I would simply point out to the mathematicians present that, should they ever think *in petto* that they are saved by the grace of mathematics (its grace – that is, not only its beauty but also its purity and its rigour) from any SPS, there are a considerable number of texts by great mathematicians which might be analysed as I have just analysed Monod's text, and it is highly probable that such an analysis would produce similar results. And to give a precise example, I call their attention to the existence of a short text by Lichnerowitz, delivered to the Société française de Philosophie on 27 February 1965. This text bears a title that I would never have dared to invent: *Mathematical Activity and its Role in our Conception of the World.* I want to point out that in the subsequent debate Cartan made some very interesting comments. In this discussion, the roles were clearly demarcated. Lichnerowitz's arguments were openly *idealist,* those of Cartan were rather *materialist.* They may rest assured: mathematicians too have an SPS. They too, in their SPS, are contradictory representatives of tendencies that transcend them and confront each other: the materialist (Element 1) and the idealist (Element 2). And to ensure that no one feels left out, I will say: philosophers too, but in the case of philosophers, their SPP is not a philosophy but their world-view.

3. Philosophy

After all I have just said, I will speak only briefly of the two last characters in our little theatre: philosophy and world-view.

Philosophy is present in Monod's lecture in two forms: first in the form of *philosophical terms borrowed from existing philosophies,* which function in the interior of his spontaneous philosophy. In so far as these terms are borrowed from existing philosophies, they refer back to those philosophies.

Philosophy is also present in the form of *explicit philosophical arguments.* Monod knows what philosophies are, or at least knows that they exist and are particularly concerned with what happens in the sciences. In this connection he cites Aristotle, the philosophies of Kant and Hegel, dialectical materialism, Engels (whom he attacks with particular violence), Nietzsche and Teilhard de Chardin. Monod is particularly perspicacious in his materialist moment – that is, in his attack on Teilhard. He says that this philosophy is not new – an insight

---

4. Jean-Paul Sartre, *Words,* Harmondsworth 1964.

which pleases us but will by no means please everyone. Monod is not content simply to cite philosophers; he does philosophy. He even proposes a definition of philosophy, by saying that its function is 'above all to establish a system of values' and contrasting it with the sciences, which have nothing to do with values. On this theme, he develops a whole philosophical argument.

The most remarkable philosophical terms present in Monod's course are the following: noosphere/biosphere (Teilhard, condemned as a philosophical exploiter of biology, resurfaces as the positive philosopher of the noosphere – that is, of human history); alienation, praxis, nothingness (in Nietzsche's sense), etc. Further, an entire series of apparently innocent notions are employed and function philosophically in Monod: for example, the notion of *man*, in the phrase: '*it is language that seems to have created man rather than man language*'. There is no need to go further. We are in a philosophical atmosphere with an idealist allure (certain words are never pronounced: materialism, dialectical, etc.) or, more precisely, with an existentialist–spiritualist–Nietzschean–*atheist* allure. A self-declared *atheism* emerges in the final words, in which Sartre, like Nietzsche, would find it as difficult to disown their child as to recognize him: '*What ideal may we propose to men today, an ideal which is both above them and beyond them, if not the conquest through knowledge of the nothingness they themselves have discovered?*'

More interesting is the fact that Monod has given us a genuine chapter of philosophy in the strong sense: that is, a chapter of philosophy that bears directly on the relation between philosophy and the sciences. A distinction between philosophy and the sciences. Knowledge, not values, belongs to the sciences. Values belong to philosophy. A distinction between scientific method and scientific ethics: '*Even today, the ethics of knowledge is often confused with scientific method itself. But method is a normative epistemology, not an ethics. Method tells us to seek. But what commands us to seek and to adopt a method, and the asceticism it implies, in order to seek?*' Sciences, scientific method, normative epistemology, ethics of knowledge, values, philosophy. Monod has done his philosophical work very well: he draws lines of demarcation and proposes a line that is for him, and for any philosopher, a 'correct line'.

There is no point in quibbling over certain of Monod's philosophical expressions, for he is not a professional philosopher and that would be unfair. On the contrary, we should be very grateful to him for having expounded his philosophy and, through it, his relation to the existing philosophical tendencies.

Monod's philosophical tendency (resulting from the comparison between the kind of terms he borrows and the philosophical argument he puts forward): an idealist–spiritualist tendency accompanied by a categorical declaration of *atheism*. The result: the primacy of an atheist *ethics*. Spiritualism is severed from its religious moorings by the declaration of atheism, leaving, in the final analysis, an atheist *ethics*: a morality of science or, more precisely, an ethics of scientific practice. An ascetic morality, austere, aristocratic in its austerity, without any other object of reference than the practice of knowledge (a refusal to give this morality the foundation of human happiness, its material power, or a 'know thyself ').

What interests us in a very precise sense *is the organic relation that exists between Monod's philosophy and his SPS.*

The same atheist idealist tendency. The same accent on scientific practice. In philosophy as in the SPS, the presence of an objectivist *materialist* reference, the ultimate core of which is *scientific knowledge and its practice*; while at the same time, in philosophy as in the SPS, the materialist tendency is surrounded by the idealist tendency that dominates it. We have seen how this investment is carried out in Monod's SPS. We have established the existence of the same idealist investment in Monod's *philosophy*; but what is extremely remarkable – and I ask you to note this point because it is of the greatest importance – this siege does not take the form of an *inversion of meaning* whose moments and terms we might observe and describe in detail, empirically. There is a certain tension, and therefore a certain presence of the tendential struggle between idealism and materialism, in Monod's philosophy (the fact that he speaks of science might be considered an echo of the *materialist tendency*, especially in that he rejects religion; his morality might be considered an overt and dominant representation of the *idealist tendency*). But it is clear that this tension, and the outcome of this conflict, have been *decided in advance* in favour of the *idealist tendency*, which triumphs without a struggle in the exaltation of the ethics of knowledge. What is the underlying element in these links, which are merely statements of objective relations, that *binds* Monod's philosophy to his SPS? Essentially, what they have *in common* or, to be more specific, what his philosophy has in common with Element 2 of the SPS: an idealist philosophy of *science* that allows the extension of biological categories to the 'noosphere', authorizing a conception of the 'noosphere' based on an idealist theory of history, which permits the exaltation of the ethics of knowledge to a place in the philosophy of science. Their common content can be written in the form of a sequence of transformed identities:

(emergence of the noosphere) History = noosphere = realm of
(scientific) knowledge = scientific activity = ethics of scientific
knowledge.

This sequence, which we could examine in detail, rests in the last resort
on the two following identities: *history* = *noosphere* = (the) *science*(s).

What therefore permits Monod's philosophy in the last resort to
communicate with his SPS is the philosophical *operator* '*noosphere*',
whose meaning (the effect of its intervention) may be simply understood
by saying that it represents a conception of history classic since the
eighteenth century, since the *Aufklärung*, wherein it is the sciences that
are the motor of history, and history is ultimately reducible to the history
of knowledges, of the sciences and scientific ideas.

But Monod's philosophy of science is not merely a *philosophy of
science*: like every philosophy of science, it is *a more or less openly
avowed philosophy of history*. If Monod is exemplary here, it is because
he openly avows his *philosophy of history*. It is through it that we shall
enter into the last object of our analysis: his *world-view*.

4. Monod's World-View (WV)

Remember what we have said about the difference that distinguishes a
philosophy from a world-view. A world-view may well deal with
science, but a world-view is never centred on science as philosophy is. It
does not maintain the same relations with the sciences as philosophy
does. A world-view is centred on something other than the sciences: on
what we have called the values of *practical ideologies*. A world-view
expresses tendencies that traverse practical ideologies (religious, juridical, political, etc.). A WV is always directly or indirectly concerned
with the questions that pertain to these domains: problems of religion,
morality, politics, and ultimately with the problem of the meaning of
history, of the salvation of human history. Every WV finally expresses a
certain tendency of a *political character* or appearance.

What is remarkable about Monod is that this is all in the open.

At the centre of his WV, the problem of the *alienation* of the modern
world, and of the salvation of the modern world.

The alienation of the modern world: created, woven by science, it is a
stranger in its own land. Why?

*The alienation of modern man from the scientific culture that has none the less
woven his universe is revealed in forms other than that of the naive horror
expressed by Verlaine. I see in this dualism one of the most profound evils*

afflicting modern societies, an evil that is bringing about a disequilibrium so serious that it threatens the future realization of the great dream of the nineteenth century: the future emergence of a society no longer constructed against man but for him.

The alienation of the modern world therefore threatens the great socialist dream itself. Monod is for socialism, but concerned for its future.

Alienation: dualism. Between the science and scientific culture that have woven the modern world, on the one hand, and traditional values ('ideas rich in ethical content'), on the other.

We are therefore faced with the following contradiction: modern societies still live, assert and teach – without believing in them – value-systems whose base has been destroyed, but, having been woven by science, those same societies owe their emergence to the adoption, usually implicitly and by a very small number of men, of an ethics of knowledge of which they know nothing. That is the very root of modern alienation.

Double contradiction:

— modern science and outdated religious moral values whose base has been destroyed;
— modern science and the failure of men, and even scientists themselves, to recognize that these sciences and their practice imply a moral discipline, a veritable ethics of knowledge.

Now, in the contradiction of the modern world between contemporary science and earlier anachronistic values, there is both *extreme alienation* and the *means of salvation*, which are contained in an ethics of scientific knowledge.

What is this theory of the *alienation* of the modern world? Apparently a description of a certain number of empirical facts. In reality, two things:

1. *a theory of history*;
2. *a politics.*

The theory of history may be summarized thus. Monod knows that human history is not exclusively constituted by what happens in the order of scientific knowledge. There also exists an order of 'praxis', of material power, of religious, moral and political passions. But Monod thinks that what is specific to man, what makes him a social and historical being, what constitutes the 'noosphere', is language and the scientific knowledge which emerges from it at a certain moment. In any event, it is clear to Monod that in the *modern* world science is the basis of history, that the activity of the scientist weaves the modern world, and that its salvation lies in a scientific ethics.

This theory of history opens on to a politics: a politics of the elaboration and diffusion of the ethics of knowledge.

The basis of the *modern* world is scientific knowledge. The motor of the salvation of *modern* history may be the ethics of knowledge. Monod therefore advances a WV that proposes *a* politics of education, communication and moral propaganda. A specific moral doctrine, but a moral doctrine just the same, from which he expects political effects – including, if I understand him correctly, the hope of the advent of socialism.

There are two points to be noted:

1. In Monod's WV there exists an internally consistent unity between a philosophy of history (an idealist philosophy which makes knowledge the essence and lever of history) and a politics (an ethical politics). Every WV is directly or indirectly related to *a certain politics*. Every WV advances, directly or indirectly, explicitly or implicitly, *a certain politics*. This is true of all world-views. A religious WV emphasizes religion, religious values: it proposes a choice between different values, it proposes a politics that can be translated into deeds. *Idem* a moral WV. The same is true of a juridical WV (to emphasize law, seen as the essential factor in the dialectic of history, is to seek to produce certain historical effects: this kind of WV is common amongst jurists, but it is not unique to them). A political WV emphasizes political values: it assumes that politics constitutes the essential factor in history, that politics is the motor of history, etc., and from this it expects certain effects.

2. A WV does not exist in isolation: it exists only in a defined field in which it seeks to *situate itself vis-à-vis* existing world-views, and therefore to distinguish itself from existing WVs, to define itself as different in relation to them, including *by opposition* to certain of them. A WV is posited only by opposing and, ultimately, by struggling against the WVs different from it. In his WV, Monod manifestly attempts to distinguish himself from two world-views: from the *religious* WV (of the Teilhard variety) and the *Marxist* WV.

Against the *religious* WV he asserts that neither religious values, nor traditional moral values based on religion, can save the modern world (hence a struggle against religious WVs), but only a new morality, a non-religious, atheistic, ascetic morality based on scientific practice, the morality of scientists.

Against the *Marxist* WV he asserts that it is the development of knowledge and the values proper to it which are the motor of modern history, and therefore that what will put an end to the alienation of the modern world is a certain subjective aristocratic–intellectual morality, and not the 'Marxist morality' based on the proletarian class struggle. Note this very important point: Monod does not *differentiate* himself in the same way from the two world-views. He differentiates himself from the religious WV by *struggling* against it overtly, to suppress it, for he sees it as harmful and outdated. He also differentiates himself from the Marxist WV, but *without seeking to suppress it.* He declares war on the first but not on the second. He has not renounced the dream it still embodies for him, the dream of 'socialism'.

Monod's world-view is thus very specific. It is a WV which proposes a theory or a philosophy of history capable of furnishing an interpretation of the present historical conjuncture and the means of exiting from it; this naturally results in a politics. As a WV this conception takes sides, and is necessarily situated *among the existing WVs.* It takes a position between a traditionalist WV, dominated by a religious moral politics, and a Marxist WV, dominated by what we might call a *political* 'morality'.

But here we find that everything changes, not from the point of view of Monod's *declarations* but from the point of view of the real content of his theoretical theses. For this intermediate position is not equal. Monod's position is not equidistant from the two WVs. What separates Monod from the religious WV, which he combats so resolutely, does not call into question the validity of *morality* as the motor of history; it is simply that the morality he proposes is not a religious morality but an atheist morality centred on the spontaneous ethics of scientific knowledge; this morality, however, remains a morality. What separates Monod from the Marxist WV, on the other hand, is much more important. It is a serious difference over the question of the *role of morality in history.* For Monod, morality is considered to be, and is then proposed as, the means of salvation for modern history and therefore as the motor, if not of history, at least of modern history. For Marxism, morality, even a political morality, *is not the motor of history,* past or modern. In the expression I have just used, 'political morality', it is the word *political* that counts for Marxists; and politics means 'class struggle of the masses', as defined by the two great principles of Marxism: (1) it is the masses that make history (not individuals, intellectuals or even scientists); (2) it is the class struggle that is the motor of history, not morality – not even an atheist, ascetic morality, a pure and disinterested morality of the most disinterested of intellectuals, scientists.

What divides the WVs is definitely something that goes beyond their ideological content and touches upon their political tendency. Idealism = the belief that *ideas rule the world*/Materialism = the belief *that the class struggle of the masses is the motor of history*. On this fundamental point Monod's theoretical theses enter into contradiction with the way he has *situated* his WV *vis-à-vis* the religious and Marxist WVs. The contradiction, the essential opposition, concerns not the religious WV but the Marxist WV; not idealism but materialism.

One last word: how is the relationship between Monod's WV and his philosophy established? Through the intermediary of the ethics of scientific knowledge. Monod's philosophy is a philosophy of science; his WV is a WV of scientific ethics. Monod's philosophy and his WV have *science* in common. *Science* lies at the heart of Monod's SPS. And finally, *science* is Monod's activity.

And one last conclusion: if these four characters or elements that we have identified in Monod's text (science, SPS, philosophy, WV) are plotted on a graph, a very particular overlapping may be seen to occur.

1. NUCLEUS 1. = *the reality of science* that exists in the reality of the scientific findings Monod describes, which allude to the reality of scientific practice, and to the reality of the history of the production of biological knowledges. The *materialist* tendency.

This nucleus 1 irradiates the set with its materialist–dialectical tendency. It is present in the tendency of *Element 1* of Monod's SPS. It is present, in a very modified and extremely attenuated fashion, in Monod's philosophy. There are some negative traces (atheistic morality) in Monod's WV.

2. NUCLEUS 2. = *reality*, what is at the heart of Monod's WV: a *political prise de position* against other political positions. An idealist

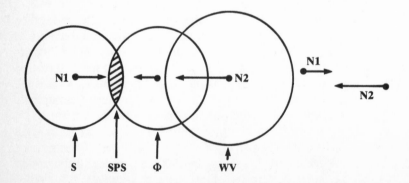

Representing the existence of *two irradiating nuclei*.

tendency that asserts itself in a subordinate fashion against the religious–spiritualist tendency, but asserts itself in a dominant fashion against the materialist tendency of the class struggle.

This nucleus 2 irradiates the entire set of elements present in Monod's text: its irradiating tendency is idealist. It is idealist in an inverse way, in an increasingly attenuated fashion, but the filiation and the dependence are clearly recognizable: it is dependent on *philosophy* (the idealist philosophy of science); on *Element 2* of the SPS: an idealist interpretation of the materialist content of Element 1.

This result is simple but very important: two irradiating nuclei, centres of opposed tendencies – a *materialist tendency* radiating from the material–objective nucleus of scientific practice and science itself (*nucleus 1*); and an *idealist tendency* radiating from Monod's ideological position in the face of 'values' implied by the social–political–ideological problems that divide the modern world (*nucleus 2*).

Monod's SPS, philosophy and WV are, in their various ways and depending upon their proximity to these two nuclei, *compromises* between these two tendencies.

The point at which the two tendencies clash most openly *is the SPS*; in the contradiction between Element 1 and Element 2. In this contradiction, the dominant element is Element 2. Here too, when we closely examine the confrontation of the two tendencies and the realist–materialist nucleus – that is, scientific practice – we find the law which I stated earlier: the domination of Element 1 by Element 2; the exploitation of Element 1 by Element 2.

4

Lenin and Philosophy*

Lénine et la philosophie, François Maspero, Paris 1969. Translated by Ben Brewster.

May I thank your Society for the honour it has done me in inviting me to present to it what it has called since it came into existence, and will doubtless long continue to call, by a disarmingly nostalgic name: a communication.[1]

I

A scientist is justified in presenting a communication before a scientific society. A communication and a discussion are possible only if they are *scientific*. But a philosophical communication and a philosophical discussion?

Philosophical communication. This term would certainly have made Lenin laugh, with that wholehearted, open laugh by which the fishermen of Capri recognized him as one of their kind and on their side. This was exactly sixty years ago, in 1908. Lenin was then at Capri, as a guest of Gorky, whose generosity he liked and whose talent he admired, but whom he treated nevertheless as a petty-bourgeois revolutionary. Gorky had invited him to Capri to take part in philosophical discussions with a small group of Bolshevik intellectuals whose positions Gorky shared, the *Otzovists*. 1908: the aftermath of the first October Revolution, that of 1905, the ebb-tide and repression of the workers' movement. And also disarray among the 'intellectuals', including the Bolshevik intellectuals. Several of them had formed a group known to history by the name '*Otzovists*'.

Politically, the Otzovists were leftists, in favour of radical measures: recall (*otzovat'*) of the Party's Duma Representatives, rejection of every form of legal action and immediate recourse to violent action. But these leftist proclamations concealed rightist *theoretical* positions. The Otzovists were infatuated with a fashionable philosophy or philosophical fashion, 'empirio-criticism', which had been updated in form by the famous Austrian physicist Ernst Mach. This physicists' and physiologists' philosophy (Mach was not just anybody: he has left his name in the

---

1. A communication presented to the Société française de Philosophie on 24 February 1968 and reproduced with the permission of its president, M. Jean Wahl.

history of the sciences) was not without affinity with other philosophies manufactured by scientists like Henri Poincaré, and by historians of science like Pierre Duhem and Abel Rey.

These are phenomena which we are beginning to understand. When certain sciences undergo important revolutions (at that time Mathematics and Physics) there will always be professional *philosophers* to proclaim that the 'crisis in science', or mathematics, or physics, has begun. These philosophers' proclamations are, if I may say so, normal: for a whole category of philosophers spend their time predicting (i.e. awaiting) the last gasp of the sciences, in order to administer them the last rites of philosophy, *ad majorem Dei gloriam.*

But what is more curious is the fact that, at the same time, there will be *scientists* who talk of a crisis in the sciences, and suddenly discover a surprising philosophical vocation – in which they see themselves as suddenly converted into philosophers, although in fact they were always 'practising' philosophy – in which they believe they are uttering revelations, although in fact they are merely repeating platitudes and anachronisms which come from what philosophy is obliged to regard as its history.

We are philosophers by trade, so we are inclined to think that if there is a 'crisis' it is a visible and spectacular philosophical crisis into which these scientists have worked themselves up when faced with the growth of a science which they have taken for its conversion, just as a child can be said to have worked itself up into a feverish crisis. Their spontaneous, everyday philosophy has simply become *visible to them.*

Mach's empirio-criticism, and all its by-products – the philosophies of Bogdanov, Lunacharsky, Bazarov, etc. – represented a philosophical crisis of this kind. Such crises are chronic occurrences. To give some contemporary idea of this, other things being equal, we can say that the philosophy which certain biologists, geneticists and linguists today are busy manufacturing around 'information theory' is a little philosophical 'crisis' of the same kind, in this case a euphoric one.

Now what is remarkable about these scientists' philosophical crises is the fact that they are always orientated philosophically in one and the same direction: they revive and update old *empiricist* or *formalist* (i.e. *idealist*) themes; they are therefore *always* directed against *materialism.*

So the Otzovists were empirio-criticists, but since (as Bolsheviks) they were Marxists, they said that Marxism had to rid itself of that pre-critical metaphysics, 'dialectical materialism', and that in order to become the Marxism of the twentieth century it had at last to furnish itself with the philosophy it had always lacked, precisely this vaguely neo-Kantian idealist philosophy, remodelled and authenticated by scientists: *empirio-criticism.* Some Bolsheviks of this group even wanted to integrate into

Marxism the 'authentic' humane values of religion, and to this end called themselves 'God-builders'. But we can ignore this.

So Gorky's aim was to invite Lenin to discuss philosophy with the group of Otzovist philosophers. Lenin laid down his conditions: Dear Alexei Maximovich, I should very much like to see you, but I refuse to engage in *any philosophical discussion.*[2]

To be sure, this was a tactical attitude: since political unity among the Bolshevik *émigrés* was essential, they should not be divided by a philosophical dispute. But we can discern in this tactic much more than a tactic, something I should like to call a '*practice*' of philosophy, and the consciousness of what practising philosophy means; in short, the consciousness of the ruthless, primary fact that philosophy *divides*. If science unites, and if it unites without dividing, philosophy divides, and it can unite only by dividing. We can thus understand Lenin's laughter: there is no such thing as philosophical communication, no such thing as philosophical discussion.

All I want to do today is to comment on that laughter, which is a thesis in itself.

I venture to hope that this thesis will lead us somewhere.

And it leads me straight away to ask myself the question which others cannot fail to ask: if no philosophical communication is possible, then what kind of talk can I give here? It is obviously a talk to philosophers. But as clothes do not make the man, the audience does not make a talk. My talk will therefore not be philosophical.

Nevertheless, for necessary reasons linked to the point we have reached in theoretical history, it will be a talk *in* philosophy. But this talk in philosophy will not quite be a talk *of* philosophy. It will be, or rather will try to be, a talk *on* philosophy. Which means that by inviting me to present a *communication*, your Society has anticipated my wishes.

What I should like to say will indeed deserve that title if, as I hope, I can communicate to you something *on* philosophy – in short, some rudimentary elements towards the idea of a *theory* of philosophy. Theory: something which in a certain way anticipates a science.

That is how I ask you to understand my title: Lenin *and* Philosophy. Not Lenin's philosophy, but Lenin *on* philosophy. In fact, I believe that what we owe to Lenin – something which is perhaps not completely unprecedented, but certainly invaluable – is the beginnings of the ability to talk a kind of discourse which anticipates what will one day perhaps be a non-philosophical theory of philosophy.

---

2. See Lenin's letters to Gorky of January, February, March and April 1908, in *Collected Works*, vol.34, Moscow 1966, pp. 372–4, 377–82, 385–91, 393–4. [Ed.]

II

If such is really Lenin's greatest merit with respect to our present concern, we can perhaps begin by quickly settling an old, open dispute between academic philosophy – including French academic philosophy – and Lenin. As I too am an academic and teach philosophy, I am among those who should wear Lenin's 'cap', if it fits.

To my knowledge, with the exception of Henri Lefebvre, who has devoted an excellent little book to him,[3] French academic philosophy has not deigned to concern itself with the man who led the greatest political revolution in modern history and who, in addition, made a lengthy and conscientious analysis in *Materialism and Empirio-criticism* of the works of our compatriots Henri Poincaré, Pierre Duhem and Abel Rey, not to speak of others.

I hope that any of our luminaries whom I have forgotten will forgive me, but it seems to me that if we except articles by Communist philosophers and scientists, I can hardly find more than a few pages devoted to Lenin in the last half-century: by Sartre in *Les Temps modernes* in 1946 ('Matérialisme et Révolution'), by Merleau-Ponty (in *Les Aventures de la dialectique*) and by Ricoeur (in an article in *Esprit*).[4]

In the last-named, Ricoeur speaks of *State and Revolution* with respect, but he does not seem to deal with Lenin's 'philosophy'. Sartre says that the materialist philosophy of Engels and Lenin is 'unthinkable' in the sense of an *Unding*, a thought which cannot stand the test of mere thought, since it is a naturalistic, pre-critical, pre-Kantian and pre-Hegelian metaphysic; but he generously concedes that it may have the function of a Platonic 'myth' which helps proletarians to be revolutionaries. Merleau-Ponty dismisses it with a single word: Lenin's philosophy is an 'expedient'.

It would surely be unbecoming on my part, even given all the requisite tact, to open a case against the French philosophical tradition of the last one hundred and fifty years, since the silence in which French philosophy has *buried* this past is worth more than any *open* indictment. It must really be a tradition which hardly bears looking at, for to this day no prominent French philosopher has dared publicly to write its history.

Indeed it takes some courage to admit that French philosophy, from Maine de Biran and Cousin to Bergson and Brunschvicg, by way of Ravaisson, Hamelin, Lachelier and Boutroux, can be *salvaged* from its

---

3. *La Pensée de Lénine*, Paris 1957. [Ed.]
4. See Jean-Paul Sartre, 'Materialism and Revolution', *Literary and Philosophical Essays*, London 1968, pp. 185–239, and Maurice Merleau-Ponty, *Adventures of the Dialectic* (1955), Evanston 1973, pp. 59–65. [Ed.]

own history only by the few great minds against whom it set its face, like
Comte and Durkheim, or buried in oblivion, like Cournot and Couturat;
by a few conscientious historians of philosophy, historians of science and
epistemologists who worked patiently and silently to educate those to
whom in part French philosophy owes its renaissance in the last thirty
years. We all know these names; forgive me if I cite only those who are
no longer with us: Cavaillès and Bachelard.[5]

After all, this French academic philosophy, profoundly religious,
spiritualist and reactionary one hundred and fifty years ago, then in the
best of cases conservative, finally belatedly liberal and 'personalist', this
philosophy which magnificently ignored Hegel, Marx and Freud, this
academic philosophy which seriously began to read Kant, then Hegel
and Husserl, and even to discover the existence of Frege and Russell
only a few decades ago, and sometimes less, why should it have
concerned itself with this Bolshevik, revolutionary, and politician,
Lenin?

Besides the overwhelming class pressures on its strictly philosophical
traditions, besides the condemnation by its most 'liberal' spirits of
'Lenin's unthinkable pre-critical philosophical thought', the French
philosophy which we have inherited has lived in the conviction that it
can have nothing philosophical to learn either from a politician or from
politics. To give just one example, it was only a little while ago that a few
French academic philosophers first turned to the study of the great
theoreticians of political philosophy: Machiavelli, Spinoza, Hobbes,
Grotius, Locke and even Rousseau, 'our' Rousseau. Only thirty years
earlier, these authors were abandoned to literary critics and jurists as
leftovers.

But French academic philosophy was not mistaken in its radical
refusal to learn anything from politicians and politics, and therefore
from Lenin. Everything which touches on politics may be fatal to
philosophy, for philosophy lives on politics.

Of course, it cannot be said that, if academic philosophy has ever
read him, Lenin did not more than repay it in kind, 'leaving it the
change'! Listen to him in *Materialism and Empirio-criticism*, invoking
Dietzgen, the German proletarian who Marx and Engels said had
discovered '*dialectical materialism*' 'all by himself', as an autodidact,
because he was a proletarian militant:

'*Graduated flunkeys*', who with their talk of '*ideal blessings*' stultify the
people by their tortuous '*idealism*' – that is J. Dietzgen's opinion of the

5. Now, alas, we have to add the name of Jean Hyppolite to this list.

professors of philosophy. '*Just as the antipodes of the good God is the devil,
so the professorial priest had his opposite pole in the materialist.*' The
materialist theory of knowledge is '*a universal weapon against religious
belief*', and not only against the '*notorious, formal and common religion of
the priests, but also against the most refined, elevated professorial religion of
muddled idealists*'. Dietzgen was ready to prefer '*religious honesty*' to the
'*half-heartedness*' of free-thinking professors, for '*there a system prevails*',
there we find integral people, people who do not separate theory from
practice. For the Herr Professors '*philosophy is not a science, but a means of
defence against Social-Democracy*'.

'*Those who call themselves philosophers – professors and university
lecturers – are, despite their apparent freethinking, more or less immersed in
superstition and mysticism ... and in relation to Social-Democracy constitute
a single ... reactionary mass.*' '*Now, in order to follow the true path, without
being led astray by all the religious and philosophical gibberish, it is necessary
to study the falsest of all false paths [der Holzweg der Holzwege],
philosophy*'.[6]

Ruthless though it is, this text also manages to distinguish between 'free-
thinkers' and 'integral people', even when they are *religious*, who have a
'system' which is not just speculative but inscribed in their practice. It is
also lucid: it is no accident that it ends with an astonishing phrase of
Dietzgen's, which Lenin quotes: we need to follow a true path; but in
order to follow a true path it is necessary to *study* philosophy, which is
'*the falsest of all false paths*'*[der Holzweg der Holzwege]*. Which
means, to speak plainly, that there can be no true path (sc. in the
sciences, but above all in politics) without a study, and, eventually, a
theory of philosophy as a false path.

In the last resort, and more important than all the reasons I have just
evoked, this is undoubtedly why Lenin is *intolerable* to academic
philosophy and, to avoid hurting anyone, to the vast majority of
philosophers, if not to all philosophers, whether academic or otherwise.
He is, or has been on one occasion or another, philosophically intolerable to everyone (and obviously I also mean myself). Intolerable,
basically, because despite all they may say about the pre-critical character of his philosophy and the summary aspect of some of his categories,

6. *Materialism and Empirio-criticism, Collected Works*, vol.14, Moscow 1962,
pp. 340–41. I have italicized Lenin's quotations from Dietzgen. Lenin himself stressed the
key phrase '*der Holzweg der Holzwege*'. [For Engels's comments on Dietzgen's *Das Wesen
der menschlichen Kopfarbeit* ('The Nature of Mental Work'), see *Ludwig Feuerbach and
the End of Classical German Philosophy*, in Karl Marx and Frederick Engels, *Selected
Works*, vol.3, Moscow 1970, p. 362; and his letter to Marx of 6 November 1868 in *Selected Correspondence*, Moscow 1975, pp. 203–04. [Ed.]

philosophers feel and know that this is not *the* real question. They feel and know that Lenin is profoundly indifferent to their objections. He is indifferent, first, because he foresaw them long ago. Lenin said himself: I am not a philosopher, I am badly prepared in this domain (Letter to Gorky, 7 February 1908).[7] Lenin said: I know that my formulations and definitions are vague, unpolished; I know that philosophers are going to accuse my materialism of being 'metaphysical'. But he adds: that is not the question. Not only do I not 'philosophize' with their philosophy, I do not 'philosophize' like them at all. Their way of 'philosophizing' is to expend fortunes of intelligence and subtlety for no other purpose than to *ruminate in* philosophy. Whereas I treat philosophy differently, I *practise* it, as Marx intended, in obedience to what it is. That is why I believe I am a 'dialectical materialist'.

Materialism and Empirio-criticism contains all this, either directly or between the lines. And that is why Lenin the philosopher is intolerable to most philosophers, who do not want to know (i.e. who realize without admitting it) that this is *the real question*. The real question is not whether Marx, Engels and Lenin are or are not real philosophers, whether their philosophical statements are formally irreproachable, whether they do or do not make foolish statements about Kant's 'thing-in-itself', whether their materialism is or is not pre-critical, etc. For all these questions are and always have been posed inside a certain *practice* of philosophy. The real question bears precisely on this traditional practice which Lenin brings back into question by proposing a *quite different* practice of philosophy.

This different practice contains something like a promise or outline of an *objective knowledge* of philosophy's mode of being. A knowledge of philosophy as a *Holzweg der Holzwege*. But the last thing philosophers and philosophy can bear, the intolerable, is perhaps precisely the idea of this knowledge. What philosophy cannot bear is the idea of a theory (i.e. of an objective knowledge) of philosophy capable of changing its traditional practice. Such a theory may be fatal for philosophy, since it lives by its denegation.

So academic philosophy cannot tolerate Lenin (or Marx, for that matter) for two reasons, which are really one and the same. On the one hand, it cannot bear the idea that it might have something to learn from politics and from a politician. And on the other hand, it cannot bear the idea that philosophy might be the object of a theory, i.e. of an objective knowledge.

That *into the bargain*, it should be a politician like Lenin, an

7. *Collected Works*, vol.34, p. 381. [Ed.]

'innocent' and an autodidact in philosophy who had the audacity to suggest the idea that a theory of philosophy is essential to a really conscious and responsible *practice* of philosophy, is obviously too much....

Here, too, philosophy, whether academic or otherwise, is not mistaken: it puts up such a stubborn resistance to this apparently accidental encounter in which a mere politician suggests to it the beginnings of a knowledge of what philosophy is, because this encounter *hits the mark*, the most sensitive point, the point of the intolerable, the point of the *repressed*, which traditionally philosophy has merely ruminated – precisely the point at which, in order to know itself in its theory, philosophy has to recognize that it is no more than a certain investment of politics, a certain continuation of politics, a certain rumination of politics.

Lenin happens to have been the first to say so. It also happens that he *could* say so only because he was a politician, and not just any politician but a *proletarian leader*. That is why Lenin is intolerable to philosophical rumination, as intolerable – and I choose my words carefully – as Freud is to psychological rumination.

It is clear that between Lenin and established philosophy there are not just misunderstandings and incidental conflicts, not even just the philosophy professors' reactions of wounded sensibility when the son of a teacher, a petty lawyer who became a revolutionary leader, declares bluntly that most of them are petty-bourgeois intellectuals functioning in the bourgeois education system as so many ideologists inculcating the mass of student youth with the dogmas – however critical or post-critical – of the ideology of the ruling classes.[8] Between Lenin and established philosophy there is a peculiarly intolerable connection: the connection in which the reigning philosophy is touched to the quick of what it represses: politics.

III

But before we can really see how the relations between Lenin and philosophy reached this point, we must go back a little and, before discussing Lenin and philosophy in general, we have to establish Lenin's place in Marxist philosophy and therefore to raise the question of the state of Marxist philosophy.

I cannot hope to outline the history of Marxist philosophy here. I am

---

8. See the Appendix, pp. 201–2 below.

in no position to do so, and for an altogether determinant reason: I should have to know precisely what was this X whose history I proposed to write, and if I knew that, I would also have to be in a position to know whether this X has or has not a History, i.e. whether it has or has not the right to a History.

Rather than outlining, even very roughly, the 'history' of Marxist philosophy, I should like to demonstrate the existence of a symptomatic difficulty, in the light of a sequence of texts and works in History.

This difficulty has given rise to famous disputes which have lasted to the present day. The names most often given to these disputes signal its existence: what is the core of Marxist theory? a science or a philosophy? Is Marxism at heart a philosophy, the 'philosophy of praxis' – but then what of the scientific claims made by Marx? Is Marxism, on the contrary, at heart a science, historical materialism, the science of history – but then what of its philosophy, dialectical materialism? Or again, if we accept the classical distinction between historical materialism (science) and dialectical materialism (philosophy), how are we to think this distinction: in traditional terms or in new terms? Or again, what are the relations between materialism and the dialectic in dialectical materialism? Or again, what is the dialectic: a mere method? or philosophy as a whole?

This difficulty which has provided the fuel for so many disputes is a *symptomatic* one. This is intended to suggest that it is the evidence for a partly enigmatic reality, of which the classical questions I have just recalled are a certain treatment, i.e. a certain interpretation. Speaking very schematically, the classical formulations interpret this difficulty solely in terms of *philosophical* questions, i.e. inside what I have called philosophical rumination – whereas it is undoubtedly necessary to think these difficulties, and the philosophical questions which they cannot fail to provoke, in quite different terms: in terms of a *problem*, i.e. of objective (and therefore scientific) knowledge. Only on this condition, certainly, is it possible to understand the confusion that has led people to think in terms of prematurely philosophical questions the essential theoretical contribution of Marxism to philosophy, i.e. the insistence of a certain *problem* which may well produce philosophical effects, but only in so far as it is not itself in the last instance a philosophical *question*.

If I have deliberately used terms which presuppose certain distinctions (scientific problem, philosophical question), this is not so as to pass judgement on those who have been subject to this confusion, for we are all subject to it and we all have every reason to think that it was and still is inevitable – so much so that Marxist philosophy itself has been and still is caught in it, for necessary reasons.

For finally, a glance at the theatre of what is called Marxist philosophy since the *Theses on Feuerbach* is enough to show that it presents a rather curious spectacle. Granted that Marx's early works do not have to be taken into account (I know that this is to ask a concession which some people find difficult to accept, despite the force of the arguments I have put forward) and that we subscribe to Marx's statement that *The German Ideology* represented a decision to 'settle accounts with [his] erstwhile philosophical consciousness',[9] and therefore a rupture and conversion in his thought, then when we examine what happens between the *Theses on Feuerbach* (the first indication of the 'break', *1845*) and Engels's *Anti-Dühring (1877)*, the long interval of philosophical emptiness cannot fail to strike us.

The XIth Thesis on Feuerbach proclaimed: 'The philosophers have only interpreted the world in various ways; the point is to change it.'[10] This simple sentence seemed to promise a new philosophy, one which was no longer an *interpretation*, but rather a *transformation* of the world. Moreover, that is how it was read more than half a century later by Labriola, and then following him by Gramsci, both of whom defined Marxism essentially as a new philosophy, a 'philosophy of praxis'. Yet we have to face the fact that this prophetic sentence produced no new philosophy immediately, at any rate no new philosophical discourse – quite the contrary, it merely initiated a long philosophical silence. This silence was broken publicly only by what had all the appearances of an unforeseen accident: a precipitate intervention by Engels, forced to do ideological battle with Dühring, constrained to follow him on to his own 'territory'[11] in order to deal with the political consequences of the 'philosophical' writings of a blind teacher of mathematics who was beginning to exercise a dangerous influence over German socialism.

Here we have a strange situation indeed: a Thesis which seems to announce a revolution in philosophy – then a thirty-year-long philosophical silence, and finally a few improvised chapters of philosophical polemic published by Engels, for political and ideological reasons, as an introduction to a remarkable summary of Marx's scientific theories.

Must we conclude that we are the victims of a retrospective philosophical illusion when we read the XIth Thesis on Feuerbach as the proclamation of a philosophical revolution? Yes and no. But *first*, before saying no, I think it is necessary to say yes, seriously: *yes, we are essentially the victims of a philosophical illusion.* What was announced

9. Preface to *A Contribution to the Critique of Political Economy*, Karl Marx, *Early Writings*, Harmondsworth 1975, p. 426. [Ed.]

10. *Early Writings*, p. 423. [Ed.]

11. See Engels's 1878 Preface to *Anti-Dühring*, Moscow 1947, p. 10. [Ed.]

in the *Theses on Feuerbach*, was, in the necessarily philosophical language of a declaration of rupture with all 'interpretative' philosophy, something quite different from a new philosophy: a new science, the science of history, whose first, still infinitely fragile foundations Marx was to lay in *The German Ideology*.

The philosophical emptiness which followed the proclamation of Thesis XI was thus the fullness of a science, the fullness of the intense, arduous and protracted labour which put an unprecedented science on to the stocks, a science to which Marx was to devote all his life, down to the last drafts for *Capital*, which he was never able to complete. It is this scientific fullness which represents the first and most profound reason why, even if Thesis XI did prophetically announce an event which was to make its mark on philosophy, it could not give rise to a philosophy, or rather *had* to proclaim the radical suppression of all existing philosophy in order to give priority to the work needed for the theoretical gestation of Marx's scientific discovery.

This radical suppression of philosophy is, as is well known, inscribed in so many words in *The German Ideology*. It is essential, says Marx in that work, to get rid of all philosophical fancies and turn to the study of positive reality, to tear aside the veil of philosophy and at last see reality for what it is.[12]

The German Ideology bases this suppression of philosophy on a theory of philosophy as a hallucination and mystification, or to go further, as a *dream*, manufactured from what I shall call the day's residues of the real history of concrete men, day's residues endowed with a purely imaginary existence in which the order of things is inverted. Philosophy, like religion and ethics, is only ideology; it has no history, everything which seems to happen in it really happens outside it, in the only real history, the history of the material life of men. Science is then the real itself, known by the action which reveals it by destroying the ideologies that veil it: foremost among these ideologies is philosophy.

Let us halt at this dramatic juncture and explore its meaning. The theoretical revolution announced in Thesis XI is in reality the foundation of a new science. Employing a concept of Bachelard's,[13] I believe we can think of the theoretical event which inaugurates this new science as an 'epistemological break'.

---

12. See Karl Marx and Frederick Engels, *The German Ideology, Collected Works*, vol.5, London 1976, pp. 36–7. [Ed.]

13. See, for example, Gaston Bachelard, *Le Rationalisme appliqué*, Paris 1949, pp. 102 ff. [Ed.]

Marx founds a new science, i.e. he elaborates a system of new scientific concepts where previously there prevailed only the manipulation of ideological notions. Marx founds the science of history where there were previously only philosophies of history. When I say that Marx organized a theoretical system of scientific concepts in the domain previously monopolized by philosophies of history, I am extending a metaphor which is no more than a metaphor: for it suggests that Marx replaced ideological theories with a scientific theory in a uniform space, that of History. In reality, this domain itself was reorganized. But with this crucial reservation, I propose to stick to the metaphor for the moment, and even to give it a still more precise form.

If in fact we consider the great scientific discoveries of human history, it seems that we might relate what we call *the sciences*, as a number of *regional* formations, to what I shall call the great theoretical *continents*. The distance that we have now obtained enables us, without anticipating a future which neither we nor Marx can 'stir in the pot', to pursue our improved metaphor and say that, before Marx, two continents *only* had been opened up to scientific knowledge by sustained epistemological breaks: the *continent of Mathematics* with the Greeks (by Thales or those designated by that mythical name) and the *continent of Physics* (by Galileo and his successors). A science like chemistry, founded by Lavoisier's epistemological break, is a regional science within the continent of physics: everyone now knows that it is inscribed in it. A science like biology, which came to the end of the first phase of its epistemological break, inaugurated by Darwin and Mendel, only a decade ago, by its integration with molecular chemistry, also becomes part of the continent of physics. Logic in its modern form becomes part of the continent of Mathematics, etc. On the other hand, it is probable that Freud's discovery has opened a new continent, one which we are only just beginning to explore.[14]

If this metaphor stands up to the test of its extension, I can put forward the following proposition. Marx has opened up to scientific knowledge a new, third scientific continent, the continent of History, by an epistemological break whose first still uncertain strokes are inscribed in *The German Ideology*, having been announced in the *Theses on Feuerbach*. Obviously this epistemological break is not an instantaneous event. It is even possible that one might, by recurrence and where some of its *details* are concerned, assign it a sort of premonition of a past. At any rate, this break becomes *visible* in its first signs, but these signs only

---

14. For Althusser's appreciation of Freud's 'revolutionary discovery', see 'Freud and Lacan' (1964), *Essays on Ideology*, London 1984, pp. 141–71. [Ed.]

inaugurate the beginning of an endless history. Like every break, this break is actually a sustained one within which complex reorganizations can be observed.

In fact, the operation of these reorganizations, which affect essential concepts and their theoretical components, can be observed empirically in the sequence of Marx's writings: in the *Manifesto* and *The Poverty of Philosophy* (1847), in *A Contribution to the Critique of Political Economy* (1859), in *Wages, Price and Profit* (1865), in the first volume of *Capital* (1867), etc. Other reorganizations and developments have followed in the works of Lenin, especially in that unparalleled work of economic sociology, unfortunately ignored by sociologists, called *The Development of Capitalism in Russia*, in *Imperialism*, etc. Whether or not we accept the fact, we are still inscribed today in the theoretical space marked and opened by this break. Like the other breaks which opened up the other two continents that we know, this break inaugurates a history which will never come to an end.

That is why we should not read the XIth Thesis on Feuerbach as the announcement of a new philosophy, but as that necessary declaration of rupture with philosophy which clears the ground for the foundation of a new science. That is why, from the radical suppression of all philosophy to the unforeseen 'accident' which induced the philosophical chapters in *Anti-Dühring*, there is a long philosophical silence during which only the new science speaks.

Of course, this new science is materialist, but so is every science, and that is why its general theory is called 'historical materialism'. Here materialism is quite simply the strict attitude of the scientist to the reality of his object which allows him to grasp what Engels called 'nature just as it exists without any foreign admixture'.[15]

In the slightly odd phrase 'historical materialism' (we do not use the phrase 'chemical materialism' to designate chemistry) the word materialism registers both the initial rupture with the idealism of philosophies of history and the installation of scientificity with respect to history. Historical materialism thus means: science of history. If the birth of something like a Marxist philosophy is ever to be possible, it would seem that it must be from the very gestation of this science – a quite original sister, certainly, but in its very strangeness a sister of the existing sciences, after the long interval which always divides a philosophical reorganization from the scientific revolution which induced it.

Indeed, in order to go further into the reasons for this philosophical

---

15. See Engels, *Dialectics of Nature*, Moscow 1954, p. 198 (translation modified). [Ed.]

silence, I am driven to put forward a thesis concerning the relations between the sciences and philosophy without going further than to illustrate it with empirical data. Lenin began his book *State and Revolution* with this simple empirical comment: the State has not always existed; the existence of the State is observable only in class societies.[16] In the same way, I shall say: philosophy has not always existed; the existence of philosophy is observable only in a world which contains what is called a science or a number of sciences. A science in the strict sense: a theoretical, i.e. ideal [*idéelle*] and demonstrative discipline, not an aggregate of empirical results.

Here, in brief, are my empirical illustrations of this thesis.

If philosophy is to be born, or reborn, one or more sciences must exist. Perhaps this is why philosophy in the strict sense only began with Plato, its birth induced by the existence of Greek mathematics; was overhauled by Descartes, its modern revolution induced by Galilean physics; was recast by Kant under the influence of Newton's discovery; and was remodelled by Husserl under the impetus of the first axiomatics, etc.

I suggest this theme, which needs to be tested, only in order to point out, in the empirical mode still, that ultimately Hegel was not wrong to say that philosophy takes wing *at dusk*:[17] when science, born at dawn, has already lived the time of a long day. Philosophy is thus always a long day behind the science which induces the birth of its first form and the rebirths of its revolutions, a long day which may last years, decades, a half-century or a century.

We should realize that the shock of a scientific break does not make itself felt at once, that time is needed for it to reorganize philosophy.

We should also conclude, no doubt, that the work of philosophical gestation is closely linked with the work of scientific gestation, each being at work in the other. It is clear that the new philosophical categories are elaborated in the work of the new science, but it is also true that in certain cases (to be precise, Plato, Descartes) what is called philosophy also serves as a theoretical laboratory in which the new categories required by the concepts of the new science are brought into focus. For example, was it not in Cartesianism that a new category of causality was worked out for Galilean physics, which had run up against Aristotelian cause as an 'epistemological obstacle'? If we add to this the

---

16. *The State and Revolution, Collected Works*, vol.25, Moscow 1964, p. 387. See also Engels, *The Origin of the Family, Private Property and the State*, London 1972, p. 232. [Ed.]

17. Cf. Hegel's Preface to the *Philosophy of Right*, ed. T.M. Knox, Oxford 1967, p. 13. [Ed.]

fact that the great philosophical events with which we are familiar (ancient philosophy descending from Plato, modern philosophy descending from Descartes) are clearly related to inducements from the opening of the two scientific continents, Greek mathmatics and Galilean physics, we can pronounce (for this is all still empirical) certain inferences about what I think we can call Marxist philosophy. Three inferences:

First inference. If Marx really has opened up a new continent to scientific knowledge, his scientific discovery ought to induce some kind of important reorganization in philosophy. The XIth Thesis was perhaps ahead of its time, but it really did announce a major event in philosophy. It seems that this may be the case.

Second inference. Philosophy exists only by virtue of the distance it lags behind its scientific inducement. Marxist philosophy should therefore lag behind the Marxist science of history. This does indeed seem to be the case. The thirty-year desert between the *Theses on Feuerbach* and *Anti-Dühring* is evidence of this, as are certain long periods of deadlock later, periods in which we and many others are still marking time.

Third inference. There is a chance that we shall find more advanced theoretical elements for the elaboration of Marxist philosophy than we might have expected in the gestation of Marxist science, given the distance we now have on its lag. Lenin used to say that one should look in Marx's *Capital* for his dialectic – by which he meant Marxist philosophy itself.[18] *Capital* must contain something from which to complete or forge the new philosophical categories: they are surely at work in *Capital*, in the 'practical state'. It seems that this may be the case. We must read *Capital* in order to find out.

The day is always long, but as luck would have it, it is already far advanced, look: dusk will soon fall. Marxist philosophy will take wing.

Taken as guidelines, these inferences introduce, if I may say so, a kind of order into our concerns and hopes, and also into certain of our thoughts. We can now understand that the ultimate reason why Marx – trapped as he was in poverty, fanatical scientific work and the urgent demands of political leadership – never wrote the Dialectic (or Philosophy) he dreamed of, was not, *whatever he may have thought*, that he

---

18. *Philosophical Notebooks, Collected Works*, vol.38, Moscow 1961, p. 319. [Ed.]

never 'found the time'.[19] We can now understand that the ultimate
reason why Engels – suddenly confronted with the necessity, as he
writes, of 'having his say on philosophical questions' – could not satisfy
the professional philosophers, was not the improvised character of a
merely ideological polemic. We can now understand that the ultimate
reason for the philosophical limitations of *Materialism and Empirio-
criticism* was not just a matter of the constraints of the ideological
struggle.

We can now say it. The time that Marx could not find, Engels's
philosophical extemporization, the laws of the ideological struggle in
which Lenin was forced merely to turn his enemy's own weapons against
him, each of these is a good enough excuse, but together they do not
constitute a reason.

The ultimate reason is that the times were not ripe, that dusk had not
yet fallen, and that neither Marx himself, nor Engels, nor Lenin could
yet write the great work of philosophy which Marxism–Leninism lacks.
If they did come well after the science on which it depends, in one way
or another they all still came *too soon* for a philosophy, which is indispensable but cannot be born without a necessary *lag*.

Given the concept of this necessary 'lag', everything should become
clear, including the misunderstanding of those like the young Lukács
and Gramsci, and so many others without their gifts, who were so
impatient with the slowness of the birth of this philosophy that they
proclaimed that it had already long been born, from the beginning, from
the *Theses on Feuerbach*, i.e. well *before* the beginnings of Marxist
science itself – and who, to prove this to themselves, simply stated that
since every science is a 'superstructure', and every existing science is
therefore basically positivist because it is bourgeois, Marxist 'science'
could not but be *philosophical*, and Marxism a philosophy, a post-
Hegelian philosophy or 'philosophy of praxis'.

Given the concept of this necessary 'lag', light can be cast on many
other difficulties, too, even in the *political* history of Marxist organizations, their defeats and crises. If it is true, as the whole Marxist tradition
claims, that the greatest event in the history of the class struggle – i.e.
practically in human history – is the union of Marxist theory and the
workers' movement, it is clear that the internal balance of that union
may be threatened by those failures of theory known as *deviations*,
however trivial they may be; we can understand the political scope of
the unrelenting theoretical disputes unleashed in the socialist and then in

---

19. Cf. Marx's letter to Engels of 14 January 1858, *Selected Correspondence*, p. 93.
[Ed.]

the Communist movement, over what Lenin calls mere 'shades of opinion', for, as he said in *What is to be Done?*: '*The fate of Russian Social-Democracy for very many years to come may depend on the strengthening of one or the other "shade".*'[20]

Therefore, Marxist theory being what it is, a science and a philosophy, and the philosophy having necessarily lagged behind the science, which has been hindered in its development by this, we may be tempted to think that these theoretical deviations were, at bottom, *inevitable*, not just because of the effects of the class struggle on and in theory, but also because of the dislocation [*décalage*] inside theory itself.

In fact, to turn to the past of the Marxist workers' movement, we can call by their real names the theoretical deviations which have led to the great historical defeats for the proletariat – that of the Second International, to mention only one. These deviations are called economism, evolutionism, voluntarism, humanism, empiricism, dogmatism, etc. Basically, these deviations are *philosophical* deviations, and were denounced as such by the great workers' leaders, starting with Engels and Lenin.

But this now brings us quite close to understanding why they overwhelmed even those who denounced them: were they not in some way inevitable, precisely as a function of the necessary *lag* of Marxist philosophy?

To go further: if this is the case, and even in the deep crisis today dividing the international Communist movement, Marxist philosophers may well tremble before the task – unanticipated because so long anticipated – which history has assigned and entrusted to them. If it is true, as so many signs indicate, that today the lag of Marxist philosophy can in part be overcome, doing so will not only cast light on the past, but also perhaps transform the future.

In this transformed future, justice will be done equitably to all those who had to live in the contradiction of political urgency and philosophical lag. Justice will be done to one of the greatest: to Lenin. Justice: his philosophical work will then be perfected. Perfected, i.e. completed and corrected. We surely owe this service and this homage to the man who was lucky enough to be born in time for politics, but unfortunate enough to be born too early for philosophy. After all, who chooses his own birth date?

----

20. *What is to be done?*, *Collected Works*, vol.5, Moscow 1961, p. 370 (Althusser's emphasis). [Ed.]

IV

Now that the 'history' of Marxist theory has shown us why Marxist philosophy lags behind the science of history, we can go directly to Lenin and into his work. But then our philosophical 'dream' will vanish: things do not have its simplicity.

Let me anticipate my conclusion. No, Lenin was not born too soon for philosophy. No one is ever born too soon for philosophy. If philosophy lags behind, if this lag is what makes it philosophy, how is it ever possible to lag behind a lag which has no history? If we absolutely must go on talking of a lag, it is we who are lagging behind Lenin. Our lag is simply another name for a mistake. For we are philosophically mistaken about the relations between Lenin and philosophy. The relations between Lenin and philosophy are certainly expressed *in* philosophy, inside the 'game' which constitutes philosophy as philosophy, but these relations are not philosophical, because this 'game' is not philosophical.

I want to try to expound the reasons for these conclusions in a concise and systematic – and therefore necessarily schematic – form, taking as the object of my analysis Lenin's great 'philosophical' work, *Materialism and Empirio-criticism*. I shall divide this exposition into three moments:

1. *Lenin's great philosophical Theses.*
2. *Lenin and philosophical practice.*
3. *Lenin and partisanship in philosophy.*

In dealing with each of these points, I shall be concerned to show what was new in Lenin's contribution to Marxist theory.

1. Lenin's Great Philosophical Theses

By Theses I mean, like anyone else, the philosophical positions taken by Lenin, registered in philosophical pronouncements. For the moment I shall ignore the objection which has provided academic philosophy with a screen or pretext for its failure to read *Materialism and Empirio-criticism*: Lenin's categorial terminology, his historical references, and even his ignorances.

It is a fact itself worthy of a separate study that, even in the astonishing 'In Lieu of an Introduction' to *Materialism and Empirio-criticism* which takes us brusquely back to Berkeley and Diderot, Lenin in many respects situates himself in the *theoretical space of eighteenth-century empiricism,* i.e. in a philosophical problematic which is 'officially' pre-critical – if it is assumed that philosophy became 'officially' critical with Kant.

Once we have noted the existence of this reference system, once we know its structural logic, we can explain Lenin's theoretical formulations as so many effects of this logic, including the incredible contortions which he inflicts on the categorial terminology of empiricism in order to turn it against empiricism. For if he does think *in* the problematic of objective empiricism (Lenin even says 'objective sensualism') and if the fact of thinking in that problematic often affects not just the formulations of his thought, but even some of its movements, no one could deny that Lenin does *think*, i.e. thinks systematically and rigorously. It is this thought which matters to us, in that it pronounces certain Theses. Here they are, pronounced in their naked essentials. I shall distinguish three of them:

Thesis I. Philosophy is not a science. Philosophy is distinct from the sciences. Philosophical categories are distinct from scientific concepts.

This is a crucial thesis. Let me indicate the decisive point in which its destiny is at stake: the category of *matter,* surely the touchstone for a materialist philosophy and for all the philosophical souls who hope for its salvation, i.e. its death. Now Lenin says in so many words that the distinction between the philosophical category of matter and the scientific concept of matter is vital for Marxist philosophy:

Matter is a philosophical category. (*Materialism and Empirio-criticism,* p. 130)

The sole property of matter with whose recognition philosophical materialism is bound up is the property of being an objective reality. (ibid., pp. 260–61)

It follows that the philosophical *category* of matter, which is conjointly a Thesis of *existence* and a Thesis of *objectivity,* can never be confused with the contents of the scientific *concepts* of matter. The scientific concepts of matter define knowledges, relative to the historical state of the sciences, about the objects of those sciences. The content of the scientific concept of matter changes with the development, i.e. with the deepening of scientific knowledge. The meaning of the philosophical category of matter does not change, since it does not apply to any object of science but affirms the *objectivity* of all scientific knowledge of an object. The category of *matter* cannot change. It is 'absolute'.

The consequences which Lenin draws from this distinction are crucial. First, he re-establishes the truth about what was then called the 'crisis of physics': physics is not in crisis, but in growth. Matter has not 'disappeared'. The scientific concept of matter alone has *changed in*

content, and it will always go on changing in the future, for the process
of knowledge is infinite in its object itself.

The scientific pseudo-crisis of physics is only a *philosophical* crisis or
fright in which ideologists, even though some of them are also scientists,
are openly attacking materialism. When they proclaim the disappearance of matter, we should hear the silent discourse of their wish: *the
disappearance of materialism*!

And Lenin denounces and knocks down all those ephemerally philosophical scientists who thought their time had come. What is left of these
characters today? Who still remembers them? We must concede at least
that this philosophical ignoramus Lenin had good judgement. And what
professional philosopher was capable, as he was, of committing himself
without hesitation or delay, so far and so surely, absolutely alone,
against everyone, in an apparently lost cause? I should be grateful if
anyone could give me one name – other than Husserl, at that time
Lenin's objective ally against empiricism and historicism – but only a
temporary ally and one who could not *meet* him, for Husserl, as a good
'philosopher', believed he was going 'somewhere'.

But Lenin's Thesis goes further than the immediate conjuncture. If it
is absolutely essential to distinguish between the philosophical category
of matter and every scientific concept, it follows that those materialists
who apply philosophical categories to the objects of the sciences as if
they were concepts of them are involved in a case of 'mistaken identity'.
For example, anyone who wants to make *conceptual* use of *categorial*
oppositions like matter/mind or matter/consciousness is only too likely
to lapse into *tautology*, for the

> antithesis of matter and mind has absolute significance only within the
> bounds of a very limited field – in this case exclusively within the bounds of
> the fundamental epistemological problem of what is to be regarded as primary
> and what as secondary [i.e. in philosophy]. Beyond these bounds [i.e. in the
> sciences] the relative character of this antithesis is indubitable. (*Materialism
> and Empirio-criticism*, p. 147)

I cannot go into other very wide-ranging consequences, e.g. into the
fact that from Lenin's point of view the distinction between philosophy
and the sciences necessarily opens up the field of a theory of the history
of knowledges; or the fact that Lenin announces in his theory the
historical *limits* of all truth (sc. all scientific knowledge) which he thinks
as a theory of the distinction between *absolute truth and relative truth*
(in this theory a single opposition of categories is used to think both the
distinction between philosophy and the sciences, and the necessity for a
theory of the history of the sciences).

I would just ask you to note what follows. The distinction between philosophy and the sciences, between philosophical categories and scientific concepts, constitutes at heart the adoption of a radical philosophical position *against all forms of empiricism and positivism*: against the empiricism and positivism even of certain materialists, against naturalism, against psychologism, against historicism (on this particular point see Lenin's polemical violence against Bogdanov's historicism).

It must be admitted that this is not so bad for a philosopher whom it is easy to dismiss as pre-critical and pre-Kantian on the grounds of a few of his formulations – indeed, it is far rather astonishing, since it is clear that in 1908 this Bolshevik leader had never read a line of Kant and Hegel, but had stopped at Berkeley and Diderot. And yet, for some strange reason, he displays a 'critical' feeling for his positivist opponents and a remarkable strategic discernment within the religious concert of the 'hypercritical' philosophy of his day.

The most amazing thing of all is the fact that Lenin manages the *tour de force* of taking up these *anti-empiricist positions precisely in the field of an empiricist reference problematic.* It certainly is a paradoxical exploit to manage to be anti-empiricist while thinking and expressing oneself in the basic categories of empiricism, and must surely pose a slight 'problem' for any philosopher of good faith who is prepared to examine it.

Does this by any chance mean that the field of the philosophical problematic, its categorial formulations and its philosophical pronouncements, are relatively indifferent to the philosophical positions adopted? Does it mean that at heart nothing essentially happens in what seems to constitute philosophy? Strange.

Thesis 2. If philosophy is distinct from the sciences, there is a privileged link between philosophy and the sciences. This link is represented by the materialist thesis of objectivity.

Here, two points are essential.

The first concerns the nature of scientific knowledge. The suggestions contained in *Materialism and Empirio-criticism* are taken up, developed and deepened in the *Philosophical Notebooks*: they give their full meaning to the anti-empiricism and anti-positivism which Lenin shows within his conception of *scientific practice*. In this respect, Lenin must also be regarded as a witness who speaks of scientific practice as a genuine practitioner. A reading of the texts he devoted to Marx's *Capital* between 1898 and 1905, and his analysis of *The Development of Capitalism in Russia*, is enough to show that his scientific practice as a Marxist theoretician of history, political economy and sociology was constantly accompanied by acute epistemological reflections which his philosophical texts simply take up in a generalized form.

What Lenin reveals, and here again using categories which may be contaminated by his empiricist references (e.g. the category of reflection), is the anti-empiricism of scientific practice, the decisive role of scientific abstraction – or rather, the role of conceptual systematicity, and in a more general way, the role of theory as such.

Politically, Lenin is famous for his critique of 'spontaneism',[21] which, it should be noted, is not directed against the spontaneity, resourcefulness, inventiveness and genius of the masses of the people but against a political ideology which, screened by an exaltation of the spontaneity of the masses, exploits it in order to divert it into an incorrect politics. But it is not generally realized that Lenin adopts exactly the same position in his conceptions of scientific practice. Lenin wrote: *'without revolutionary theory there can be no revolutionary movement.'*[22] He could equally have written: *without scientific theory there can be no production of scientific knowledges.* His defence of the requirements of theory in scientific practice precisely coincides with his defence of the requirements of theory in political practice. His anti-spontaneism then takes the theoretical form of anti-empiricism, anti-positivism and anti-pragmatism.

But just as his political anti-spontaneism presupposes the deepest respect for the spontaneity of the masses, his theoretical anti-spontaneism presupposes the greatest respect for *practice* in the process of knowledge. Neither in his conception of science nor in his conception of politics does Lenin for one moment fall into *theoreticism.*

This first point enables us to understand the *second.* Materialist philosophy is, in Lenin's eyes, profoundly linked to scientific practice. This thesis must, I believe, be understood in two senses.

First in an extremely classical sense which illustrates what we have been able to observe empirically in the history of the relations which link all philosophy to the sciences. For Lenin, what happens in the sciences is a crucial concern of philosophy. The great scientific revolutions induce important reorganizations in philosophy. This is Engels's famous thesis: materialism changes in form with each great scientific discovery.[23] Engels was fascinated by the philosophical consequences of discoveries in the natural sciences (the cell, evolution, Carnot's principle, etc.), but Lenin defends the same thesis in a better way by showing that the

21. See, e.g., ibid., pp. 373–97. [Ed.]

22. Ibid., p. 369 (Althusser's emphasis). [Ed.]

23. See, e.g., *Ludwig Feuerbach and the End of Classical German Philosophy*, p. 349. [Ed.]

decisive discovery which has induced an obligatory reorganization of materialist philosophy does not come so much from the sciences of nature as from the *science of history*, from historical materialism.

In a second sense, Lenin invokes an important argument. Here he no longer talks of philosophy in general, but of materialist philosophy. The latter is particularly concerned with what happens in scientific practice, but in a manner peculiar to itself, because it *represents*, in its materialist thesis, the '*spontaneous*' convictions of scientists about the existence of the objects of their sciences, and the objectivity of their knowledge.

In *Materialism and Empirio-criticism*, Lenin constantly repeats the statement that most specialists in the sciences of nature are 'spontaneously' materialistic, at least in *one of the tendencies* of their spontaneous philosophy. While fighting the ideologies of the spontaneism of scientific practice (empiricism, pragmatism) Lenin recognizes in the experience of scientific practice a spontaneous materialist tendency of the highest importance for Marxist philosophy. He thus interrelates the materialist theses required to think the specificity of scientific *knowledge* with the spontaneous materialist tendency of the *practitioners* of the sciences: as expressing both practically and theoretically one and the same materialist thesis of existence and objectivity.

Let me anticipate and say that the Leninist insistence on affirming the privileged link between the sciences and Marxist materialist philosophy is evidence that here we are dealing with a decisive nodal point, which, if I may, I shall call *Nodal Point No. 1*.

But precisely in this mention of the spontaneous philosophy of the scientist something important is emerging which will bring us to another decisive nodal point of a quite different kind.

Thesis 3. Here, too, Lenin is taking up a classical thesis expounded by Engels in *Ludwig Feuerbach and the End of Classical German Philosophy*,[24] but he gives it an unprecedented scope. This thesis concerns the history of philosophy conceived as the history of an age-old struggle betweeen two tendencies: idealism and materialism.

It must be admitted that in its bluntness, this thesis runs directly counter to the convictions of the great majority of professional philosophers. If they are prepared to read Lenin – and they will all have to some day – they will all admit that his philosophical theses are not so summary as reputation makes them. But I am afraid that they will stubbornly resist this last thesis, for it threatens to wound them in their most profound convictions. It appears far too crude, fit only for public (i.e.

---

24. Ibid., pp. 345–6. [Ed.]

ideological and political) disputes. To say that the whole history of philosophy can be reduced in the last instance to a struggle between materialism and idealism seems to cheapen all the wealth of the history of philosophy.

In fact, this thesis amounts to the claim that essentially *philosophy has no real history*. What is a history which is no more than the repetition of the clash between two fundamental tendencies? The forms and arguments of the fight may vary, but if the whole history of philosophy is merely the history of these forms, they have only to be reduced to the immutable tendencies that they represent for the transformation of these forms to become a kind of *game for nothing*. Ultimately, philosophy has no history; philosophy is that strange theoretical site where nothing really happens, nothing but this *repetition* of nothing. To say that nothing happens in philosophy is to say that philosophy *leads nowhere because it is going nowhere*: the paths it opens really are, as Dietzgen said, long before Heidegger, '*Holzwege*': paths that lead nowhere.

Besides, that is what Lenin suggests *in practice*, when, right at the beginning of *Materialism and Empirio-criticism*, he explains that Mach merely *repeats* Berkeley, and himself counterposes to this his own *repetition* of Diderot. Worse still, it is clear that Berkeley and Diderot *repeat* each other, since they are in agreement about the matter/mind opposition, merely arranging its terms in a different way. The nothing of their philosophy is only the nothing of this inversion of the terms in an immutable categorial opposition (Matter/Mind) which represents in philosophical theory the play of the two antagonistic tendencies in confrontation in this opposition. The history of philosophy is thus nothing but the nothing of this repeated inversion. In addition, this thesis would restore a meaning to the famous phrases about Marx's inversion of Hegel, the Hegel whom Engels himself described as no more than a previous inversion.[25]

On this point it is essential to recognize that Lenin's insistence has absolutely no limits. In *Materialism and Empirio-criticism*, at least (for his tone changes on this point in the *Philosophical Notebooks*), he jettisons all the theoretical nuances, distinctions, ingenuities and subtleties with which philosophy tries to think its 'object': they are nothing but sophistries, hair-splitting, professorial quibbles, accommodations and compromises whose only aim is to mask what is really at stake in the dispute to which all philosophy is committed: the basic struggle between the tendencies of materialism and idealism. There is no third way, no

---

25. See Marx's 1873 Postface to the Second German Edition of *Capital*, vol. 1, Harmondsworth 1976, pp. 102–3 and cf. Engels, *Ludwig Feuerbach*, p. 348. [Ed.]

half-measure, no bastard position, any more than there is in politics. Basically, there are only idealists and materialists. All those who do not openly declare themselves one or the other are 'shamefaced' materialists or idealists (Kant, Hume).

But we must therefore go even further and say that if the whole history of philosophy is nothing but the re-examination of arguments in which one and the same struggle is carried to its conclusion, then philosophy is nothing but a tendency struggle, the *Kampfplatz* that Kant discussed[26] – which, however, throws us back on to the subjectivity pure and simple of ideological struggles. It is to say that *philosophy strictly speaking has no object,* in the sense that a science has an object.

Lenin goes as far as this, which proves that Lenin was a *thinker.* He declares that it is impossible to prove the ultimate principles of materialism, just as it is impossible to prove (or refute, to Diderot's annoyance) the principles of idealism. It is impossible to prove them because they cannot be the object of a knowledge, meaning by that a knowledge comparable with that of science which does prove the properties of its objects.

So philosophy has no object. But now everything fits. If nothing happens in philosophy, it is precisely because philosophy has no object. If something actually does happen in the sciences, it is because they do have an object, knowledge of which they can increase, *which gives them a history.* As philosophy has no object, nothing can happen in it. The nothing of its history simply repeats the nothing of its object.

Here we are beginning to get close to *Nodal Point No. 2,* which concerns these famous *tendencies.* Philosophy merely re-examines and ruminates over arguments which represent the basic conflict of these tendencies in the form of categories. It is their conflict, unnameable *in* philosophy, which sustains the eternal null inversion for which philosophy is the garrulous theatre, the inversion of the fundamental categorial opposition between matter and mind. How, then, is the tendency revealed? In the hierarchic order it installs between the terms of the opposition: an order of domination. Listen to Lenin:

Bogdanov, pretending to argue only against Beltov and cravenly ignoring Engels, is indignant at such *definitions,* which, don't you see, 'prove to be simple *repetitions*' of the 'formula' (of Engels, our 'Marxist' forgets to add) that for one trend in philosophy matter is primary and spirit secondary, while for the other trend the reverse is the case. All the Russian Machists exultantly echo Bogdanov's 'refutation'! But the slightest reflection could have shown

---

26. See *Critique of Pure Reason,* London 1929, pp. 7, 666–9.

these people that *it is impossible, in the very nature of the case, to give any definition of these two ultimate concepts of epistemology, except an indication which of them is taken as primary.* What is meant by giving a 'definition'? It means essentially to bring a given concept within a more comprehensive concept.... The question then is, are there more comprehensive concepts with which the theory of knowledge could operate than those of being and thinking, matter and sensation, physical and mental? No. These are the ultimate, most comprehensive concepts, which epistemology has in point of fact so far not surpassed (apart from changes in *nomenclature*, which are always possible). One must be a charlatan or an utter blockhead *to demand a 'definition' of these two 'series' of concepts of ultimate comprehensiveness which would not be a 'mere repetition': one or the other must be taken as primary.* (*Materialism and Empirio-criticism*, p. 146)

The inversion which is formally the nothing which happens in philosophy, in its explicit discourse, is not null – or rather, it is an effect of annulment, the annulment of a previous hierarchy replaced by the opposite hierarchy. What is at stake in philosophy, in the ultimate categories which govern all philosophical systems, is therefore the sense of this hierarchy, the sense of this location of one category in the dominant position; it is something in philosophy which irresistibly recalls a seizure of power or an *installation in power*. Philosophically, we should say: an installation in power is without an *object*. An installation in power – is this still a purely theoretical category? A seizure of power (or an installation in power) is political, it does not have an object, it has a stake, precisely the power, and an aim: the effects of that power.

Here we should stop for a moment to see what is new in Lenin's contribution with respect to Engels's. His contribution is enormous if we are really prepared to weigh up the effects of something which has too often been taken for a mere shade of opinion.

Ultimately, although Engels has strokes of astonishing genius when he is working on Marx, his *thought* is not comparable with Lenin's. Often he manages only to juxtapose theses – rather than managing to *think* them in the unity of their relations.

Worse still: he never really rid himself of a certain positivist theme from *The German Ideology*. For although he recommends its systematic study, for him philosophy has to disappear: it is merely the craftsman's laboratory in which the philosophical categories necessary to science were forged in the past. These times have gone. Philosophy has done its work. Now it must give way to science.[27] Since the sciences are scientifically capable of presenting *the organic unitary system of their*

---

27. *Ludwig Feuerbach*, p. 342. [Ed.]

relations, there is no longer any need either for a *Naturphilosophie* or for a *Geschichtsphilosophie*.

What is left for philosophy? An object: the dialectic, the most general laws of nature (but the sciences provide them) and of thought. There thus remains the laws of thought which can be disengaged from the history of the sciences. Philosophy is thus not really separate from the sciences; hence the positivism that insinuates itself into certain of Engels's formulations when he says that to be a materialist is to admit nature as it is 'without any foreign admixture', despite the fact that he knows that the sciences are a process of knowledge. That is why philosophy does have an object for all that: but paradoxically, it is then *pure thought*, which would not displease idealism. For example, what else is Lévi-Strauss up to today, on his own admission, and by appeal to Engels's authority? He, too, is studying the laws – let us say the structures – *of thought*. Ricœur has pointed out to him, correctly, that he is Kant minus the transcendental subject. Lévi-Strauss has not denied it.[28] Indeed, if the object of philosophy is pure thought, it is possible to appeal to Engels and find oneself a Kantian, minus the transcendental subject.

The same difficulty can be expressed in another way. The dialectic, the object of philosophy, is called a *logic*. Can philosophy really have the object of Logic for its object? It seems that Logic is now moving further and further away from philosophy: it is a science.

Of course, *at the same time*, Engels also defends the thesis of the two tendencies, but materialism and dialectics on the one hand, tendency struggle and philosophical advance exclusively determined by scientific advance on the other hand, are two things very hard to think together – i.e. to *think*. Engels tries, but even if we are prepared not to take him literally (the least that can be asked where a non-specialist is concerned) it is only too clear that he is *missing* something *essential*.

Which is to say that he is *missing* something essential to his thought if he is to be able to think. Thanks to Lenin, we can see that this is a matter of an *omission*. For Engels's thought is missing precisely what Lenin adds to it.

Lenin contributes a profoundly consistent thought, in which are located a number of radical theses that undoubtedly circumscribe emptinesses, but precisely *pertinent* emptinesses. At the centre of his thought is the thesis that philosophy *has no object*, i.e. philosophy is not to be

---

28. See Paul Ricœur, 'Symbole et temporalité', *Archivio di Filosofia* 1–2, Rome 1963, p. 24; cf. Claude Lévi-Strauss, *The Raw and the Cooked* (1964), Harmondsworth 1986, p. 11. [Ed.]

explained merely *by the relationship it maintains with the sciences.*

We are getting close to *Nodal Point No. 2.* But we have not got there yet.

2. Lenin and Philosophical Practice

In order to reach this *Nodal Point No. 2* I shall enter a new domain, that of philosophical practice. It would be interesting to study Lenin's philosophical practice in his various works, but that would presuppose that we already knew what philosophical practice is as such.

Now it so happens that on a few rare occasions Lenin was forced, by the exigencies of philosophical polemic, to produce a kind of *definition of his philosophical practice.* Here are the two clearest passages:

> You will say that this distinction between relative and absolute truth is indefinite. And I shall reply: it is sufficiently 'indefinite' *to prevent science from becoming a dogma in the bad sense of the term,* from becoming something dead, frozen, ossified; but at the same time it is sufficiently 'definite' to enable us to *draw a dividing-line in the most emphatic and irrevocable manner* between ourselves and fideism and agnosticism, between ourselves and philosophical idealism and the sophistry of the followers of Hume and Kant. (*Materialism and Empirio-criticism,* p. 136)

> Of course, we must not forget that the criterion of practice can never, in the nature of things, either confirm or refute any human idea completely. This criterion too is sufficiently 'indefinite' not to allow human knowledge to become 'absolute', but at the same time it is sufficiently definite to wage a ruthless fight on all varieties of idealism and agnosticism. (ibid., pp. 142–3)

Other passages confirm Lenin's position. These are clearly not rash or isolated formulations, but the expressions of a profound thought.

Lenin thus defines the ultimate essence of philosophical practice as an *intervention* in the theoretical domain. This intervention takes a double form: it is theoretical in its formulation of definite categories; and practical in the function of these categories. This function consists of 'drawing a dividing-line' inside the theoretical domain between ideas declared to be true and ideas declared to be false, between the scientific and the ideological. The effects of this line are of two kinds: positive in that they assist a certain practice – scientific practice – and negative in that they defend this practice against the dangers of certain ideological notions: here those of idealism and dogmatism. Such, at least, are the effects produced by *Lenin's* philosophical intervention.

In this drawing of a dividing-line we can see the two basic tendencies we have discussed confronting one another. It is materialist philosophy that draws this dividing-line in order to protect scientific practice against the assaults of idealist philosophy, the scientific against the assaults of the ideological. We can generalize this definition by saying: all philosophy consists of drawing a major dividing-line by means of which it repels the ideological notions of the philosophies that represent the opposing tendency; the stake in this act of drawing (i.e. in philosophical practice) is scientific practice, scientificity. Here we rediscover my *Nodal Point No. 1*: the privileged relation of philosophy to the sciences.

We also rediscover the paradoxical game of the inversion of terms in which the history of philosophy is annulled in the nothing it produces. This nothing is not null, since its stake is the fate of the scientific practices, of the scientific, and of its partner, the ideological. Either the scientific practices are exploited or they are assisted by the philosophical intervention.

We can thus understand why philosophy can have a history, and yet nothing occurs in that history. For the intervention of each philosophy, which displaces or modifies existing philosophical categories and thus produces those changes in philosophical discourse in which the history of philosophy proffers its existence, is precisely the philosophical nothing whose insistence we have established, since a dividing-line actually is nothing; it is not even a line or a drawing, but the simple fact of being divided, i.e. *the emptiness of a distance taken.*

This distance leaves its *trace* in the distinctions of the philosophical discourse, in its modified categories and apparatus; but all these modifications are nothing in themselves since they act only outside their own presence, in the distance or non-distance which separates the antagonistic tendencies from the scientific practices, the stake in their struggle.

All that can be truly philosophical in this operation of a null drawing is its displacement, but that is relative to the history of the scientific practices and of the sciences. For there is a history of the sciences, and the lines of the philosophical front are displaced according to the trans-formations of the scientific conjuncture (i.e. according to the state of the sciences and their problems), and according to the state of the philo-sophical apparatuses that these transformations induce. The terms that designate the scientific and the ideological thus have to be *rethought* again and again.

Hence there is a history *in* philosophy rather than a history *of* philosophy: a history of the displacement of the indefinite repetition of a null trace whose effects are real. This history can be read profitably in all the great philosophers, even the idealist ones – and in the one who sums up the whole history of philosophy, Hegel. That is why Lenin read

Hegel, with astonishment – but this reading of Hegel is also a part of Lenin's *philosophical practice*. To read Hegel as a materialist is to draw dividing-lines within him.[29]

No doubt I have gone beyond Lenin's literal meaning, but I do not think that I have been unfaithful to him. At any rate, I say simply that Lenin offers us something with which we can begin to think the specific form of *philosophical practice* in its essence, and give a meaning retrospectively to a number of formulations contained in the great texts of classical philosophy. For, in his own way, Plato had already discussed the struggle between the Friends of the Forms and the Friends of the Earth, declaring that the true philosopher must know how to demarcate, incise and draw dividing-lines.

However, one fundamental question remains: what of the two great tendencies which confront one another in the history of philosophy? Levin gives this question a wild answer [*une réponse sauvage*], but an answer none the less.

3. Partisanship in Philosophy

The answer is contained in the thesis – famous and, it must be said, shocking to many people – of partisanship in philosophy.

This word sounds like a *directly* political slogan in which partisan means a political party, the Communist Party.

Yet any halfway close reading of Lenin – not only of *Materialism and Empirio-criticism* but also, and above all, of his analyses in the theory of history and of the economy – will show that it is a concept and not just a slogan.

Lenin is simply observing that all philosophy is partisan, as a function of its basic tendency, against the opposing basic tendency, via the philosophies which represent it. But at the same time he is observing that the vast majority of philosophers put a great price on being able to declare publicly and prove that *they are not partisan because they do not have to be partisan*.

Thus Kant: the '*Kampfplatz*' he discusses is all right for other, precritical philosophers, but not for critical philosophy. His own philosophy is outside the '*Kampfplatz*', somewhere else, whence it assigns itself precisely the function of arbitrating the conflicts of metaphysics in the

---

29. For Lenin's reading of Hegel, see especially the 'Conspectus of Hegel's Book *The Science of Logic*' (1914–16), *Philosophical Notebooks*, pp. 85–238. Cf, Althusser's lecture 'Lenin before Hegel' (1969), in *Lenin and Philosophy and Other Essays*, London 1971, pp. 103–20. [Ed.]

name of the interests of Reason. Ever since philosophy began, from Plato's $\Theta \varepsilon \omega \rho \varepsilon \hat{\iota} \nu$ to Husserl's philosopher as 'civil servant of humanity', and even to Heidegger in some of his writings, the history of philosophy has also been dominated by this repetition, which is the repetition of a contradiction: *the theoretical denegation of its own practice, and enormous theoretical efforts to register this degenation in consistent discourses.*

Lenin's response to this surprising fact, which seems to be constitutive of the vast majority of philosophies, is simply to say a *few words* to us about the insistence of these mysterious tendencies in confrontation in the history of philosophy. In Lenin's view these tendencies are finally related to class positions, and therefore to class conflicts. I say *related to* [*en rapport*], for Lenin says no more than that, and besides, he never says that philosophy can be reduced to the class struggle pure and simple, or even to what the Marxist tradition calls the ideological class struggle. Not to go beyond Lenin's declarations, we can say that in his view, philosophy *represents* the class struggle: i.e. politics. It *represents* it, which presupposes *an instance with* [*auprès de*] *which* politics is thus represented: this instance is the sciences.

Nodal Point No. 1: the relation between philosophy and the sciences. *Nodal Point No. 2*: the relationship between philosophy and politics. Everything revolves around this double relation.

We can now advance the following proposition: philosophy is a certain continuation of politics, in a certain domain, *vis-à-vis* a certain reality. Philosophy represents politics in the domain of theory or, to be more precise: *with the sciences* – and, vice versa, philosophy represents scientificity in politics, with the classes engaged in the class struggle. How this representation is governed, by what mechanisms this representation is assured, by what mechanisms it can be falsified or faked and *is falsified as a general rule*, Lenin does not tell us. He is clearly profoundly convinced that in the last resort no philosophy can run ahead of this condition, evade the determinism of this double representation. In other words, he is convinced that philosophy exists somewhere as a third instance between the two major instances which constitute it as itself an instance: the class struggle and the sciences.

One more word is enough: if *Nodal Point No. 1*, the instance of the Sciences, is to be found in Engels, *Nodal Point No. 2*, the instance of Politics, is not, despite his mention of tendency struggles in philosophy. In other words, Lenin is not just a commentator on Engels; he has contributed something new and decisive in what is called the domain of Marxist philosophy: what was *missing* from Engels.

One more word and we are through. For the knowledge of this double representation of philosophy is only the hesitant beginning of a *theory of philosophy*, but it really is such a beginning. No one will dispute the fact that this theory is an embryonic one, that it has hardly even been outlined in what we thought was a mere polemic. At least these suggestions of Lenin's, if accepted, have the unexpected result that they *displace the question into a problem*, and remove what is called Marxist philosophy from the rumination of a philosophical practice which has always and absolutely predominantly been that of the *denegation* of its real practice.

That is how Lenin responded to the prophecy in the XIth Thesis, and he was the first to do so, for no one had done it before him, not even Engels. He himself responded in the 'style' of his philosophical practice. A wild practice [*une pratique sauvage*] in the sense in which Freud spoke of a wild analysis, one which does not provide the theoretical credentials for its operations and raises screams from the philosophy of the 'interpretation' of the world, which might be called the philosophy of *denegation*. A wild practice, if you will, but what did not begin by being wild?

The fact is that this practice is a *new* philosophical practice: *new* in that it is no longer that rumination which is no more than the practice of denegation, where philosophy, constantly intervening 'politically' in the disputes in which the real destiny of the sciences is at stake, between the scientific that they install and the ideology that threatens them, and constantly intervening 'scientifically' in the struggle in which the fate of the classes is at stake, between the scientific that assists them and the ideological that threatens them – none the less stubbornly denies in philosophical 'theory' that it is intervening in these ways: *new* in that it is a practice which has renounced denegation, and, knowing what it does, *acts according to what it is.*

If this is indeed the case, we may surely suspect that it is no accident that this unprecedented effect was induced by Marx's *scientific* discovery, and thought by a *proletarian political* leader. For if philosophy's birth was induced by the first science in human history, this happened in Greece, in a class society, and knowing just how far class exploitation's effects may stretch, we should not be astonished that these effects, too, took a form which is classical in class societies, in which the ruling classes *denegate* the fact that they rule, the form of a philosophical denegation of philosophy's domination by politics. We should not be astonished that only the scientific knowledge of the mechanisms of class rule and all their effects, which Marx produced and Lenin applied, induced the extraordinary displacement in philosophy that shatters the phantasms of the denegation in which philosophy tells itself, so that men will believe it and so as to believe it itself, that it is above politics, just as it is above classes.

Only with Lenin, then, could the prophetic sentence in the XIth Thesis on Feuerbach at last acquire body and meaning. (Until now) 'the philosophers have interpreted the world in various ways; the point is to change it'. Does this sentence promise a new *philosophy*? I do not think so. Philosophy will not be suppressed: philosophy will remain philosophy. But knowing what its practice is and knowing what it is, or beginning to know it, it can be slowly transformed by this knowledge. Less than ever can we say that Marxism is a new philosophy: a philosophy of praxis. At the heart of Marxist theory, there is a science: a quite unique science, but nevertheless a science. What is new in Marxism's contribution to philosophy is a new *practice of philosophy. Marxism is not a (new) philosophy of praxis, but a (new) practice of philosophy.*

This new practice of philosophy can transform philosophy, and in addition it can to some extent *assist* in the transformation of the world. Assist only, for it is not theoreticians, scientists or philosophers, nor is it 'men', who make history – but the 'masses', i.e. the classes allied in a single class struggle.

February 1968

APPENDIX

To avoid any misunderstanding of the meaning of this condemnation of philosophy teachers and of the philosophy they teach, attention should be paid to the date of the text and to certain of its expressions. Echoing Dietzgen, Lenin condemns philosophy teachers *as a mass*, not all philosophy teachers without exception. He condemns their philosophy, but he does not condemn philosophy itself. He even recommends the *study* of their philosophy, so as to be able to define and pursue a different practice from theirs in philosophy. A triple observation, therefore, in which in the end the date and circumstances change nothing of substance.

1. Philosophy teachers are teachers, i.e. intellectuals employed in a given education system and subject to that system, performing, as a mass, the social function of inculcating the 'values of the ruling ideology'. The fact that there may be a certain amount of 'play' in schools and other institutions, which enables individual teachers to turn their teaching and reflection against these established 'values', does not change the *mass* effect of the philosophical teaching function. Philosophers are intellectuals and therefore petty bourgeois, subject as a mass to bourgeois and petty-bourgeois ideology.

2. That is why the ruling philosophy, whose representatives or supports the mass of philosophy teachers are, even in their 'critical' freedom, is subject to the ruling ideology, defined by Marx from *The German Ideology* onwards as the ideology of the ruling class. This ideology is dominated by idealism.

3. This situation, shared by those petty-bourgeois intellectuals, the philosophy teachers, and by the philosophy they teach or reproduce in their own individual form, does not mean that it is impossible for certain intellectuals to escape the constraints that dominate the mass of intellectuals, and, if philosophers, to adhere to a materialist philosophy and a revolutionary theory. The *Communist Manifesto* itself evoked this possibility. Lenin returns to it, adding that the collaboration of these intellectuals is indispensable to the workers' movement. On 7 February 1908 he wrote to Gorky:

> The significance of the intellectuals in our Party is declining; news comes from all sides that the intelligentsia is *fleeing* the Party. And a good riddance to these scoundrels. The Party is purging itself from petty-bourgeois dross. The workers are having a bigger say in things. The role of the worker-professionals is increasing. All this is wonderful.[30]

Gorky, whose co-operation Lenin was asking for, protested, so Lenin replied on 13 February 1908:

> I think that some of the questions you raise about our differences of opinion are a sheer misunderstanding. Never, of course, have I thought of 'chasing away the intelligentsia', as the silly syndicalists do, or of denying its necessity for the workers' movement. There can be no divergence between us on any of *these* questions.

On the other hand, in the same letter, the philosophical divergencies persist: 'It is in regard to materialism as a world outlook that I think I disagree with you in substance.'[31] This is hardly surprising, for Gorky was pleading the cause of empirio-criticism and neo-Kantianism.

---

30. *Collected Works*, vol.34, p. 379. [Ed.]
31. Ibid., pp. 385–6. [Ed.]

5

Is it Simple to be a Marxist in Philosophy?*

*Est-il simple d'être marxiste en philosophie?, La Pensée 183, October 1975.
Translated by Grahame Lock.

The following text contains the main arguments with which Louis Althusser accompanied his submission, at the University of Picardy, of certain of his earlier Writings[1] for the degree of doctorat d'État.

1. *Montesquieu: Politics and History* (1959) (in *Montesquieu, Rousseau, Marx,* London 1982, pp. 9–109); Ludwig Feuerbach, *Manifestes philosophiques. Textes choisis (1839–1845)*, ed. and trans. Louis Althusser (Paris 1960); *For Marx* (1965) (London 1979); 'Part I: From *Capital* to Marx's Philosophy' and 'Part II: The Object of *Capital*', in *Reading Capital* (1965) (London 1979, pp. 11–198). [Ed.]

The dialectical form of exposition is only correct when it knows its limits.

> Marx, *A Contribution to the Critique of Political Economy*

I think that I shall neither surprise nor upset anyone when I confess that I wrote none of these texts – the little *Montesquieu*, the articles in *For Marx*, the two chapters in *Reading Capital* – with a view to presenting them as a university thesis. It is, however, true that twenty-six years ago, in 1949–50, I did place before M. Hyppolite and M. Jankélévitch a project for a *grande thèse* (as it used to be called) on politics and philosophy in the eighteenth century in France with a *petite thèse* on Jean-Jacques Rousseau's *Second Discourse.* And I never really abandoned this project, as my essay on Montesquieu shows. Why do I mention this point? Because it concerns the texts placed before you. I was already a Communist, and I was therefore trying to be a Marxist as well – that is, I was trying, to the best of my ability, to understand what Marxism *means.* Thus I intended this work on philosophy and politics in the eighteenth century as a necessary propaedeutic to an understanding of Marx's thought. In fact, I was already beginning to practise philosophy in a certain way, a way which I have never abandoned.

First of all I was beginning to make use of the eighteenth-century authors as a *theoretical detour*, a process which seems to me indispensable not only to the understanding of a philosophy but to its very existence. A philosophy does not make its appearance in the world as Minerva appeared to the society of Gods and men. It exists only in so far as it occupies a position, and it occupies this position only in so far as it has conquered it in the thick of an already occupied world. It therefore exists only in so far as this conflict has made it something distinct, and this distinctive character can be won and imposed only in an indirect way, by a detour involving ceaseless study of other, existing positions. This detour is the form of the conflict which determines what side a philosophy takes in the battle and on the *Kampfplatz* (Kant), the battle-field which is philosophy. Because if the philosophy of philosophers is this perpetual war (to which Kant wanted to put an end by introducing the everlasting peace of his own philosophy), then no philosophy can exist within this theoretical relation of force except in so far as it marks itself off from its opponents and lays siege to that part of the positions which they have had to occupy in order to guarantee their power over the enemy whose impress they bear.

If – as Hobbes says, speaking perhaps to empty benches, and with reference as much to philosophy as to the society of men – war is a generalized state, and leaves nowhere in the world for a shelter, and if it produces its own condition as its own result, which means that every war is essentially *preventive*, it is possible to understand that the war of philosophies, in which systems come into conflict, presupposes the preventive strike of positions against one another, and thus the necessary use by a philosophy of a detour via other philosophies in order to define and defend its own positions. If philosophy is, in the last instance, class struggle at the level of theory, as I have recently argued, then this struggle takes the form, proper to philosophy, of theoretical demarcation, detour and production of a distinctive position. To prove it, I need only refer, aside from the whole of philosophical history, to Marx himself, who was able to define himself only by reference to Hegel and by marking himself off from Hegel. And I think that, from afar, I have followed his example, by allowing myself to refer back to Spinoza in order to understand why Marx had to refer back to Hegel.

Of course this conception of philosophy as struggle – and, in the last instance, as class struggle in theory – implied a reversal of the traditional relation between philosophy and politics. So I went to work on a study of political philosophers and 'ordinary' philosophers, from Machiavelli to Hegel, via Hobbes, Spinoza, Locke, Montesquieu, Rousseau and Kant. I claimed that it was necessary to get rid of the suspect division between philosophy and politics which at one and the same time treats the political figures as inferior – that is, as non-philosophers or Sunday-afternoon philosophers – and also implies that the political positions of philosophers must be sought *exclusively* in the texts in which they talk explicitly about politics. On the one hand I was of the opinion that every political thinker, even if he says almost nothing about philosophy, like Machiavelli, can nevertheless be considered a philosopher in a strong sense; on the other hand I held that every philosopher, even if he says almost nothing about politics, like Descartes, can nevertheless be considered a political thinker in a strong sense, because the politics of philosophers – that is, the politics which make philosophies what they are – are something quite different from the political ideas of their authors. For if philosophy is in the last instance class struggle at the level of theory, the politics which constitute philosophy (like the philosophy which supports the thought of political thinkers) cannot be identified with such and such an episode of the political struggle, nor even with the political inclinations of the authors. The politics which constitute philosophy bear on and revolve around a quite different question: *that of the ideological hegemony of the ruling class*, whether it is a question of organizing it, strengthening it, defending it or fighting against it. Here I am using formulae which I was not earlier in a position to put forward. But if I may say so, I was little by little discovering, as I challenged some accepted ideas, something resembling what I later called a 'new practice of philosophy', and having discovered the need for this new practice, I immediately started, for better or worse, to put it into practice – with the result, in any case, that it did later provide me with a special way of approaching Marx.

If I seemed to abandon this eighteenth-century theoretical propaedeutic, which in fact continued to inspire me, it was certainly not exclusively for personal reasons. What are called circumstances – those which I mention in the Preface to *For Marx*, what after the Twentieth Congress of the CPSU was baptized by the name (without a concept) of the 'personality cult', together with the rightist interpretations which then engulfed Marxism, celebrating or exploiting liberation or the hope of its coming in philosophies of man, of his freedom, of his designs, of transcendence, etc. – these circumstances obliged me to throw myself into the battle. Keeping everything in proportion, you might say that like the young Marx, writing for the *Rheinische Zeitung*, who was 'forced to give an opinion on some practical questions' (the theft of wood or the Prussian censorship), I too was soon forced – on pain of being misunderstood on account of my silence – to 'give an opinion' on some burning questions of Marxist theory. The occasion for me to do so was accidental; that is, it happened that in 1960 I had to write a simple review, for the journal *La Pensée*, of an international collection of articles on the young Marx.[2] This review became a counterattack, which did not simply take the accepted theses to task but attacked them from the flank; thus I displaced the ground of the debate and to this end proposed a certain number of theses which since that time I have continued to argue, to work on and then to rectify.

The reason I recall these circumstances is that I want to make a second remark about the polemical or – to put it bluntly – the political character of my philosophical essays. Those essays which are now placed before you had to declare openly that struggle is at the heart of every philosophy. Of course, what I have just said should make it clear that they are not made up of politics in the raw, since they are philosophical, nor are they simply polemical, a war of words, since they come out of a

---

2. 'On the Young Marx', *For Marx*, pp. 49–86. [Ed.]

reasoned argument, and because the whole meaning of the effort is to put forward and defend the simple idea that a Marxist cannot fight, in what he writes or in what he does, *without thinking out the struggle*, without thinking out the conditions, the mechanisms and the stakes of the battle in which he is engaged and which engages him. These texts are thus explicit interventions in a definite conjuncture: political interventions in the existing world of Marxist philosophy, directed at one and the same time against dogmatism and the rightist critique of dogmatism; and also philosophical interventions in politics, against economism and its humanist 'appendix'. But since they appealed to the history of the labour movement and to Marx, they could not be reduced to a simple commentary on the conjuncture. And I want to say this: whatever might be thought about its weaknesses and its limits, this philosophical intervention was the work of a member of the Communist Party, acting – even if I was at first isolated, even if I was not always listened to, even if I was then and still am criticized for what I said – within the labour movement and for it; thus the work of a militant trying to take politics seriously in order to think out its conditions, limits and effects within theory itself, trying in consequence to define the line and forms of intervention. It cannot be denied that such an initiative involved great efforts and risks. And since I am talking about risks, I may be allowed to talk about one of them (leaving the others undiscussed), the one which concerns the theoretical *position* of my essays.

Here it is. In the debate in which I became involved, I chose, with respect to *certain* politically and theoretically strategic points, to defend radical theses. These, literally stated, looked paradoxical and even theoretically provocative. Two or three examples, to illustrate this choice.

I argued and wrote that 'theory is a practice', and proposed the category of theoretical practice, a scandalous proposal in some people's eyes. Now this thesis, like every thesis, has to be considered in terms of its effect in drawing a demarcation line – that is, in defining a position of opposition. Its first effect was, *in opposition to all forms of pragmatism*, to justify the thesis of the relative autonomy of theory and thus the right of Marxist theory not to be treated as a slave to tactical political decisions, but to be allowed to develop, in alliance with political and other practices, without betraying its own needs. But at the same time this thesis had another effect, *in opposition to the idealism of pure theory*, of stamping theory with the materialism of practice.

Another radical formulation: the internal character of the criteria of validation of theoretical practice. I was able to cite Lenin, who himself put forward this provocative thesis (among so many others): 'Marx's theory is all-powerful because it is true'[3] (it is not because it is verified by its successes and failures that it is true, but because it is true that it is verifiable by its successes and failures). But I brought in other arguments: that mathematics does not require the application of its theorems in physics and chemistry in order to prove it; that the experimental sciences do not require the technical application of their results in order to prove them. For demonstration and proof are the product of definite and specific material and theoretical apparatuses and procedures, internal to each science. There again it is the relative autonomy of theory which was at stake, not this time in opposition to theoretical idealism but in opposition to the pragmatic and empiricist lack of discrimination which made it impossible to distinguish practices from one another, like the cows in the Hegelian night.

One last example: I argued the thesis of Marx's theoretical anti-humanism. A precise thesis, but one whose precise meaning some people did not want to understand, and which roused against me all the world's bourgeois and social-democratic ideology, even within the international labour movement. Why did I take up such radical positions? I shall not shelter behind the argument of manifest ignorance, which can still be useful, but at the proper time. I want first of all to defend the principle of taking up these radical positions, because obviously they were met with cries of dogmatism, speculation, scorn for practice, for the concrete, for man, etc. This indignation was not without a certain piquancy.

For my part, since I was not unaware of the relation which I mentioned above between philosophy and politics, I remembered Machiavelli, whose rule of Method, rarely stated but always practised, was that one must think *in extremes*, which means within a position from which one states borderline theses, or, to make the thought possible, one occupies the place of the impossible. What does Machiavelli do? In order to change something in his country's history, therefore in the minds of the readers whom he wants to provoke into thought and so into volition, Machiavelli explains, off-stage as it were, that one must rely on one's own strength – that is, in fact, *not rely on anything*, neither on an existing State nor on an existing Prince, but on the nonexistent impossibility: a new Prince in a new principality.[4]

I found an echo of and a basis for this argument in Lenin. He, of course, a few years after *What is to be Done?*, in response to certain

---

3. 'The Three Sources and Component Parts of Marxism', *Collected Works*, vol.19, Moscow 1963, p. 23 (translation modified). [Ed.]

4. Althusser's interpretation of Machiavelli may be consulted in 'Machiavelli's Solitude' (1977), *Economy and Society*, vol.17, no.4, November 1988. [Ed.]

criticisms which had been made of his formulae, replied in the form of
the theory of the bending of the stick.[5] When a stick is bent in the wrong
direction, said Lenin, it is necessary, if you want to put matters right –
that is, if you want to straighten it and keep it straight – to grasp it and
bend it durably in the opposite direction. This simple formula seems to
me to contain a whole theory of the effectiveness of speaking the truth, a
theory deeply rooted in Marxist practice. Contrary to the whole
rationalist tradition, which requires only a straight, true idea in order to
correct a bent, false idea, Marxism considers that ideas have a historical
existence only in so far as they are taken up and incorporated in the
materiality of social relations. Behind the relations between simple ideas
there thus stand relations of force, which place certain ideas in power
(those which can be schematically called the ruling ideology) and hold
other ideas in submission (which can be called the oppressed ideology),
until the relation of force is changed. It follows that if you want to
change historically existing ideas, even in the apparently abstract domain
called philosophy, you cannot content yourself with simply preaching
the naked truth, and waiting for its anatomical obviousness to 'enlighten'
minds, as our eighteenth-century ancestors used to say: you are forced,
since you want to force a change in ideas, to recognize the force which is
keeping them bent, by applying a counterforce capable of destroying
this power and bending the stick in the opposite direction so as to put
the ideas right.

All this outlines the logic of a social process whose scope is obviously
wider than any written text. But in a written text like *What is to be
Done?* the only form which this relation of forces can take is its
presence, its recognition and its anticipation in certain radical formulae,
which cause the relation of force between the new ideas and the
dominant ideas to be felt in the very statement of the theses themselves.
If I might, in my own modest way, allow myself to be inspired and
empowered by these examples, I would say: yes, I did consciously
confront and deal with the relation between ideas as a relation of force,
and yes, I did consciously 'think in extremes' about some points which I
considered important and bend the stick in the opposite direction. Not
for the pleasure of provocation, but to alert my readers to the existence
of this relation of forces, to provoke them in this connection and to
produce definite effects – not in function of some belief in the omnipotence of theory, for which I have been reproached by certain 'head-
masters' of the school of philosophy, but on the contrary in the materialist

---

5. See Lenin's 1907 Preface to the collection *Twelve Years, Collected Works*, vol.13,
Moscow 1962, pp. 94–113. [Ed.]

knowledge of the weakness of theory left to itself – that is, in the consciousness of the conditions of force which theory must recognize and to which it must defer if it is to have a chance of transforming itself into a real power.

As a proof of what I have been saying, I would be happy, when the opportunity offers itself, to argue the point that this relation of force, counterbending and bending, this *extremism* in the formulation of theses, belongs quite properly to philosophy, and that even if they did not admit as much, as Lenin did in passing and from behind the shelter of a common maxim, the great philosophers always practised it, whether they hid this fact behind an idealist disclaimer or brought it out into the full light of day in their treatment of the 'scandals' of materialism.

It remains true that in bending the stick in the opposite direction, you run a risk: of bending it too little, or too much, the risk which every philosopher takes. Because in this situation, in which social forces and interests are at stake but can never be untangled with absolute certainty, there is no court of final appeal. If you intervene too abruptly, you run the risk of not immediately finding the mark; if you bend the stick too little or too much, you run the risk of finding yourself being pulled back into error. This, as you perhaps know, is what I publicly admitted to have happened to some extent in my own case, when I recognized in 1967 and explained more recently in the *Elements of Self-Criticism*[6] that my writings of 1965, which have been laid before you, were impaired by a theoreticist tendency and just a little compromised by a flirt with structuralist terminology. But to be able to explain these failings I needed the perspective of time – not just a ten-year interval but the experience of the effects caused by my writings, of further work and of self-criticism. It has been written: you need to understand. I would add: especially to understand what you yourself have written.

Before discussing the detailed argument of my essays, a word about their very general objective.

This objective can be made out from the titles of my books: *For Marx, Reading Capital.* For these titles are slogans. I think that I can speak here for figures of my generation, who have lived through Nazism and Fascism, the Popular Front, the Spanish War, the War and the Resistance, and the Stalin period. Caught up in the great class struggles of contemporary history, we had engaged ourselves in the struggles of the labour movement and wanted to become Marxists. Now it was not easy to be a Marxist and to find one's feet within Marxist theory, even

---

6. See *Essays in Self-Criticism*, London 1976, pp. 101-61. [Ed.]

after the Twentieth Congress, since the dogmatism of the preceding period lived on, now in conjunction with its counterpoint, all that 'Marxist' philosophical twaddle about man. And since this twaddle was based on the letter of the works of the young Marx, it was necessary to return to Marx in order to throw a little light on ideas clouded over by the trials of history. I do not want to lay stress on the political importance of this operation; it did, however, have something original about it, for which I have never been forgiven, in that it criticized dogmatism not from the right-wing positions of humanist ideology but from the left-wing positions of theoretical anti-humanism, anti-empiricism and anti-economism. I was not alone in the operation: as I later found out, others – not only Della Volpe in Italy but also certain young Soviet thinkers whose writings have not been widely published – had also, in their own manner, set out on the same path. We were attempting to give back to Marxist theory, which had been treated by dogmatism and by Marxist humanism as the first available ideology, something of its status as a theory, a revolutionary theory. Marx had expressed the hope, in the Preface to *Capital,* for 'a reader who is willing ... to think for himself'.[7] In order to try to understand what Marx had thought, the very least we had to do was to return to Marx and 'think for ourselves' about what he had thought.

Thus, in opposition to the subversion to which Marx's thought had been subjected, it seemed to me indispensable to lay stress on one simple idea: the unprecedented and revolutionary character of this thought. *Unprecedented,* because Marx had – in a work of conceptual elaboration which begins with *The German Ideology* and culminates in *Capital* – founded what we might call, as a first approximation, the science of history. *Revolutionary,* because this scientific discovery which armed the proletariat in its struggle caused a complete upset in philosophy: not only by causing philosophy to revise its categories in order to bring them into line with the new science and its effects, but also and above all by giving philosophy the means, in the form of an understanding of its real relation to the class struggle, of taking responsibility for and transforming its own practice.

It is this innovation, this radical difference between Marx and his predecessors, that I wanted not only to bring out but also to clarify and if possible to explain, because I considered it to be politically and theoretically *vital* for the labour movement and its allies, and still do consider it vital *for this difference to be grasped.* To this end I had to establish myself at the level of the new philosophy, produced by Marx in

---

7. *Capital,* vol.1, Harmondsworth 1976, p. 90. [Ed.]

the course of his scientific revolution, and in a movement of thought close to Spinoza and sanctioned by Marx to try to grasp this difference on the basis of the newly acquired truth. But to the same end I had to grasp the philosophy capable of grasping the difference – that is, I had to obtain a clear view of Marx's own philosophy. Now everyone knows that the mature Marx left us nothing in this line except the extraordinary 1857 Introduction to *A Contribution to the Critique of Political Economy* and the intention, which he never realized, of writing a dozen pages on the dialectic. No doubt Marx's philosophy is, as Lenin said, contained in *Capital*[8] but in a practical state, just as it is also contained in the great struggles of the labour movement. I decided that it had to be extracted, and basing myself on the available fragments and examples, I tried to give it a form resembling its concept. That is why the question of Marxist philosophy naturally occupied the centre of my attention. I did not make it the centre of the world, I did not raise philosophy to the level of command, but I had to make this philosophical detour in order to grapple with the radical character of Marx's work.

This conviction has always been with me. I would now formulate it differently from in *For Marx* and *Reading Capital*, but I consider that I made no mistake in locating philosophy as the place from which Marx can be understood, because that is where his *position* is summed up.

The 'Last Instance ...'

I now suggest to you that my essays should be approached by three rough paths which travel across them and intersect.

I will first take the path of the 'last instance'.

We know that Marx and Engels argued the thesis of the determination by the economy *in the last instance.* This little phrase, which seems like nothing at all, in fact upsets the whole ruling conception of society and of history. Not enough attention has been paid to the figure or metaphor in which Marx presents his conception of a society in the Preface to the 1859 *Contribution.*[9] This figure is that of a *topography*: that is, of a spatial apparatus which assigns positions in space to given realities.

The Marxist topography presents society in terms of the metaphor of an edifice whose upper floors rest, as the logic of an edifice would have

---

8. 'Plan of Hegel's Dialectics [Logic]', *Philosophical Notebooks, Collected Works*, vol.38, Moscow 1961, p. 319. [Ed.]

9. See Marx, *Early Writings*, Harmondsworth 1975, pp. 425–6. [Ed.]

it, on its foundation. The foundation is in German *die Basis* or *die Struktur*, which is traditionally translated as *base* or more often *infrastructure*: it is the economy, the unity of the productive forces and relations of production under the dominance of the relations of production. From the base of the ground floor rise the upper floor or floors of the *Überbau*, in translation the legal-political and ideological superstructure.

A simple image, it will be said, representing realities. Agreed: but it also *distinguished these realities*, which is very important – for example by placing positive law, which Hegel includes within civil society, in the category of the superstructure, and thus distinguishing something very different from simple realities: their *efficacy* and its *dialectic.*

When Marx says that the base or infrastructure is determinant in the last instance, he implies that what it determines is the superstructure.

For example:

The specific economic form in which unpaid surplus labour is pumped out of the direct producers determines the relationship of domination and servitude, as this grows directly out of production itself and reacts back on it in turn as a determinant.[10]

But the determination of which Marx is thinking here is determination only *in the last instance.* As Engels wrote (in a letter to Bloch):

According to the materialist conception of history, the *ultimately* determining element in history is the production and reproduction of real life. More than this neither Marx nor I have ever asserted. Hence if somebody twists this into saying that the economic element is the *only* determining one, he transforms that proposition into a meaningless, abstract, senseless phrase.[11]

---

10. *Capital,* vol.3, Harmondsworth 1981, p. 927. Marx continues:

On this is based the entire configuration [*Gestaltung*] of the economic community arising from the actual relations of production, and hence also its specific political form [*Gestalt*]. It is in each case the direct relationship of the owners of the conditions of production to the immediate producers – a relationship whose particular form naturally corresponds always to a certain level of development of the type and manner [*Art und Weise*] of labour, and hence its social productive power – in which we find the innermost secret [*innerste Geheimnis*], the hidden basis [*Grundlage*] of the entire social edifice [*Konstruktion*], and hence also the political form of the relationship of sovereignty and dependence, in short, the specific form of state in each case.

11. Engels continues:

The economic situation is the basis, but the various elements of the superstructure – political forms of the class struggle and its results, such as constitutions established by

In the determination of the topography, the last *instance* really is the *last* instance. If it is *the last one*, as in the legal image which it invokes (court of the last instance), that is because there are *others*, those which figure in the legal-political and ideological superstructure. The mention of the last instance in determination thus plays a double role: it divides Marx sharply off from all mechanistic explanations, and opens up within determination the functioning of different instances, the functioning of a real difference in which the dialectic is inscribed. The topography thus signifies that the determination in the last instance by the economic base can be grasped only within a differentiated, therefore complex and articulated whole (the *'Gliederung'*), in which the determination in the last instance fixes the real difference of the other instances, their relative autonomy and their own mode of reacting on the base itself.

Before drawing the consequences, I would like to underline the decisive theoretical importance of this category of the *'last instance'*, too often considered as a philosophical approximation or popularization. To argue for the determination in the last instance *by the economy* is to mark oneself off from all idealist philosophies of history; it is to adopt a materialist position. But to talk about the determination by the economy *in the last instance* is to mark oneself off from every mechanistic conception of determinism and to adopt a dialectical position. However, when you are working in Hegel's shadow you must be on your guard against the idealist temptations involved in the dialectic. And Marx is on his guard, because when he inscribes the dialectic within the functioning of the instance of a topography, he effectively protects himself from the illusion of a dialectic capable of producing its own material content in the spontaneous movement of its self-development. In submitting the dialectic to the constraints of the topography, Marx is submitting it to the real conditions of its operation, he is protecting it from speculative folly, he is forcing it into a materialist mould, forcing it to recognize that its own figures are prescribed by the material character of its own conditions. I agree that this inscription and this prescription are not in

---

the victorious class after a successful battle, etc., juridical forms, and especially the reflexes of all these real struggles in the brains of the participants, political, legal, philosophical theories, religious views and their further development into systems of dogmas – also exercise their influence upon the course of the historical struggles and in many cases preponderate in determining their *form*.

(Letter to Joseph Bloch, 21 September 1890, *Selected Correspondence*, Moscow 1975, pp. 394–5; translation modified.)

(Note that the French version of Engels's letter renders 'the *ultimately* determining element in history' by 'le facteur déterminant dans l'histoire est, en dernière instance, . . .'– whence the Althusserian category. [Ed.])

themselves sufficient to provide us with the figures of the materialist dialectic in person, but they do save us from at least one temptation: that of seeking these figures ready-made in Hegel.

In this manner we come back to the themes developed in my essays, whose object was to differentiate between Marx and Hegel. I have stated elsewhere what debt Marx owed to Hegel, and also why he was constantly forced to make the detour via Hegel in order to find his own way forward.[12]

Yes, Marx was close to Hegel, but above all *for reasons which are not mentioned,* for reasons which go back further than the dialectic, for reasons which relate to Hegel's critical position in respect to the theoretical presuppositions of classical bourgeois philosophy, from Descartes to Kant. To sum it up in a few words: Marx was close to Hegel in his insistence on rejecting every philosophy of the Origin and of the Subject, whether rationalist, empiricist or transcendental; in his critique of the *cogito*, of the sensualist-empiricist subject and of the transcendental subject, thus in his critique of the idea of a theory of knowledge. Marx was close to Hegel in his critique of the legal subject and of the social contract, in his critique of the moral subject, in short of every philosophical ideology of the Subject, which whatever the variation involved gave classical bourgeois philosophy the means of *guaranteeing* its ideas, practices and goals by not simply reproducing but philosophically elaborating the notions of the dominant legal ideology. And if you consider the grouping of these critical themes, you have to admit that Marx was close to Hegel just in respect to those features which Hegel had openly borrowed from Spinoza, because all this can be found in the *Ethics* and the *Tractatus Theologico-politicus*. These deep-rooted affinities are normally passed over in pious silence; they nevertheless constitute, from Epicurus to Spinoza and Hegel, the premises of Marx's materialism. They are hardly ever mentioned, for the simple reason that Marx himself did not mention them, and so the whole of the Marx–Hegel relationship is made to hang on the dialectic, because this Marx did talk about! As if he would not be the first to agree that you must never judge someone on the basis of his own self-conscious image but on the basis of the whole process which, behind this consciousness, produces it.

I hope I shall be excused for laying so much stress on this point, but it is the key to the solution of very many problems, real or imaginary, concerning Marx's relation to Hegel, and within Marx concerning *the*

---

12. Cf. 'Marx's Relation to Hegel' (1968), *Montesquieu, Rousseau, Marx*, pp. 163–86; and *Elements of Self-Criticism*, pp. 133–41.

relation of the dialectic to materialism. In fact I believe that the question of the Marxist dialectic cannot be properly posed unless the dialectic is *subjected to the primacy of materialism*, and a study is made of what forms this dialectic must take in order to be the dialectic of *this* materialism. From this point of view it is easy to understand how the idea of the dialectic could have imposed itself on a philosophy like that of Hegel, not only because the dramatic turmoil of the French Revolution and its after-effects provided the hard lesson, but also because the dialectic was the only means of thinking within a philosophy which had very good reasons for originally refusing (even if it later transformed and reintroduced them) the use and guarantee of the categories of Origin and Subject. Of course, Hegel did not apply himself to the search for the dialectic only after rejecting Origin and Subject. In a single movement he created the dialectic which he needed to differentiate himself from the classical philosophies, and, to force it to serve his ends, he 'mystified' the dialectic, to use Marx's words.[13] But that does not mean that the Hegelian mystification itself is not witness to a relation constant since the time of Epicurus, and perhaps before him, *between materialism –* which can play its role only by drawing a demarcation line between itself and every philosophy of the Origin, whether of Being, of the Subject or of Meaning – *and the dialectic.* To make the matter clearer in a few words: when you reject the radical origin of things, whatever the figure used, you need to create quite different categories from the classical ones in order to get a grasp on those notions – essence, cause or liberty – whose authority is drawn from this origin. When you reject the category of origin as a philosophical issuing bank, you have to refuse its currency too, and put other categories into circulation: those of the dialectic. That is in outline the profound relation linking the premisses of the materialism to be found in Epicurus, Spinoza and Hegel, which governs not only everything about the dialectic but also the dialectic itself.

It is this which seems to me important, much more than the 'conclusions without premisses' which are the only judgements made by Marx on Hegel and where he raises *only and for its own sake* the question of the dialectic. He does this, of course, in order to recognize in Hegel the merit of having – I quote – 'been the first to express the general movement of the dialectic', which is correct and certainly a rather reserved statement, but also in order to argue, this time without any reservations, that Hegel had 'mystified' it, and that Marx's own dialectic was not only not that of Hegel, but 'its exact opposite'. But we also know that according to Marx it was enough, in order to demystify

---

13. Postface to the Second Edition of *Capital*, vol.1, pp. 102–3. [Ed.]

the Hegelian dialectic, to invert it. I have argued enough in the past
about the fact that this idea of inversion did not do the job and was only
a metaphor for a real materialist transformation of the figures of the
dialectic,[14] about which Marx promised us a dozen pages which he never
wrote. This silence was surely not accidental. It was doubtless a consequence of the need to trace a line back from the conclusions to the
materialist premisses of the dialectic, and on the basis of these premisses
to think out, in the strong sense, the new categories which they imply
and which can be found in operation in *Capital* and in Lenin's writings,
but do not always or do not yet clearly bear their name.

I became involved in this problem when I started to look for the
difference, in their very proximity, between Marx and Hegel. It is quite
obvious that if Marx borrowed from Hegel the word and the idea of the
dialectic, he nevertheless could not possibly have accepted this doubly
mystified dialectic – mystified not only in the idealist attempt to produce
its own material content, but also and above all in the figures which
realize the miracle of its self-incarnation: negation and the negation of
the negation, or *Aufhebung*. Because if the Hegelian dialectic rejects
every Origin – which is what is said at the beginning of the *Logic*, where
Being is immediately identified with Nothingness – it projects this into
the End of a Telos which in return creates, within its own process, its
own Origin and its own Subject. There is no assignable Origin in Hegel,
but that is because the whole process, which is fulfilled in the final
totality, is indefinitely, in all the moments which anticipate its end, its
own Origin. There is no Subject in Hegel, but that is because the
becoming-Subject of substance, as an accomplished process of the
negation of the negation, is the Subject of the process itself. If Marx took
over the idea of the dialectic from Hegel, he not only 'inverted' it in
order to rid it of the pretension or fantasy of self-production, but also
had to transform its figures so that they should cease to produce the
implied effects. Lenin made the point again and again during the years
1918–23 that if socialism does not succeed in transforming petty
commodity production, then as long as it is allowed to exist, petty
commodity production will continue to give rise to capitalism. One
might say, in the same manner: as long as Marxism does not succeed in
transforming the figures of the dialectic mystified by Hegel, these figures
will continue to give rise to Hegelian, mystified effects. Now this *transformation* was not to be found in my head, nor only in the future, but
out in the open in the texts of Marx and Lenin and the practice of the
proletarian class struggle.

---

14. See especially 'Contradiction and Overdetermination' (1962) and 'On the Materialist Dialectic' (1963), *For Marx*, pp. 87–128, 161–218. [Ed.]

I was therefore simply trying to formulate conceptually what already existed in the practical state.

That, to approach the matter from this direction, is why I claimed that Marx did not have the same idea of the nature of a social formation as Hegel, and I believed that I could demonstrate this difference by saying that Hegel thought of society as a *totality*, while Marx thought of it as a complex whole, structured in dominance. If I may be allowed to be a little provocative, it seems to me that we can leave to Hegel the category of *totality*, and claim for Marx the category of the *whole*. It might be said that this is a verbal quibble, but I do not think this is entirely true. If I preferred to reserve for Marx the category of the whole rather than that of the totality, it is because within the totality a double temptation is always present: that of considering it as a pervasive essence which exhaustively embraces all of its manifestations, and – what amounts to the same thing – that of discovering in it, as in a circle or a sphere (a metaphor which makes us think of Hegel once again), a centre which would be its essence.

On this point I believed that I had found an important difference between Marx and Hegel. For Hegel, society, like history, is made up of circles within circles, of spheres within spheres. Dominating his whole conception is the idea of the expressive totality in which all the elements are total parts, each expressing the internal unity of the totality which is only ever, in all its complexity, the objectification-alienation of a simple principle. And in fact, when you read the *Rechtsphilosophie*, you find that Hegel is deploying, in the dialectic of the Objective Spirit which produces them, the spheres of abstract law, of *Moralität* and *Sittlichkeit*, so that each produces the other through the negation of the negation so as to find their truth in the State. There are many differences between them, but since their relation is always one of 'truth', these differences are always affirmed only to be denied and transcended in other differences, and this is possible because in each difference there is already present the in-itself of a future for-itself. And when you read the Introduction to the *Philosophy of History*, you find the same process, one might even say the same procedure: each moment of the development of the Idea exists in its States, which realize a simple principle – the beauty of individuality for ancient Greece, the legal spirit for Rome, etc. And borrowing from Montesquieu the idea that in a historical totality all concrete determinations, whether economic, political, moral or even military, express one single principle, Hegel conceives history in terms of the category of the expressive totality.

For Marx, the differences are real, and they are not only differences in spheres of activity, practices and objects: they are differences in *efficacy*. The last instance operates here in such a way that it explodes

the peaceful fiction of the circle or the sphere. It is not an accident that
Marx abandons the metaphor of the circle for that of the edifice. A
circle is closed, and the corresponding notion of totality presupposes
that one can grasp all the phenomena, exhaustively, and then reassemble
them within the simple unity of its centre. Marx, on the other hand,
presents us with an edifice, a foundation, and one or two upper floors –
exactly how many is not stated. Nor does he say that everything must fall
into these categories, that everything is either infrastructure or superstructure. You could even argue for the idea, essential to *Capital*, that
the Marxist theory of societies and of history implies a whole theory of
their incidental costs and their failures. Marx says only that you must
distinguish, that the distinctions are real, irreducible, that in the order of
determination the share of the base and that of the superstructure are
unequal, and that this inequality or unevenness in dominance is constitutive of the unity of the whole, which therefore can no longer be the
expressive unity of a simple principle all of whose elements would be the
phenomena.

That is why I talked about *a whole*, to make it clear that in the
Marxist conception of a social formation everything holds together, that
the independence of an element is only ever the form of its dependence,
and that the interplay of the differences is regulated by the unity of a
determination in the last instance; but that is why I did not talk about a
totality, because the Marxist whole is complex and uneven, and stamped
with this unevenness by the determination in the last instance. It is this
interplay, this unevenness, which allow us to understand that something
real can happen in a social formation and that through the political class
struggle it is possible to get a hold on real history. I made the point in
passing: no politics have ever been seen in the world which were
inspired by Hegel. For where can you get a hold on the circle when you
are caught in the circle? Formally, the Marxist topography gives an
answer when it says: *this* is what is determinant in the last instance – the
economy, therefore the economic class struggle, extended into the
political class struggle for the seizure of State power – and *this* is how
the class struggle in the base is linked (or is not linked) to the class
struggle in the superstructure. But that is not all. In pointing this out, the
Marxist topography refers any questioner to his place in the historical
process: *this* is the place which you occupy, and *this* is where you must
move to in order to change things. Archimedes wanted only a single
fixed point in order to lift up the world. The Marxist topography names
the place where you must fight because that is where the fight will take
place for the transformation of the world. But this place is no longer a
point, nor is it fixed – it is an articulated system of positions governed by
the determination in the last instance.

All this remains formal, no one will deny it, in the Preface to the *Contribution* to which I have alluded. But the *Communist Manifesto* called things by their names, and *Capital* repeated them. *Capital* is full of examples of the topographical figure. It is through the use of this figure that theoretical determination can become practical decision, because it arranges things in such a way that the workers, to whom Marx was talking, can seize them. The concept which is grasped [*Begriff*] becomes in Marx the theoretical-practical apparatus of a topography, a means of practically grasping the world.

It is easy to see that in this new whole, the dialectic at work is not at all Hegelian. I tried to show this in connection with the question of contradiction, by pointing out that if you take seriously the nature of the Marxist whole and its unevenness, you must come to the conclusion that this unevenness is necessarily reflected in the form of the *overdetermination* or of the *underdetermination* of contradiction. Of course, it is not a question of treating overdetermination or underdetermination in terms of the addition or subtraction of a quantum of determination, a quantum added or subtracted from a pre-existing contradiction – that is, one leading a *de jure* existence somewhere. Overdetermination or underdetermination are not exceptions in respect to a pure contradiction. Just as Marx says that man can be alone only within society, just as Marx says that the existence of simple economic categories is an exceptional product of history, in the same way a contradiction in the pure state can exist only as a determinate product of the impure contradiction.

The effect of this thesis is quite simply to change the reference points from which we look at contradiction. And, in particular, it warns us against the idea of what I have called simple contradiction, or more exactly contradiction in the logical sense of the term, whose terms are two equal entities each simply bearing one of the contrary signs + or −, A or not-A. If I might now go a little further than I did in my first essays, but in the same direction, I should say that contradiction, as you find it in *Capital*, presents the surprising characteristic of being *uneven*, of bringing contrary terms into operation which you cannot obtain just by giving the second a sign obtained by negating that of the first. This is because they are caught up in a *relation of unevenness* which continuously reproduces its conditions of existence just on account of this contradiction. I am talking, for example, about the contradiction within which the capitalist mode of production exists and which, tendentially, condemns it to death, the contradiction of the capitalist *relation of production*, the contradiction which divides classes into classes, in which two quite unequal classes confront each other: the capitalist class and the working class. Because the working class is not the opposite of the capitalist class, it is not the capitalist class negated, deprived of its capital and its powers – and the capitalist class is not the working class plus something else, namely riches and power. They do not share the same history, they do not share the same world, they do not lead the same class struggle, yet they do come into confrontation, and this certainly is a contradiction since the *relation of confrontation reproduces the conditions of confrontation* instead of transcending them in a beautiful Hegelian exaltation and reconciliation.

I think that if you keep in sight this special characteristic of Marxist contradiction – that it is *uneven* – you will come up with some interesting conclusions, not only about *Capital* but also about the question of the struggle of the working class, of the sometimes dramatic contradictions of the labour movement, and of the contradictions of socialism. For if you want to understand this unevenness, you will have to follow Marx and Engels in taking seriously the conditions which make the contradiction uneven – that is, the material and structural conditions of what I have called the structured whole in dominance – and here you will get a glimpse into the theoretical foundations of the Leninist thesis of uneven development. Because in Marx all development is uneven, and here again it is not a question of additions to or subtractions from a so-called even development, but of an essential characteristic. Every development is uneven, because it is contradiction which drives development, and because contradiction is uneven. That is why, alluding to the *Discourse on the Origin of Inequality* by Rousseau, who was the principal theoretician of alienation before Hegel, I once added as a subtitle to my article 'On the Materialist Dialectic' the phrase: 'On the Unevenness of Origins', signifying by the plural, *origins*, that there is no Origin in the philosophical sense of the term, and that every beginning is marked with unevenness.

I have only sketched out a few themes, simply to indicate the critical importance of the thesis of the last instance for understanding Marx. And it is of course true that every interpretation of Marxist theory involves not only theoretical stakes but also political and historical. These theses on the last instance, on the structured whole in dominance, on the unevenness of contradiction, had an immediate principal objective, which governed the way in which they were expressed: that of recognizing and indicating the place and the role of theory in the Marxist labour movement, not just by taking note of Lenin's famous slogan 'Without revolutionary theory there can be no revolutionary movement',[15] but by going into detail in order to free theory from confusions, mystifications and manipulations. But beyond this primary

---

15. *What is to be Done?*, *Collected Works*, vol.5, Moscow 1961, p. 369. [Ed.]

objective, my theses had other, more important aims, bearing on the temptations faced by the labour movement: the temptation of a messianic or critical idealism of the dialectic, which has haunted intellectuals in revolt from the time of the young Lukács and even of the old and new Young Hegelians; the temptation of what I called the poor man's Hegelianism, the evolutionism which has always, in the labour movement, taken the form of economism.

In both cases, the dialectic functions in the old manner of pre-Marxist philosophy as a philosophical guarantee of the coming of revolution and of socialism. In both cases, materialism is either juggled away (in the case of the first hypothesis) or reduced to the mechanical and abstract materiality of the productive forces (in the case of the second hypothesis). In all cases the practice of this dialectic runs up against the implacable test of the facts: the revolution did not take place in nineteenth-century Britain, nor in early twentieth-century Germany; it did not take place in the advanced countries at all, but elsewhere, in Russia, then later in China and Cuba, etc.

How can we understand this displacement of the principal contradiction of imperialism on to the weakest link, and correlatively how can we understand the stagnation in the class struggle in those countries where it appeared to be triumphant, without the Leninist category of uneven development, which refers us back to the unevenness of contradiction and its over- and underdetermination? I am deliberately stressing underdetermination, because while certain people easily accepted a simple supplement to determination, they could not accept the idea of underdetermination – that is, of a threshold of determination which, if it is not crossed, causes revolutions to miscarry, revolutionary movements to stagnate or disappear, and imperialism to rot while still developing, etc. If Marxism is capable of registering these facts, but not capable of understanding them, if it cannot grasp, in the strong sense, the 'obvious' truth that the revolutions which we know are either premature or miscarried, but from within a theory which dispenses with the normative notions of prematurity and of miscarriage – that is, with a normative standpoint – then it is clear that something is wrong on the side of the dialectic, and that it remains caught up in a certain idea which has not yet definitively settled accounts with Hegel.

That is why I think that in order to see more clearly what makes Marx different, one must put into its proper perspective the immediate formulation in which he expressed his relation to the Hegelian dialectic. To do so one must first consider how Marx's materialism is expressed, because the question of the dialectic depends on this. And there is a rather good way of dealing with this problem, which I have just tried to follow: that which uses the category of determination in the last instance.

On the Process of Knowledge

I now want, much more briefly, to take another path across my essays in
order to look at another group of theses developed there on the question
of 'knowledge'.

I cannot hide the fact that in this matter I depended heavily on
Spinoza.[16] I said a moment ago that Marx was close to Hegel in his
critique of the idea of a theory of knowledge, but this Hegelian critique
is already present in Spinoza. What does Spinoza in fact mean when he
writes, in a famous phrase, '*Habemus enim ideam veram* ...'?[17] That we
have a true idea? No: the weight of the phrase lies on the '*enim*'. It is *in
fact* because and only because we have a true idea that we can produce
others, according to its norm. And it is *in fact* because and only because
we have a true idea that we can know that it is true, because it is '*index
sui*'. Where does this true idea come from? That is quite a different
question. But it is a fact that we do have it (*habemus*), and whatever it
may be that produces this result, it governs everything that can be said
about it and derived from it. Thus Spinoza *in advance* makes every
theory of knowledge, which reasons about the *justification* of
knowledge, dependent on the *fact* of the knowledge which we already
possess. And so every question of the Origin, Subject and Justification
of knowledge, which lie at the root of all theories of knowledge, is
rejected. But that does not prevent Spinoza from talking about
knowledge: not in order to understand its Origin, Subject and Justification but in order to determine the process and its moments, the
famous 'three levels', which moreover appear very strange when you
look at them close up, because the first is properly the lived world, and
the last is specially suited to grasping the 'singular essence' – or what
Hegel would in his language call the 'concrete universal' – of the Jewish
people, which is heretically treated in the *Theologico-Political Treatise*.

I am sorry if some people consider, apparently out of theoretical
opportunism, that I thus fall into a heresy, but I would say that Marx –
not only the Marx of the 1857 Introduction, which in fact opposes Hegel
through Spinoza, but the Marx of *Capital*, together with Lenin – is in
fact on close terms with Spinoza's positions. For while they too reject
every theory of the Origin, Subject and Justification of knowledge, *they
too talk* about knowledge. And the fact that Lenin claims for Marxism

16. Althusser's 'detour via Spinoza' is further discussed in *Elements of Self-Criticism*,
pp. 132–41. [Ed.]
17. Spinoza, *On the Improvement of the Understanding*, in *On the Improvement of the
Understanding/The Ethics/Correspondence*, New York 1955, p. 12. [Ed.]

the expression 'theory of knowledge'[18] is not an embarrassment when you realize that he defines it as ... the dialectic. In fact Marx and Lenin talk about knowledge in very general terms, to describe the general aspects of its process. One must be suspicious of those passages in which Marx states such generalities. There is at least one case, among others, with respect to which he did explain himself: that of *'production'*.[19] At one and the same time he outlines the general characteristics of production and yet argues that general production and, *a fortiori*, production in general do not exist, because only particular modes of production exist within concrete social formations. This is one way of saying that everything takes place within the concrete structure of particular processes, but that in order to be able to grasp what is happening you need the help of that minimum of nonexistent generality without which it would be impossible to perceive and understand what does exist. Well, I think that the 1857 Introduction is in this vein. I think that it introduces neither a 'theory of knowledge' nor its surrogate, an epistemology: I think that it only expresses that minimum of generality without which it would be impossible to perceive and understand the concrete processes of knowledge. But just like the general concept of production, the general concept of knowledge is there only to disappear in the concrete analysis of concrete processes: in the complex history of the processes of knowledge.

In the whole of this affair I based myself as closely as possible on Marx's 1857 Introduction, and if I used it to produce some necessary effects of theoretical provocation, I think I did nevertheless remain faithful to it.

I was directly and literally inspired by Marx, who several times uses the concept of the *'production'* of knowledge, to argue my central thesis: the idea of knowledge as *production*. I obviously also had in mind an echo of Spinozist 'production', and I drew on the double sense of a word which beckoned both to labour, practice, and to the display of truth. But essentially – and in order to provoke the reader – I held closely, I would even say mechanically, to the Marxist concept of production, which literally suggests a process and the application of tools to a raw material. I even outbid Marx by presenting a general concept of 'practice', which reproduced the concept of the labour process to be found in *Capital*; and, referring back to theoretical practice, I used and no doubt forced a little Marx's text in order to arrive at the distinction between the three

18. For example, in the *Philosophical Notebooks*, p. 319. [Ed.]
19. See the *Grundrisse*, Harmondsworth 1973, pp. 83–8. [Ed.]

generalities,[20] the first of which functioned as the theoretical raw material, the second as the instruments of theoretical labour, and the third as the concrete-in-thought or knowledge. I admit that Spinoza was involved in this affair, too, because of his 'three levels of knowledge', and the central role of the second: scientific abstraction.

What interested me above all else in Marx's text was his radical double opposition to empiricism and to Hegel. In opposition to empiricism, Marx argued that knowledge does not proceed from the concrete to the abstract but from the abstract to the concrete, and that all this takes place, I quote '*in thought*', while the real object, which gives rise to this whole process, exists outside thought. In opposition to Hegel, Marx argued that this movement from the abstract to the concrete was not a manner of producing reality but of coming to know it. And what fascinated me in all this argument was that *one had to begin with the abstract.* Now Marx wrote that knowledge is '*a product of thinking, of comprehension ... a product of the assimilation and transformation [ein Produkt der Verarbeitung]* of perceptions and images *into concepts*', and also that 'it would seem to be the proper thing *to start with the real and concrete elements ... e.g.* to start in the sphere of economy with population.... Closer consideration shows, however, that this is wrong. *Population is an abstraction.*'[21] I concluded that perceptions and images [*Anschauung und Vorstellung*] were treated by Marx as abstractions, and I attributed to this abstraction the status of the concrete or of experience as you find it in Spinoza's first level of knowledge – that is, in my language, the status of the ideological. Of course I did not say that Generalities II, working on Generalities I, work only on ideological material, because they could also be working on abstractions which are already scientifically elaborated, or on both together. But there did remain this borderline case of a purely ideological raw material, a hypothesis which allowed me to introduce the science/ideology antithesis, and the epistemological break, which Spinoza, long before Bachelard, inserted between his first and second levels of knowledge; and thus I produced a certain number of ideological effects, which, as I have pointed out in my *Elements of Self-Criticism*,[22] were not free of all theoreticism.

But of course, since I suffer from what Rousseau called something like 'the weakness of believing in the power of consequences', I did not

20. Compare 'On the Materialist Dialectic', pp. 182–93, with *Capital*, vol.1, pp. 283–92. [Ed.]
21. Introduction to *A Contribution to the Critique of Political Economy*, Moscow 1971, p. 205; cf. *Grundrisse*, pp. 100–02. [Ed.]
22. *Elements of Self-Criticism*, pp. 119–25. [Ed.]

stop there, but drew an important distinction: that between *the real object and the object of knowledge.*[23] This distinction is contained in the very phrases in which Marx deals with the process of knowledge. As a materialist, he argues that knowledge is knowledge of a real object (Marx says: a real subject), which (I quote) 'remains, after as before, outside the intellect and independent of it'.[24] And a little later, in reference to the subject of investigation, society, he writes (I quote) that it 'must always be envisaged therefore as the precondition of comprehension'. Marx therefore poses, as a precondition of the whole process of knowledge of a real object, the existence of this real object outside thought. But this exteriority of the real object is affirmed at the same time as he affirms the specific character of the process of knowledge, which is 'the product of the assimilation and transformation' of perceptions and images into concepts. And at the end of the process, the thought-concrete, the thought-totality, which is its result, presents itself as knowledge of the real-concrete, of the real object. The distinction between the real object and the process of knowledge is indubitably present in Marx's text, as is the reference to the work of elaboration and the diversity of its moments, and the distinction between the thought-concrete and the real object, of which it gives us knowledge.

I used this text not in order to construct a 'theory of knowledge' but in order to stir something within the world of the blindly obvious, into which a certain kind of Marxist philosophy retreats in order to protect itself from its enemies. I suggested that if all the knowledge which we possess really is knowledge of a real object which remains 'after as before' independent of the intellect, there was perhaps some point in thinking about the interval separating this '*before*' from the '*after*', an interval which is the process of knowledge itself, and in recognizing that this process, defined by the 'work of elaboration' of successive forms, was inscribed precisely, from beginning to end, in a transformation which bears not on the real object[25] but only on its stand-ins: first of all on the perceptions and images, then on the concepts which come out of them. Thus I arrived at my thesis: if the process of knowledge does not transform the real object, but only transforms its perception into concepts and then into a thought-concrete, and if all this process takes place, as Marx repeatedly points out, '*in thought*', *and not in the real*

---

23. See, for example, *Reading Capital*, pp. 40–43. [Ed.]

24. Introduction to *A Contribution to the Critique of Political Economy*, p. 207 (translation modified); cf. *Grundrisse*, p. 101. [Ed.]

25. 'That is, so long as the intellect adopts a purely speculative, purely theoretical attitude' (Marx). He distinguishes between the theoretical attitude (*knowledge* of the real object) and the practical attitude (*transformation* of the real object).

object, this means that, with regard to the real object, in order to know it, 'thought' operates on the transitional forms which designate the real object in the process of transformation in order finally to produce a concept of it, the thought-concrete. I referred to the set of these forms (including the last one) produced by this operation in terms of the category 'object of knowledge'. In the movement which causes the spontaneous perceptions and images to become the concept of the real object, each form does indeed relate to the real object, but without becoming confused with it. But neither can the thought-concrete which is finally produced be confused with the real, and Marx attacks Hegel precisely for allowing this confusion to take place. Once again Spinoza came to mind, and the memory of his haunting words: the idea of a circle is not the circle, the concept of a dog does not bark – in short, you must not confuse the real thing and its concept.[26]

Of course, if this necessary distinction is not solidly supported it may lead to nominalism, even to idealism. It is generally agreed that Spinoza fell into nominalism. But he did in any case take measures to protect himself from idealism, both in developing his theory of a substance with infinite attributes, and in arguing for the parallelism of the two attributes *extension* and *thought*. Marx protects himself in another way, more securely, by the use of the thesis of the *primacy of the real object over the object of knowledge*, and by the *primacy of this first thesis over the second: the distinction between the real object and the object of knowledge*. Here you have that minimum of generality – that is, in the case in question, of materialist theses, which, by drawing a line between themselves and idealism, open up a free space for the investigation of the concrete processes of the production of knowledge. And finally, for whoever wants to make the comparison, this thesis of the distinction between real object and object of knowledge 'functions' in a very similar manner to Lenin's distinction between absolute truth and relative truth, and to a very similar purpose.

Lenin wrote:

> You will say that this distinction between relative and absolute truth is indefinite. And I shall reply: it is sufficently 'indefinite' *to prevent science from becoming a dogma in the bad sense of the term*, from becoming dead, frozen, ossified; but at the same time it is sufficiently 'definite' to enable us to *draw a dividing-line in the most emphatic and irrevocable manner* between ourselves

26. See, for example, Spinoza, *On the Improvement of the Understanding*, p. 12; cf. *Reading Capital*, pp. 40–41, 105. [Ed.]

and fideism and agnosticism, between ourselves and philosophical idealism and the sophistry of the followers of Hume and Kant.[27]

Which means, to put it bluntly: our thesis is precise enough not to fall into idealism, precise enough to draw a line between itself and idealism – that is, correct enough in its generality to prevent the living freedom of science from being buried under its own results.

The same is true, keeping everything in proportion, of my thesis on the difference between the real object and the object of knowledge. The stakes were considerable. It was a question of preventing the science produced by Marx from being treated 'as a dogma in the bad sense of the term'; it was a question of bringing *to life* the prodigious work of criticism and elaboration carried out by Marx, without which he would never have been able – to put it in his way, which remains classical – to discover behind the appearance of things, and in diametrical opposition to this appearance, their unrecognized 'intimate relations'. It was a question of getting people to understand and to appreciate the unprece- dented break which Marx had to make with the accepted world of appearances – that is, with the overwhelmingly 'obvious truths' of the dominant bourgeois ideology. And since we were ourselves involved in this matter, it was a question of turning this truth into a living and active truth for us, because we had to break with other 'obvious truths', sometimes couched in Marx's own vocabulary, whose meaning the dominant ideology or deviations in the labour movement had distorted. It was a question of recalling that if, as Lenin said, 'the living soul of Marxism is the concrete analysis of a concrete situation',[28] then know- ledge of the concrete does not come at the beginning of the analysis, it comes *at the end*, and the analysis is possible only on the basis of Marx's concepts, and not on the basis of the immediate, 'obvious' evidence of the concrete – which one cannot do without, but which cannot really be understood from the marks it bears on its face.

Finally – and this was not the least important aspect – it was a question of recalling with Marx that knowledge of reality changes something in reality, because it *adds* to it precisely the fact that *it* is known, though everything makes it appear as if this *addition* cancelled itself out in its result. Since knowledge *of* reality belongs in advance to reality, since it is knowledge *of nothing but* reality, it adds something to

27. *Materialism and Empirio-criticism, Collected Works*, vol.14, Moscow 1962, p. 136 (Althusser's emphasis). [Ed.]

28. *'Kommunismus', Collected Works*, vol.31, Moscow 1966, p. 166. Cf., for exam- ple, *For Marx*, p. 206. [Ed.]

it only on the paradoxical condition of adding *nothing* to it,[29] and once
produced it reverts to it without need of sanction, and disappears in it.
The process of knowledge adds to reality at each step its own knowledge
of that reality, but at each step reality puts it in its pocket, because this
knowledge is its own. *The distinction between object of knowledge and
real object presents the paradox that it is affirmed only to be annulled.
But it is not a nullity*: because in order to be annulled it must be
constantly affirmed. That is normal, it is the infinite cycle of all
knowledge, which adds something to reality – precisely, knowledge of
reality – only to give it back, and the cycle is only a cycle, and therefore
living, *as long as it reproduces itself*, because only the production of new
knowledge keeps old knowledge alive. These things happen more or less
as in Marx's text, which says: living labour must 'add new value to
materials' in order that the value of the 'dead labour' contained in the
means of production should be preserved and transferred to the
product, since (I quote) it is 'by the simple addition of a certain quantity
of labour [that] ... the original values of the means of production are
preserved in the product'.[30]

What is at stake with regard to these theses? Let us take Marxist
science and suppose that political conditions are such that no one works
on it any more, no one is adding any new knowledge. Then the old
knowledge that reality has pocketed is there, within it, in the form of
enormous and dead 'obvious' facts, like machines without workers, no
longer even machines but things. We could no longer in this case be
sure, as Lenin puts it, of preventing science 'from becoming a dogma in
the bad sense of the term, from becoming dead, frozen, ossified'. Which
is another way of saying that Marxism itself risks repeating truths which
are no longer any more than the names of things, when the world is
demanding new knowledge, about imperialism *and* the State *and*
ideologies *and* socialism *and* the labour movement itself. It is a way of
recalling Lenin's astonishing remark that Marx *only laid the foundation
stones* of a theory which we must at all costs develop in every
direction.[31] It is a way of saying: *Marxist theory can fall behind history,
and even behind itself, if ever it believes that it has arrived.*

---

29. Cf. Engels, *Dialectics of Nature* (Moscow 1954, p. 198): 'knowledge of nature just
as it is, *without any foreign addition*' (translation modified). Cf. also the Leninist theory of
reflection.

30. Marx, *Capital*, vol.1, p. 309. [Ed.]

31. See 'Our Programme', *Collected Works*, vol. 4, Moscow 1960, pp. 211–12. [Ed.]

Marx and Theoretical Humanism

I now want, very briefly, to follow one last path across my essays, in
order to test out another provocative thesis: that of Marx's theoretical
anti-humanism. I would say that just for the pleasure of watching the
ideological fireworks with which it was met, I would have had to invent
this thesis if I had not already put it forward.[32]

It is a serious thesis, as long as it is seriously read, and above all as
long as serious attention is paid to one of the two words which make it
up – and not the diabolical one, but the word '*theoretical*'. I said and
repeated that the concept or category of man did not play a theoretical
role in Marx. But unfortunately this term 'theoretical' was ignored by
those who did not want to understand it.

Let us try to understand it.

And, to that end, let me first say a word about Feuerbach, some of
whose texts I translated. No one will deny that Feuerbach's philosophy is
openly a theoretical humanism. Feuerbach says: every new philosophy
announces itself under a new name. The philosophy of modern times,
my philosophy, he says, announces itself under the name 'Man'.[33] And
in fact man, the human essence, is the central principle of the whole of
Feuerbach's philosophy. It is not that Feuerbach is not interested in
nature, because he does talk about the sun and the planets, and also
about plants, dragonflies and dogs, and even about elephants in order to
point out that they have no religion. But he is first of all preparing his
ground, if I may put it that way, when he talks about nature, when he
calmly tells us that each species has its own world, which is only the
manifestation of its essence. This world is made up of objects, and
among them there exists one object *par excellence* in which the essence
of the species is accomplished and perfected: its essential object. Thus
each planet has the sun as an essential object, which is also the essential
object of the planet, etc.

Now that the ground is prepared, we can turn our attention to man.
He is the centre of his world as he is at the centre of the horizon that
bounds it, of his *Umwelt*. There is nothing in his life which is not *his*: or
rather nothing which is not *him*, because all the objects of his world are
his objects only in so far as they are the realization and projection of his
essence. The objects of his perception are only his manner of perceiving
them, the objects of his thought are only his manner of thinking them,

---

32. See especially 'Marxism and Humanism' (1964), *For Marx*, pp. 219–47. [Ed.]
33. 'Preliminary Theses on the Reform of Philosophy' (1842), Thesis 63, in *The Fiery
Brook: Selected Writings of Ludwig Feuerbach*, New York 1972, p. 170. [Ed.]

and the objects of his feelings are only his manner of feeling them. All his objects are essential in so far as what they give him is only ever his own essence. Man is always in man, man never leaves the sphere of man, because – in a simple little phrase which the young Marx took over from Feuerbach, and which provoked some scholarly discussion among the participants in last summer's Hegel Congress in Moscow – the world is the world of man and man is the world of man.[34] The sun and the stars, the dragonflies, perception, intelligence and passion are only so many transitions on the road to the decisive truths: man's specific characteristic, unlike the stars and the animals, is to have his own species, the essence of his species, his whole generic essence as the object, and in an object which owes nothing to nature or religion.

By the mechanism of objectification and inversion, the generic essence of man is given to man, unrecognizable in person, in the form of an exterior object, of another world, in religion. In religion, man contemplates his own powers, his productive forces as powers of an absolute other before whom he trembles and kneels down to implore pity. And this is perfectly practical, because out of it came all the rituals of religious worship, even the objective existence of miracles, which really do take place in this imaginary world since they are only, in Feuerbach's words (and I quote), 'the realization of a desire' [*Wunscherfüllung*].[35] The absolute object which is man thus comes up against the absolute in God, but does not realize that what he comes up against *is himself*. The whole of this philosophy, which does not limit itself to religion but also deals with art, ideology, philosophy, and in addition – a fact which is too little known – with politics, society, and even history, thus rests on the identity of essence between subject and object, and this identity is explained by the power of man's essence to project itself in the self-realization which constitutes its objects, and in the alienation which separates object from subject, makes the object exterior to the subject, reifies it, and inverts the essential relation, since scandalously enough the Subject finds itself dominated by itself, in the form of an Object, God or the State, etc., which is, however, nothing but itself.

It must not be forgotten that this discourse, of which I can only sketch the premises here, had a certain grandeur, since it called for the inversion produced by religious or political alienation to be itself

---

34. Cf. Marx, 'A Contribution to the Critique of Hegel's Philosophy of Right. Introduction', *Early Writings*, p. 244. [Ed.]
35. Ludwig Feuerbach, *The Essence of Christianity*, New York 1957, chapter XIII, pp. 128–9. [Ed.]

inverted; in other words, it called for an inversion of the imaginary domination of the attributes of the human subject; it called on man finally to claim back possession of his essence, alienated in his domination by God and the State; it called on man finally – no longer in the imaginary world of religion, in the 'heaven of the State', or in the alienated abstraction of Hegelian philosophy, but on the earth, here and now, in real society – to realize his true human essence, which is the human community, 'Communism'.[36]

Man at the centre of his world, in the philosophical sense of the term, the originating essence and the end of his world – that is what we can call a theoretical humanism in the strong sense.

It will be agreed, I think, that Marx, having originally espoused Feuerbach's problematic of the generic essence of man and of alienation, later broke with him; and also that this break with Feuerbach's theoretical humanism was a radical event in the history of Marx's thought.

But I would like to go further, for Feuerbach is a strange philosophical personality with this peculiarity (if I may be allowed the expression) of 'blowing the gaff'. Feuerbach is a *confessed* theoretical humanist, but behind him stands a whole row of philosophical precursors who, while they were not so brave as to confess it so openly, were working on a philosophy of man, even if in a less transparent form. Far be it from me to denigrate this great humanist tradition, whose historical merit was to have struggled against feudalism, against the Church, and against their ideologists, and to have given man a status and dignity. But far be it from us, I think, to deny the fact that this humanist ideology, which produced great works and great thinkers, is inseparably linked to the rising bourgeoisie whose aspirations it expressed, translating and transporting the demands of a commercial and capitalist economy sanctioned by a new system of law, the old Roman law revised as bourgeois commercial law. Man as a free subject, free man as a subject of his actions and his thoughts, is first of all man free to possess, to sell and to buy, the subject of law.

I will cut matters short and put forward the claim here that, with some untimely exceptions, the great tradition of classical philosophy has reproduced in the categories of its systems *both* the right of man to know, out of which it has made the subject of its theories of knowledge, from the *cogito* to the empiricist and the transcendental subject; *and* the

36. Cf. Feuerbach, 'Principles of the Philosophy of the Future' (1843), para.59, *The Fiery Brook*, p. 244; and '*The Essence of Christianity* in Relation to *The Ego and its Own*' (1845), translated in *Philosophical Forum*, vol. VIII, 1974, p. 91. [Ed.]

right of man to act, out of which it has made the economic, moral and political subject. I believe, but obviously cannot prove it here, that I have the right to claim the following: in the form of the different subjects in which it is both divided up and disguised, the category of man, of the human essence, or of the human species, plays an essential *theoretical* role in the classical pre-Marxist philosophies. And when I talk about the *theoretical* role which a category plays, I mean that it is intimately bound up with the other categories, that it cannot be cut out of the set without altering the functioning of the whole. I think I can say that, with a few exceptions, the great classical philosophy represents, in implicit form, an indisputably humanist tradition. And if in his own way Feuerbach 'blows the gaff', if he puts the human essence squarely at the centre of the whole thing, it is because he thinks he can escape from the constraint which caused the classical philosophies to hide man behind a division into several subjects. This division – let us say into two subjects, in order to simplify matters – which makes man a subject of knowledge and a subject of action is a characteristic mark of classical philosophy and prevents it from coming out with Feuerbach's fantastic declaration. Feuerbach himself thinks he can overcome this division: for the plurality of subjects he substitutes the plurality of attributes in the human subject; and he thinks he can settle another politically important problem, the distinction between individual and species, in terms of sexuality, which suppresses the individual because it requires that there should always be at least two of them, which already makes a species. I think that it becomes obvious from the manner in which Feuerbach proceeds that even before him the main concern of philosophy was man. The difference was that man was divided up between several subjects, and between the individual and the species.

It follows that Marx's theoretical anti-humanism is much more than a settling of accounts with Feuerbach: it is directed at one and the same time *both* against the existing philosophies of society and history *and* against the classical tradition of philosophy, and thus through them against the whole of bourgeois ideology.

I would say that Marx's theoretical anti-humanism is above all a *philosophical* anti-humanism. If what I have just said has any truth in it, you have only to compare it with what I said earlier about Marx's affinities with Spinoza and Hegel in their opposition to philosophies of the Origin and the Subject to see the implications. And in fact if you examine the texts which might be considered the authentic texts of Marxist philosophy, you do not find the category of man or any of its past or possible disguises. The materialist and dialectical theses which make up the whole of what little Marxist philosophy exists can give rise to all kinds of interpretations. But I do not see how they can allow any humanist interpretation: on the contrary, they are designed to exclude it, as one variety of idealism among others, and to invite us to think in a *quite different* manner.

But we still have not finished, because we still have to understand the theoretical anti-humanism of historical materialism – that is, the elimination of the concept of man as a central concept by the Marxist theory of social formations and of history.

Perhaps we ought first of all to deal with two objections. In fact, we certainly ought to try, because they come up again and again. The first concludes that any Marxist theory conceived in the above manner ends by despising men and paralysing their revolutionary struggle. But *Capital* is full of the sufferings of the exploited, from the period of primitive accumulation to that of triumphant capitalism, and it is written for the purpose of helping to free them from class servitude. This, however, does not prevent Marx, but on the contrary *obliges* him to abstract from concrete individuals and to treat them theoretically as simple 'supports' of relations – and this in the same work, *Capital*, which analyses the mechanisms of their exploitation.[37] The second objection opposes to Marx's theoretical anti-humanism the existence of humanist ideologies which, even if they do in general serve the hegemony of the bourgeoisie, may also, in certain circumstances and within certain social strata, and even in a religious form, express the revolt of the masses against exploitation and oppression. But this raises no difficulty as soon as you realize that Marxism recognizes the existence of ideologies and judges them in terms of the role they play in the class struggle.

What is at stake here is something quite different: the *theoretical* pretensions of the humanist conception to explain society and history, starting out from the human essence, from the free human subject, the subject of needs, of labour, of desire, the subject of moral and political action. I maintain that Marx was able to found the science of history and to write *Capital* only because he broke with the *theoretical* pretensions of all such varieties of humanism.

In opposition to the whole of bourgeois ideology, Marx declares: 'A society is not composed of individuals' (*Grundrisse*), and: 'My analytic method does not start from Man but from the economically given period of society' (*Notes on Wagner's Textbook*). And against the humanist and Marxist socialists who had proclaimed in the *Gotha Programme* that 'labour is the source of all wealth and all culture', he argues: 'The bourgeois have very good grounds for falsely ascribing supernatural creative power to labour'.[38] Can one imagine a more distinct break?

---

37. Cf. Marx's Preface to the first edition of *Capital*, vol.1, p. 92. [Ed.]

The effects can be seen in *Capital.* Marx shows that what in the last instance determines a social formation, and allows us to grasp it, is not any chimerical human essence or human nature, nor man, nor even 'men', but a *relation*, the production relation, which is inseparable from the base, the infrastructure. And, in opposition to all humanist idealism, Marx shows that this relation is not a relation between men, a relation between persons, nor an intersubjective or psychological or anthropological relation, but a double relation: a relation between groups of men concerning the relation between these groups of men and things, the means of production. It is one of the greatest possible theoretical mystifications you can imagine to think that social relations can be reduced to relations between men, or even between groups of men: because this is to suppose that social relations are relations which involve only *men*, whereas actually they also involve *things*, the means of production, derived from material nature.

The production relation is, says Marx, a relation of distribution: it distributes men among classes at the same time and according as it attributes the means of production to a class. The classes are born out of the antagonism in this distribution, which is also an attribution. Naturally, human individuals are parties to this relation, therefore active, but first of all in so far as they are held within it. It is because they are parties to it, as to a freely agreed contract, that they are held within it, and it is because they are held within it that they are parties to it. It is very important to understand why Marx considers men in this case only as 'supports' of a relation, or 'bearers' of a function in the production process, determined by the production relation. It is not at all because he reduces men in their concrete life to simple bearers of functions: he considers them as such in this respect because the capitalist production relation reduces them to this simple function within the infrastructure, in production; that is, in exploitation.

In effect, the man of production, considered as an agent of production, *is only that* for the capitalist mode of production; he is determined as a simple 'support' of a relation, as a simple 'bearer of functions', completely anonymous and interchangeable, for if he is a worker he may be thrown into the street, and if he is a capitalist he may make a fortune or go bankrupt. In all cases he must submit to the law of a production

---

38. Marx, *Grundrisse*, p. 265; 'Marginal Notes on Adolph Wagner's *Lehrbuch der politischen Ökonomie*', translated in *Theoretical Practice* 5, 1972, p. 52; 'Critique of the Gotha Programme', *The First International and After*, Harmondsworth 1974, p. 341 (translation modified). [Ed.]

relation, which is a relation of exploitation, therefore an antagonistic class relation; he must submit to the law of this relation and its effects. If you do not submit the individual concrete determinations of proletarians and capitalists, their 'liberty' or their personality to a theoretical 'reduction', then you will understand nothing of the terrible practical 'reduction' to which the capitalist production relation submits individuals, treating them only as bearers of economic functions and nothing else.

But to treat individuals as simple bearers of economic functions has consequences for the individuals. It is not Marx the theoretician who treats them as such, but the capitalist production relation! To treat individuals as bearers of interchangeable functions is, within capitalist exploitation, which is the fundamental capitalist class struggle, *to mark them* irreparably in their flesh and blood, to reduce them to nothing but appendices of the machine, to cast their wives and children into the hell of the factory, to extend their working day to the maximum, to give them just enough to reproduce themselves, and to create that gigantic reserve army from which other anonymous bearers can be drawn in order to put pressure on those who are in employment, who are lucky enough to have work.

But at the same time it is to create the conditions for an organization of struggle of the working class. For it is the development of the capitalist class struggle – that is, of capitalist exploitation – which itself creates these conditions. Marx continually insisted on the fact that it was the capitalist organization of production which *forcibly taught the working class the lesson of class struggle*, not only in concentrating masses of workers in the place of work, not only in mixing them together, but also and above all in imposing on them a terrible discipline of labour and daily life, all of which the workers suffer only to turn it back in common actions against their masters.

But in order for all this to happen, the workers must be party to and held within *other relations*.

The capitalist social formation, indeed, cannot be reduced to the capitalist production relation alone, therefore to its infrastructure. Class exploitation cannot continue – that is, reproduce the conditions of its existence – without the aid of the superstructure, without the legal-political and ideological relations, which in the last instance are determined by the production relation. Marx did not enter into this analysis, except in the form of a few brief remarks. But from everything he said we can conclude that these relations too treat concrete human individuals as 'bearers' of relations, as 'supports' of functions, to which men are parties only because they are held within them. Thus, legal relations abstract from the real man in order to treat him as a simple 'bearer of the legal relation', as a simple subject of law, capable of owning property, even if the only property which he possesses is that of his naked labour-power. Thus too political relations abstract from the living man in order to treat him as a simple 'support of the political relation', as a free citizen, even if his vote only reinforces his servitude. And thus too the ideological relations abstract from the living man in order to treat him as a simple subject either subjected to or rebelling against the ruling ideas.[39] But all these relations, each of which uses the real man as its support, nevertheless determine and brand men in their flesh and blood, just as the production relation does. And since the production relation is a relation of class struggle, it is the class struggle which in the last instance determines the superstructural relations, their contradiction, and the overdetermination with which they mark the infrastructure.

And just as the capitalist class struggle creates, within production, the conditions of the workers' class struggle, so you can see that the legal, political and ideological relations can contribute to its organization and consciousness, through the very constraints which they impose. For the proletarian class struggle really did learn politics within the framework of bourgeois relations, and via the bourgeois class struggle itself. Everyone knows very well that the bourgeoisie was able to overthrow the old regime, its production relation and its State, only by engaging the popular masses in its struggle, and everyone knows that the bourgeoisie was able to defeat the great landowners only by enrolling the workers in its political battle – afterwards, of course, massacring them. Through its law and its ideology as well as through its bullets and its prisons, the bourgeoisie educated them in the political and ideological class struggle, among other ways by forcing them to understand that the proletarian class struggle had nothing to do with the bourgeois class struggle, and to shake off the yoke of its ideology.

It is here that the last instance, and the contradictory effects which it produces within the 'edifice', intervenes to account for the dialectic of these paradoxical phenomena, which Marx grasps not with the help of the ridiculous concept of man, but with quite different concepts: production relation, class struggle, legal, political and ideological relations. Theoretically, the functioning of the last instance allows us to account for the difference and unevenness between the forms of the class struggle, from the economic struggle to the political and ideological

---

39. For Althusser's theory of ideology, see 'Ideology and Ideological State Apparatuses' (1970), in *Essays on Ideology*, London 1984, pp. 1–60, and 'Note on the ISAs' (1976), *Economy and Society*, vol.12, no.4, 1983, pp. 455–65. [Ed.]

struggle, and thus for the interplay existing between these struggles and for the contradictions existing in this struggle.

Marx's theoretical anti-humanism, as it operates within historical materialism, thus means a refusal to root the explanation of social formations and their history in a concept of man with theoretical pretensions – that is, a concept of man as an *originating subject*, one in whom originate his needs (*Homo oeconomicus*), his thoughts (*Homo rationalis*), and his acts and struggles (*Homo moralis, juridicus* and *politicus*]. For when you begin with man, you cannot avoid the idealist temptation of believing in the omnipotence of liberty or of creative labour – that is, you simply submit, in all 'freedom', to the omnipotence of the ruling bourgeois ideology, whose function is to mask and to impose, in the illusory shape of man's power of freedom, another power, much more real and much more powerful: that of capitalism. If Marx does not start with man, if he refuses to derive society and history theoretically from the concept of man, it is in order to break with this mystification which expresses only an ideological relation of force, based in the capitalist production relation.

Marx therefore starts out from the structural cause producing this effect of bourgeois ideology which maintains the illusion that you should start with man: Marx starts with the given economic formation, and in the particular case of *Capital*, with the capitalist production relation and the relations which it determines in the last instance in the superstructure. And each time he shows that these relations determine and brand men, and how they brand them in their concrete life, and how, through the system of class struggles, living men are determined by the system of these relations. In the 1857 Introduction Marx said: the concrete is a synthesis of many determinations.[40] We might paraphrase him and say: men in the concrete sense are determined by a synthesis of the many determinations of the relations in which they are held and to which they are parties. If Marx does not start out from man, which is an empty idea – that is, one weighed down with bourgeois ideology – it is in order finally to reach living men; if he makes a detour via these relations of which living men are the 'bearers', it is in order finally to be able to grasp the laws which govern both their lives and their concrete struggles.

We should note that at no time does this detour via relations estrange Marx from living men, because at each moment of the process of knowledge – that is, at each moment in his analysis – Marx shows how each relation – from the capitalist production relation, determinant in the last instance, to the legal-political and ideological relations – brands

---

40. See *Grundrisse*, p. 101. [Ed.]

men in their concrete life, which is governed by the forms and effects of the class struggle. Each of Marx's abstractions corresponds to the 'abstraction' imposed on men by these relations, and this terribly concrete 'abstraction' is what makes men into exploited workers or exploiting capitalists. We should also note that the final term of this process of thought, the 'thought-concrete', to which it leads, is that synthesis of many determinations which defines concrete reality.

Marx thus placed himself on class positions, and he had in view the *mass* phenomena of the class struggle. He wanted to aid the working class to understand the mechanisms of capitalist society and to discover the relations and laws within which it lives, in order to reinforce and orientate its struggle. He had no object other than the class struggle; his aim was to help the working class to make revolution and thus finally, under Communism, to suppress the class struggle and classes.

The only more or less serious objection which can be made to the thesis of Marx's theoretical anti-humanism is – I must be honest enough to admit it – related to those texts which, in *Capital,* return to the theme of alienation. I say deliberately: the *theme,* because I do not think that the passages in which this theme is taken up have a *theoretical* significance. I am suggesting that alienation appears there not as a really considered concept but as a substitute for realities which had not yet been thought out sufficiently for Marx to be able to refer to them: the forms, still on the horizon, of organization and struggle of the working class. The theme of alienation in *Capital* could thus be said to function as a substitute for a concept or concepts not yet formed, because the objective historical conditions had not yet produced their object. If this hypothesis is correct, it becomes possible to understand that the Commune, in answering Marx's expectations, rendered the theme of alienation superfluous, as did the whole of Lenin's political practice. In fact alienation disappears from Marx's thought after the Commune, and never appears in Lenin's immense work.

But this problem does not just concern Marxist theory; it also involves the historical forms of its fusion with the labour movement. This problem faces us openly today: we shall have to examine it.

6

The Transformation of Philosophy*

*La Transformación de la filosofia, Universidad de Granada, Granada 1976.
Translated by Thomas E. Lewis.

With your permission, I should like to offer some reflections on Marxist philosophy.

We live in a historical period in which the fact that Marxism – Marxist theory and Marxist philosophy – forms part of our culture does not mean that it is integrated into it. On the contrary, Marxism (dis)functions in our culture, as an element and force of division. That Marxism is an object of conflict, a doctrine defended by some and violently attacked and deformed by others, should surprise no one. Because Marxism – its theory and its philosophy – tables the question of class struggle. And we know full well that behind the theoretical options opened up by Marxism there reverberates the reality of political options and a political struggle.

Nevertheless, despite its great interest, I shall leave aside this aspect of the question and focus on the paradoxical characteristics of Marxist philosophy.

Marxist philosophy presents an internal paradox that is initially bewildering, and whose elucidation turns out to be enigmatic. This paradox can be stated simply by saying: Marxist philosophy exists, yet has never been produced as 'philosophy'. What does this mean? All the philosophies with which we are familiar, from Plato to Husserl, Wittgenstein and Heidegger, have been produced as 'philosophies' and have themselves furnished the proofs of their philosophical existence by means of rational theoretical systems that generate discourses, treatises, and other systematic writings which can be isolated and identified as 'philosophy' in the history of culture. This is not all: such systematic and rational theoretical systems have always furnished the proof of their philosophical existence by means of the knowledge, or the discovery, of an object of their own (whether that object is the idea of the Whole, of Being, of Truth, of the a priori conditions of any knowledge or possible action, of Origin, of Meaning, or of the Being of Being). All known philosophies, then, have presented themselves in the history of our culture as 'philosophies', within the field of the 'history of philosophy', in the form of discourses, treatises, or rational systems that convey the knowledge of an object of their own.

But we must go further. In constituting themselves as 'philosophies' within the field of culture, all known philosophies have carefully differentiated themselves from other discursive forms or other bodies of written work. When Plato writes his dialogues or his didactic works, he takes great care to differentiate them from any other literary, rhetorical or sophistic discourse. When Descartes or Spinoza writes, no one can mistake it for 'literature'. When Kant or Hegel writes, we are not dealing with a moral exhortation, a religious sermon, or a novel. Thus philosophy produces itself by radically distinguishing itself from moral, political, religious or literary genres. But what is most important is that philosophy produces itself, as 'philosophy', by distinguishing itself from the sciences. Here one of the most crucial aspects of the question arises. It seems as if the fate of philosophy is profoundly linked to the existence of the sciences, since the existence of a science is required to induce the emergence of philosophy (as in Greece, when geometry induces Platonic philosophy). And this bond within a common destiny is all the more profound inasmuch as philosophy cannot arise without the guaranteed existence of the rational discourse of a pure science (the case of geometry *vis-à-vis* Plato, analytic geometry and physics *vis-à-vis* Descartes, Newtonian physics *vis-à-vis* Kant, etc.). Philosophy can exist (and be distinct from myth, religion, moral or political exhortation, and the aesthetic) only on the absolute precondition of being itself able to offer a pure rational discourse – that is, a rational discourse whose model philosophy can find only in the rigorous discourse of existing sciences.

But at this point things undergo a surprising inversion: philosophy borrows the model of its own pure rational discourse from existing pure sciences (think of the tradition that runs from 'let no one enter philosophy who is not a geometer', to Spinoza's injunction to 'heed geometry', to Husserl's 'philosophy as a rigorous science'), yet this very same philosophy completely inverts in philosophy its relationship with the sciences. That is, philosophy separates itself rigorously from the real sciences and their objects and declares that it is a science, not in the sense of the vulgar sciences (which know not what they speak of) but rather in the sense of the supreme science, the science of sciences, the science of the a priori conditions of any science, the science of the dialectical logic that converts all real sciences into mere determinations of the intellect, etc. In other words, philosophy borrows the model for its pure rational discourse from the existing sciences. Thus it is subjected to the 'real sciences', which are its condition of possibility. Yet within its own discourse, an inversion occurs: philosophical discourse transforms its act of submission to the sciences and situates itself, as 'philosophy', above the sciences, assuming power over them.

Thus it is that in Plato mathematics is relegated to the subordinate order of the 'dianoia', the hypothetical disciplines, subjected to the anhypothetical disciplines which are the object of philosophy. So it is that in Descartes the sciences are only branches growing from the trunk of metaphysics. So it is that in Kant, Hegel and Husserl philosophy is what has the last word as regards the sciences – that is, it pronounces on their validity, their meaning in the dialectic of pure logic, their meaning in relation to their origin in the concrete transcendental subject. The singular and highly contradictory bond uniting philosophy with the sciences (this operation that transforms philosophy's conditions of existence, and hence those of the sciences, into determinations subordinated to philosophy itself, and through which philosophy, declaring that it alone possesses their truth, installs itself in power over the sciences, which supply the model of its own rational and systematic discourse) – this forms part of the production of philosophy as 'philosophy'. And it leads us to suspect that between the first demarcation we have indicated (via which philosophy distinguishes itself from myth and religion, from moral exhortation and political eloquence, or from poetry and literature) and the second, to which we have just alluded (which concerns the sciences), there exists a profound bond. For if we examine the question closely, we shall come to realize that philosophy is satisfied neither with dominating the sciences nor with 'speaking' the truth of the sciences. Philosophy equally imposes its dominion over religion and morality, politics and aesthetics, and even economics (beginning with Plato, in whom we find a surprising theory of wages, and Aristotle, with his appraisals of 'value' and the 'slave system').

Philosophy thus appears as the science of the Whole – that is to say, of all things. Philosophy enunciates the truth of all external objects, reveals what such objects are incapable of articulating by themselves: it 'speaks', it reveals, their essence. And we may legitimately infer that the formula used with respect to sciences ('let no one enter philosophy who is not a geometer') equally applies to other subjects. In order to speak of religion the philosopher should be moral, in order to speak of politics the philosopher should be a politician, in order to speak of art the philosopher should be an aesthetician, etc. The same type of inversion that we have seen at work on the terrain of the sciences is likewise operative, only mutely, with respect to all other objects – 'objects' which, in a particular way, inhabit the space of philosophy. Except that philosophy allows them to accede to it only on condition that it has previously imposed its dominion over them. In a few words: the production of philosophy as 'philosophy' concerns all human ideas and all human practices, but always subordinating them to 'philosophy' – that is to say, subjecting them to a radical 'philosophical form'. And it is this process of the 'subordination' of human practices and ideas to 'philosophical form' which we see realized in philosophical dialogues, treatises and systems.

It might seem rather simplistic to put the question like this: why does philosophy need to exist as a distinct thing? Why does it need to speak with the utmost care to distinguish itself from the sciences and from every other idea or social practice? Why, philosophy speaks only of them! Let us say that the question is not so simple. That philosophy feels the need to speak, or rather, assumes the responsibility of speaking and consigning what it has to say to separate, identifiable treatises, derives from the fact that, in its profound historical conviction, it considers it has an irreplaceable task to accomplish. This is to speak the Truth about all human practices and ideas. Philosophy believes that no one and nothing can speak in its name, and that if it did not exist, the world would be bereft of its Truth. Because for the world to exist, it is necessary for such truth to be spoken. This truth is *logos*, or origin, or meaning. And since there are common origins between *logos* and speech (between *logos* and *legein*, Truth and discourse, or, put another way, since the specific, stubborn existence of *logos* is not materiality or practice or any other form, but speech, voice, word), there is only one means of knowing *logos*, and hence Truth: the form of discourse. This intimacy between *logos* and speech means that truth, *logos*, can be entirely enclosed or captured and offered up only in the discourse of philosophy. For this reason philosophy can in no way transcend its own discourse. Accordingly, it is clear that its discourse is not a medium, or an intermediary between it and truth, but the very presence of truth as *logos*.

But now the strange paradox of Marxist philosophy is upon us. Marxist philosophy exists, yet it has not been produced as philosophy in the sense we have just analysed. We do not need to go very far to be convinced of this. Apart from the brief sentences, brilliant and enigmatic, of the *Theses on Feuerbach*, which announced a philosophy that never arrived; apart from the scathing philosophical critiques in *The Germany Ideology* directed against the neo-Hegelians, who limited themselves to plunging all philosophy into the misty nothingness of ideology; and apart from the celebrated allusions to Hegel in the Postface to the second German edition of *Capital*, Marx left us no philosophical treatise or discourse. Twice, in two letters, he promised a score or so pages on the dialectic, but they never materialized; we may assume that they were scarcely easy to write. No doubt Engels left us his philosophical critique of Dühring, and Lenin his *Materialism and Empiriocriticism* – another critique. Many elements can doubtless be drawn from a critique, but how is it to be thought? How are we to structure it 'theoretically'? Are we dealing with the elements of a whole, albeit an absent whole, without effective presence – elements which it would suffice to re-elaborate according to traditional models, as in the case of Marxist philosophies that remain immersed in 'ontology'? Or, on the contrary, is it a question of elements which must be interrogated and deciphered, 'asked' precisely why they remain only, and uniquely, 'elements'? Of course, we also possess Lenin's *Notebooks* on Hegel. But the same questions arise here, too: what meaning can be given to simple reading notes, to these brilliant but enigmatic pointers? In short, we are forced to conclude in every instance that Marx, and even Engels and Lenin, left us nothing even remotely comparable to the classical forms of philosophical discourse.

Now, the extent of this paradox still lies ahead of us. It resides in the fact that the absence of a philosophical discourse within Marxism has nevertheless produced prodigious philosophical effects. No one can deny that the philosophy we have inherited, the great classical philosophical tradition (from Plato to Descartes, from Kant to Hegel and Husserl), has been shaken in its very foundations (and in all its pretensions) by the impact of that ungraspable, almost formless encounter suddenly produced by Marx. Yet it never presented itself in the direct form of a philosophical discourse, but quite the reverse: in the form of a text like *Capital.* In other words, not a 'philosophical' text but a text in which the capitalist mode of production (and, through it, the structures of social formations) is investigated; a text, ultimately, which deals only with a scientific knowledge linked to the class struggle (a scientific knowledge which thus offers itself to us as simultaneously part of the proletarian class struggle – i.e. the very thing represented in *Capital*). So: how do we grasp such a paradox?

I would like to resolve this paradox by taking the shortest route, even if it is not exactly that of actual history.

Hence, I would say at the outset that for all their brevity and incompletion, the *Theses on Feuerbach* contain the sketch of a cardinal suggestion. When Marx writes in Thesis I:

> The chief defect of all hitherto existing materialism (that of Feuerbach included) is that the thing, reality, sensuousness, is conceived only in the form of the *object, or of contemplation*, but not as *sensuous human activity, practice*, not subjectively),[1]

he no doubt employs formulae that can be interpreted in the sense of a transcendental philosophy of practice. And some have persisted in resorting to this active subjectivity, conceiving it as legitimizing a humanist philosophy, while Marx is referring to something different,

---

1. Ist Thesis on Feuerbach, Karl Marx, *Early Writings*, Harmondsworth 1975, p. 421. [Ed.]

since he expressly declares it to be 'critical' and 'revolutionary'. But in
this enigmatic sentence, in which practice is specifically opposed to the
'object-form' and the 'contemplation-form', Marx has not introduced
any philosophical notion on a par with the 'object-form' and the
'contemplation-form', and hence destined to replace them in order to
establish a new philosophy, to inaugurate a new philosophical discourse.
Instead, he establishes a reality that possesses the particularity of being at
one and the same time presupposed by all traditional philosophical
discourses, yet naturally excluded from such discourses.

What I am saying here is inferred not only from the Ist Thesis on
Feuerbach but also from all Marx's work, from *Capital* and the writings
that deal with the class struggle of the workers' movement. This
irruption of practice into the philosophical tradition – even the materialist philosophical tradition (given that eighteenth-century materialism
was not a materialism of practice) – constitutes at base a radical critique
of that classical form of the existence of philosophy which I have defined
as the production of philosophy as 'philosophy'. What in fact are the
'object-form' and the 'contemplation-form'? Now in the guise of the
metaphor of vision (a metaphor interchangeable with the metaphor of
presence or that of the speech of the *logos*), they are the very
condemnation of the claim of any philosophy to maintain a relation of
discursive presence with its object. A moment ago I suggested that the
peculiarity of the philosophical conception of the truth is its inability to
exist in any other form than that of the object, or of contemplation. In
both cases we confront the same privilege, the same claim. For
philosophy men live and act subjected to the laws of their own social
practices; they know not what they do. They believe they possess truths;
they are not aware of what they know. Thank God philosophy is there,
that it sees for them and speaks for them, tells them what they do and
what they know. Well now, the irruption of practice is a denunciation of
philosophy produced as this kind of 'philosophy'. That is to say, it
opposes philosophy's claim to embrace the ensemble of social practices
(and ideas), to see the 'whole', as Plato said, in order to establish its
dominion over these same practices. It is counter to philosophy that
Marxism insists that philosophy has an 'exterior' – or, better expressed,
that philosophy exists only through and for this 'exterior'. This exterior
(which philosophy wishes to imagine it submits to Truth) is practice, the
social practices.

The radicalism of this critique must be acknowledged if its consequences are to be understood.

In contrast to the *logos* (that is, to a representation of something
supreme, to what is called 'Truth', whose essence is reducible to 'speech'
– whether in the immediate presence of sight or voice) practice, which

is utterly foreign to the *logos*, is not Truth and is irreducible to – does not realize itself in – speech or sight. Practice is a process of transformation which is always subject to its own conditions of existence and produces, not the Truth, but rather 'truths' (or the truth, let us say, of results or of knowledge, all within the field of its own conditions of existence). And if practice has agents, it nevertheless does not have a subject as the transcendental or ontological origin of its objective, its project; nor does it have a goal as the truth of its process. It is a process without subject or goal.[2]

If we take the term Truth in its philosophical sense, from Plato to Hegel, and if we confront it with practice – a process without subject or goal, according to Marx – it must be affirmed that there is no truth of practice.

Accordingly, there is a problem involved in assigning practice the role of Truth, of foundation, of origin, in a new philosophy that would be a philosophy of praxis (if I cite this expression it is not against Gramsci, who never envisaged this). Practice is not a substitute for Truth for the purposes of an immutable philosophy; on the contrary, it is what knocks philosophy off balance. Whether in the case of errant matter or the class struggle, practice is what philosophy, throughout its history, has never been able to incorporate. Practice is that other thing, on the basis of which it is possible not only to knock philosophy off balance, but also to begin to see clearly into the interior of philosophy.

I suggested earlier that practice compels philosophy to recognize that it has an exterior. Maybe philosophy has not introduced into the domain of its thought the totality of what exists, including mud (of which Socrates spoke), or the slave (of which Aristotle spoke), or even the accumulation of riches at one pole and of misery at the other (of which Hegel spoke)? For Plato, philosophy observes the whole; for Hegel, philosophy thinks the whole. In fact, all the social practices are there in philosophy – not just money, wages, politics and the family, but all social ideas, morality, religion, science and art, in the same way that the stars are in the sky. If everything is there, if everything is perfectly collected and united in the interior of philosophy, where is its exterior space? Is it perhaps that the real world, the material world, does not exist for all philosophies? Berkeley, for example, was a bishop for whom, in Alain's phrase, 'the meal was already cooked'. Yet this bishop was a man like any other, and did not equivocate about the existence of 'roast beef', i.e.

---

2. See Althusser's 'Remark on the Category "Process without a Subject or Goal(s)"', *Essays on Ideology*, London 1984, pp. 133–9. [Ed.]

the existence of the external world.[3]

In what, then, does this malign process operative in philosophy consist? In the interests of precision, there is a small nuance which must detain us here. In order to make all social practices and ideas enter its domain, and in order to impose itself upon these social practices and ideas with the aim of speaking their truth for them, philosophy plays tricks. That is, when philosophy absorbs and re-elaborates them in accordance with its own philosophical form, it scarcely does it with scrupulous respect for the reality (the particular nature) of such social practices and ideas. On the contrary, in affirming its power of Truth over them, philosophy compels them to undergo a veritable transformation, although this truth is usually imperceptible. What else can it do to adjust them to, and think them under, the unity of one and the same Truth? Nor is it necessary to proceed very far to be convinced of this: the same impulse is evident in Descartes *vis-à-vis* Galileo's physics (which is without a doubt something more than experimentation!); in Kant's little operation on chemistry and psychology; to say nothing of Plato's and Hegel's manoeuvres with morality and politics or economics. When confronted with the objection that it has an exterior space, philosophy is right to protest and to respond that it does not, since it takes command of everything. In truth, philosophy's exterior space must be sought within philosophy itself, in this appropriation of extra-philosophical space to which social practices are subjected, in this operation of exploitation, and hence deformation, of social practices that permits philosophy to unify such practices under the Truth.

Philosophy's true exterior space, then, is within philosophy itself. In other words, this separation, this distance between the deformation and the actual practice, is the commitment to exist over and above such exploitation and transformation: it is resistance to philosophical violence.

But the most important thing remains to be said. Because what has been said so far could be interpreted in terms of the will to power, accounting for the history of philosophy somewhat in Nietzsche's manner: at a given moment there existed men motivated by *ressentiment* who, wounded by the world, set about dominating it through thought – in short, making themselves the masters of the world, conceiving it exclusively through their own thought. The philosophers were precisely

---

3. For a more extended discursion of the idea that 'Nature is always too strong for principle' by a contemporary of Berkeley; see David Hume, *Enquiry Concerning Human Understanding* (1748), third edn, Oxford 1975, Section XII, 'Of the Academical or Sceptical Philosophy', pp. 149–65. [Ed.]

these specialists in the violence of the concept, of *Begriff*, of appropriation, who asserted their power by subjecting to the law of Truth all the social practices of men, who became sadder and sadder and lived on in the night. We know that such a perspective is not foreign to some of our contemporaries who, naturally enough, discover in philosophy the archetype of power, the model of all power. They themselves write the equation knowledge = power and, in the style of modern and cultivated anarchists, affirm: violence, tyranny, state despotism are Plato's fault – just as they used to say a while back that the Revolution was Rousseau's fault.[4]

The best way to respond to them is to go further than they do and introduce the scandalous fracture of practice into the very heart of philosophy. This is where Marx's influence is perhaps most profoundly felt.

Hitherto we have let it be believed that philosophy was content to introduce the totality of human practices and ideas into its thought, in order to enunciate Truth with it. And we have provisionally assumed that if philosophy, having absorbed the totality of the social practices, deformed them, it was to a certain extent for logical and technical reasons – in order to be able to unify them. If we wish to add a certain number of objects to an already full suitcase, it is necessary to fold and deform them. If we wish to imagine the social practices under the unity of the Good, a large number of deformations will be required in order to mould them into this unity. Engels said something similar somewhere, when he asserted that all philosophy was systematic as a function of the 'imperishable desire of the human mind ... to overcome all contradictions'.[5] Well, I do not think this is entirely correct. I think, rather, that these unifying or contradictory deformations uniquely concern the peculiar logic of philosophical discourse.

I am perfectly well aware that in every philosopher, as in every mathematician who knows how to appreciate the elegance of a proof, there slumbers a lover of the arts, and there is no shortage of philosophers who have believed, with Kant, that the construction of a system was a question not only of logic, but of aesthetics as well. When logic does not suffice (or in order to make it digestible) a little aesthetics is thrown in – namely the Beautiful and the Good, which historically have

---

4. The reference is to the so-called New Philosophers, c.1976 *le dernier cri* in Parisian philosophy. See especially André Glucksmann, *The Master Thinkers* (1977), Hassocks 1981. [Ed.]

5. *Ludwig Feuerbach and the End of Classical German Philosophy*, in Marx and Engels, *Selected Works*, vol.3, Moscow 1970, pp. 341–2. [Ed.]

had the habit of appearing in public together, so as to be noticed by polite society.

But here we have to do with the foibles of philosophers, and one should not judge philosophy on the basis of them, just as mathematics should not be judged on the basis of the elegance of mathematicians.

The truth is another thing: to reach it, not only must the psychology of philosophers be scorned, but also the illusion in which philosophy finds its repose: the illusion of its own power over the social practices. Because – and it is here that everything is decided – what is important is not that philosophy exercises power over social practices and ideas. What matters is that philosophy does not incorporate social practices under the unity of its thought in gratuitous fashion, but by removing the social practices from their own space, by subjecting this hierarchy to an internal order that constitutes its true unification.

In other words, the world thought by philosophy is a unified world in so far as it is disarticulated and rearticulated – i.e. reordered – by philosophy. It is a world in which the different social practices, decomposed and recomposed, are distributed in a certain order of distinction and hierarchy which is significant. What makes it significant is not that philosophy dominates its objects but that it decomposes and recomposes them in a special order of internal hierarchy and distinction – an order which endows the whole operation of philosophy with significance. Of course, in order to realize this entire operation, in order to distribute its objects in this order, philosophy has to dominate them. Or, put another way, this necessity compels philosophy 'to take power' over them.

But let us always bear in mind that 'power' never signifies 'power for power's sake', not even in the political arena. Quite the reverse: power is nothing other than what one does with it – that is, what it produces as a result. And if philosophy is that which 'sees the whole', it sees it only for the purposes of reordering it, i.e. imposing a determinate order upon the diverse elements of the whole.

I cannot enter into details here. Thousands of examples could easily be offered, but let me rely on one that is unequivocal: the respective 'place' accorded by Descartes, Kant and Hegel to what they conceive of as morality and religion. Evidently, this 'place' (which is never identical in the totality of each of these systems) has profound repercussions upon each of their doctrines. Or, to take another more abstract example, let us recall how the presence of a theory of knowledge in Descartes and Kant, and its absence in Spinoza and Hegel, attest to their different treatments of scientific practice and derive from the overall orientation of each of these doctrines.

I cannot go more deeply into this type of clarification now, but I do want to attend to one consequence of what has just been said. When the hypothesis is advanced that philosophy makes use of social practices and ideas in order to impose upon them a specific meaning in the interior of its system, it is clear that philosophy first has to decompose, and subsequently recompose, such practices. That is, philosophy needs to dissect the social practices in a certain way so that it can retain only those elements which it considers the most significant for its enterprise, subsequently recomposing such practices on the basis of those elements. Hence, starting from the reality of scientific practice, each philosopher fashions an idea of science; starting from the reality of ethical practice, an idea of morality; etc.

This systematic deformation (let us be clear I intend deformation in the strongest sense of the word), provoked by the system (I mean not a logical system, but a system of domination, imposing a significance – a Truth – on the social practices), produces philosophical objects that resemble real objects, but are different from them. Only there is something more important still – namely: in order to cause the appearance of the Truth it wishes to impose in the interior of social practices or ideas, and in order to maintain the whole in one single block, philosophy finds itself obliged to invent what I would call philosophical objects, without a real, empirical referent – for example, Truth, Oneness, Totality, the *cogito*, the transcendental subject, and many other categories of the same kind that do not exist outside philosophy.

Years ago I wrote: philosophy does not have an object in the sense that a science has an object; or, although philosophy has no object, there exist philosophical objects.[6] Philosophy has its objects within itself, and it works on them interminably. It modifies them, it takes them up again, it cannot do without them, because such philosophical objects (which are nothing more than the object of philosophy) are the means by which philosophy achieves its objectives, its mission: to impose upon the social practices and ideas that figure in its system the deformation imposed by the determinate order of that system. I was talking just now about the theory of knowledge and I said that its presence in Descartes and Kant, like its absence in Spinoza and Hegel, has a meaning: the theory of knowledge is one of those objects of philosophy which does not belong to anything but philosophy and *vis-à-vis* which philosophers can situate themselves. From the moment we encounter this object we are in the heart of what constitutes the peculiarity of philosophy, the objects that

---

6. See *Philosophy and the Spontaneous Philosophy of the Scientists*, below, p. 77. [Ed.]

are its and its alone and in which all the destiny of its activity is played out.

If we pursue this course, we will be in a better position to understand how practice irrupts to take philosophy from behind and to show that it has an exterior. Its exterior space, once again, is what takes place within it: not only logical deformations of the social practices in order to subject them to the non-contradictory formal unity of a systematic thought that encompasses the totality, but also dismemberment and reconstruction, the ordered rearrangement of these same deformed social practices – a double deformation, then, dictated by the exigencies of that ordering which ultimately dominates everything and imparts to philosophy its meaning.

What might this meaning be? Because up to this point everything has taken place in written texts, in abstract discourses, that seem very distant from real social practices which only appear in philosophy in the form of categories and notions. Of course, this whole mental operation can satisfy its author with a beautiful conceptual unity, responding to his or her need for a 'search for truth'. After all, collectors and chess players are numerous. But what can this little private conceptual matter have to do with history, once its procedures are unmasked, once one no longer believes that it has any vocation to speak the Truth? In reality, this is where things get serious – and this we owe to Marx. What I am about to say is not entirely in Marx, of course, but without him we could not say it.

No one will deny that, at least in certain areas, history knows perfectly well how to select and to recognize its own. And it is surely not fortuitous that this has consecrated the historical existence of philosophy. It is not by chance that philosophy survives, that these sacred abstract texts, interminably read and reread by generations of students, incessantly commented upon and glossed, can weather the storms and high seas of our cultural universe, to play their part in it. And since it is not the love of art that inspires their reading or fidelity to their history, if such texts survive, paradoxical as it may seem, it is because of the results they produce; and if they produce results, it is because these are required by the societies of our history.

The whole question consists in knowing precisely what these results are and to what order they pertain. I want to warn the audience that what I am about to say cannot pretend to exhaust the subject. Like any other social and cultural reality, philosophy *par excellence* is over-determined. But I wish to foreground what I consider to be its essential determination, its determination in the last instance.

Because we have hitherto forgotten a fundamentally important reality. To wit: philosophy, which pretends to enunciate the Truth of things once and for all, embodies this paradoxical characteristic of being, in its essence, conflictual, and perpetually so. Kant said of philosophy – the philosophy that preceded his own – that it was a battlefield.[7] And all the philosophers who preceded and succeeded him have proved him right, since they have never written anything which did not make war upon one or another of their predecessors. Thus philosophy (and with an insistence and a constancy so striking as to reveal its nature) is a perpetual war of ideas. Why this war? It cannot be put down to neurasthenia in susceptible personalities. The innumerable sub-philosophers, rule-of-thumb philosophers, or tear-out-your-hair philosophers (as Marx used to say), who entered the war out of sheer contrariness, as failed authors spoiling for a fight, have left no traces in history. But on the other hand, all those who have remained in history have done nothing more than fight among themselves, and, as shrewd combatants, knew how to find support against their principal adversary in the arguments of their secondary adversaries, how to make allies, bestowing insults and praise; adopting, in short, positions – and bellicose positions, without any ambiguity. It is on the basis of this general struggle that we must try to understand the results produced by the existence of historical philosophy. And this is where Marx's thought becomes decisive.

In the Preface to the 1859 *Contribution*,[8] Marx ventured the idea that a social formation rests upon its economic infrastructure – that is, on the unity of the productive forces and the relations of production. In the infrastructure is rooted the class struggle, which pits the owners of the means of production against the directly exploited workers. And Marx added that above this infrastructure there was erected a whole superstructure, comprising law and the State on the one hand, and the ideologies on the other. The superstructure does nothing more than reflect the infrastructure. Evidently, life must be breathed into this topography, which offers a short cut in the history of a social formation, and it must be granted that if a social formation exists, in the strong sense, it is because it is capable, like every living being, of reproducing itself, but, unlike other living beings, of also reproducing its own conditions of existence. The material conditions of reproduction are secured by production itself, which also secures a considerable proportion of the conditions of reproduction of the relations of production. But the economic and political conditions of reproduction are secured by law and the State. As far as the ideologies are concerned, they participate in the relations of production and in the ensemble of social

---

7. See the *Critique of Pure Reason*, London 1929, pp. 7, 666–9. [Ed.]
8. See *Early Writings*, pp. 425–6. [Ed.]

relations, securing the hegemony of the dominant class at the level of ideas or culture. Among these ideologies are, in general, to be found legal ideology, political ideology, ethical ideology, religious ideology, and what Marx calls philosophical ideology.

With regard to these ideologies, Marx says that it is in them that men become conscious of their class conflict and 'fight it out'. I leave to one side the question of whether Marx's term – 'philosophical ideology' – exactly covers what has been designated here as 'philosophy'. But I shall retain two essential pointers: first, what occurs within philosophy maintains an intimate relation with what occurs in the ideologies; second, what occurs within the ideologies maintains a close relation with the class struggle.

Up to now, and for simplicity's sake, I have spoken above all of the social practices, saying that philosophy proposed to state their Truth, since it considered itself alone capable of so doing. But at the same time I have referred to social practices *and* ideas so as to highlight the fact that philosophy is not concerned solely with the production of a manufactured object. Equally, I have attempted to underline that neither is philosophy concerned exclusively with the practice of the production of knowledge (whether scientific or of some other type), as one observes in all our authors; and nor does it concern itself exclusively with juridical, ethical or political practice, nor any other practice tending to transform or to conserve something in the world. I have indicated all this because, while it is concerned with social practices, philosophy is also interested in the ideas that men form of these practices: ideas that in some cases will be used to condemn or criticize, in others to approve, but which in the final analysis are useful for proposing a new interpretation, a new Truth. This is because, in reality, the social practices and the ideas men form of them are intimately linked. It can be said that there is no practice without ideology, and that every practice – including scientific practice – realizes itself through an ideology.[9] In all the social practices (whether they pertain to the domain of economic production, of science, of art or law, of ethics or of politics), the people who act are subjected to corresponding ideologies, independently of their will and usually in total ignorance of the fact.

Having reached this point, I think I can advance the idea that philosophy satisfies itself only by acting upon the contradictory set of existing ideologies, acting upon the background of class struggle and its historical agency. Such action is by no means nugatory. No Marxist can

---

9. See 'Ideology and Ideological State Apparatuses', *Essays on Ideology*, pp. 39 ff., for Althusser's elaboration of this thesis. [Ed.]

defend the idea that the action exercised upon the practices by ideology suffices to change their nature and general orientation. This because it is not ideology which is determinant in the last instance. Nevertheless, the efficacy of ideology is far from negligible. On the contrary, it can be quite considerable and (in keeping with real historical experiences) Marx therefore acknowledged its highly significant role in the reproduction and transformation of social relations. Ideology's potential effectivity upon the social practices can be formally conceived as that of conferring a certain unity and direction upon them at a given stage of the class struggle.

If the set of ideologies is capable of such action, and if the peculiarity of philosophy consists in acting upon the ideologies and, through them, upon the ensemble of social practices and their orientation, then the *raison d'être* and scope of philosophy can be better appreciated.

But I want to insist upon this point: its *raison d'être* is comprehensible only in formal terms, because as yet we have not understood why it is imperative for the set of ideologies to receive from philosophy, under the categories of Truth, this unity and its direction.

In order to understand this it is necessary, in Marx's perspective, to introduce what I would call the political form of the existence of ideologies in the ensemble of social practices. It is necessary to foreground class struggle and the concept of the dominant ideology. If the society in question is a class society, political power – the power of the State – will be held by the exploiting class. To preserve its power (and this we knew long before Marx, ever since Machiavelli inaugurated political theory) the dominant class must transform its power from one based upon violence to one based upon consent. By means of the free and habitual consent of its subjects, such a dominant class needs to elicit an obedience that could not be maintained by force alone. This is the purpose served by the ever contradictory system of ideologies.

This is what, following Gramsci, I have called the system of the Ideological State Apparatuses,[10] by which is meant the set of ideological, religious, moral, familial, legal, political, aesthetic, etc., institutions via which the class in power, at the same time as unifying itself, succeeds in imposing its particular ideology upon the exploited masses, as their own ideology. Once this occurs the mass of the people, steeped in the truth of the ideology of the dominant class, endorses its values (thus giving its consent to the existing order), and the requisite violence can either be dispensed with or utilized as a last resort.

However, this state of affairs – which, other than in exceptional

---

10. Ibid., *passim.* [Ed.]

periods, has been achieved only tendentially – presupposes (contrary to what is believed) something that is not so evident – namely, the existence of a dominant ideology. As Marx said, the dominant ideology is the ideology of the dominant class. This is bound to be the outcome of a struggle, but an extraordinarily complicated struggle. And historical experience shows that it takes time – sometimes a good deal of it – for a dominant class that has seized power to succeed in forging an ideology which finally becomes dominant. Take the bourgeoisie: it needed no fewer than five centuries, from the fourteenth century to the nineteenth, to achieve this. And even in the nineteenth century, when it had to confront the first struggles of the proletariat, it was still fighting against the ideology of the landed aristocracy, the heir of feudalism. From this digression we should retain the notion that the constitution of a dominant ideology is, for the dominant class, a matter of class struggle; in the case of the nineteenth-century bourgeoisie, a matter of class struggle on two fronts. Now, this is not all. It is not simply a question of manufacturing a dominant ideology because you have need of one, by decree; nor simply of constituting it in a long history of class struggle. It must be constructed at the basis of what already exists, starting from the elements, the regions, of existing ideology, from the legacy of the past, which is diverse and contradictory, and also through the unexpected events that constantly occur in science as well as politics. An ideology must be constituted, in the class struggle and its contradictions (on the basis of the contradictory ideological elements inherited from the past), which transcends all those contradictions, an ideology unified around the essential interests of the dominant class in order to secure what Gramsci called its hegemony.

If we understand the reality of the dominant ideology in this way, we can – at least, this is the hypothesis I wish to advance – grasp the function peculiar to philosophy. Philosophy is neither a gratuitous operation nor a speculative activity. Pure, unsullied speculation indulges its self-conception. But the great philosophers already had a very different consciousness of their mission. They knew that they were responding to the great practical political questions: how could they orientate themselves in thought and in politics? What was to be done? What direction should they take? They even knew that these political questions were historical questions. That is, although they lived them as eternal questions, they knew that these questions were posed by the vital interests of the society for which they were thinking. But they certainly did not know what Marx enables us to understand and which I should like to convey in a few words. Indeed, it seems to me that one cannot understand the task, determinant in the last instance, of philosophy except in relation to the exigencies of the class struggle in ideology – in other words, the central question of hegemony, of the constitution of the dominant ideology. What we have seen occurring in philosophy – that reorganization and ordered positioning of social practices and ideas within a systematic unity under its Truth – all this, which apparently transpires very far from the real, in philosophical abstraction, we can of course see being produced in a comparable, almost superimposed (but not simultaneous), form in the ideological class struggle.

In both cases it is a question of reorganizing, dismembering, recomposing and unifying, according to a precise orientation, a whole series of social practices and their corresponding ideologies, in order to make sovereign, over all the subordinate elements, a particular Truth that imposes on them a particular orientation, guaranteeing this orientation with that Truth. If the correspondence is exact, we may infer that philosophy, which continues the class struggle as befits it, in theory, responds to a fundamental political necessity. The task which it is assigned and delegated by the class struggle in general, and more directly by the ideological class struggle, is that of contributing to the unification of the ideologies within a dominant ideology and of guaranteeing this dominant ideology as Truth. How does it contribute? Precisely by proposing to think the theoretical conditions of possibility of reducing existing contradictions, and therefore of unifying the social practices and their ideology. This involves an abstract labour, a labour of pure thought, of pure and, hence, a priori theorization. And its result is to think, under the unity and guarantee of an identical orientation, the diversity of the different practices and their ideologies. In responding to this exigency, which it lives as an internal necessity but which derives from the major class conflicts and historical events, what does philosophy do? It produces a whole apparatus of categories which serve to think and position the different social practices in a determinate location under the ideologies – that is, in the place they must necessarily occupy in order to play the role expected of them in the constitution of the dominant ideology. Philosophy produces a general problematic: that is, a manner of posing, and hence resolving, the problems which may arise. In short, philosophy produces theoretical schemas, theoretical figures that serve as mediators for surmounting contradictions and as links for reconnecting the different elements of ideology. Moreover, it guarantees (by dominating the social practices thus reordered) the Truth of this order, enunciated in the form of the guarantee of a rational discourse.

I believe, then, that philosophy can be represented in the following manner. It is not outside the world, outside historical conflicts and events. In its concentrated, most abstract form – that of the works of the great philosophers – it is something that is on the side of the ideologies, a kind of theoretical laboratory in which the fundamentally political

problem of ideological hegemony – i.e. of the constitution of the
dominant ideology – is experimentally perfected in the abstract. Therein
are perfected the theoretical categories and techniques that will make
ideological unification – an essential aspect of ideological hegemony –
possible. Because the work accomplished by the most abstract philosophers does not remain a dead letter: what philosophy has received as a
necessity from the class struggle it returns in the form of thoughts that
are going to work on the ideologies in order to transform and unify
them. Just as the conditions of existence imposed on philosophy can be
empirically observed in history, so philosophy's effects on the ideologies
and the social practices can be observed. It suffices to think of
seventeenth-century rationalism and Enlightenment philosophy, to take
two well-known examples: the results of the work of philosophical
elaboration are given in ideology and in the social practices. These two
phases of bourgeois philosophy are two of the constitutive moments of
bourgeois ideology as a dominant ideology. This constitution was
accomplished in struggle, and in this struggle philosophy played its role
as a theoretical foundation for the unity of this ideology.

If everything that has just been said can be granted – and, above all, if
it has been possible to say it because of Marx's discovery of the nature of
class society, of the role of the State and of the ideologies in the
superstructure – the question of Marxist philosophy becomes even more
paradoxical. Because if, in the last instance, philosophy plays the role of
laboratory for the theoretical unification and foundation of the dominant ideology, what is the role of philosophers who refuse to serve the
dominant ideology? What is the role of a man like Marx, who declares
in the Postface to the second German edition that *Capital* is 'a critique
[that] represents a class ... whose historical task is the overthrow of the
capitalist mode of production and the final abolition of all classes'?[11] Put
another way: if what I have proposed is plausible, how is a Marxist
philosophy conceivable?

In order to grasp its possibility, it is sufficient to reflect on the fact
that the expression 'dominant ideology' has no meaning if it is not set
against another expression: the dominated ideology. And this derives
from the very question of ideological hegemony. The fact that, in a
society divided into classes, the dominant class must forge an ideology
that is dominant (in order to unify itself and to impose it in turn on the
dominated classes) issues in a process that unfolds with a good deal of
resistance. Particularly because, in addition to the ideology of the old
dominant class, which still survives, there exist in class society what

---

11. *Capital*, vol. 1, Harmondsworth 1976, p. 98. [Ed.]

Lenin called 'elements' of another distinct ideology, that of the exploited class. The ideology of the dominant class does not constitute itself as dominant except over and against the ideological elements of the dominated class. A similar opposition can be found within philosophy itself, as one element of the hegemonic problem that philosophy is a war of all against all, that perpetual war which is the effect and the echo of the class struggle in philosophy. Thus the antagonistic positions of the antagonistic ideologies are represented within philosophy itself. Philosophy, which works in its own theoretical laboratory to the benefit of the ideological hegemony of the ascendant or dominant class, without realizing it, confronts its own adversaries, generally under the name of materialism.

In principle, there occurs in philosophy something analogous to what takes place in class society: in the same way that the unity and the struggle of the exploited class are organized under class domination, the forms of philosophical partisanship for the dominated class are represented in the forms that constitute philosophy as philosophy, and hence under the forms of the question of ideological hegemony. Thus it is that the entire history of philosophy resounds deafeningly with the echo of the exploited or the opponents. Some, such as the eighteenth-century materialists, went so far as to oppose their own system of truth to the representatives of the dominant class. But rather than the eighteenth-century materialists (who did not represent the exploited class, but a new class of exploiters – the bourgeoisie then attempting to achieve an alliance with the aristocracy on the English model), perhaps those who ought to interest us are the ones who only half succeeded (or hardly succeeded) in imparting to their opposition the form of a philosophy produced as 'philosophy'. For my part I would closely investigate the cases of Epicurus and Machiavelli, to cite only them. But if I do so, it is only to try to understand Marx: that is, his silence.

Basically, the whole paradox of Marx lies here. He who had received a philosophical formation refused to write philosophy. He who almost never spoke about philosophy (but had shaken the foundations of all traditional philosophy when he wrote the word 'practice' in the Ist Thesis on Feuerbach), none the less, in writing *Capital*, practised the philosophy he never wrote. And in writing *Capital* Marx has left us, as no one before him had, the keys to beginning to understand what is at stake within philosophy itself – that is, to being able to begin to elaborate something like a theory of philosophy. After him, both Engels and Lenin wrote nothing but critiques and isolated fragments. So again: how are we to understand this paradox? Can it be understood on the basis of what has been proposed here?

I shall attempt to set out what I believe in this regard, without concealing the fact that I am taking the risk of stating a very daring hypothesis. But I believe it is worth running the risk.

When we observe the history of the Marxist workers' movement through the prism of the philosophical forms in which it has recognized itself, we encounter two typical situations. In the first we find ourselves with Marx, Engels, Lenin, Gramsci and Mao, who, in one way or another, always give the impression of distrusting like the plague anything that might appear to be a philosophy produced as such, as 'philosophy', in the forms of ideological hegemony we have analysed. By contrast, we find ourselves in the second situation with people like Lukács – although he is not decisive – and above all with Stalin (who was indeed decisive in opening the highway for a Marxist philosophy produced as 'philosophy'). Stalin did this by re-inflecting some unfortunate sentences of Engels's regarding 'matter and motion', etc., and by orientating Marxist philosophy towards a materialist ontology or metaphysics in which philosophical theses are realized through matter.[12] It is clear that Stalin did not possess the great circumspection of Marx, Lenin and Gramsci, and that his philosophical positions originated in his political line and terrorist practices, since it is not difficult to show that Stalinist philosophical positions are not only *not* foreign to the political line of Stalinism, but that they were even perfectly serviceable for it. Nor would it be difficult to show how, within the profound Stalinist crisis from which we are scarcely now beginning to recover, Stalin's philosophical positions started Marxist 'philosophy' on its way.

Thus it is as if the history of the Marxist workers' movement, at a point that is still obscure, had experimentally vindicated Marx, Lenin and Gramsci, contradicting Plekhanov, Bogdanov, and especially Stalin. It is as if (owing to the extreme haziness, yet great discretion, of their directly philosophical interventions, together with their constant practice of a philosophy that they never wanted to write), Marx, Lenin and Gramsci had suggested that the philosophy required by Marxism was by no means a philosophy produced as 'philosophy', but rather a new practice of philosophy.

In order to understand what lies at the root of this, we may start from Marx's contrast, in the Postface to the second German edition of *Capital*, between two conceptions of the dialectic. In the first conception, the dialectic serves – and I quote – 'to glorify the existing order of things'; hence it involves an apologia for the dominant class. In the second, the dialectic is 'critical and revolutionary'.[13] It is this latter conception alone

---

12. See Engels, *Dialectics of Nature*, Moscow 1954, pp. 243–51; and cf. Stalin, *Dialectical and Historical Materialism*, Moscow 1941. [Ed.]

13. *Capital*, vol.1, p. 103. [Ed.]

which is capable of serving the proletariat. To simplify, one could say that it is correct to think that Stalin regressed to the first conception and that, in order to avoid this peril, Marx steadfastly held to the second and never wrote philosophy as 'philosophy'.

Marx manifestly considered that to produce philosophy as 'philosophy' was a way of entering into the adversary's game; that even in an oppositional form it meant playing by the rules of hegemony and contributing, indirectly, to a confrontation with bourgeois ideology which accepts the validity of its form of philosophical expression; that to dress up proletarian ideology in forms demanded by the question of bourgeois ideological hegemony was to compromise the future – and thus the present – of proletarian ideology; and finally, that it was to risk succumbing, within philosophy, to the party of the State.

Because the history of the relations between philosophy and the State is, as the philosopher Paul Nizan likewise saw,[14] a long history. I referred to this when I alluded to the question of the dominant ideology. The dominant ideology is the ideology of the dominant class, therefore of the class which holds State power. From Plato to Descartes, Spinoza, Kant, Hegel and even Husserl, philosophy is obsessed by the question of the State, generally in the form of a nostalgic call by the philosopher to the State that it might see fit to listen to him – when it is not in the form of a dream of the philosopher as Head of State.

By contrast, with a very sure political instinct, Marx clearly understood the political and philosophical significance of the question of the State. He not only thought about the existing bourgeois State (of which Dietzgen – with Lenin's approval – said, in words famous for their severity, that philosophy professors were its flunkeys).[15] He not only thought about the bourgeois State, 'the first ideological power', in Engels's words, capable of imposing the form of its ideology on all philosophical production. Marx saw much further. He thought about the form of the future State, the one which it would be necessary to construct after the Revolution, of which the experience of the Commune had given him a first idea and which had to be, not a State but a 'community' or (as Engels put it) 'no longer a State in the proper sense of the word'.[16] In short: a totally new form that would induce its own disappearance, its own extinction. Naturally, this strategic viewpoint of

---

14. See Paul Nizan, *The Watchdogs; Philosophers and the Established Order* (1932), New York 1971. [Ed.]

15. See 'Lenin and Philosophy', above, p. 173. [Ed.]

16. See Marx, 'The Civil War in France', *The First International and After*, Harmondsworth 1974, pp. 206 ff.; and Engels, Letter to August Bebel, 18–28 March 1875, in Marx and Engels, *Selected Correspondence*, Moscow 1975, p. 275. [Ed.]

Marx's, which entirely subverted the conventional conception of the State (which is still in evidence today) was no chimera, but rested upon one of his profound convictions: that the proletariat, as it had been produced and concentrated by the capitalist mode of production, as it was educated by its great class struggles, possessed capacities that were totally foreign to the bourgeois world – above all, the ability to invent mass-based forms of organization, such as the Paris Commune and the Soviets of 1905 and 1917, which are a good example of forms of organization that enable the proletariat to exist at the margin of the State. Of course, Marx's strategic vision, which foresaw the destruction of the State, encompassed the whole superstructure, including the ideologies (and thus the dominant ideology, quite inseparable from the State). It is quite possible that Marx always had the same distrust of philosophy and the State (for the reasons that connect traditional philosophy with the State and caused him to foresee the abolition of the State). In no way did this involve an anarchist rejection of the State, despite certain affinities between Marx and the anarchists; nor, by the same token, did it involve a rejection of philosophy. On the contrary, it involved a profound mistrust of an institution – the State – and a form of unification of the dominant ideology – philosophy – which appeared to Marx to be profoundly linked, in so far as both are involved in the same mechanism of bourgeois class domination. For my part, I believe that this is why Marx abstained from all philosophy produced as 'philosophy': in order not to fall into the 'glorification of the existing order of things'.

If this is true, Marx has bequeathed Marxists (cruelly instructed by the counter-experience of Stalinist ontology) an especially difficult undertaking. Just as he left the workers' movement with the task of inventing new forms of 'commune' that would convert the State into something superfluous, so Marx left Marxist philosophers with the task of inventing new forms of philosophical intervention to hasten the end of bourgeois ideological hegemony. In sum: the task of inventing a new practice of philosophy.

To support our argument by comparison with the revolutionary State, which ought to be a State that is a 'non-State' – that is, a State tending to its own dissolution, to be replaced by forms of free association – one might equally say that the philosophy which obsessed Marx, Lenin and Gramsci ought to be a 'non-philosophy' – that is, one which ceases to be produced in the form of a philosophy, whose function of theoretical hegemony will disappear in order to make way for new forms of philosophical existence. And just as the free association of workers ought, according to Marx, to replace the State so as to play a totally different role from that of the State (not one of violence and repression), so it can be said that the new forms of philosophical existence linked to the future of these free associations will cease to have as their essential function the constitution of the dominant ideology, with all the compromises and exploitation that accompany it, in order to promote the liberation and free exercise of social practices and human ideas.

And as with the perspectives on the State, the task assigned Marxist philosophy is not one for the distant future. It is an undertaking for the present, for which Marxists ought to be prepared. Marx was the first to show us the way by putting philosophy into practice in a new and disconcerting form, refusing to produce a philosophy as 'philosophy' but practising it in his political, critical and scientific work – in short, inaugurating a new, 'critical and revlutionary' relation between philosophy and the social practices, which are at one and the same time the stakes and the privileged site of class struggle. This new practice of philosophy serves the proletarian class struggle without imposing upon it an oppressive ideological unity (we know where that oppression has its roots), but rather creating for it the ideological conditions for the liberation and free development of social practices.

7

Marxism Today*

*Le Marxisme aujourd'hui, published in Italian under the title Un balancio critico as part of the article Marxismo, in Enciclopedia Europea, vol. VII, Aldo Garzanti, Milan 1978. Translated by James H. Kavanagh.

Can we, 130 years after the *Communist Manifesto* and 110 years after *Capital*, outline something like a balance sheet of what is called 'Marxism'? Certainly, for we have not only a historical perspective on Marxism but the long experience of its victories, defeats and tragedies. Perhaps, too, because we are henceforth living within a crisis, within its crisis – a situation conducive to dispelling all illusions and concentrating minds on the pitiless test of reality.

Today, then, what can we retain of Marx that is essential, and has possibly not always been understood?

There is, first of all, one simple fact: Marx said that he was 'not a Marxist'.[1] This remark, which has been taken as the quip of a free spirit who required readers to 'think for themselves',[2] actually carries great weight. Marx was not only protesting in advance against the interpretation of his work as a system, as a new philosophy of history, or as the finally discovered science of political economy – an *œuvre* with the unity of a total theory ('Marxism') produced by an 'author' (Marx). Marx was not only rejecting this pretension in declaring *Capital* not 'science' but 'critique of political economy'.[3] But in so doing he was changing the very meaning of the term 'criticism' or 'critique'. Upon this notion – charged with delivering the true from the false, or denouncing the false in the name of the true, by the rationalist tradition – Marx was imposing an entirely different mission, founded on *the class struggle*: 'such a critique represents one class … the proletariat'.[4] And with these words, he rejected the idea that he might, in the traditional sense, be the intellectual 'author' of such a critique.

These reflections return us to another fact: it was within the working-class movement – by participating in its practice, its hopes, and its struggles – that the thought of Marx and Engels changed fundamentally, became 'critical and revolutionary'.[5] This is not just a simple point in the history of ideas. In the history of Marxism it has become the stake of

---

1. See Engels's letter of 5 August 1890 to Conrad Schmidt, in Marx and Engels, *Selected Correspondence*, Moscow 1975, p. 393. [Ed.]
2. Preface to the first edition of *Capital*, vol. 1, Harmondsworth 1976, p. 90. [Ed.]
3. The subtitle of *Capital*. [Ed.]
4. *Capital*, vol.1, p. 98. [Ed.]
5. Ibid., p. 103. [Ed.]

crucially significant theoretico-political debates. When, in the full bloom of German Social-Democracy (1902), Kautsky affirmed that Marxist theory had been produced by the '*bourgeois intelligentsia*', the sole guardians of 'science', and 'introduced into the proletarian class struggle from without'; when, in an entirely different context (the struggle against 'economism'), even Lenin picked up Kautsky's formulation,[6] they were implicating Marx's thought in the most questionable kind of interpretation. A formulation is only a formulation. But it can crystallize a political tendency, as well as justify and reinforce certain historical practices. Behind this view of a scientific theory produced by bourgeois intellectuals, and 'introduced ... from without' into the working-class movement, lies a whole conception of the relations between theory and practice, between the Party and the mass movement, and between party leaders and simple militants, which reproduces bourgeois forms of knowledge and power in their separation.

There is no question that Marx and Engels were academically trained bourgeois intellectuals, but origin is not necessarily destiny. The real destiny that defined Marx and Engels in their historical role as intellectuals of the working class was played out in their direct experience – Marx's experience of the political struggles of Communist and socialist organizations in France, and Engels's experience of working-class exploitation and Chartism in England. The stages of their progressive commitment can be tracked in the contradictions of their 'early works'; and we can even locate the 'moment' – after the dramatic confrontation of philosophy and political economy in the 1844 *Manuscripts* – of their 'consciousness' of the need radically to question the principles of their formation, to think in an entirely different way, to 'change terrain' and, in order so to do, to 'settle accounts with [their] former philosophical conscience'.[7] This 'moment' begins to take shape in the striking, enigmatic sentences on the *Theses on Feuerbach* (1845) – only the first stage in an endless research that continued, after the political struggles of 1848–49, in *The Class Struggles in France* (1850), *The Eighteenth Brumaire* (1852), *A Contribution to the Critique of Political Economy* (1859), the foundation of the First International (1864), then in *Capital* itself (1867) and in *The Civil War in France* (1871). We can respond to Kautsky's formula as follows: Marx's thought was formed and developed *inside the working-class movement*, on the basis of that movement and its positions. It was from within the working-class movement,

---

6. See *What is to be Done?*, *Collected Works*, vol.5, Moscow 1961, pp. 383–4, where Karl Kautsky (*Neue Zeit*, XX, I, no.3, 1901–02, p. 79) is quoted approvingly. [Ed.]

7. Preface to *A Contribution to the Critique of Political Economy*, in Karl Marx, *Early Writings*, Harmondsworth 1975, p. 427. [Ed.]

paying its way through struggles and contradictions, that Marx's thought was diffused from the first Marxist circles to the great mass parties.

We find the same dubious interpretation in Engels's famous thesis, systematically repeated by Kautsky and invoked by Lenin, of the 'three sources' of Marxism.[8] Marx and Engels were indeed among those intellectuals informed by German philosophy, English political economy, and French socialism (our 'three sources'). To reduce Marx's thought to the confluence of these three currents, however, is to succumb to the platitude of a history of ideas, incapable of accounting for the politico-theoretical foundation that forced this encounter and transformed it into a 'revolutionary critique' of its elements. Hegel, Smith and Ricardo, Proudhon, etc., certainly constituted Marx's historical horizon – which he could not ignore, from which he had to begin – and were the raw material upon which he was obliged to work – but in order to penetrate its ideological façade, to shake up its principles, to perceive its other side, its hidden reality. To get to the other side is precisely to 'change terrain' and to adopt another position – a 'critique [that] represents ... the proletariat'. To reduce the history of this revolution in thought to the simple confluence of 'three sources' is ultimately to see Marx as an 'author' who knew how to combine the elements that converged in him – for example, to make a 'metaphysics of political economy' by applying Hegel to Ricardo. It is to see Marx as putting each of these three elements 'on its feet' with their structures intact – constituting political economy as a science, philosophy as dialectical materialism, and the visions of French socialism as a 'materialist' philosophy of history or – the practical version of this messianism – as a scientific socialism.

We know that these formulae, in this finished form, are not to be found in Marx. Rather, they belong to the history of Marxism, where, from the Second International onwards, they represented the official definition of Marxism: dialectical materialism, historical materialism, scientific socialism. Nevertheless we do find in Marx, who battled within the contradiction of having to think something which had no name, elements that license the appearance of these formulae. We find the (Feuerbachian) theme of the 'inversion' of Hegelian philosophy, of putting the Hegelian dialectic 'back on its feet'.[9] We do find – increasingly criticized yet always present as a motif – the idea of a philosophy

---

8. See especially V.I. Lenin, 'The Three Sources and Three Component Parts of Marxism', *Collected Works*, vol.19, Moscow 1968, pp. 23–8. [Ed.]

9. See *Capital*, vol.1, pp. 102–03; 'on its feet' [*sur les pieds*] derives from the French translation of *Capital* by Joseph Roy (see Althusser's comments in *For Marx*, London 1979, p. 89 n.2). [Ed.]

of history, of a meaning of history embodied in the succession of 'progressive epochs' of determinate modes of production, leading to the transparence of Communism.[10] We find in Marx this idealist represent-ation of the 'realm of freedom' succeeding the 'realm of necessity'[11] – the myth of a community wherein the 'free development' of individuals *takes the place of social relations*, which become as superfluous as the State and commodity relations.

The latent or manifest idealism of these themes haunts not only *The German Ideology* (a veritable 'materialist' philosophy of history) but also the evolutionism of the 1859 Preface (the 'progressive' succession of modes of production) and the tautological finalism of the famous sentences that delighted Gramsci: 'No social order is ever destroyed before all the productive forces for which it is sufficient have been developed. . . . Mankind thus inevitably sets itself only such tasks as it is able to solve'.[12] In an infinitely more subtle form, the same idealism haunts *Capital* itself. We have learned to recognize in *Capital*'s 'mode of exposition', however impressive, the fictive unity imposed upon it from the outset by the requirement of beginning with the abstraction of value – i.e. with the homogeneity presupposed by the field of commensurabil-ity – without having previously posited capitalist relations of exploitation as the condition of its process.[13]

If the question of the 'beginning' represented a burden for Marx ('Beginnings are always difficult in all sciences'[14]); if he imposed on himself the idea of a mandatory starting point with the ultimate abstraction of value, this was also a function of a certain conception of science [*Wissenschaft*] – that is, a conception of the formal conditions to which every thought process [*Denkprozess*] must submit in order to be true (e.g. that all knowledge, and hence its exposition, must proceed from the abstract to the concrete). Clearly, Hegel is still present in this illusion of the necessary presentation [*Darstellung*], or exposition, of the True.

The effects of this philosophical conception of the formation of True thought can be located at precise points in *Capital*: for example, in the arithmetical presentation of surplus-value as the difference between the

---

10. Cf. Preface to *A Contribution to the Critique of Political Economy*, pp. 425–6. [Ed.]

11. See Marx, *Capital*, vol.3, Harmondsworth 1981, pp. 958–9. [Ed.]

12. Preface to *A Contribution to the Critique of Political Economy*, p. 426. [Ed.]

13. For a more extended discussion of these issues, see Althusser's 'Avant-Propos' to Gérard Duménil, *Le Concept de loi économique dans 'Le Capital'*, Paris 1978, pp. 7–26. [Ed.]

14. Preface to the first edition of *Capital*, vol.1, p. 89. [Ed.]

value produced and the variable capital advanced in the process of production.[15] Imposed in this form by deduction from the order of exposition, this presentation can lead to an economistic interpretation of exploitation. Exploitation, however, cannot be reduced to this surplus-value, but must be thought in its concrete forms and conditions. That is to say, it must be thought within the implacable constraints of the labour process (extension, intensification, compartmentalization) and the division and discipline of the organization of labour, on the one hand; and the conditions of the reproduction of the labour force (consumption, housing, family, education, health, questions of women, etc.), on the other. Undoubtedly, Marx did not identify exploitation solely with the arithmetical subtraction of value. He speaks of the various forms of surplus-value (absolute, relative), just as he speaks of forms of exploitation in the labour process and in the reproduction of labour-power. But he does this in chapters that have always appeared strange, 'historical' and 'concrete' rather than abstract, and *on the margin* of the dominant mode of exposition[16] – as if he had to break off or interrupt this mode in order to impart its meaning to it!

Many other examples of difficulties and contradictions might be given where Marx gets caught in the self-imposed trap of commencing with the abstraction of value. To cite just two: the thorny question of the preservation/transference of the value of the means of production in their operation by labour-power; or the question of the transformation of values into prices of production, where Marx is caught in a faulty line of reasoning – as if one did not have to go back even further to understand the point.[17]

So we see: however consciously posed, the obvious need to 'change terrain', to adopt a position that 'represents ... the proletariat', did not in itself serve from the outset 'to settle accounts with our former philosophical conscience'. The materialism advocated by Marx also applies to him: consciousness is not practice; consciousness is not even thought in its real forms. We might note as a sign of this unavoidable gap the fact that apart from the brief, enigmatic proclamation of the *Theses on Feuerbach*, Marx himself would never clearly explain his new

---

15. See *Capital*. vol.1, Part Three, chapter 11, 'The Rate and Mass of Surplus-Value', pp. 417–26. [Ed.]

16. For example, chapters 10 ('The Working Day') and 15 ('Machinery and Large-Scale Industry'), and Part Eight ('So-Called Primitive Accumulation'). [Ed.]

17. See *Capital*, vol.1, Part Three, chapter 8, 'Constant Capital and Variable Capital', pp. 307–19; and vol.3, Part Two, chapter 9, 'Formation of a General Rate of Profit (Average Rate of Profit), and Transformation of Commodity Values into Prices of Production', pp. 254–72. [Ed.]

positions on 'his' philosophy. He had promised Engels a dozen pages on the dialectic; he never wrote them. And he 'omitted' the 1857 Introduction – the most elaborated statement of his position – saying: 'it seems to me confusing to anticipate results which still have to be substantiated'.[18] Everything happened in his work and in his struggle: an interminable struggle to insure the new positions against the return of the old – a battle that was always in doubt, even when it seemed won; a struggle to find words that do not yet exist in order to think what was concealed by some omnipotent words. (The struggle is also fought over words.) Witness the most profound hesitations in *Capital,* where 'alienation' continues to haunt the text in the theory of fetishism, the opposition between dead and living labour, the domination of the conditions of production over the worker, and the figure of Communism. Alienation: an old word, an old, all-purpose, idealist concept, manifestly there to think something else – something which is unthought, and has remained so.

Here is another example of how history, in good materialist fashion, surprised and overtook Marx. Marx is distinguished from all idealist political philosophy in that he never entertained any illusions about the 'omnipotence of ideas', his own included. (It was Lenin who, in the heat of polemic, unwisely wrote that 'the Marxist doctrine is omnipotent because it is true'.[19]) From the *Manifesto* onwards, Marx's position is clear and was never to change: it is the general movement of the class struggle of the proletariat against the capitalists that will open the path to Communism as a 'real movement'.[20] The influence of ideas is only the secondary expression of a balance of class forces.

The extraordinary thing is that Marx takes account of this materialist thesis in the position of his own ideas. This is clear in the *Manifesto* as well as the 1859 Preface, where the exposition takes the form of a topography. Thus Marx expounds his own ideas twice, in two very different forms. He first presents them as principles of comprehensive analysis (whether of a global conjuncture, as in the *Manifesto,* or of the structure of a social formation, as in the 1859 Preface). His ideas are thus present – and present in their theoretical form – everywhere, since they are the means of explaining a global reality. But Marx's ideas make a second appearance, when he situates them in a position determined and limited by this global reality – in the formula of the 1859 Preface, among the 'ideological forms in which men become conscious of [class]

---

18. Preface to *A Contribution to the Critique of Political Economy*, p. 424. [Ed.]
19. 'The Three Sources and Three Component Parts of Marxism', p. 23. [Ed.]
20. See *Manifesto of the Communist Party*, in Karl Marx *The Revolutions of 1848*, Harmondsworth 1973, p. 80. [Ed.]

conflict and fight it out'.[21] In thus situating his ideas in a (superstructural) position defined by social and class relations, Marx no longer considers them as principles of explanation of the given whole, but solely in terms of their possible effect in the ideological struggle. Therewith the ideas change their form; they pass from 'theoretical form' to 'ideological form'.

The measure of Marx's materialism is less the materialist content of his theory than the acute, practical consciousness of the conditions, forms and limits within which these ideas can become active. Hence their double inscription in the topography. Hence the essential thesis that ideas, no matter how true and formally proven, can never be historically active in person but only in the form of a mass ideology, adopted in the class struggle.

Yet by an incredible historical irony, Marx was not in a position to conceive the possibility that his own thought might itself be diverted to serve the ends of the 'omnipotence of ideas' and used as its politics. It is not a question of putting Marx on trial here and judging him on the basis of something other than his own history, upon which we must reflect. Still, we may note one piece of evidence: in all that Marx left us, there is very little concerning what he called the 'superstructure' – meaning law, the State, and 'ideological forms'. And until Gramsci (whose contribution remains limited) the Marxist tradition added nothing to what Marx left us. Moreover, it is a surprising paradox that from a theoretical point of view Marxism is still at the stage of Marx, or rather somewhere short of him. His thought has given rise to commentaries and illustrations (sometimes brilliant, most often dull) and to some applications, and it has of course been plunged into sharp conflicts of interpretation in the course of revolutionary political action. Yet for the most part Marxism has been repeated, and distorted or ossified in the process. This is an astonishing phenomenon, given that Marxism presented itself not as utopian but as scientific, and that no science in the world lives without progressing – progress which involves critically questioning its first forms of expression, its 'beginning'. Nothing of the sort occurred in the case of Marxism: only Rosa Luxemburg had the courage to attempt a critique of the reproduction schemas in Volume 2 of *Capital*,[22] but that was erroneous. Up until recent years, when a movement of critical research finally seems to be taking shape, Marxist theory has never been recommenced or developed. Now, this paradox refers us not only to the incontestable effects of the class struggle and the domination of bourgeois

---

21. Preface to *A Contribution to the Critique of Political Economy*, p. 426. [Ed.]
22. In *The Accumulation of Capital* (1913), London 1951. [Ed.]

ideology, which have kept Marxism on the defensive, theoretically; it also refers us to the lacunae in Marx, which we must be careful not to judge in the name of the Idea of a Theory in itself, something that should be 'complete', without gaps or contradictions.

The materialism of the double position of ideas in the topography, and of the subordination of ideas to the class struggle, does not actually suffice to think the effectivity of ideas in the class struggle. It is also necessary for ideas to be taken up in mass 'ideological forms', something which is not possible through pure and simple propaganda but requires organizations of class struggle. 'Workers of the world unite!' effectively means 'Organize!' Now it seems that the exigency of organization did not pose a particular theoretical problem for Marx: the whole problem was resolved in advance through the transparency of a conscious, voluntary community constituted by free and equal members – a prefiguration of the free community of Communism, a community *without social relations.* The idea – which the working class would have to confront in its historical experience – that every organization must furnish itself with an apparatus so as to ensure its own unity of thought and action, that there is no organization without an apparatus, and that the division between apparatus and militants could reproduce the bourgeois division of power and cause problems so serious as to end in tragedy – this was inconceivable to Marx. But his successors did not tackle it as a theoretical problem either – not even Rosa Luxemburg, who had sensed the danger.[23] And Marx, besides having a transparent notion of organization, never abandoned his old transparent conception of ideology as 'consciousness' or 'system of ideas', and never succeeded in conceiving its materiality – that is to say, its realization in practices governed by apparatuses functioning as forms of dominant ideology, dependent upon the State.[24] Most of Marx's successors have done nothing but repeat (i.e. gloss or interpret) Marx himself, and blindly plunged into the darkness of night: in the dark on the State, in the dark on ideology, in the dark on the Party, in the dark on politics – at the extreme, toppling Marx's thought into something utterly alien to him.

It has been said that Marxism is 'not a dogma but a guide to action' – proof that the temptation of dogma haunts its denial.[25] Lenin himself did

23. See, for example, 'Organizational Questions of Russian Social Democracy' (1904) and 'The Russian Revolution' (1918), in M.-A. Waters, ed., *Rosa Luxemburg Speaks*, New York 1970, pp. 112–30, 365–95. [Ed.]

24. Cf. Louis Althusser, 'Ideology and Ideological State Apparatuses', *Essays on Ideology*, London 1984, pp. 1–60. [Ed.]

25. For example, in the Conclusion to the *History of the Communist Party of the Soviet Union (Bolsheviks) – Short Course*, Moscow 1939, p. 356. [Ed.]

not hesitate to affirm that 'the Marxist doctrine is omnipotent because it is true', and that 'Marxism is cast in a block of steel'. Of course, we must remember the context in which these statements were made, and realize that Lenin deliberately 'bent the stick' in the other direction;[26] but history transforms the context, while the words remain. Marxism was turned into an evolutionist philosophy of history (Kautsky, Plekhanov), *Capital* into a treatise on political economy. To fix the unity of this enterprise, some unfortunate texts of Engels's (like *Ludwig Feuerbach* or the *Dialectics of Nature*) were utilized to construct 'the' Marxist philosophy – dialectical materialism – which Lenin, conferring an absolute guarantee, declared 'the only wholly consistent philosophy'. At the end of this line of development, Marxism became a philosophy (dialectical materialism) of which historical materialism was an 'integral part' and scientific socialism the application. In Marx's name, for years and years Stalin fixed the formulae of this poor man's Hegelianism,[27] this Absolute Knowledge without exterior, from which any topography had disappeared – and for good reason. Since 'the cadres decide everything',[28] the definition of the True was the prerogative of the leaders, the bourgeois ideology of the omnipotence of ideas triumphed in the monstrous unity of State–Party–State ideology, the masses had only to submit in the very name of their liberation.

The influence of bourgeois ideology on the working-class movement is insufficient to account for this enormous distortion; the reproduction of its forms within the workers' movement must also be explained. Here a theory of ideology – not only in relation to the State, to its material existence in certain apparatuses, but also in relation to the Party itself – is indispensable. Marxist leaders have always been sensitive to the influence of (dominant) bourgeois ideology on political tendencies within the working-class movement. Yet they always conceived it mechanically, and invariably ultimately identified it as the sole cause of all the movement's difficulties and 'deviations'. *This influence alone.* Engaged in and blinded by the practical, immediate problems of the class struggle, these leaders were not advised that any organization of struggle secretes a specific ideology designed to defend and ensure its own unity. If they did indeed recognize that Marxist theory had to find mass-based 'ideological forms' in order to become politically active, they did not really take into account the fact of the difference and potential

---

26. See Lenin's 1907 Preface to the collection *Twelve Years, Collected Works*, vol.13, Moscow 1962, pp. 94–113. [Ed.]

27. See especially *Dialectical and Historical Materialism*, Moscow 1941. [Ed.]

28. See Stalin's 'Report to the Eighteenth Congress of the CPSU(B)' (1939), *Problems of Leninism*, Peking 1976, p. 919. [Ed.]

contradiction between Marxist ideology and the ideology required for the existence, unity and defence of the organization. Lacking a theory of the Party, and of the effects produced by the structure of its apparatus, they could not conceive that Marxist ideology might be deformed by the ideology necessary for the Party as such. The latter prerequisite is reflected in Lenin's formulae on the 'omnipotence' and 'steel block' of Marxism. For the Party to be unified in its organizational practice, certain of its cause and its future in a critical period, nothing less than the proclaimed guarantee of the Truth of its ideology, and of the unfailing unity of its theory and its practice, was demanded. And since the Party is an apparatus, there was a great temptation for the leadership to attribute to itself the ideological guarantee of a kind of Absolute Knowledge, to the point of no longer perceiving the ideological function of this knowledge, confused with its power, and hence its risks – even to the extent of not realizing that this unrecognized function of ideology could end up reproducing in the Party itself, in the difference between its leaders and its militants, the structure of the bourgeois State.[29]

Yet in order to perceive that the acknowledged influence of bourgeois ideology on the working-class movement is not simply a matter of 'ideas' or of 'tendencies' but is also reflected in the materiality of organizational structures that tend to reproduce the structure of the State, a materialist theory of ideology, of the State, of the Party, and of politics would have been required. In the practice of its organizations, Marxism has constantly encountered these realities: it has had to resolve the problems posed by them, but gropingly and as if blind. This constitutes the grandeur and pathos of Lenin's work and action: that he was acutely aware of the existence of these questions and did not cease to rectify and change his thinking when confronted with the gigantic task of founding a new party and a new State, and to involve the masses in the ideological renewal of a cultural revolution. Lenin's prodigious experience in the practice of revolution as a long and contradictory process is indeed a corrective to the mythic notion of it as a total and immediate mutation, but does not lead to a theory of State, ideology and Party. This constitutes the grandeur and pathos of Gramsci: to have sensed the importance and political weight of these questions, but without being able to extricate himself from a historical research still caught up in a philosophy of history. This is what constitutes the grandeur of Mao: that he practically questioned the metaphysical idea of

---

29. For Althusser's analysis of this in the case of the French Communist Party, see 'What Must Change in the Party', *New Left Review* 109, May/June 1978, especially pp. 26–39. [Ed.]

the dialectic by audaciously *submitting the dialectic to the dialectic* (in his theory of 'contradiction'), and thus broached the nature of ideological relations and put his finger on the separation and power of the party apparatus, in the ambitious project of a cultural revolution, designed to change the relation between Party and masses. Here too, however, practice did not lead to a theory.

This testimony should not be a judgement in disguise. That would be to fall back into a subtle form of the 'omnipotence of ideas', to assign responsibility for what has happened in history to the *absence of a theory* of ideology, State, Party, and politics. That would be to assume that a '*complete*' Marxist theory could have mastered history and, beyond this idealism of historical mastery, to suppose another idealism: that a theory 'represent[ing] ... the proletariat' in its class struggle is not born out of this struggle and subject to the history of this struggle, under the power of the State and the dominant ideology, is not dependent on the structure of its organizations, and of the ideological conditions of their constitution and their struggle. In its discoveries, as in its lacunae and contradictions, Marxist theory is subject to this struggle, just as it is implicated in the deformations and tragedies of its history.

Marxism will not rid itself of the tragedies of its history by condemning or deploring them; that way lie moralism and theoretical and political abdication. It is vital for Marxism to recognize these tragedies, to take responsibility for them, put them on its agenda, and forge the theoretical means required to understand them at their roots. Nor does this have anything to do with the intellectual curiosity of illuminating an irreversible past. At stake in such a radical reflection is *Marxism today*: let it finally begin to know itself as it is, and it will change.

For theoretical problems do not gambol in the heads of intellectuals, who determine neither their sudden appearance, nor their position, nor their unlocking. To be materialist today, we must first of all recognize that if we can sketch a first and fragile reckoning of Marx's thought – its lacunae, contradictions and illusions – it is because the situation imposes this task upon us and enables us to acquit it. The gigantic development of working-class and popular struggles in the world and in our countries, replying with unprecedented possibilities to the imperialist offensive; finally makes *the general crisis of Marxism* – political, ideological and theoretical – *explode in the full light of day* with its contradictions, confusions, impasses and tragedies. Without going back any further, we can say that this crisis was blocked and sealed up for us in the forms of Stalinist State dogmatism, which doomed all who tried to approach the problem to condemnation and political isolation. Today – and this is a novelty, of considerable importance – the forms of this blockage are breaking up, and the elements of the crisis are – even in their dispersion

– becoming *visible* to the popular masses. The demands of the crisis make us see what is missing in Marx, because henceforth we urgently need to see clearly into the State, ideology, the Party, and politics. We have only to read Marx and Lenin to see that Marxism, even when it was living, was always in a *critical* position (in both senses of the word: fighting the illusions of the dominant ideology, and incessantly threatened in its discoveries) because it was always engaged in – and surprised by – mass movements, and open to the demands of the unpredictable history of their struggles. Now more than ever, even in the midst of the worst contradictions, the masses are on the move.

Perhaps for the first time in its history, Marxism is on the verge of profound changes, of which the first signs are visible. Today Marxist theory can and must readopt Marx's old dictum – and not forsake it: we must 'settle accounts with our former philosophical conscience' – and first of all, with that of Marx. And we should realize that this is not only the business of philosophers, intellectuals, leaders – nor even of single parties. For 'all men are "philosophers"' (Gramsci[30]). In the last resort it is the business of the popular masses in the ordeal of their struggle.

---

30. *Prison Notebooks*, London 1971, p. 323. [Ed.]

Index